Rabbit (Un)Redeemed

Rabbit (Un)Redeemed

The Drama of Belief
in John Updike's Fiction

Peter J. Bailey

Madison • Teaneck
Fairleigh Dickinson University Press

Associated University Presses
2010 Eastpark Boulevard
Cranbury, NJ 08512

The paper used in this publication meets the requirements of the American National Standard for Permanence of Paper for Printed Library Materials Z39.48-1984.

Library of Congress Cataloging-in-Publication Data

Bailey, Peter J., 1946–
    Rabbit (un)redeemed : the drama of belief in John Updike's fiction / Peter J. Bailey.
        p.   cm.
    Includes bibliographical references and index.
    ISBN 0-8386-4053-2 (alk. paper)
    1. Updike, John—Criticism and interpretation.   2. Updike, John—
Characters—Harry Angstrom.   3. Angstrom, Harry (Fictitious character).
4. Belief and doubt in literature.   5. Middle class men in literature.   I. Title.
PS3571.P4Z54   2006
813'.54—dc22   2005018159

For Lucretia Bailey Yaghjian,
sister, spiritual advisor, Christian

and

In memory of
Professore Jackson I. Cope,
mentor

"What else you think you are, champ?" Charlie Stavros asks Harry.

In response, Harry thinks, "A God-made one-of-a-kind with an immortal soul breathed in. A vehicle of grace. A battlefield of good and evil. An apprentice angel. All those things they tried to teach you in Sunday school, or really didn't try very hard to teach you, just let them drift in and out of the pamphlets, back there in that church basement buried deeper in his mind than an air-raid shelter."

Rabbit at Rest, 1265.

As I've said before, my religious sensibility operates primarily as a sense of God the creator, which is fairly real to me, and secondly as a sense of the mystery and irreducibility of one's own identity, mixed in with the fear of the identity being an illusion or being squelched.

Jeff Campbell, "Interview with John Updike," *Conversations with John Updike*, 103.

[Clark] didn't know what to believe—he only knew he was going to die someday.

In the Beauty of the Lilies, 408.

Contents

Acknowledgments

IN *SELF-CONSCIOUSNESS: MEMOIRS,* UPDIKE WROTE OF SHILLINGTON, Pennsylvania, his home town, "the horse-chestnut trees, the telephone poles, the porches, the green hedges recede to a calm point that in my subjective geography is still the center of the world." Barry Nelson, Updike's Shillington High classmate and the editor of a Shillington history newsletter, generously escorted me on an expert's tour of the place that, for him, remained a fully objective residence. His insights into Shillington's past and the nature of Updike's appropriation of it deepened my understanding of the Olinger Stories and of Rabbit's Pennsylvania-generated anxieties, and I'm grateful, as well, for Mr. Nelson's willingness to continue our conversation by mail.

David Shields offered rigorous and invariably insightful critiques of numerous drafts of the chapters here, and he deserves my thanks for that kindness and for two decades' worth of wonderful intellectual exchange and friendship. Frances Weller Bailey hasn't consistently shared my enthusiasm for Updike's work over the past thirty years (and was, therefore, a hugely helpful critic of the manuscript), but she has shared every other part of my life, for which I couldn't be more grateful. I'm grateful, too, to St. Lawrence University for the sabbatical that enabled me to complete this project, and I want to mention as well those often unwitting beneficiaries of my Updike fixation, my students at St. Lawrence, who have made the profession of teaching literature and fiction writing a pleasure and a source of great satisfaction.

Rabbit (Un)Redeemed

Prologue: Granting the Individual Soul its Due

> The refusal to rest content, the willingness to risk excess on behalf
> of one's obsessions, is what distinguishes artists from entertainers,
> and what makes some artists adventurers on behalf of us all.
> —Updike, review of *Franny and Zooey*

AT ITS MOST VITAL, SINGLE AUTHOR LITERARY CRITICISM ILLUMI-
nates the human drama of an individual novelist's book-by-book
struggle—the artist's "adventure" that Updike posits here—with the
preoccupations that compel her to keep returning to fiction for one
more go at focusing and clarifying obsessions that, translated into literary terms, constitute her works' themes. That struggle is significant
to us nonwriters not because the author is a prodigy or celebrity, but
because—to paraphrase the closing line of Ralph Ellison's *Invisible
Man*—perhaps on the lower levels, he speaks for us. Like the medicine
man in native cultures who enacts in dance the spiritual realities and
conflicts of his tribe, the novelist uses her linguistically heightened
sensibility to give us the news of our cultural moment, to express
through dramatic plots the tensions and contradictions engendering
themselves on the lower levels of our lives.

To cite Ellison's novel as an example, *Invisible Man* can be interpre-
ted as having made visible the critical discontinuity in American culture between sociological conceptions of race and the discourse of
existentialism. One of that novel's great ambitions, arguably, is to reconcile the relativistic language of self with the moral imperatives of
liberal race ideologies, and the narrator's failure to negotiate effectively this antinomy consigns him in the novel's conclusion to the
basement of his invisibility while apparently sentencing as well the
author of the most celebrated American novel of the second half of
the twentieth century to a career-spanning novelistic silence. What
Ellison's novel embodies is an intensely focused exploration of cultural discontinuities we readers experience but are markedly less
adept at articulating; as numerous Ellison critics have argued, the
course his literary career took seems inextricably linked to his novel's
inability to resolve those cultural contradictions. This is not to say

13

that Ellison's protagonist *is* Ellison, of course, but is, instead, to read the novel as Robert Frost read a poem—"as a figure of the will braving alien entanglements."[1] That "will" is where protagonist and author meet and share whatever agency they can muster against the "alien entanglements" the world imposes and which generate plots in fiction. To acknowledge that Ellison never published another finished novel after *Invisible Man* is neither to diminish his accomplishment nor to fetishize melodramatically literary silence—it simply allows us to better appreciate how profound is the not-merely-literary corner the narrator of *Invisible Man* paints himself into in his Harlem basement. I will attempt in *Rabbit (Un)Redeemed* to discover an analogously significant drama in the markedly more prolific career of John Updike.

Working from an extensive knowledge of his subject's oeuvre, the literary critic can, I think, make a significant contribution to the more casual reader's appreciation of a writer's work and career, the cultural contradictions they express, delineate, and illuminate. By providing that reader with a plausibly substantiated, nuanced version of the complex story the novelist's career has been enacting from book to book, the critic seeks ultimately to locate through the medium of the author's narrative designs a larger pattern delineating the story of the author's "will braving alien entanglements." That story exists not only in the pages of the texts the author has written, of course, but in the writer's life as well, and offering a compelling characterization of the relationship between the writer's life and work has become one of the necessities of postmodern literary criticism in its reaction against the narrow hermeneutics of the New Criticism.

The risks this form of criticism runs are two: it can gravitate toward reductionism by foregrounding one major pattern or conflict in the author's work at the expense of the many others discernible there, and it also tends to isolate the writer by sealing him off in a conversation with himself rather than apprehending him more broadly in the context of the other writers of his era.[2] I'll attempt to resist the first tendency by extensively acknowledging critical projections of John Updike—particularly those focusing, as do I, upon the *Rabbit* tetralogy—that construe him and the significance of his literary career differently from the way I read it. Succumbing to the second risk, on the other hand, seems somehow inescapable when dealing with Updike because of three significant characteristics of his career: his unique position among contemporary American fiction writers as a self-professed Christian novelist,[3] the existence of more than three thousand pages of Updike's own essays and literary criticism and the crosslights they shed upon his own oeuvre, and his work's thoroughly related and very intentional celebration of the individual self. In his *New Yorker* review of Knut Hamsun's *Victoria*, Updike approvingly cites Hamsun's "determination to grant the individual soul its due,"[4] and although he never hazards a guess as to what the individual soul's due is, his commendation of this and other protagonist-centered works of Hamsun's and of other European and American writers mirrors his own literary penchant for consistently filtering the world through the prism of a single individual's vision of it. As A. O. Scott aptly characterized his work, "Updike writes from the inside out, his realism bound not so much to the earth as to the person, to the phenomenological welter of individual consciousness and sensation. His most consistent (and consistently controversial) preoccupations—sex and religion—are at bottom complementary manifestations of an overriding concern with what it means—what it is like—to be a self."[5] One of my basic contentions here is that the affirmation of self is simultaneously the most consistently pervasive thematic element of Updike's work, and a primary source of most of its drama and many of its contradictions. It is also—as David Foster Wallace and Sven Birkerts have testified with Oedipally triumphant zeal[6]—a significant cause of the occasional misfires in Updike's oeuvre for the reason that, as Updike admitted in a 1971 interview, "Like it or not, we have all arrived at a moment when the single, personal unit seems inadequate, selfish, and solipsistic."[7]

The Rabbit novels, which I treat in *Rabbit (Un)Redeemed* as the nucleus of Updike's work, constitute Updike's fifteen-hundred-page elegy to American individualism. Harry Angstrom's tetralogy-spanning theme song, expressed early in the first novel, is "If you have the guts to be yourself, other people'll pay your price" (129). The emblematic nature of Rabbit's claim is suggested by the fact that he is, with no deliberation on his part, echoing Ralph Waldo Emerson's argument that "If the single man plant himself indomitably on his instincts, and there abide, the huge world will come round to him."[8] In moments of extremity, Rabbit's cultivated egocentricity slides resistlessly into solipsism: while he waits for Janice to give birth, "everything seems unreal that is outside of his sensations" (169), and, with the exception of narrative passages depicting the perspectives of Ruth, Lucy Eccles, Janice, and Nelson, the Rabbit tetralogy's fifteen-hundred pages indefatigably register nothing other than those thoroughly subjective sensations and perceptions of Harry Angstrom's. Consequently, the narrative strategy of the tetralogy corroborates Harry's response to Janice's plea in *Rabbit, Run* that he consider how she, having just given birth, feels: "I can. I can but I don't want to, it's not the thing, the thing is what *I* feel" (213). At the other end of the quartet of novels, Harry's mistress, Thelma Harrison, tells her lover in the last months of his life, "Harry, you're not actually the center of the universe, it only feels that way to you"[9] (*Rest*, 201), and the tetralogy is as tireless in documenting how accurately Thelma has diagnosed Harry's egocentricity as it is in tentatively validating his psychic disposition.

Throughout these novels, Rabbit responds instinctively against attempts to limit his individual human freedom, reacting with particular virulence against the Christian/humanist infringement upon it epitomized in Reverend Eccles's assertion that "with my church, I believe that we are all responsible beings, responsible for ourselves and for each other" (132). Harry can never quite articulate his objection to the secular creed that underlies Eccles's pious sentiments, but Updike can: "In fact, there is an easy humanism that insists that man is an animal that feeds and sleeps and defecates and makes love and isn't that nice and natural and let's have more of that. But this is omitting intrinsic stresses in the human condition—you foresee things, for example, you foresee your own death. You have really been locked out of the animal paradise of unthinking natural reflex."[10]

Save for a brief appearance in *Rabbit Redux*, Eccles disappears from the Rabbit saga, but his collectivist/humanist vision survives in a number of other characters whose major role is similarly to question and contest Rabbit's egotistic/existentialist creed. Primary among these antagonists is Harry's son, Nelson, who from *Rabbit, Run* forward imposes upon his father both Oedipal opposition and the cloying demands of familial obligation before himself becoming a New Age family counselor possessed of a therapeutic lexicon reminiscent of the secular humanism of Eccles that Harry can never conceptualize but feels "squeezed" by nonetheless. Harry's commitment to his family is vexed and inconstant, largely because he is so clearly a projection of Updike's own conflicted attitude toward familial responsibilities.

One of the epigraphs of Updike's first story collection, *The Same Door*, quotes T. S. Eliot's celebration of family from *The Family Reunion*, but the book's best stories—"The Alligators" and "The Happiest I've Been" in particular—close on ringing affirmations of the human psychic necessity to resist or escape familial imperatives. "There should be, in a man's life," reasons the protagonist of another *The Same Door* story, "A Gift from the City," "hours when he has never married, and his wife walks in magic circles she herself draws. It was little enough to ask; he had sold his life, his chances, for her sake."[11] Updike concludes an early memoir/essay, "My Uncle's Death," with an assessment of his ultimate impression from a visit of relatives: the experience "suggested to me that in the depth of the mystery called 'family' there lay, necessarily, an irrevocable mistake."[12] In one of the Maples stories, "Separating," Joan Maple berates her adulterous husband Richard's perception of their children as "a corporate obstacle to your freedom,"[13] which is precisely how Harry frequently perceives Janice, Nelson, and company, and the demands they incessantly make. "These [familial] debts are real," Updike acknowledged in his memoirs, *Self-Consciousness* (hereafter referred to as *S-C*), "but realer still is a certain obligation to our own selves, the obligation to live. We are social creatures, but unlike ants and bees, not just that; there is something intrinsically and individually vital which must be defended against the claims even of virtue."[14] In *Memories of the Ford Administration*, Alf Clayton translates the New Hampshire state motto into a epigram summarizing the conflict never resolved in Updike's work: "Live free or go home."[15] The drama of Rabbit Angstrom's four-volume existence consists largely in his struggle to conciliate his self-seeking impulses—the internal imperative to "live free"—with his familial obligations, with the human necessity of remaining a "social creature"—the responsibility to "go home."

Although Harry's life does contain social episodes—in *Rabbit Redux*, he inadvertently becomes breadwinner to a 1960s style commune precipitated by Janice's desertion of him and Nelson, and with the prosperity of *Rabbit is Rich* he gains a "gang" of country club Yuppie friends with whom to socialize—his more customary state in the tetralogy is a solitary one, three of the four novels culminating in Rabbit's desperate isolation and aloneness. (The outlier, *Rabbit Redux*, confounds the affirmativeness of its closing reunion of Janice and Harry through the narrator's concluding equivocation, "OK?"— a question, Updike has maintained, "not meant to have an easy answer."[16]) "Harry embodies the human problem of why am I me rather than somebody else," Updike explained in an interview following the fourth volume's publication. "He feels to be himself is immensely precious and important; the longer he lives, the less evidence there is to support his sensation that he's wonderful."[17] As the passage of years distances him from the only real "wonderfulness" he ever knows—as a high school basketball star, he approached the women he desired as "a winner"—Harry's experiences of external narcissistic corroboration decline, throwing increasingly into doubt his egotistical self-perception. Nonetheless, the ultimate tenacity of Harry's commitment to self is signaled in *Rabbit at Rest*, when, recuperating from angioplasty, he experimentally imagines his life in Brewer, Pennsylvania, as "a brick of sorts, set in place with a slap in 1933 and hardening ever since, just one life in rows and blocks of lives." The analogy provides him with a "faint faroff communal thrill," but the thrill is distinctly short-lived. Perceiving himself as one among many bricks proves to be "hard to sustain over against his original and continuing impression that Brewer and all the world beyond are just frills upon himself, like the lace around a plump satin valentine. . . ." As he sometimes does in *Rabbit, Run*, Harry proceeds to compare himself to the Dalai Lama, whose reported offer to resign his divinely ordained position in Tibet has been met with expressions of horror by his followers: "[T]he Dalai Lama," Harry concludes, "can no more resign godhead than Harry can resign selfhood"[18] (1317).

Harry's association of selfhood with godhead isn't a casually-conceived analogy on Updike's part, since for author and protagonist alike, awareness of self is inextricably linked to a sustained belief in "an unseen world" (201), causally connected to "furtive sensations of the invisible . . ." (201–2). In a way that few Christians and fewer churches are likely to sanction, Harry's intuitions of a divine presence in his life are indistinguishable from egotism, his conviction that a just and morally centered universe surrounds him depending more than most believers would endorse on the quality of Rabbit's self-esteem at any given moment. Even Janice, the least theologically inclined character in the tetralogy, recognizes the link between belief and self-esteem, musing in "Rabbit Remembered" that she "has never not believed in a God of some sort but on the other hand never made a thing out of it like Mother or in his weird way Harry. They felt something out there, reflecting back from their own good sense of themselves."[19] In *Rabbit is Rich*, Harry admonishes his family, "what I think about religion is . . . without a little of it you'll sink" (800), but on the subjective balance sheet on which he totes up all significant scores, this affirmation translates to "without a little religion, *I'll* sink." Harry never once opens a Bible in the tetralogy, and he is anything but a doctrinally oriented believer: his theological curiosity seems nearly exhausted by his recollection of Lutheran minister Fritz Kruppenbach's Sunday school lesson "that life has no terrors for those with faith but for those without faith there can be no salvation and no peace. *No* peace" (684). In acting out this thoroughly subjective religious sensibility, one strongly influenced by Kruppenbach's dreadful either/or, Rabbit has as his sole barometer of faith his nerve endings. That thoroughly subjective basis of belief is one Updike's work consistently, albeit equivocally, endorses.

"Much of religious loyalty," Updike asserted in an essay on "The Future of Faith," "is, after all, a mode of defiance, insisting *This is what I am*."[20] To deny the spiritual, in Updike's view, is to repudiate the self: "it appeared to me that when we try in good faith to believe in materialism, in the exclusive reality of the physical, we are asking our selves to step aside; we are disavowing the very realm where we exist and where things precious are kept—the realm of emotion and conscience, of memory and intention and sensation" (*S-C*, , 250). In an essay on Whitman, Updike applied to the "Song of Myself" poet a term, "egotheism" (which *Webster's Unabridged Dictionary* defines as "deification of self") in response to his sense that "egoism" doesn't really convey the religious quality of Whitman's—or, I'm adding, Rabbit's—self-preoccupation. Updike's description of egoism in that essay, however, *does* convey that quality: "By 'egoism' I mean not the egotist's overvaluation of his own attributes . . . but a recognition of each man's immersion in a unique and unexchangeable ego which is, in a sense, all he's got, but something he indeed does, short of madness and the grave, have."[21] In characterizing the diminishing confirmations of his "wonderfulness that the world mirrors back to Harry," Updike continued, "Nevertheless, he does cling to this [self-perception], and in some way only the God within can confirm this feeling that each of us is somehow the center of the universe."[22] The validity of Rabbit's *Run*-concluding conviction that "Goodness lies inside, there is nothing outside" (264) is constantly contested throughout the tetralogy, but the idea is nonetheless one that Updike, simultaneously conjuring his debts to Freud and Kierkegaard, has consistently affirmed in essays. "In loving," Updike contended in a book review of Denis de Rougemont's *More Love in the Western World*, "the lover's own self becomes lovely. The selfish and altruistic threads in these emotions are surely inseparable."[23] If love for another is indistinguishable from narcissism, faith in God's love, for both Rabbit and Updike, is equally inseparable from egotism. As Updike argued in *Self-Consciousness*, "Billions of consciousnesses silt history full, and every one of them the center of the universe. What can we do in the face of this unthinkable truth but scream or take refuge in God?" (40). Who, then, is God?: "God is the self projected onto reality by our natural and necessary optimism. He is the not-Me personified." In a note to this sentence, Updike appends a passage from his "Emersonianism" essay, which concludes, "It was Emerson's revelation that God and the self are of the same substance" (*S-C*, 218). "The vitalities of human selfhood," Ralph C. Wood argued, "far from undermining confidence in God, are for Updike the surest sign of His reality."[24]

For both Harry and Updike, I'll contend in these pages, belief in God is inseparable from belief in the self's integrity and value, and in mourning God's withdrawal from his life, Harry is actually mourning the passing of the source of his sensations of human specialness, the loss of the childhood security that he recalls in *Rabbit is Rich* as a conviction that his soul was "central and dramatic and invisibly cherished" (743). One of my primary purposes in this study will be to demonstrate how significantly Updike's egotheism—this unique convergence of the secular and religious, this identification of selfhood with the sacred—plays out in Updike's fiction in general, in the Rabbit tetralogy in particular, and in Updike's literary career as well. "I feel that to be a person," Updike once told an interviewer, "is to be in a situation of tension, is to be in a dialectical situation"[25]; the dialectical situation at the center of Updike's work, I maintain, consists in egoistic impulses encountering, converging with, and often contending with religious belief.

"The mystery that more puzzled me as a child," Updike acknowledged in "The Dogwood Tree: A Boyhood," "was the incarnation of my ego—that omnivorous and somehow pre-existent I—in a speck so specifically situated amid the billions of history. Why was I I? The arbitrariness of it astounded me; in comparison, nothing was too marvelous."[26] That marvelousness, however, demands a source beyond the self: "Our eager, innate life, rebounding from the exterior world, affirms itself, and the quality of affirmation is taken to be extrinsic, immanent, divine. I needed God to exist."[27] It is remarkable how frequently God is accounted for in Updike's work, as He is here, as the fulfillment of a human need rather than as an autonomous, preexisting Being or eternal presence.

As Roger Lambert imagines Dale Kohler's religious sensibility in *Roger's Version*, "What was this desolation in Dale's heart, I thought, but the longing for God—that longing which is, when all is said and done, our only evidence of His existence? Why do we feel such loss, but that there was Something to lose?"[28]

This is the most that can be said of God, Updike insists and Rabbit intuits, and although Rabbit never characterizes the object of his belief in other than metaphoric terms, Updike's description of Melville's belief summarizes accurately the faiths of both author and protagonist: "Melville is a rational man who wants God to exist. He wants him to exist for the same reasons we all do: to be our rescuer and appreciator, to act as confidant in our moments of crisis and to give us reassurance that, over the horizon of our deaths, we will survive."[29] It's difficult to imagine a definition of God more narcissistic or solipsistic, but Updike's Lutheranism converges with his embrace of Paul Tillich's "I-Thou" theology and Kierkegaard's egocentrically defined relationship to divinity to produce a highly personalistic faith,[30] one practically devoid of the communitarian impulses that inspire Eccles's "busybody" theology.

To return to *Roger's Version*, a novel which, as *In the Beauty of the Lilies*, allows Updike to expound upon theological issues that the Rabbit tetralogy, because of Harry's instinctual barometer of faith, can be approached only through oblique dramatization, Dale Kohler's faith is imagined by Roger Lambert, who projects his adversary's conception of God similarly in terms of human need: "Without it, I become too frightened. I become so frightened I can't act. I get terribly lethargic, as if I'm at the bottom of the sea. . . . Without it—faith, I mean—there's this big hole, and what's strange, the hole is a certain shape, that it just exactly fills. That He just exactly fills."[31] Rabbit's realization while waiting for Janice to give birth at the hospital— *"There is no God; Janice can die"*—makes him feel similarly underwater, and his confused and frightened agnosticism in *Rabbit Redux* renders him too passive to save Jill Pendleton from a drug-induced self-destruction. The entanglement of self-affirmation with faith in Updike's work inevitably leaves the doubter of divinity doubting his own value, significance, and integrity, and leaves Rabbit during his angioplasty procedure in *Rest* realizing that the underwater world he found so terrifying is himself: "Harry has trouble believing how his life is tied to all this mechanics—that the *me* that talks inside him all the time scuttles like a water-striding bug above this pond of body fluids and their slippery conduits. How could the flame of him ever have ignited in such wet straw?" (1295). The unanswerability of that question left the author of *Rabbit at Rest*, in one of the most dramatic convergences between creator and protagonist, producing "a depressed book about a depressed man written by a depressed man."[32]

By emphasizing this essential convergence in Updike's work between egotism and religious belief, I am able to give equal weight to the two conceptual positions—Freudianism and Christianity—that most significantly underlie his fiction and that are too often in Updike criticism considered in isolation from each other. More dramatically, this egotheistically syncretic approach to Updike's oeuvre permits me to illuminate the darkening landscape of Rabbit's subjective impressions as well as the deepening spiritual/theological skepticism in Updike's fiction—and nonfiction—that culminates with such profound eloquence in Clarence Wilmot's reflections on his eclipsed belief at the beginning of *In the Beauty of the Lilies*. "Life's sounds all rang with a curious lightness and flatness, as if a resonating base beneath them had been removed," Updike writes: "They told Clarence Wilmot what he had long suspected, that the universe was utterly indifferent to his states of mind and as empty of divine content as a corroded kettle. All its metaphysical content had leaked away, but for cruelty and death, which without the hypothesis of a God, became unmetaphysical; they became simply facts, which oblivion would in time obliviously erase. Oblivion became a singular comforter."[33]

It is my basic argument that the Updike works I emphasize here—three David Kern/Olinger narratives, the Rabbit tetralogy and its "sequel," "Rabbit Remembered," *Self-Consciousness: Memoirs, The Afterlife* stories, and *In the Beauty of the Lilies*—are among his most compelling writings precisely because their characters' preoccupations with personal oblivion oblige Updike to challenge his own assumptions about the at-one-ness of self and spirit and to place at risk his own Christian beliefs. (Hesitant as I am to offer any generalization estimating the solidity of Updike's faith, I'd locate it somewhere between his characterizations of two other writers' states of spirituality: "A very vivid ghost of Christianity stares out at us from [Hawthorne's] prose, alarming and odd in not being evenly dead, but alive in some limbs and amputate in others, blurred in some aspects and otherwise basilisk-keen. Hawthorne's creed perhaps begins with this: he feels himself delicate, fragile, and threatened. . . ."[34] And, "In the interminable rain of [Proust's] prose I felt goodness. Proust was one of those men—increasingly rare, as faith further ebbs—who lost the consolations of belief but retained the attitudes and ambitions of a believer."[35]) Updike's work is most compelling, I'm suggesting, when it puts in play questions like the one David Kern asks his pantheist mother in "Pigeon Feathers": "good grief, don't you see . . . if when we die there's nothing, all your fields and sun and what not are, ah, horror? It's just an ocean of horror"[36] (pp. 137–38). These characters' terror of death and fears of being forgotten, of being absorbed tracelessly into history's compost heap, analogously call into question the worth of Updike's tenaciously prolific literary career, implicitly precipitating the question that Ben Turnbull asks himself in *Toward the End of Time*: "What is wrong with me, that I want to leave a trace, by scribbling these disjunct and jumpy notes concerning my idle existence?"[37] That question is central to my seventh chapter, which draws from Alf Clayton's thoughts on the writing of history in *Memories of the Ford Administration* to illuminate *In the Beauty of the Lilies,* a novel that seeks to compensate for the dispossession of transcendent understandings of time with historical reconstructions of the past.[38] In their relentless confrontation with questions of ultimacy, these works, perhaps even more than other Updike texts, comprise what Updike intended as his individual "fortress against death" like the one that David Kern seeks to build in "Pigeon Feathers": "Nowhere in the world of other people would he find the hint, the nod he needed

to begin to build his fortress against death. They none of them believed. He was alone. In that deep hole" (139). Out of that deep hole
of anguished spiritual doubt have emerged some of Updike's most
resonant fictions, works that affirm the integrity, sacredness, and irreducible solitude of the human spirit, while questioning the efficacy of
any humanly created fortress against death. These works are among
Updike's most compelling texts specifically because their celebration
of the individual trails in its wake expressions of the anxiety that Emerson voiced in his nearly self-recantatory essay, "Experience": "The
individual is always mistaken." What this would mean in terms of
Updike's career would be that his most unsympathetic critics, from
Norman Mailer to John W. Aldridge to David Foster Wallace, have
been right all along—that all his lapidary prose does is call attention
to itself, and that there's no escape from narcissism in his work for
either protagonist or author.

Whether these deliberately selected works are Updike's most effective or significant matters to me far less than that they constitute
deeply felt confrontations of his greatest hopes with his darkest fears,
works that, placed in dialogue with each other, literarily materialize
Updike's profoundly unresolved debate over the value of human self-
consciousness—which is to say, the value of his own prodigious literary production. These are the Updike texts that most dramatically
question whether, in generating all those works of literary art over all
those years, he has been a Salingerian "adventurer on behalf of us all,"
or—as David Foster Wallace has contended—only another literary
egotist spuriously affirming his lonely belief that he is the center of
the universe.

The tension in Updike's fiction between egotism and religious belief that I'm positing at the center of his literary career significantly
influences the critical method with which I'm approaching his work.
My interpretive strategy is dictated by the character of Updike's texts,
which are shaped by his religious sensibility, but also by his education, and—according to *Self-Consciousness*—by his skin. In an apparently autobiographical essay collected in *Museums and Women*,
Updike describes how difficult it would be for him to convey the virtues of his education to politically inclined students of the early sev-
enties: "Could I explain to a crowd of riot-minded guitarists, how
real, if imperfectly read, these great names [Milton, Donne, Keats,
Eliot, Lowell] were to us? Or with what zest we executed the academic exercise, by now perhaps as obsolete as diagrammatic parsing,
called *explication*?" So fond is Updike's memory of the pleasures of
this "academic exercise" that his panegyric continues: "To train one's
mind to climb, like a vine on a sunny wall, across the surface of a

poem by George Herbert, seeking the handhold crannies of pun, ambiguity and buried allusion; to bring forth from the surface sense of
the poem an altogether other, hidden poem of consistent metaphor
and, as it were, verbal subversion; to feel, in Eliot's phrase, a thought
like an emotion; to explicate—this was life lived on the nerve ends."[39]

In spite of the often well-founded critiques of the limitations of formalist interpretation and the deconstructions of its ideological assumptions that were just beginning to accumulate when Updike
wondered whether that interpretive mode had become obsolescent,
the best Updike criticism retains significant formalist tendencies,
largely because his fiction demands such a critical strategy. To "bring
forth from the surface sense of the poem an altogether other, hidden
poem of consistent metaphor and, as it were, verbal subversion" is
the method of the most illuminating Updike criticism from Alice and
Kenneth Hamilton through Thomas Edwards, Charles Thomas Samuels, George Hunt, Joyce B. Markle, Judie Newman, John Neary, Edward P. Vargo, Donald J. Greiner, Mary O'Connell, and Marshall
Boswell—the fact that the "hidden poems" these critics uncover in
his texts are often "altogether other" reflect both the irreducible individualism of the explicators as well as the metaphoric density of the
poems Updike has provided them with which to work.

That literary works contain "an altogether other, hidden poem," or
"secrets," is one of Updike's most consistent assertions about them,[40]
and he ascribes the presence of secrets in his own literary texts as
much to physiology as to art. In *Self-Consciousness*, he suggested that,
"Having so long carried a secret [psoriasis] behind my clothes, I had
no trouble with the duplicity that creates plots and surprises and
symbolism and layers of meaning; dualism, indeed, such as existed between my skin and myself, appeared to me the very engine of the
human" (75). The explication of these "surprises and symbolism and
layers of meaning" is, unavoidably, what Updike criticism must devote itself to, with two important caveats: first, few contemporary
American writers' styles provide the well-intentioned *explicator de
texte* with such opportunities to exceed the reader's curiosity about
subtextual implications, and a major test of the effectiveness of Updike criticism seems to me the critic's ability to resist the temptation
of sacrificing her/his ongoing illumination of the "hidden poem" to
excessive exegesis of the synapses of language—motif and metaphor—so generously latent in Updike novels. What Updike said of
fiction in an interview is equally true of critiques of it: "Detail is bear-
able only if you feel it's strung or bestowed on some sort of general
seizable form; otherwise, it becomes suffocating and you're lost in
it."[41]

My second source of wariness toward formalism in general and my own explicatory impulses in particular derives from my sense of an additional limitation of New Critical analysis: it too seldom questions the values underlying its operations. If this reading of Updike's work is effective, that will be partly because *Rabbit (Un)Redeemed* consistently implicates its critical method in the issues of meaning it repeatedly interrogates. Updike contributed an epigraph to James Yerkes's *John Updike and Religion* delineating his sense of the interpenetrations between literary form and the possibility of cosmic meaning. "Fiction is rooted in an act of faith," Updike suggested, "a presumption of an inherent significance in human activity, that makes human life worth dramatizing and particularizing. There is even a shadowy cosmic presumption that the universe—the totality of what is, which includes our subjective impressions as well as objective data—composes a narrative and contains a poem, which our own stories and poems echo."[42] Conventional New Critical strategies content themselves with explicating "our own stories and poems"; Updike's assertion here ups the ante for both his works and their would-be critics by analogizing the presence of subtexts in fiction to his hope of the existence of cosmic patterns of order, intelligibility, and meaning. "For the assertion 'God exists' is a drastic one that imposes upon the universe a structure," Updike wrote in an introduction to F. J. Sheed's *Soundings in Satanism*; "given this main beam, subordinate beams and joists, if reason and logic are anything, must follow."[43] It is this very tentatively affirmed structure that the shapes of literary works must, for Updike, seek to approximate. Accordingly, Rabbit's pursuit of "something that wants me to find it" in the tetralogy necessarily finds its literary correspondences in "[a]ll the little congruences and arabesques [Updike] prepared with such delicate anticipatory pleasure"[44] in composing the Rabbit novels, and determining how to read Updike's webs of subtext constitutes one of the reader/critic's chief pleasures in reading his work. It is a primary purpose of this book to offer some suggestions as to whether Updike offers these subtextual convergences and consonances as reflections of cosmic unities, or, more secularly, as the fruits of an aesthetic strategy having no resonances beyond the artfulness of the literary craftsman. My explication of motif and metaphor in these texts, then, cannot merely be an analysis of—to cite one image pattern to which I devote a substantial amount of critical energy—sky imagery in the Rabbit tetralogy, but must never lose sight of the relationship between Harry's mutating perceptions of the sky's meaning for him and the novels' cumulative response to the eschatological questions they pose and structurally dramatize.

If I have one fundamental insight to contribute to the extensive literary critiques of Updike's language, literature, and tetralogy, it consists in my argument for the convergence between the workings of Rabbit's consciousness and the crisis Updike has experienced in his sense of the value of his own literary representations of reality. In other words, Rabbit's deepening incapacity to believe that "Goodness lies inside, there is nothing outside" (264) finds its corollary in the evolution delineated in Updike's work transforming it from the "song of joy" in affirmation of creation, which "The Blessed Man of Boston" narrator David Kern invokes as his literary purpose, to *In the Beauty of the Lilies*, with its chronological reconstruction of history as attempted compensation for a relinquished belief in time's spiritual significance, and "Rabbit Remembered," in which Harry's survivors live on in a world largely gutted of transcendent presence. If the patterns delineated by the artist's literary craft are reflective of nothing more than the convergences created by pun, allusion, and repeated, resonating linguistic motifs, fiction, in Updike's view, becomes nothing more than what *Toward the End of Time* protagonist Ben Turnbull perceives it as being: "I never read fiction," Turnbull admits, "after all its little hurly-burly what does it amount to but more proof that we are of all animals the most miserable?" (46). After his prostate operation, too, Turnbull again rejects fiction, "avoiding the emotional stresses of fiction—that clacking, crudely carpentered old roller coaster, every up and down mocked by the triviality, when all is said and done, of human experience, its Sisyphean repetitiveness"[45] (277).

Consequently, this study of Updike's fiction fails if it loses sight of the profoundly dark human spiritual drama the Updike works I address here create, enact, and seek aesthetically to resolve.

1

The Truth that Shall Make You Free

> My art is Christian only in that my faith urges me to tell the truth,
> however painful and inconvenient, and holds out hope that the
> truth—reality—is good. Good or no, only the truth is useful.
> —Jeff Campbell, "Interview with John Updike"
> in *Conversations with John Updike*

IN MY READING OF THE RABBIT TETRALOGY, HARRY EXPERIENCES NO
more harrowing fear than the triad of anxieties he contemplates in
Rabbit, Run: that "the world arches over a pit, that death is final, that
the wandering thread of his feelings leads nowhere" (201).[1] As *Rabbit, Run* engendered sequel after sequel, the saga's proliferation deepened Updike's obligation to offer some form of literary judgment
upon whether Rabbit's meticulously evoked feelings lead anywhere,
the conception of *Rabbit at Rest* further committing him to determine dramatically whether those feelings' termination enacts conso-
nant closure or death's heedless imposition of "the rest is silence."
Significantly, Rabbit's anxiety about the value of the workings of his
individual consciousness has its corollary in teleological questions
frequently raised in our politically charged literary climate: of what
value is the extended adumbration of an individual, irremediably subjective perspective to the understanding of complex social dynamics
of a mass society? That question, in turn, represents a less theologically inflected way of asking the one with which the Lutheran minister, Fritz Kruppenbach, silences the humanistically inclined Reverend
Eccles in *Rabbit, Run*: "How big do you think your little friends look
among the billions God sees?" (146). Updike's fiction constitutes his
cumulative evolutionary response to this crucial challenge to protagonist-centered literary representation, one as central to his aesthetic as
self-affirmation is to Harry Angstrom's philosophy of life. Characterizing that aesthetic in his foreword to *Hugging the Shore*, Updike
wrote, "A fervent relation to the world: I suppose this is my critical
touchstone, with its old-fashioned savor of reverence and Creation

and the truth that shall make you free."[2] I'll let the first of Rabbit's lessons in "learning to die" dramatize the concurrence between Harry and Updike on the individual's ultimate existential imperative—truth-telling—and its capacity to "make you free."

When, in *Rabbit, Run*, Ruth and Rabbit[3] climb Mt. Judge on a Sunday afternoon outing, Rabbit embarks upon the spiritual experience he is about to have with characteristic impiety. "His day has been bothered by God," the narrator explains in the novel's pervasive third-person limited narration:[4] "Ruth mocking, Eccles blinking—why did they teach you such things if no one believed them?" Leaving this central question of the tetralogy gapingly unanswered, Updike has Rabbit take in his surroundings. As he looks down upon Brewer from this vantage point, "the city is huge in the middle view, and he opens his lips as if to force the lips of his soul to receive the taste of truth about it, as if truth were a secret in such low solution that only immensity can give us a sensible taste. Air dries his mouth." The desiccating truth with which he is confronted is that "someone is dying. The thought comes from nowhere: simple percentages. Someone in some house along those streets, if not this minute, then the next, dies; and in that suddenly stone chest the heart of this flat prostrate rose seems to him to be."

For Updike's protagonist at this moment, the reality of Brewer is incarnated in the "suddenly stone heart" of the someone he imagines has died, all contesting evidence of human vitality having been subsumed in this intuition of life's sudden termination and its overwhelming significance. Terrified by this visual experience of death's power to annihilate the "flower pot city" that sustains his life, Rabbit begs Ruth, "Put your arm around me." Given no physical evidence that there *is* anyone dying in Brewer, this moment manifests Rabbit's religious sensibility in telling ways: his spirituality is thoroughly subjective, triggered by his own imaginings more than by external actualities, and his belief that reality's central truth can be encompassed by a single individual reflects little human sympathy for death's prey but instead manifests the Freudian assumption—one clearly endorsed by Updike—that one's most profound empathy is ultimately with oneself and the terror of his own personal extinction. Rabbit's subsequent response to his utterly intuitive confrontation with death's reality seems an act of gratuitous cruelty: he asks Ruth, of whose high school reputation for promiscuity he is aware, "Were you really a hooer?"[5] (99).

Rabbit's importunate question is patently heartless, and, because it follows an instant in which he experiences a "return of security" about Brewer as his home and "shelter of love," smugly moralizing;

but it is reflective as well of his—and Updike's—response to what Michael Novak termed the "experience of nothingness": it provokes in him an attempt to pursue, confront, and articulate the truth. His reckless pursuit of truth here is freeing only in the limited sense that his question—and the response it provokes from Ruth, "Are you really a rat?"—establishes a firmer ground of truthfulness for their nascent relationship; more significantly, the episode anticipates the novel's cemetery scene in which Harry's articulation of the truth is more palpably and more ambiguously liberating. For Rabbit, as for Updike, even the most obviously self-serving impulses toward the apprehension and expression of truth are never completely separable from religious affirmation, and Rabbit's spirituality is most consistently enacted in the novels through his insistence upon speaking the truth he perceives. Updike's fiction operates upon the same principle.[6]

In an interview with T. M. McNally and Dean Stover conducted while he was writing *Rest*, Updike asserted that "One thing that's given me courage in writing has been the belief that the truth, what is actual, must be faced and is somehow holy. That is, what exists is holy and God knows what exists; He can't be shocked, and He can't be surprised. There is some act of virtue in trying to get things down exactly as they are: how people talk, how they act, how they smell. So I have felt empowered in some way to be as much of a realist as I could be, to really describe life as I see it."[7] Although articulated through a more literary idiom than Rabbit's devotion to truth ever is, Updike's realist disposition, clearly, derives from the same feeling of extremity, the same religious impulse that inspires Rabbit heedlessly to demand the absolute truth of Ruth's past. Harry and Updike share, also, a distinctly antagonistic conviction that others must be as willing as they are to confront the truth: a tense moment in *Rabbit Redux* is suddenly leavened by the question Skeeter poses to Nelson, "Who's your gruesome friend?" Rabbit, Jill, Skeeter, and Nelson laugh at this "unexpected illumination" of Nelson's friend Billy Fosnacht, whose only compensation for being the butt of this moment is that "their laughter makes a second wave to reassure him that they are not laughing at him, they are laughing in relief at the gift of truth"[8] (451). Updike seems no more solicitous of readers' sensibilities than Rabbit is to Ruth's feelings or the Penn Villas contingent is to Billy's when he commends Graham Greene's adherence to the idea that "It is a novelist's exact duty, to 'rub our noses' in his apprehensions of the truth, paradoxical and dismal though they may be."[9]

Author and protagonist, as we'll see, come increasingly to question the spiritual sanction of that truth-affirming impulse—Rabbit in the tetralogy and Updike in the evolution of his fiction. Rabbit's declining faith in the mystical validity of his impulses serves, I'm arguing, as a fictional barometer of Updike's progressive doubts that the truth he is recording is "holy," his increasing, deeply reluctant succumbing to the possibility that literature can approach nothing more transcendent than the achievement of "some virtue" in "getting things down exactly as they are." If literary realism is all that human beings are capable of achieving, Updike nominates as his aesthetic mentor Walt Whitman: "Whatever may have been the case in years gone by," Updike quotes Whitman, "the true use for the imaginative faculty of modern times is to give ultimate vivification to facts, to science, to common lives, endowing them with glows and glories and final illustriousness which belong to every real thing, and to real things only." Updike proceeds enthusiastically to endorse Whitman's argument: "The mystery of Me proclaimed, what Emerson called the 'other Me'—the world itself—can be sung in its clean reality, and real things assigned the sacred status that in former times was granted to mysteries. If there is a distinctive 'American realism,' its metaphysics are Whitman's."[10]

Significantly, Updike has come increasingly in interviews and essays to align himself with literary realists such as William Dean Howells and Henry James; whether Updike's fiction ever persuades his reader—or himself—that "real things" can credibly be "assigned the sacred status that in former times was granted to mysteries" is another matter. Updike's conflict between creating an eschatalogically inspired mimesis and a historically based realism is the aesthetic drama I seek to illuminate at the heart of his literary career; the Rabbit tetralogy, I'm assuming throughout *Rabbit (Un)Redeemed*, is the site in his oeuvre where he hazards most in juxtaposing Rabbit's deepening agnosticism against his own declining faith.

If Rabbit is a deeply conflicted Christian, Updike is, I'm contending, an analogously conflicted realist, a writer whose interviews as often affirm the value of literary mimesis as they insist that literary reproduction of the real is, in itself, insufficient, inadequate.[11] In considering Updike's pursuit of "the truth that shall set you free," then, it is necessary to distinguish between human truth approachable in literary fiction and a more transcendent conception of truth that dwarfs mere realism. There is reproductive accuracy of the kind that Updike exercises in meticulously detailing Rabbit's journeys south in *Run* and *Rest*; but his work also aspires to a more elevated notion of truth. "*Rabbit, Run*," Updike told Jan Nunley, "is a fairly deliberate attempt to examine the human predicament from a theological standpoint. I'm not trying to force a message on the reader, but I am trying to give human behavior theological scrutiny as it's seen from above. . . ."[12] The centrality and complexity of this tension between conceptions of truth-telling or—to use more sacramental language—witnessing that pervades Updike's work is epitomized by his equivocal response to the question posed by *Life Magazine* to a number of writers, "Why Are We Here?" "Ancient religion and modern science agree," Updike suggested, "we are here to give praise. Or, to slightly tip the expression, to pay attention. Without us, the physicists who have espoused the anthropic principle tell us, the universe would be unwitnessed, and in a real sense not there at all. It exists, incredibly, for us."

Clearly, the difference between "giving praise" and "paying attention" is substantial. There is a sense of obligation invoked in "giving praise" that seems incontestably religious; "paying attention" has divested the formulation of its transitive character. Many of Updike's essays and reviews, in fact, invoke a writer whose cosmological beliefs terminate at "paying attention," one whose aesthetic pronouncements celebrate the patient, almost devotional literary description/replication of the surfaces and textures of reality. In the mid-1980s, Updike undertook a literary rediscovery of the fiction of William Dean Howells, his Harvard University Howells centennial essay and introduction to *Indian Summer* serving as both celebration of Howells and as vehicles affirming (a bit resignedly) his self-enlistment in the ranks of American realists.

In "Howells as Anti-Novelist," Updike endorsed the ordinariness of the world Howells's prose exhaustively limns by approvingly quoting Howells's Kitty Ellison's description of the ideal fiction: "If I were to write a story, I should want to take the slightest sort of plot, and lay the scene in the dullest sort of place, and then bring out the possibilities." (Brewer, Pennsylvania, it may occur to Updike's reader, qualifies nicely, especially after it has been divested, in "Rabbit Remembered," of the title protagonist of Updike's tetralogy for whom its sacred character consists in his having been born there.) The work, Kitty continues, need contain "nothing extraordinary, little everyday things told so exquisitely, and all fading naturally away without any particular result, only the full meaning of everything brought out."[13] Updike then enlists Henry James in support of the somewhat equivocal brief for literary realism he is mounting: "[Howells] reminds us of how much our native grown imaginative effort is a matter of details, of fine shades, of fine colors, a making the small things do great service. Civilization with us is monotonous," James complained, "and in the way of contrasts, of salient points, of chiaroscuro, we have to take what we can get. We have to look for these things in fields where a less devoted glance would see little more than an arid blank, and, at the last, we manage to find them. All this refines and sharpens our perceptions, makes us, in a literary way, on our own scale, very delicate" (173).

James, clearly, is as dissatisfied with fiction that merely "refines and sharpens our perceptions" as are those Updike detractors who find in his work sensibility without substance, delicacy of perception concealing the fact that "Mr. Updike has nothing to say."[14] If it manages the trick at all, Howellsian realism, James believed, only manages at the last second to redeem us from that "arid blank" and—as he argued elsewhere—never transcends completely American civilization's monotony but confirms it. His sincere expository obeisances to Howells between the writing of *Rich* and *Rest* notwithstanding, Updike ultimately judged Howellsian realism to be no less wanting than James does. In his "Special Message" prefacing the Franklin Library edition of *Rabbit at Rest*, Updike admitted that "Plain realism has never seemed to me enough—all those 'he said's' and 'she said's,' those obligatory domestic crises and chapter concluding private epiphanies. Novel readers must have a plot, no doubt, and a faithful rendering of the texture of the mundane; but a page of printed prose should bring to its mimesis something extra, a kind of supernatural, as it were, to lend everything roundness—a fine excess that corresponds with the intricacy and opacity of the real world."[15] That "something extra, a kind of supernatural" is Updike's literary version of Rabbit's faith in "something that wants me to find it," and I maintain throughout this study that Rabbit's dwindling belief in his "something" corresponds to Updike's declining belief that literature can achieve "something extra" beyond verisimilar rendering.

The point is crucial enough to my argument to justify amplification through another example. Updike reconfigured the difference between profane and sacred limnings of truth in an omnibus review of books dealing with contemporary conceptions of evil: he began by citing George Steiner's comment that, "To have neither heaven nor hell is to be intolerably deprived and alone in a world gone flat." (I'll argue in my concluding chapters that Steiner's description aptly characterizes the world of "Rabbit Remembered.") Updike then appends Edmund Wilson's qualifier, "The answer to [T. S.] Eliot's assertion that 'it is doubtful whether civilization can endure without religion' is that we have to make it endure. But mere endurance," Updike glosses, "is bleak fare after the heady wine of religious consolation"[16] The central tension, I believe, being played out in Updike's fiction, on both dramatic and aesthetic plains, consists between the hope that the vineyards of the "heady wine of religious consolation" continue to exist and the deepening anxiety that the best we can hope for is "the bleak fare of mere endurance."

In order to plot what I am delineating as the reluctantly expanding secularism of Updike's aesthetic, we need to consider where it began. In "Midpoint," the 1969 autobiographical poem he characterized as summarizing his "philosophy,"[17] Updike affirmed his hope that what he witnesses not be an "arid blank" or mere passing show:

> Humble
> as a glow-worm, my boneless ego asked
> only to witness, to serve as the hub
>
> of a whirling spectacle that would not pass.

The art that would be his medium of witnessing must be as exacting as Howells's, and as austere, because only then might it accomplish its mimesis-transcending purpose:

> I sought in middling textures part-
> icles of iridescence, scintillae
> in dullish surfaces; and pictured art
>
> as descending, via pencil, into dry
> exactitude.

That exactitude in registering the world in words is crucial because of what it holds out the promise of glimpsingly revealing: that

> The beaded curtain
> Of Matter hid a knowing Eye.[18]

As Updike continued to explain in the "Why Are We Here?" response for *Life Magazine* I truncated above, "This formulation (knowing what we know of the universe's ghastly extent), is more incredible to our sense of things than the Old Testament hypothesis of a God willing to suffer, coddle, instruct, and even, in the Book of Job, to debate with men, in order to realize the meagre benefit of worship, of praise of His Creation. What we beyond doubt do have is our instinctive intellectual curiosity about the universe from the quasars down to the quarks, our wonder at existence itself, and an occasional surge of sheer blind gratitude for being here."[19]

With its conflicting impulses toward affirming realistic representation and disparaging it in the name of more sacramental artistic ambitions, this paragraph effectively epitomizes the way in which literary

representation and eschatology often converge—and sometimes contend—with each other in Updike's fiction and expository prose. The
only meaning the universe can be said to have, the "anthropic principle" suggests, is its being witnessed by humanity. For Updike, this
leaves perception—and the literary forms it generates—culminating
in works (in the words of Howells's Kitty Ellison) "all fading naturally away without any particular result." Thus Updike described his
artistic mission in "Midpoint":

> Some task remains, whose weight I can't forget,
> Some package, anciently addressed, of praise,
> That keeps me knocking on the doors of days. (44)

Significantly, and very characteristically of Updike, both the "Why
Are We Here?" passage and the "Midpoint" stanza leave ambiguous
what it is that we attendants are obliged to praise. For himself, a personal aesthetic commitment was clearly laid out in "Midpoint":

> An easy Humanism plagues the land;
> I choose to take an otherworldly stand. (38)

Updike is unwilling to settle for the "anthropic principle," and consequently, in the "Why Are We Here?" passage, he moves through a
syntactically torturous route of associations to posit God at the center
of it all commanding only the "meagre benefit of worship." Mirroring
an attitude adopted with significantly less self-consciousness by his
scripturally uninformed, Bible-shunning protagonist, Updike suggests that the universe's existence is far more astounding than the biblical narratives evolved in the human effort to account for the miracle.
While we may have doubts that there is a being compelling our praise
for his creation, Updike implies, we cannot doubt "our intellectual
curiosity" about the universe—which, assumedly, inspires us to further witnessing of it in hopes of understanding more. Updike's final
sentence ambiguously elides its object again: to what or to whom we
experience "sheer blind gratitude" for being here remains uncertain.

The two points I want to make arising from my comparison of Updike's "Why Are We Here?" meditation and "Midpoint" contempla-
tions are these: that the oscillation discernible here between the
endorsement of witnessing the universe for its own sake and ever-so-
tentatively affirming faith transcending mere witnessing is thoroughly
typical of Updike's pronouncements and of his fiction, and that, for
all the manifest dissimilarities between him and his protagonist, the

conflicted attitude expressed here between witnessing and worshipping is one that Updike and Rabbit share.

As the tetralogy evolved, and Rabbit's role in the novels as initiator
of action gradually diminished, the protagonist's entrance into middle
and later middle age obliged him increasingly to embrace the role of
witness as the only one left to him.[20] *Rabbit is Rich* and *Rabbit at Rest*
are novels dominated by Rabbit's constant attentiveness to the world
around him, the former dramatizing a man experiencing comfort-
inspired equanimity toward what he witnesses, the latter projecting
one obsessed with the failure of that disintegrating outer world to
sustain the life he knows he's losing. Despite his darkening vision of
things, Rabbit's characteristic tropism, like that of his creator, is to
praise: in response to a beautiful day in *Rest*, Harry thinks that
"there's a grace of sorts" in the solar system "that chimes with the
excessive beauty of this crystalline late-summer day. He needs to
praise" (1423). The terror that their expressions of praise echo emp-
tily in a universe devoid of a creator is, I think, one that Rabbit and
Updike share, and that the Rabbit tetralogy constitutes Updike's
most significant literary configuring of that spiritual anxiety.

Rabbit Angstrom is not, of course, a Pulitzer Prize winning novelist nor the preeminent American man of letters of his era; Joyce Carol
Oates's excellent essay, "Updike's American Comedies," gauged the
relationship exactly in her suggestion that "*Rabbit, Run* explored,
quite remorselessly, the consequences of a reduced, secularized, 'un-
imagined' world, Updike's conception of Updike-without-talent,
Updike trapped in quantity."[21] Rabbit does, nonetheless, allow Updike to dramatize his existential anxieties through a persona less gifted
than is his creator in articulating and conceptualizing them.[22] Primary
among those anxieties, for my purposes, is the spiritual question of
the significance of human witnessing. In creating Rabbit, Updike intentionally divested himself both of the literary vocation that provides his own fundamental rationale for bearing witness and the
intellectual polish and eloquence that sometimes smooth his path
through existential thickets. As far as Rabbit knows, "the wandering
thread of his feelings" constitutes no more than—to use a word he
never would—solipsism; he is the only audience of his thoughts and
perceptions which, he is often convinced, circle meaninglessly on
themselves and will expire pointlessly when he does.[23] Harry Angstrom's struggle in the Rabbit tetralogy consists between the need to
believe that his acts of attentiveness count for something—"His feeling that there is an unseen world is instinctive, and more of his actions
than anyone suspects constitute transactions with it" (201)—and his
fear that his consciousness is a meaningless chaos: "I think I'm going

crazy down here," he tells his daughter-in-law, Pru, when she in-
trudes via telephone upon his Deleon solitude at the end of *Rest*: "My
dreams—they're like cut-up comic strips" (1500). If the Rabbit novels
are Updike's most significant literary accomplishment, it may be because through imposing Harry Angstrom's perceptual limitations
upon his own stylistic gifts, Updike set himself the toughest trial of
his ethical and aesthetic creed of the spirit-affirming capacities of
human witnessing.

The convergences between author's and character's apprehensions
over the value of witnessing are clearly signaled in one of Updike's
more expansive comments on his artistic mission, one that clearly
predicates his literary output on the existence of what the narrator of
Run refers to as Rabbit's "transactions with the unseen world." His
youthful self, Updike explained in "The Dogwood Tree," "saw art—
between drawing and writing he ignorantly made no distinction—as
a method of riding a thin pencil line out of Shillington, out of time
altogether, into an infinity of unseen and even unborn hearts. . . . I
reasoned thus: just as the paper is the basis for the marks upon it,
might not events be contingent upon a never expressed (because fea-
tureless) ground? Is the true marvel of Sunday skaters the pattern of
their pirouettes or the fact that they are silently upheld?" As if contradicting James's positing of the world as an "arid blank," Updike
insisted that, "Blankness is not emptiness; we may skate upon an intense radiance we do not see because we see nothing else. And in fact
there is a color, a quiet but tireless goodness that things at rest, like a
brick wall or a small stone, seem to affirm. A wordless reassurance
these things are pressing to give. An hallucination?"

That question elicited the one that seems to me at the heart of Updike's fiction, a question most compellingly dramatized in his work
through Rabbit's increasing doubts that there is any point in his continuing to perceive what he perceives. "To transcribe middleness with
all its grits, bumps, and anonymities, in its fullness of satisfaction and
mystery," Updike asked himself: "is it possible or, in view of the suffering that violently colors the periphery and that at all moments
threatens to move into the center, worth doing?" Updike's answer to
that question is characteristically equivocal, but if affirmation is to be
wrung from the query, it must ride—as affirmation always does for
Rabbit—on the energy of self-assertion, on the dynamism of egotism:
"Possibly not; but the horse-chestnut trees, the telephone poles, the
porches, the green hedges [of Shillington] recede to a calm point that
in my subjective geography is still the center of the world."[24]

Given my prologue's discussion of the centrality of self in Updike's
aesthetic, it isn't surprising to find him locating the worthiness of

"transcribing middleness with all its grits, bumps, and anonymities" in the affirmation of personal memory, in the "calm point" that Shillington inhabits in his "subjective geography." Unlike Updike, however, Harry Angstrom isn't transcribing middleness but living in its midst, passively registering the flow of it that, he becomes increasingly terrified, must ultimately submerge him. Rabbit is Updike's most significant creation, I contend, because in the first novel in which he appears, he is already, at the age of twenty-six, questioning the Wordsworthian affirmation of witness Updike offers in "The Dogwood Tree." In Mt. Judge, Pennsylvania, the geographical place that was his life's inception, Harry finds no "calm point" or sustaining center, but only an overwhelming sense of loss and betrayal at the hands of nature. Taking Nelson to a playground in *Run* shortly after Janice has returned from the hospital with Becky, Harry is besieged by memories of his childhood: "He feels the truth: the thing that has left his life has left irrevocably; no search would recover it. No flight would reach it. It was here, beneath the town, in these smells and these voices, forever behind him."[25] Whereas Updike built a literary career on the inspiration which was Shillington, Pennsylvania, Rabbit intuits only the negations of literary naturalism underlying his home: "The fullness ends when we give Nature her ransom, when we make children for her. Then she is through with us, and we become, first inside, then outside, junk. Flower stalks" (193–94).

Since Updike's style is his primary means of undertaking his literary acts of witnessing, it needs to be more clearly linked to the thematic exploration I claim these novels enact.[26] The deliberate, highly sensual accumulation of impression and subjective detail—say—of Rabbit's spirit-stifling Wilbur Street apartment with the stultifying psychological weather that eventually sparks his flight toward his fantasy of Gulf Coast freedom is an early example. Just before embarking upon that flight, Rabbit runs his hand over the bark of trees, seeking to salve the conflicts besieging his mind with "the small answer of a texture"; in the Rabbit tetralogy, the dense word-textures so patiently woven by Updike's language are often the only answer provided.

It is a highly typical Updike paradox, however, that the heedless proliferation of these word-textures in his texts occasionally seem indistinguishable from the traps Rabbit seeks so desperately to escape. Like the map that he expects to guide him safely south at the beginning of *Rabbit, Run*, these words evocative of his conflicted sensibility sometimes come to seem "a net he is somewhere caught in"[27] (33). That first Rabbit novel opens with a powerful evocation of Harry's experience of overwhelming psychic unfreedom, the terror of which provokes his drive south; *Rabbit at Rest* ends by evoking the texture of the terrible spiritual dread Rabbit experiences in his Florida condominium to which he has fled as if in completion of that lapsed pilgrimage of thirty years earlier: "The rooms and furniture of the condo in these days he's been living here alone have taken on the tension and menace of a living person who is choosing to remain motionless. At night he can feel the rooms breathe and think. They are thinking about him" (1499). At the end of *Rest*, clearly, the "something that wants me to find it" has found him. Harry's immersion in silence and solitude renders his self-impelled flight toward death as dramatically inevitable as was his flight south to his younger trapped self. It is in Updike's ability to craft these psychic terrains, perhaps beyond any other capacity, that he surpasses his American contemporaries, but his prose isn't exclusively limited to evoking interior landscapes.

Updike's fiction is generously possessed as well of his desire—need, rather—obsessively to name the things of the world in fiction as he'd once punctiliously catalogued the hits of 1959 he heard on his radio driving the same southerly route Rabbit would take.[28] That such a need is essentially religious in nature is an argument I am not the first Updike critic to make.[29] Updike has himself attributed a parallel tendency to Proust, whose "tendrilous sentences seek out an essence so fine the search itself is an act of faith."[30] The centrality of that issue to my thesis is, however, a distinctive feature of this study, accounting for the following chapter's contextualization of the tetralogy in a discussion of the relationship between spiritual epiphany and secular ritual in "Pigeon Feathers," "Packed Dirt, Churchgoing, A Dying Cat, A Traded Car," and "The Blessed Man of Boston, My Grandmother's Thimble, and Fanning Island." One of the secondary claims the Rabbit tetralogy makes to literary endurance is its preservation in print of hundreds of the objects and popular culture icons that permeated middle-class American lives and minds in the four decades distilled by the novels and through which we who existed in these eras partially defined ourselves.[31] The driftwood lamp in Janice and Harry's Penn Villas living room that mysteriously survives the fiery cataclysm in *Rabbit Redux* is one such object. The Toyota, which takes on nearly religious significance for Rabbit throughout *Rabbit is Rich* as the source of his middle-age prosperity, reflects how serious Updike is in asserting the spiritual character objects take on in our lives. That that object—like so many objects represented in the tetralogy—proves too flimsy a ground on which to found a meaningful existence demonstrates how uncompromisingly religious is Updike's perception of human life. (Who needs the icons of religious belief, Updike asks in a sonnet, "Religious Consolation": "We do; we need more worlds. This one will fail."[32]) For both Harry and Updike, recording the physical world is potentially an act of infinite hope—thus the "small answer of a texture"—that always contains the threat of betrayal, so vulnerable is the human spirit to being overwhelmed by the pure excess of materiality. "One wonders," Updike acknowledges in "Howells as Anti-Novelist," seeming to speak for both Harry and himself, "whether Howells's tenacious artistic clinging to the surface of things doesn't show a fear of falling back into an abyss."[33]

The point demands emphasizing because Rabbit's anxieties are, in my reading of them, so often shadowy, secularized and less literary versions of Updike's own. In Updike's *Memoirs of the Ford Administration*, Alfred Clayton explains that his biography of James Buchanan failed because the biographer became so overwhelmed by his material and the commentary on the president's life that has preceded his own biographical investigations. "My attempt to bestow upon Buchanan *the award of posterity*," Clayton confesses, "collapsed when I, having imagined an eagle's-eye view that would make of his life a single fatal moment, found myself merely writing more history. . . . My opus ground to a halt of its own growing weight, all that comparing of subtly disparate secondary versions of the facts, and seeking out of old newspapers and primary documents, and sinking deeper and deeper into an exfoliating quiddity that offers no deliverance from itself, only a final vibrant indeterminacy, infinitely detailed and yet ambiguous—as unsettled, these dead facts, as if alive."[34] Clayton's biographical researches having failed to attain to the urgency and focus of "the eagle-eyed view" he hoped would distill and clarify Buchanan's personal history, the biography bogs down in the details which are its raison d'etre, his book never elucidating but only adding to the "exfoliating quiddity" of fact, assumption and speculation, which is Buchanan's exponentially accumulating posthumous life.

I'll return to Clayton's plaint in considering Updike's attempt to find, through writing *In the Beauty of the Lilies*, more meaning in historical reconstruction than does Clayton in writing Buchanan's life. Although no biographer, Rabbit's corresponding experience involves his constant complaint, particularly in *Rest*, about the excess of things in the world: "Just thinking about those old days lately depresses him; it makes him face life's constant depreciation . . . he feels a stifling uselessness in things, a kind of atomic decay whereby the precious glowing present turns, with each tick of the clock, into the leaden slag of history" (1431–2). Clayton's inability to subordinate that mass of words to an all-encompassing understanding dramatizes a fear that pervades Updike's best fiction, one obliquely embedded in Rabbit's thanatophobic moment on Mt. Judge. The possibility that the vantage point of spiritual extremity offers no illumination save an awareness of death is what prompts Rabbit to respond by confronting Ruth with a question soliciting cruel truth. The great hope underlying Updike's work is that "the truth" he pursues through fiction invokes and reveals a "knowing Eye" behind the "beaded curtain of Matter" rather than merely reproducing the superflux of material reality or meaninglessly reasserting the ephemerality of things. Alf Clayton's description of his project's failure can be read, I think, as Updike's obliquely articulated anxiety that his own work may dissolve into "an exfoliating quiddity that offers no deliverance from itself, only a final vibrant indeterminacy, infinitely detailed and yet ambiguous." Nowhere in the massive critical literature on Updike's work has anyone articulated more eloquently the risk his fiction runs—that of offering only self-enclosed fables that provide testimony to the world's opacity and unintelligibility rather than being a literary illumination of it. Clearly, he expects more of his work than that, or at least has higher hopes for it.

Writers, Updike argued in "How Does the Writer Imagine?" "must sit down in the expectation that the material will speak through us, that certain unforseeable happinesses of pattern and realization will emerge out of the blankness as we write."[35] The great fact of the Rabbit tetralogy, I suggest, is that, for the tetralogy's protagonist at any rate, the emergence of "certain unforeseeable happinesses of pattern and realization" is the rarest of occurrences, Harry progressively doubting the value of his human attentiveness as anything more than a form of solipsistic and meaningless self-diversion. Having mistakenly eaten pellets intended for the exotic birds exhibited at Jungle Gardens early in *Rest*, Harry is "suffused with a curious sensation; he feels faintly numb and sick, but beyond that, beyond the warm volume enclosed by his skin, the air is swept by a universal devaluation; for one flash he sees his life as a silly thing it will be a relief to discard" (1143).

In Rabbit Angstrom, Updike created a literary alter ego who alternately constitutes the polar opposite of Updike's literary life while embodying and exemplifying many of Updike's deeply held values and ideals. Through Rabbit, Updike confronts the voice in himself that mocks his modernist belief in the redemptiveness of art and has no answering experience to the "still center of the world" of Shillington, Pennsylvania, that launched Updike upon a fulfilling and triumphant literary career. For Rabbit, life as "a winner" largely ends in the last moments of his final basketball game for Mt. Judge High School, getting resurrected tenuously in the affluence Janice's inheritance provides him in *Rabbit is Rich*. Rabbit's faith is more ephemeral

and less eloquent than Updike's, making him more vulnerable to nihilism than Updike, whose descent into despair often seems provided
with a safety net by his ability to articulate the fall. "Rabbit is not a
formal Christian, really," Updike commented in an interview. "He's
been exposed to it, but he proceeds by a few more basic notions: an
instinctiveness that somehow his life must be important, even though
there's no eternal confirmation of this—only the belief that the reality
within must matter and must be served."[36]
     Harry and Updike shared an antipathy for the late '60s version of
America, one that sent Updike fleeing to England with his family
while it so disorients Harry that he becomes passively complicit in
the death of one of its counterculture celebrants. Updike and his protagonist experience their most striking rapprochement in *Rabbit is
Rich*, their parallel satisfactions with the prosperity that middle age
has brought getting expressed through their frequently ecstatic col-
laboration in verbally witnessing the comfortable world surrounding
Harry.[37] Throughout much of that novel, they seem to be concurring
in the idea that God's apparent withdrawal is supportable because, as
Updike explained in "The Dogwood Tree," "I got the impression of
wealth as a vast brooding presence, like God Himself."[38] By the end
of *Rabbit is Rich*, the richness has begun going sour, precipitating the
uninterrupted descent of *Rabbit at Rest*, which never seems fully to
contradict Rabbit's naturalistic conclusion in the Jungle Gardens
scene that "It's hell, to be a creature. You are trapped in yourself, the
genetic instructions, more strictly than in a cage" (1144). The medical
details of Rabbit's failing heart derived from Linda Grace Hoyer Updike's ultimately fatal coronary decline, and consequently, Updike set
Rabbit's fictional death within days of his mother's on October 10,
1989. Whereas in *Couples* and other fictions, Joyce Carol Oates ob-
served in her review of *Rest*, "John Updike explored the human body
as Eros, he now explores the body, in yet more detail, as Thanatos.
One begins virtually to share, with the doomed Harry Angstrom, a
panicky sense of the body's terrible finitude, and of its place in a
world of other, competing bodies."[39] *Rest* was, as Updike characterized it, "a depressed book about a depressed man written by a depressed man,"[40] and although "Rabbit Remembered" with hedged
cheerfulness revisits the survivors a decade after Harry's death, the
epilogue's "life goes on" aura and affirmative resolution of some of
the tetralogy's unresolved tensions doesn't entirely contravene *Rest*'s
gloomy depiction of the individual's bleak, lonely descent into obsessive physicality and death.
     Determining whether Rabbit's naturalistic dismissal of his four-
volume-long act of witness—that his life "is a silly thing which it

would be a relief to discard"—coincides with Updike's dramatized estimation of its ultimate literary value is one of my primary critical objectives in *Rabbit (Un)Redeemed: The Drama of Belief in John Updike's Fiction*. *In the Beauty of the Lilies* and "Rabbit Remembered" provide me with closing chapters and an epilogue by imaging up an America that can't even rise to the faint, fragile, and deeply intuitive faith of a Rabbit Angstrom. "Why did they teach you such things if no one believed them?" we've already watched Rabbit impatiently interrogating his Sunday school retentions immediately before his Mt. Judge epiphany with Ruth. Fifteen hundred pages of prose and thirty years of life depicted in those pages provide no very good answer to Rabbit's question. Updike's fiction, I want to show through the illumination of these selected texts, delineates more substantially than any other American writer's the cultural evolution culminating in the condition in which we currently find ourselves: the post-Christian. But, even as his fiction's surfaces reflect the incoherence and unintelligibility of lived experience—"Truly, our lives are like the universe," as Alf Clayton puts it, "nothing is lost, only transformed, in the slide toward disorder" (*Memories*, 228)—the aesthetically patterned depths of Updike's fiction embody his hope for cosmic order.

2

Where Only a Scribble Exists:
The David Kern Stories

By authentic, I mean actual. For the creative imagination, as I conceive it, is wholly parasitic upon the real world—what used to be called Creation. Creative excitement, and a sense of useful work, has invariably and only come to me when I felt I was transferring, with a lively accuracy, some piece of experienced reality to the printed page.

—"How Does the Writer Imagine?" in *Odd Jobs*

It seems to me nearly incontestable: the most compelling fiction John Updike has written dramatizes his protagonists' loss of religious faith and the personal consequences of that loss. From "Pigeon Feathers," "Packed Dirt, Churchgoing, A Dying Cat, A Traded Car," and "The Blessed Man of Boston, My Grandmother's Thimble, and Fanning Island" through the Rabbit tetralogy, *Couples*, and *A Month of Sundays*, to numerous stories in *The Afterlife and Other Stories* and the opening of *In the Beauty of the Lilies*, the erosion of his characters' belief in a God-centered universe has inspired Updike's most substantial and resonant fiction. If future generations continue to read and value Updike's oeuvre, I'd predict it will be because more than the work of any other American writer of his era, his most resonant fiction has devoted itself to the anatomization of America's evolution from a Christian to post-Christian culture and to the dramatization of the individual human cost of that spiritual transition. Of American writers, perhaps only Henry Adams in his *Education* has written as eloquently and movingly about the experience of the abrupt sensation that the natural world, rather than being imbued with divine concern, intentionality, and justice, is a chaos of forces indifferent to human desires and needs.

"What could become of such a child of the 17th and 18th centuries," Adams asks, "when he should wake up to and find himself required to play the game of the twentieth?" (In a rejected ending to

43

Self-Consciousness, Updike introduced "Oppositional Other" to critique his memoirs, his counterself mocking the book's exposition of
Updike's "wanting, on the basis of medieval or at best eighteenth-
century metaphysics, to preserve your miserable, spotty identity forever!"[1]) Adams's primary lesson of that new century was for the first
time to "feel the shell of custom broken": "He had never seen Nature—only her surface—the sugar-coating that she shows to youth.
Flung suddenly in his face, with the harsh brutality of chance, the
terror of the blow stayed by him henceforth for life." Having watched
his sister suffer through the excruciations of fatal lockjaw, Adams explains, "For the first time, the stage scenery of the senses collapsed;
the human mind felt itself stripped naked, vibrating in a void of
shapeless energies, with restless mass colliding, crushing, wasting and
destroying what these same energies had labored for centuries to
perfect. . . . For the first time in his life, Mont Blanc looked like what
it was—a chaos of anarchic and purposeless forces—and he needed
days of repose to see it clothe itself again with the illusions of his
senses, the white purity of its snows, the splendor of its light, and the
infinity of its heavenly peace."[2] As we'll see, Rabbit becomes similarly
preoccupied throughout the tetralogy—particularly in *Rabbit at
Rest*—with the "anarchic and purposeless forces" of nature, science
and technology confronting him with the same refutations of his spiritual hopes that the dynamo emblematized for Adams. In *Rabbit is
Rich*, Updike's protagonist allows the "illusions of his senses" to
imbue nature with a benignity prompting him to learn the names of
its flora, but overall he proves much less capable than Adams of settling back comfortably into a faith in "the infinity of [nature's] heavenly peace."

As an inheritor of Adams's modernist spiritual pessimism, Updike
brings to his fiction an indissoluble ambivalence about religious belief, consistently—and often ironically—depicting faith as a complex
psychological dynamic constituted of such markedly unspiritual
components as egotism, aestheticism, destructive impulses and sexuality. Because the Rabbit tetralogy is so intensely concerned with the
fluctuations of Harry's faith—his oscillations, in *Rabbit, Run*, for instance, between a belief in "something that wants me to find it" and
the necessity of killing in himself that belief because his pursuit of it
is responsible for his daughter's death—I want to use three early Updike stories, published more or less contemporaneously with the first
Rabbit novel, to establish the psychological complexity of Updike's
understanding of faith and to provide a context for the illumination
of the varieties of Rabbit's religious experience. In "Pigeon Feathers,"
Updike dramatizes his young protagonist's apparent spiritual tri-

umph over religious doubt; in "Packed Dirt, Churchgoing, A Dying Cat, A Traded Car" and "The Blessed Man of Boston, My Grandmother's Thimble, and Fanning Island," an older David Kern posits (somewhat equivocally, I'll argue) secular forms—the narratives themselves, for instance—as compensations for the dissolution of religious certainties. In addition to constituting Updike's attempt to interrogate modernism's premise that art can fill the void once occupied by faith, these stories in their self-conscious concern with recording the existence of ephemeral people and events anticipate as well his more ambitious questionings of historical reconstructions in *Memories of the Ford Administration* and *In the Beauty of the Lilies*.

At the end of his *Education*, Adams wonders whether the conflict of forces between the "old conventions and values" and the dawning technological order predicated upon power and money would "produce a new man . . . a child born of contact between the old and new energies."[3] These three Olinger stories comprise Updike's most focused attempts at reconciling the "old and new energies" of rural, Christian America and post-Christian secularism of which he is a product, their aura of palpable anguish epitomizing how painful was the cultural transition that culminated in this son of Plowville, Pennsylvania. writing "Talk of the Town" copy for the hyperurbanite *New Yorker* between 1955–57.[4] In his 1993 interview with Jan Nunley, Updike discussed what he characterized as the "crisis theology" of Barth and Tillich that provided him with a saving spiritual sustenance during the period of his life memorialized in these pivotal, definitional stories. "[P]erhaps the struggle whereby I established my theological ideas climaxed in my early twenties in a set of conclusions along the lines of crisis theology," Updike suggested. "I haven't altered those views," he added, "I haven't really refreshed them either."[5] Updike's comment about "crisis theology" establishes two important principles underlying my critical project: first, the absence of significant shifts in Updike's theological disposition allows me to move fairly freely within his oeuvre without fear of finding completely contradictory evidence. Second, the fact that these three stories address dramatically the ontological questions central to Updike's career-spanning fictional concerns while simultaneously constituting attempted aesthetic solutions to those dilemmas is another, perhaps even more compelling, justification for using them as prelude to discussing the *Rabbit Angstrom* saga and *In the Beauty of the Lilies*.

Ostensibly a narrative dramatizing the resolution of an adolescent's crisis of faith, "Pigeon Feathers" is, simultaneously, a depiction of the psychic process through which an artistic sensibility is born, and an exploration of the sexual basis of this epiphany as well. The story's

protagonist, David Kern, has been moved from his Olinger, Pennsylvania, home to a remote farm in Firetown during World War II as a
result of his mother's desire to reacquire the country house in which
she was born and raised, and the certainties that upheld his Olinger
childhood fail to survive the dislocation.[6] Not only have many of the
customs that had imposed order upon David's Olinger life been abandoned, but his sense of security in the world, exemplified by the neat
rows of brightly lit houses that lined his old street,[7] has been replaced
by the sense of alienness he feels in the "huge exhaustion" of the
farmland that stretches in all directions from his new home.

Updike has discussed the autobiographical inspiration for this
story—Linda Grace Hoyer Updike's purchasing, in 1945, of "the old
Hoyer farm" where she grew up, and her moving of her family there
against the wishes of her husband and son—so often in fiction and
nonfiction that the event comes to seem a—if not *the*—seminal psychological experience of his life. Based on the evidence of Updike's
memoirs, *Self-Consciousness*, and his other fifty-plus published
books, his mother's moving of the Updike family from Shillington to
Plowville at a particularly vulnerable point in his maturation is the
central betrayal of his life, an experience that provided inspiration for
more novels (*The Centaur*, *Of the Farm*) and more stories (those in
The Afterlife and Other Stories in particular) than any other. E. B.
White's review of Louis Bromfield's *Malabar Farm*, Updike asserted
in an appreciation of White, "gave my mother the necessary courage
to buy eighty rundown acres of Pennsylvania loam and turned me
overnight into a rural creature, clad in muddy shoes, a cloak of loneliness, and a clinging aura of apples."[8] "The underlying dramatic transaction [of his 1965 novel, *Of the Farm*], as I conceived it," he
acknowledged, "was the mutual forgiveness of mother and son, the
acceptance each of the other's guilt in taking what they had wanted,
to the discomfort, respectively, of the dead father and the divorced
wife."[9] Updike reprised the familial disputants of *Of the Farm* in
"The Sandstone Farmhouse": "This was the mother Joey had loved,"
the story's narrator explains, "the mother before they moved, before
she betrayed him with the farm and its sandstone house."[10] As the
unnamed protagonist of "The Brown Chest" recalls, it wasn't only
the farm and house that seemed a betrayal: "Country space frightened
him, much as the coal bin and the dark triangles under the attic eaves
had—spaces that didn't have enough to do with people. Fields that
were plowed one day in the spring and harvested one day in the fall,
woods where dead trees were allowed to topple and slowly rot without anyone noticing."[11] Much of the power of "Pigeon Feathers,"
consequently, is attributable to its evocation of David Kern's resent-

ment at his mother's banishing of his beloved Olinger environs and stranding of him in a place that has too little to do with people and too much to do with nature's brutal processes of destruction and renewal, and his guilt over those feelings of intense resentment.

Attempting to participate in the structuring of his new life and thereby to exorcise his feelings of disorientation in it, David sorts and shelves his mother's books, coming across H. G. Wells's account of the birth of Christianity in his *Outline of History*. Jesus, David reads, was "an obscure political agitator, a kind of hobo" who somehow survived his own crucifixion, this "freakish accident" inexplicably resulting in the formation of a religion founded upon the delusions of superstitious, credulous men. Outraged that such blasphemy can be tolerated in God's universe, David musters all his Sunday school certainties in an effort to refute Wells's cavalier dismissal of Christianity's central constitutive narrative, only to find them all too metaphorically fragile to effectively contest Wells's "engines of knowledge."

His mother, to whom David turns for eschatological reassurance, offers him only the equivocal comfort of a pantheist God capable of vouchsafing a salvageable soul to the land but not to humans; becoming a sort of all-redeeming earth mother, she offers with a consoling embrace to "receive his helplessness, all her grace, her gentleness, her love of beauty gathered into a passive intensity that made him intensely hate her."[12] His father, a high school science teacher who counters his wife's animistic conception of nature with a strictly chemical understanding, nonetheless dreads the natural world no less than David does, unwittingly reinforcing his son's terror by "comically" and, clearly, disingenuously—insisting "kill-or-be-killed, that's my motto," while contending, "Hell, I think death is a wonderful thing. I look forward to it. Get the garbage out of the way. If I had the man here who invented death, I'd pin a medal on him" (139). David's last resort in the world beyond himself is the local Lutheran minister, Reverend Dobson, the instructor of David's catechetical class, "a delicate young man with great dark eyes and small white shapely hands that flickered like protesting doves when he preached," who attempts to assuage the boy's fears by analogizing heaven to "the goodness that Abraham Lincoln did liv[ing] after him" (133). "Nowhere in the world of other people," the story's narrator explains, appropriating David's tone of bruised faith and spiritual isolation, "would he find the hint, the nod, he needed to begin to build his fortress against death. They none of them believed. He was alone. In that dark hole" (139).

The "dark hole" that David inhabits recalls the experience that escalates his religious questionings into a full-blown spiritual crisis.[13] One night shortly after reading Wells, David sees the skeleton of an insect projected on a wall by the beam of his flashlight, its appearance precipitating "an exact vision of death," the image revealing to him the awful significance of Wells's expulsion of God from the universe.[14] If there is no God, then death is final, the destination of all humans being "a long hole in the ground, no wider than your body, down which you are drawn while the white faces above recede. You try to reach them but your arms are pinned. Shovels pour dirt into your face. There you will be forever, in an upright position, blind and silent, and in time no one will remember you, and you will never be called. . . . And the earth tumbles on, and the sun expires, and unaltering darkness reigns where once there were stars." This deathly epiphany prompts David to understand that the world is "a jumble of horror" haunted by "the spectres out of science fiction, where gigantic cinder moons fill half of the turquoise sky." (For Rabbit, too, as I'll demonstrate in subsequent chapters, the sky provides a constant barometer of God's existence or absence.) "As David ran, a gray planet rolled inches behind his neck. If he looked back, he would be buried. And in the momentum of his terror, hideous possibilities— the dilation of the sun, the triumph of the insects, the crabs on the shore of *The Time Machine*—wheeled out of the vacuum of make-believe and added their weight to his impending oblivion" (123). Ralph C. Wood diagnosed David's condition with characteristic precision: "Like many adolescents, David seeks an individual rather than a social salvation, and he is obsessed with the problem of mortality rather than the problem of sin. His desire is for a faith at once biblical in its intensity and promise, and yet secular in its provenance and implication. He demands, in sum, the transcendent God proclaimed by Christian faith, but without either the historical revelation incarnate in Christ and recorded in scripture, or the communal allegiance to God found in the church."[15]

David's experience of nothingness seems an appropriately teenage version of Henry Adams's, one constituted of images derived not from the fin de siecle scientific discoveries underlying Adams's crisis but from Wellsian science fiction. Correspondingly, the solemnity of David's confrontation with death is both nicely undercut and made more poignantly real by the fact that his "exact vision" transpires in the family outhouse, its site and the metaphors through which it is presented ("The skin of his chest was soaked with the effort of rejection") suggesting that it is as much the humiliating consciousness of his own physical necessities as the awareness of death that he is struggling to expel. That being the case, it makes sense that precipitating the resolution of David's dilemma is a suggestion made by his grand-mother, the nature of the "supernatural aid" this "helpful crone" provides (to adopt Joseph Campbell's "adventure of the hero" terms[16]) being obliquely hinted at by her most salient physical fea-ture—a palsied hand that so distresses her daughter that David's mother is constantly imploring her, "Mother, put your waggler away." Updike embroiders this character's role as facilitator of Da-vid's masculine initiation by placing "cockeyed spectacles" on Gran-mom's face and by having her waggler impotently wither when David declines to accept the initiatory task she offers him, the subsequent fulfillment of which marks his attainment of masculine maturity. Whether Granmom's waggler conjures up for David's mother, who routinely wears her husband's clothes as she walks her farm, a dis-tastefully phallocentric conception of nature is less clear than that she is discomfited by her mother's highly visible deformity because it represents an indisputable repudiation of her pantheistic faith in the orderly purposefulness of nature.

Furniture from the Olinger home, banished to the barn because of the farmhouse's smaller dimensions, is being "fouled" by pigeon droppings, and David's grandmother suggests the boy use his new rifle to scatter the pests. His mother endorses the plan, agreeing that the barn has come to look like a rookery—a crow's nest, but also a place of illicit birth. Entering the barn with his gun, David sends the puppy, Copper—a companion to his innocence—back to the house and waits while his eyes adjust to the darkness, since "a barn, in day, is a small night." Taking careful aim on a pigeon outlined in the crack of the barn roof, he fires: "The slow contraction of his hand abruptly sprang the bullet; for a half-second there was doubt, and then the pi-geon fell like a handful of rags. . . ." This doubt, in its literal and figu-rative senses, is further dispelled with the death of each pigeon until the point at which David feels himself "fully master now. . . .

> He felt like a beautiful avenger. Out of the shadowy ragged infinity of the
> vast barn roof these impudent things dared to thrust their heads, pre-
> sumed to dirty its starred silence with their filthy timorous life, and he cut
> them off, tucked them back neatly into the silence. He had the sensation
> of a creator; these little smudges and flickers that he was clever to see and
> even cleverer to hit in the dim recesses of the rafters—out of each of them
> he was making a full bird. A tiny peek, probe, dab of life, when he hit it,
> blossomed into a dead enemy, falling with good, final weight. (146–47)

Exhilarated by this ceremony of murderous creation, David emerges from the barn where his mother waits, poised to confirm his transfiguration. Shying from his "carelessly held gun," she tells him, "Don't smirk. You look like your father." She and David retrieve the dead pigeons from the barn, and when he asks whether he should get her a shovel with which to bury them, she replies, "You bury them. They're your kill. And be sure to make the hole deep enough so that [Copper] won't dig them up." (Her admission that "the dog will go wild" over these corpses constitutes her reluctant acknowledgment of another face of nature she would rather ignore.) Expressing sorrow at the silence imposed by David's stilling of the pigeons' comforting cooing, she returns to the house: "Unlike her, she did not look up, either at the orchard to the right of her or at the meadow to her left, but instead held her head rigidly, tilted a little, as if listening to the ground."

Left alone, David examines his kill before burying them, noting the perfection of the wings and the beauty of the colors perfectly splayed across the bodies of these pests:

> And across the surface of the infinitely adjusted yet somehow effortless mechanics of the feathers played idle designs of color, no two alike, designs executed, it seemed, in a controlled rapture, with a joy that hung level in the air above and behind him. . . . As he fitted the last two, still pliant, on the top, and stood up, crusty coverings were lifted from him, and with a feminine, slipping sensation along his nerves that seemed to give the air hands, he was robed in this certainty: that the God who had lavished such craft upon these worthless birds would not destroy His whole Creation by refusing to let David live forever. (149–50)

Briefly sketched, an interpretation foregrounding some of the Christian elements of "Pigeon Feathers" goes something like this: the story dramatizes an ironic affirmation of God's existence through the destruction of His creatures. The barn is a symbolic church in which David is able to resurrect the universal order, the cosmic harmony that Wells's history and the insect (a dobson, perhaps) had demolished, the boy thus transcending his vision of "unaltering darkness . . . where once there were stars" by restoring the "starred silence" the pigeons had "dirtied" with their "filthy timorous life." In killing the pigeons that foul the Olinger furniture, David is avenging the pollution of his past and simultaneously avenging God by shooting Dobson (whose "great dark eyes" and "small white hands flickering like protesting doves" prefigure David's prey) and his theology-by-analogy. This creative vindication of the past precipitates the resurrection of God the creator's existence in the present (David "was robed in this certainty: that the God who had lavished such craft on these worthless birds") and the promise of an everlasting future ("would not destroy His whole Creation by refusing to let David live forever"). Through his own ceremony of creative destruction, David unwittingly reproduces the "argument from design" proof of God's existence, regenerating his faith, the orderly completion of the death and burial ritual reflecting, reconstructing, and revealing the hierarchical harmony of heaven and earth as he conceives them.[17] "I think the most important ecclesiastical fiction I ever wrote was the story 'Pigeon Feathers,'" Updike told Jan Nunley in their interview, substantiating a reading like this one. That story, he continued, "reflects my own shock when it seemed to me that the well-intentioned, sweet, bright, liberal Lutheran minister who was confirming me didn't really attach any factual reality to these concepts."[18]

As valid as such a reading of "Pigeon Feathers" might seem, its limitation consists in the paucity of metaphors and motifs of the story it incorporates and illuminates. An interpretation that acknowledges the religious elements of David's epiphany as well as the sexual and aesthetic components of his experience construes the story as a depiction of an adolescent's reconciliation with nature, which he has previously perceived as being a brutally ugly, extinction-threatening reality, his reconciliation springing from his unconscious recognition of the aesthetic/sexual impulses that are so inextricably a part of his own nature. Although David's fear of death is real enough in itself, Updike has overlaid his description of it with sufficient carnal metaphors to indicate that David is struggling as much with the embarrassing truths of his bodily existence as he is with thanatophobia.[19] In his "exact vision of death," experienced while he perches on the fetid hole of the family outhouse, David sees himself upright and stiff in a hole in the ground, the image being one of many Updike uses to elide the death fears and physical/sexual anxieties clashing in David's confused mind. The boy's burying of his kill in a hole he has himself dug—one deep enough to frustrate Copper's tooth-and-claw attempt to dig them up—represents his self-assertive appropriation of and participation in this natural process. The sexual initiatory character of this ritual is reinforced by the fact that a rifle is so central to its fulfillment: David's mother shies from the gun when David emerges from the barn, telling him the smirk he wears makes him look like his father—like a mature male capable of confronting her sexually, like one whose attainment of sexual maturity decrees that she will never again be able to "receive his helplessness, all her grace, her gentleness, her love of beauty gathered into a passive intensity," which is the relation of mother to child. The ceremony in the churchlike barn is one in which David's childlike passivity gives way to self-assertiveness:

"Fully master now," he feels himself "a beautiful avenger" of his past submissiveness to and fear of nature, and by "cutting off" the lives of the pigeons, he is able to avenge the emasculation that nature, in the form of his mother's pantheism and his father's terror of nature, had imposed upon him. (So accommodating is nature to David's act of self-regeneration that he imagines one of the pigeons he's shooting "nodding its head as if in frantic agreement" with his initiatory project, thus supplying him with what he's sought from the story's beginning: "the hint, the nod, he needed to begin to build his fortress against death.") As his mother's disappointment at David's stilling of the pigeons' cooing suggests, David has transformed nature from the comforting presence in whose name she had relocated the family to a medium of personal self-transfiguration and violent initiation.[20] As testament to her defeat, David's mother is left with nothing to listen to but the inert silence of the destination to which her pantheism sentences her—the ground.

Although David's initiatory progress seems primarily a repudiation of his mother's pantheist ethic, in another sense it derives from both that conception and from his father's self-abnegating naturalism, David's resolution conciliating their opposed positions in his own creative synthesis.[21] The act of destroying the pigeons confirms his father's "kill-or-be-killed" construal of nature, David improving on it by involving himself in the process rather than, as his father does, fleeing its nonhuman workings for the domestication of Olinger. David's fascination with the intricacies of the dead pigeons' feathers clearly partakes of his mother's all-sustaining belief in the beauty of nature, but again, he appropriates the position to transform it into something his own. When she and he debate God's existence earlier in the story, he asks her,

> "He made everything? You feel that?"
> "Yes."
> "Then who made Him?"
> "Why, Man. Man." (137)

Adopting his father's way of characterizing his mother, David dismisses this response as illogical, the conclusion of a "femme," but her answer can also serve as a useful gloss for David's discovery of the divine in the feathers of pigeons.

He studies the "infinitely adjusted yet somehow effortless mechanics of the feathers," perceiving a "controlled rapture" in their "idle designs of color," the paradoxes he intuits closely approximating the terms in which artistic creation is often described. Noting with an artist's deliberate precision differences between each bird's markings ("one broadly banded in slate shades of blue," another "mottled all over in rhythms of lilac and gray") as he drops them into the grave he has dug, he feels, as he stands up "crusty coverings being lifted from him"—coverings like the tarpaulins used when the furniture of his Olinger childhood was relegated to the barn. The "feminine, slipping sensation" that seems "to give the air hands" weaves together a number of motifs: it combines David's apprehension at the end of their discussion about God's existence that his mother would touch him in a maternally patronizing way, pitying rather than relieving his doubts, with his earlier failed attempt to feel Christ's touch on his fingertips as a failed test of the efficacy of prayer; more significantly, it recalls and fulfills David's construing of the Christian promise of eternal life as "a promise that in the most perverse way, as if the homeliest crone in the kingdom were given the Prince's hand, made every good and real thing, ball games and jokes and pert-breasted girls, possible" (135). (The dependency articulated here of "every good and real thing" on Christian redemption is an idea that permeates the layman's eschatology of Rabbit Angstrom as well, whose inability "to walk the straight line of a paradox" renders keeping the Prince's "perverse" reversal of expectation before him as a guiding spiritual truth impossible.) In one sense, then, the hands that David imagines are those of the Prince of Peace, but, given the clauses that follow, it's equally tempting to identify the hands as those of the Muse.

The beauty that David perceives as inherent in the pigeons' feathers is balanced with the aesthetic act of his destruction and subsequent appreciation of them: out of the "smudges and flickers that he was clever to see and even cleverer to hit in the dim recesses of the rafters—out of each of these he was making a full bird." Through his destructive art of transformation, David is actually improving upon by transforming the coarse stuff—"worthless birds"—of nature. His religious experience in the barn is as much a discovery of artistic sensibility as it is of the existence of divine purposefulness; the immortality he assures himself will be his is as much the product of his perceptive faculties as it is of God's grace. (At age fifteen, David hasn't yet worked out that it's only through the recording of his perceptions of the intricate beauties of actuality that he will be allowed to "live forever," Updike leaving it to David's older avatars in the *Olinger Stories* and to Peter Caldwell in *The Centaur* to articulate the totality of this modernist credo.[22]) On an unconscious level, David has intuited that it is his perception of these "birds which breed in the millions and are exterminated as pests" which makes them beautiful—"Why,

Man. Man," his mother answers when asked who created the creator of everything—and perhaps he understands in an inchoate way that the religious epiphany he is experiencing is no less an aesthetic one. In "Pigeon Feathers," David is "called" from his "deep hole" of doubt after all, rediscovering a craftsman of a God inseparable from the artistic vocation that, he intuits, will provide him with the immortality he seeks. So perfectly pitched is the story's conclusion between eschatological epiphany and the realization of artistic mission that Updike could acknowledge thirty-three years after the publication of "Pigeon Feathers" that, "At the age of sixty-two, I can scarcely improve on the vision and affirmation of the last paragraph."[23]

No other Updike story comes to quite so resounding or gratifying a spiritual climax as "Pigeon Feathers" seems to, and if the subtextual layers of David's epiphany ironize that aura of certainty, they combine nonetheless to validate the story's exemplification of one of its most eloquent assertions: "Hope bases vast premises on foolish accidents, and reads a word where in fact only a scribble exists" (120). In Updike's most interesting fiction, the scribble always contains the possibility of revealing itself as a word—even the *Word*—but, just as in David's epiphany in "Pigeon Feathers," it's never easy to distinguish the act of description itself from spiritual apprehension. In the Jan Nunley interview, Updike explains what the close of "Pigeon Feathers" so effectively dramatizes: "Any act of description is, to some extent, an act of praise, so that even when the event is unpleasant or horrifying or spiritually stunning, the very attempt to describe it is, in some way, part of that Old Testament injunction to give praise. The Old Testament God repeatedly says He wants praise, and I translate that to mean the world wants describing, the world wants to be described and 'hymned.' So there's a kind of hymning undercurrent I feel in my work."[24] Updike makes a similar argument in *Self-Consciousness: Memoirs*, providing an autobiographical source for this aesthetic in remembering that, "What I felt, in that basement Sunday school of Grace Lutheran Church in Shillington, was a clumsy attempt to extend a Yes, a blessing, and I accepted that blessing, offering in return only a nickel a week and my art, my poor little art. . . . Imitation is praise. Description expresses love. I early arrived at these self-justifying inklings."[25] In these terms, David Kern is not merely linguistically imitating the feathers of the pigeons but is praising them; in describing their "effortless mechanics," he is expressing love for the creation of which they are a microcosmic image. Updike has, with only modest irony, attributed the ceaseless proliferation of his writing to the imperatives of this aesthetic: the world contains enormous quantities of creation to describe/praise; because that description implicitly affirms the self as well as the creation being praised, "to be in print," in Updike's view, "was to be saved"; consequently, he experiences "to this moment a day when I have produced nothing printable, when I have not gotten any words out, is a day lost and damned as I feel it" (S-C, 108). Updike is also honest enough to admit that this aesthetic is pervaded by "self-justifying inklings," and it's in this acknowledgment that David Kern, Updike, and Rabbit Angstrom begin fruitfully—for my purposes—interpenetrating with each other. David's recovery of a God whose promise of individual salvation makes "every good thing . . . possible" is embedded inextricably in an unconscious ritual of masculine initiation and his realization of an artistic vocation: consequently, to know and affirm God is indistinguishable from knowing and affirming the self. Characterizing his "religious sensibility" in another interview, Updike explained that it "operates primarily as a sense of God the creator, which is fairly real to me, and secondly as a sense of the mystery and irreducibility of one's own identity, mixed in with the fear of the identity being an illusion or being squelched."[26] His fiction is remarkably disinclined to serialize the manner in which his characters apprehend these mysteries; as I've already suggested, one of Rabbit's primary psychological traits is to predicate a stable identity for himself upon God's presence, consistently interpreting his sporadic fears "of [his] identity being an illusion" as validation of God's nonexistence. Similarly, David is too delighted with his self-transformative epiphany to notice how solipsistically it circles on itself, God merging seamlessly into the artistic sensibility that will allow David immortality through his apprehension and description of God's creation. Ralph C. Wood's delineation of Updike's theology is again illuminating: "God's signature is written across the whole cosmos, Updike is reported to have said, but his lettering is illegible. It follows that faith springs neither from the revelation of God in Israel and Christ as attested by Scripture, nor from the community of belief that proclaims the Gospel through the church, but from the transcendent self's own egoistic quest."[27] In his thoroughly self-restorative epiphany, the innocent David Kern of "Pigeon Feathers" resembles the clergymen whom Henry Adams describes criticizing a St. Gaudens statue at Rock Creek Cemetery: "One after another brought companions there, and, apparently fascinated by their own reflection, broke out passionately against the expression they felt in the figure of despair, of atheism, of denial. Like the others, the priest saw only what he brought" (329).

David's older self experiences a crisis of faith in "Packed Dirt, Churchgoing, A Dying Cat, A Traded Car," similar to the one adolescent David undergoes, but he is far more conscious than he was as a teenager of the extent to which he is creating his own antidotes to faithlessness and despair, contriving for himself the structures of meaning and order through which he seeks self-redemption. He understands religion and his own attempts to compensate for its dwindling in the same terms that M. Poincare is quoted in the *Education* as perceiving mathematics: "In short, the mind has the facility of creating symbols, and it is thus that it has constructed mathematical continuity which is only a particular system of symbols."[28] In both "Packed Dirt" and "The Blessed Man of Boston, My Grandmother's Thimble, and Fanning Island," David Kern posits secular solutions to religious dilemmas, Updike in neither story unambiguously dramatizing endorsement of the compensatory alternatives to lapsed faith, which are the best the older David can manage.

In "Packed Dirt," the boy who resolved that "God who had lavished such craft on these worthless birds would not destroy His whole creation by refusing to let David live forever" has become a husband and father in his midtwenties whose insomniac and guilt-ridden sexual fantasies about women he had danced with at a party earlier that evening culminate in an episode of nocturnal terror in which "each second my agony went unanswered justified it more certainly: the God who permitted me this fear was unworthy of existence."[29] Updike in *Self-Consciousness* attributes the intensity of "Packed Dirt" and "The Blessed Man of Boston" to the asthma-inspired mortality anxieties he experienced while composing these "last, fragmentary stories in *Pigeon Feathers*," stories "which I think of, in retrospect, as my best, perhaps because the words were attained through such an oppressive blanket of funk" (97). Whereas younger David's crisis resolves itself through his unconscious discovery/creation of the perceiver/artificer in himself, older David—who has become the writer his "Pigeon Feathers" epiphany all but foreordained that he become—is much more self-conscious in positing aesthetic solutions to his spiritual dislocation, in finding sacramental consolation in the symbol systems his imagination projects.

A deliberately detailed, highly artistic description of his perception of dirt packed by the passage of human feet opens the story and provides the first manifestation of the cumulative solution to the religious crisis dramatized in "A Traded Car." "Churchgoing," significantly, also partakes of that solution, less because of the spiritual reassurance the content of the experience affords than because the institutional ritual of worship is reassuring in itself. "A Dying Cat" dramatizes the idea that "a life demands a life": while his wife is giving birth to their first child in a London hospital, David is ineffectually administering last rites to a cat that has been run over. In "A Traded Car" the experience of nothingness David suffers is deflected by the news that his father has been hospitalized, suffering heart trouble: "All day death had been advancing under cover and now it had struck, declared its position. My father had engaged the enemy and it would be defeated" (262). When he drives the car he's about to trade in to Pennsylvania to visit his father, his mother confides, "Daddy says he's lost all his faith." David's response—"Since I had also lost mine, I had nothing to say"[30](237)—marks the story's final shift away from the issue of faith to the idea that ultimately unifies the story's four narrative sections: the necessity of creating compensations for the absence of belief.

A hitchhiking sailor David picks up on his way from Massachusetts to Pennsylvania wants to know, "What's the point?" of the writing David does, to which he initially responds, "I don't know. . . . I wish I did." By the end of "Packed Dirt," David has a better answer, one that supplies the thematic resolution uniting the story's four strands: "We in America need ceremonies is I suppose, sailor, the point of what I have written" (279). Ceremonies such as footprints marking the human presence in landscapes flattened by machines: "As our sense of God's forested legacy to us dwindles, there grows, in these worn, rubbed, and patted patches, a sense of human legacy—like those feet of statues of saints which have lost their toes to centuries of kisses. One thinks of John Dewey's definition of God as the union of the actual and the ideal" (248–49). Ceremonies—such as writing a note to the cat's owners explaining how it was found and acknowledging their loss, or a final extended drive in a car that is about to be traded in and thus "dissolved back into the mineral world from which it was conjured." Cars, "the dreaming vehicles of our ideal and onrushing manhood" should not be "dismissed without a blessing, a kiss, a testament or any ceremony of farewell" any more than cats should be; David's story—and Updike's—argues for the exercise of secular sacraments, acts that commemorate the stages of the incessant passage of our lives as they shift imperceptibly from present to past. One of the pleasures of churchgoing, David asserts, is that a "resplendently robed man strives to console us with scraps of ancient epistles and halting accounts, hopelessly compromised by words, of those intimations of divine joy that are like pain in that, their instant gone, the mind cannot remember or believe them" (249); ceremonies, at least, allow us to "remember and believe" the human joys we have experienced, the cycles of beginning and ending that recur in our lives and provide them with the only order and coherence that a secular understanding recognizes. The need for ceremonies is the point of what David has written; the enactment of aesthetically constructed cere-

monies is what Updike has written in "Packed Dirt, Churchgoing, A
Dying Cat, A Traded Car," his story reluctantly affirming a modernist credo of Wallace Stevens Updike quotes in his review of *Souvenirs
and Prophecies: The Young Wallace Stevens*: "In an age of disbelief . . .
it is for the poet to supply the satisfactions of belief, in his measure
and his style."[31]

The affirmation of humanly redemptive ceremonies is clearly one
of Updike's objectives in "Packed Dirt," but the story is nonetheless
pervaded by significant reservations, by suggestions of the insufficiency of aesthetic solutions to faith's disappearance, which are
sounded even more emphatically in "The Blessed Man." Like "Pigeon Feathers," "Packed Dirt" concludes in an epiphany in which
previously established motifs contest with each other. One of the
footpaths David feels affection for seems "precious because it had
been achieved accidentally, and had about it that repose of grace
which is beyond willing" (248). The ceremonies he proceeds to ad-
umbrate lack this "repose of grace which is beyond willing" (or the
"infinitely adjusted yet somehow effortless mechanics" of pigeon
feathers) because they are so clearly and deliberately extrapolations,
faith's intentionally constructed surrogates rather than its confirmations. "Belief," David subsequently contends, "builds itself unconsciously and in consciousness is spent"; what's happening in "Packed
Dirt," arguably, is belief building itself too consciously, metaphors
drawn from religious observance masquerading as observance itself.
In childhood, David suggests, "The earth is our playmate. . . . and the
call to dinner has a piercingly sweet eschatological ring" (247); later,
"It seemed to me for this sunset hour that the world is our bride,
given to us to love, and the terror and joy of the marriage is that we
bring to it a nature not our bride's" (277–78). To move from a perception of the earth as playmate to the world as bride is to abandon an
innocent conception of unmediated human relationality to nature for
one characterized by otherness and negotiation, the loss of any sense
of divine spirit indwelling in matter necessitating that the human response to the natural world be, at best, ambivalent feelings of terror
and joy. Ceremoniously considered, the call to dinner has no ring at
all—it's just a summons to eat.[32]

For all their consolation, ceremonies, Updike makes clear, are consciousness's artifices for fulfilling its need for order; consequently,
ceremonies are as much symptoms of what has been lost as they are
antidotes to the loss, consciousness's effort to project on the world
manifestations of its own internal structures of order and reassurance.
Their consolations are as real as those of the game described in Updike's story, "Solitaire," and as utterly inconsonant with the natural

world around them: "In the rise and collapse of the alternately colored ranks of cards, in the grateful transpositions and orderly revelations and unexpected redemptions, the circuits of the mind found an
occupation exactly congruent with their own secret structure."[33] "In
plain words," Adams wrote toward the end of his *Education*, "Chaos
was the law of nature; Order was the dream of man" (451).

Whereas "Packed Dirt" reproduces, in fictional form, Updike's
own intense struggle with and equivocal success in elaborating a creed
predicated not on the assumption of universal order but on "the circuits of the mind," on the mind's capacity to project forms of compensatory and consolatory order, "The Blessed Man" dramatizes less
ambiguously the inadequacy of one specific human form to substitute
for the loss of the Word: the short story.

The aesthetic that David (who never names himself in the story, but
whose background is identical to those of the David Kerns in the
other two Olinger stories) articulates is nearly indistinguishable from
Updike's "description as an act of praise" artistic strategy. The very
ordinary man he spots as he's leaving a Red Sox game seems to him
"the happy man, the man of unceasing and effortless blessing. I
thought then to write a novel, an immense book about him, recounting his every move, his every meal, every play, pitch, and hesitation
of every ball game he attended, the number of every house he passed
as he walked Boston's Indian-colored slums. . . ." The catalogue of
the minutiae this man experiences and witnesses, which David wants
to document, continues for many more lines, coalescing in his assertion of the desire that it all be "set sequentially down with the bald
simplicity of intrinsic blessing, thousands upon thousands of pages;
ecstatically uneventful; divinely and defiantly dull" (228). David's desire to compose the absolute accounting of this blessed man's life
aligns him with Alf Clayton of *Memories of the Ford Administration*,
who, as I suggested in the first chapter, is betrayed by his similar impulse toward creating an exhaustive biography of American president
John Buchanan.[34] Updike's detractors might find David's Howellsian
description of the projected work as "ecstatically uneventful; divinely
and defiantly dull" a reasonable characterization of Updike's own literary production to date, but even his admirers must recognize in it a
rationale not only for the volume of his literary output but for its
devotion to detail as well. The difficult part of the task David sets
himself here is not recording the details but conveying through them
the quality of "the bald simplicity of intrinsic blessing" the man projects, which justifies the prolixity of detail and is the motivation for
describing him in the first place. In discussing "Packed Dirt," I suggested that the element that humanly conceived ceremonies could not

match of those markings unintentionally imposed on the earth by barefoot walkers was their quality of "that repose of grace which is beyond willing"; it is the deliberately willed character of David's "Blessed Man" project, similarly, that dooms it (and the story in which it is described) to failure.

David predicts and accounts for the story's ultimate failure in slightly different terms: "We would-be novelists," he contends in closing his "Blessed Man" narrative, "have a reach as shallow as our skins. We walk through volumes of the unexpressed and like snails leave behind a faint thread excreted out of ourselves. From the dew of the few flakes that melt on our faces we cannot reconstruct the snowstorm" (228–29). His unflattering comparison of human literary production to the minimal excrescence of snails and invocation of the incapacity of literary language to "reconstruct the snowstorm" prepare for the standard apologia he subsequently offers of the Christian artist confronted with the magnitude of God's creation: "Oh Lord, bless these poor paragraphs, that would do in their vile ignorance Your work of resurrection" (229). The remaining two "unwritten stories" of "The Blessed Man of Boston, My Grandmother's Thimble, and Fanning Island" reproduce the same disparity between imitation and creation, between human artistic conception and the invocation of otherwordly standards.

The discovery of his grandmother's thimble prompts in David the same impulse toward mimetic exhaustiveness the "blessed man" inspired in him, the desire to "tell how once there had been a woman who now was no more, how she had been born and lived in a world that had ceased to exist, though its memoes were all about us. . . ." (Updike, I'll argue in a later chapter, acted upon a parallel motivation of historical reconstruction and recovery in writing *In the Beauty of the Lilies*.) David is led to this impulse by a sensation that accompanied the finding of the thimble:

> I felt at my back that night a steep wave about to break over the world and bury us and all our trinkets of survival fathoms down. . . . it is this imminent catastrophe that makes it imperative for me to cry now, in the last second when the cry will have meaning, that once there was a woman whom one of the continents in one of its square miles caused to exist. That the land that cast her up was harsher, more sparsely exploited, more fertile than it is now. That she was unique; that she came toward the end of the time when uniqueness was possible (241–42).

His grandmother's "willed survival" is what David's attempted reconstruction of her life emphasizes, the theme providing a segue into the third of his unwritten stories. "Fanning Island" expands dramatically upon Pascal's parable of the human condition as the situation of "a number of men in chains, and all condemned to death." In David's interpolation, the "steep wave" he felt was immanent the night he found his grandmother's thimble has washed up the men on an island, the absence of women there condemning them to eventual extinction. David's outline for this story is written from the point of view of the chief's son, the island's last survivor, and the challenge of completing this narrative (as it is in those of the "blessed man" and David's grandmother, rendering them equally unresurrectable) is "the days, the evocation of the days . . . the green days. The tasks, the grass, the weather, the shades of sea and air" that fill the time the survivor has left before the "imminent catastrophe" of death. In concluding his narrative, David appraises his project unfavorably in comparison to art he considers more successful in accomplishing his ends: "a piece of turf torn from a meadow becomes a *gloria* when drawn by Dürer," he asserts. "Details. Details are the giant's fingers. He seizes the stick and strips the bark and shows, burning beneath, the moist white wood of joy." David's trio of failed narratives have shared in common not only the theme of survival, but—in the "effortless blessing" of the "happy man" and in the quizzical smile his grandmother often wore—also the notion of achieved survival being a source of joy. Thus the story ends upon David's confession, "For I thought that this story [the Fanning Island narrative specifically, but the accumulated three narratives that comprise Updike's story as well], fully told, would become without my willing it, a happy story, a story full of joy; had my powers been greater, we would know. As it is, you, like me, must take it on faith."

Human art, the story's conclusion reaffirms, cannot perform the Lord's work of resurrection; without it, these narratives cannot become "stories full of joy" because no amount of particularizing of the days and moments of witness can alter the oblivion that is their inevitable terminus. No matter how meaningful they seem to him or how beautifully he can describe them, with the chief's son's death vanish "the green days . . . the tasks, the grass, the weather, the shades of sea and air" he knows, for he is no more capable than Harry Angstrom proves to be at transforming witness into worship. In the story's wonderful closing double entendre, we must take on faith that the three narratives we have read are happy stories, for if we lack that (Christian) faith, they're not. What this complex story illustrates more effectively than any other Updike work is his own ambivalence toward the promises of his craft. The impulse exists in Updike, as it does in David Kern, to imitate exhaustively the details of lives, to use "my poor little art" to insure that "the tasks, the grass, the weather, the shades of sea and air" he has known won't disappear; but accompanying—and contesting—that impulse is the assumption that art cannot do what faith can: ensure the salvation or redemption of these lives and days. David blames artistic incapacity for the story's failure, self-deprecatingly suggesting that his literary powers are not equal to Dürer's artistic ones; I'd suggest that his story fails (as Updike's, which effectively makes this point, does not) because of David's doubts as to whether the narratives he's leaving unfinished constitute "a happy story," because of his doubts that "burning beneath" the bark of his prose is "the moist white wood of joy" rather than indeterminate accounts of meaninglessly protracted survival.

"The Blessed Man of Boston, My Grandmother's Thimble, and Fanning Island" dramatizes the either/or that underlies and informs much of Updike's serious fiction, his desire/doubt that artistic rendering is limning patterns beyond those he is deliberately creating. In the prologue, I quoted Updike's response to Jeff Campbell's question about a line from *Midpoint*, in which he—reprising David's encomia to detail—suggested that his typical strategy in writing is inductive: that citation needs to be reintroduced at greater length here. "Instead of beginning with some broad suppositions and trying to make them apply to little phenomena," Updike explained, "you look at the little phenomena and try to extract the rules that inhere from them. And so in writing I try to adhere to the verifiable, the undeniable little thing. Somehow, I hope the pattern will emerge, and I guess I must have such hope cosmically."[35]

This assertion reflects Updike's perception of his literary art as a paradigm of spirit: the writer's creation of webs of coherence in fiction approximates the intuition of equally inherent threads of cosmic meaning in the universe. That such patterns actually exist and communicate, Updike designates only as a "hope," thus imbuing his work with a spiritual equivocation that he has characterized as its "yes, but quality."[36] His fiction, then, seeks tirelessly "to read a word where only a scribble exists," and its inability, or refusal, to resolve its own ambiguous condition, perched between hope and doubt, is testament to its spiritual integrity. Flannery O'Connor expected no more of the Christian novelist than the anatomization of our faith-vexed condition Updike offers: "I don't believe that we shall have great religious fiction," O'Connor argued, "until we have again that happy combination of believing artist and believing society. Until that time, the novelist will have to do the best he can in travail with the world he has. He may find in the end that instead of reflecting the image at the heart of things, he has only reflected our broken condition, and through it, the face of the devil we are possessed by. This is a modest achievement, but perhaps a necessary one."[37] At the end of "Leaves," another story devoted to the dramatization of Updike's aesthetic, the narrator makes a similar apologia for the unresolved spiritual ambiguities of his narrative: "Can our spirits really enter Time's haven of mortality and sink composedly among the mulching leaves?" he asks. "No: we stand at the intersection of two kingdoms, and there is no advance and no retreat, only a sharpening of the edge where we stand."[38]

Which is, of course, precisely where we find—and will also leave— Rabbit Angstrom.

3

Upward Space:
Rabbit, Run

> The older Harry gets the more cynical he is; he used to be religious in a funny way.
> —Janice thinking about her husband in *Rabbit at Rest*

DAVID KERN'S EXTENDED THEOLOGICAL MEDITATIONS IN THE TWO fuguelike narratives closing *Pigeon Feathers and Other Stories* were composed after the publication of *Rabbit, Run*, but they are clearly a culmination both of an intense spiritual crisis and of Updike's second novel's impact on the evolution of his career, the dramatic eruptions of the first Rabbit book having inspired the neophyte author "to abandon a certain determined modesty in my literary ambitions."[1] David's highly civilized, eloquent self-reflectiveness about his faith seems as unlike Rabbit's largely inarticulate "furtive sensations of the invisible" as it could be, but if the two protagonists travel over different expressive highways, they nonetheless end up at basically the same place. For all of the preoccupation of "Packed Dirt" with human ultimacy, the resolving affirmation of ceremony that David offers appears lacking in any necessary spiritual dynamic. (The potential for such ceremonies generating only repetitive sterility seems to be the point of the dreary drama enacted through Harry's shopping at a drugstore for a birthday present for his dying mother early in *Redux*, his obligatory annual errand taking place on the afternoon of yet another meaningless ceremony—America's landing on the moon.) As "The Blessed Man" suggests, for Updike, fiction that falls short of revealing "the moist white wood of joy" underlying daily events does no more than register (as David finds himself reduced to doing in writing about his grandmother) that "once there was a woman whom one of the continents in one of its square miles caused to exist." Without evoking the "intimations of divine joy" that David in "Packed Dirt" hears fleetingly in the sermons of ministers, fiction in David's view—and Updike's as well—is only mimesis, the untranscendent recording of what was. As the narrator of *In the Beauty of the Lilies* remarks, "The body suffers its pain and seeks its pleasure; what more, without revelation, is there to know than this?"[2] David's desire to make his narratives into "songs of joy" commemorating those whose praise he sings must be taken on faith, his failure unambiguously to achieve his literary purpose prefiguring the close of the *Rabbit Angstrom* tetralogy in its refusal to affirm that in its pages the deceased protagonist has been resurrected in any but a strictly literary sense. The parallel spiritual/emotional trajectories of David Kern[3] and Harry are significant, then, but the proliferating absence of epiphanies of faith in Updike's fiction doesn't necessarily mean that ultimate concerns aren't being addressed, since, for him, fictional rendering and theology are inseparable.

"Why follow human adventures if the human soul is not in some way important?" Updike pondered in answer to a question posed at the University of Pittsburgh. "I think that theology is very much a part of our fictional fabric. It's very hard to write fiction without having some sort of religious sense, as Graham Greene pointed out. We all have some religious need . . . we all need to orient ourselves in terms of something bigger." Updike then proceeded to characterize Rabbit in language I quoted earlier, but which deserves repetition because of the citation's centrality to my sense of the significance Updike's protagonist has for him: "Harry embodies the human problem of why am I me rather than somebody else. He feels to be himself is immensely precious and important; the longer he lives, the less evidence there is to support his sensation that he's wonderful. Nevertheless, he does cling to this, and in some way only the God within can confirm this feeling that each of us is somehow the center of the universe."[4]

Thelma Harrison's affectionate admonishment to Harry in her final conversation with him in *Rest*, "Harry, you're not actually the center of the universe, it only feels that way to you" (*Rest*, 1990, 201) is only half right: Updike's idiosyncratic intellectual/spiritual commingling of Freudian psychology with Christianity produces a theology whose central tenet posits the experience of the indwelling of "the God within us" as proof that the individual *is* the center of the universe. Although Harry's way of formulating this idea always sounds highly narcissistic, he is actually asserting the traditional Christian belief that God's grace is experienced by the individual, one soul at a time. If it exists, in other words, grace exists for Harry as much as for any other Christian soul—the only scriptural sanction imaginable for Rabbit's mystical faith is Luke 17:20–21: "The kingdom of God is within you." Given the centrality of self-perception to faith as Updike's subjective egotheism construes it, the extended dramatic dynamic of the Rabbit tetralogy consists chiefly in Harry's waxing and waning experiences of his own spiritual worth and in the conflicts that his resulting egotism and nihilism provoke in the exterior world of communally defined values surrounding him. *Rabbit, Run* initiates this dynamic by dramatizing the two religious epiphanies constituting Harry's most profound evidence of the "invisible world" in the tetralogy. His ecstatically visualized leaps of faith will figure as crucially in my reading of *Rabbit, Run* as the absence of their repetition anywhere in the subsequent books will figure in my approach to the latter three Rabbit novels.

Rabbit Angstrom, I'm arguing, is Updike's least doctrinal Christian and therefore most effective realism surrogate, the protagonist whose proletarian skepticism and want of insulating intellectuality makes his experience and response to it an ideal fictional mediator between the secular and the spiritual. It's as though Updike decided that Rabbit, if never quite becoming a Kierkegaardian knight of faith, would nonetheless be his by-some-standards wildly inappropriate interrogator of the promises of religious belief. So ostensibly ill suited to the role, Rabbit functions remarkably effectively in this context, the protagonist raising the stakes of unbelief by inhabiting such thoroughly untranscendent environs. Rabbit's benumbingly mundane middle-class circumstances and environment practically defy the faith-affirming conclusion Rabbit reaches while he stands with Ruth on Mt. Judge, overlooking dreary Brewer, Pennsylvania: "if there's this floor there is a ceiling, that the true space in which we live is upward space" (98). Updike's most concerted and ambitious literary task, I'm arguing, has been his three decades-spanning effort to illuminate the "intimations of the infinite" that occasionally invigorate the egotistical sybarite Rabbit Angstrom, and to dramatize the immanence of spirit underlying the soul-crushingly secular American reality he inhabits. It is with an exploration of the nature of Rabbit's religious intuitions—his belief that "the true space in which we live is upward space"—that I'll begin my discussion of *Rabbit, Run*.

Harry Angstrom's religious faith in the tetralogy's opening novel is a tenuously maintained complex of sensations and impulses that has the singular advantage of confirming his sense of his own individual specialness in the face of "external circumstances" evincing the contrary, of keeping alive a spark of the uniqueness he knew on the Mt. Judge High School gym as a basketball star. As is the case with young David Kern's initiatory ceremony of belief resurrection in "Pigeon Feathers," Rabbit's faith is never completely distinguishable from

egocentricity nor carnal impulses, and its primary medium of validation is similarly visual. Although he never evolves into the artist that
adult David becomes (and is arguably Updike's most compelling protagonist for precisely that reason), Rabbit's faith has a distinctly aesthetic quality, a fact suggested by his scrutiny of visual manifestations
of spirit as he approaches Reverend Eccles's church during his short-
lived attempt to cleave to the "straight path" of moral rectitude following Becky's birth and his reunion with Janice:

> He hates all the people on the street in dirty everyday clothes, advertising
> their belief that the world arches over a pit, that death is final, that the
> wandering thread of his feelings leads nowhere. Correspondingly he loves
> the ones dressed for church: the pressed business suits of portly men give
> substance and respectability to his furtive sensations of the invisible; the
> flowers in the hats of their wives seem to begin to make it visible; and their
> daughters are themselves whole flowers, their bodies each a single flower,
> petaled in gauze and frills, a bloom of faith, so even the plainest walk in
> Rabbit's eyes glowing with beauty, the beauty of belief. He could kiss
> their feet in gratitude, they release him from fear. By the time he enters
> the church he is too elevated with happiness to ask forgiveness. (201–2)

It's for the lies he has been feeding customers in foisting "clunkers
with 80,000 miles" on them at Fred Springer's used car lot this
week—his first in his father-in-law's employ—that Rabbit initially intended to ask forgiveness. There is nothing more characteristic of his
faith than that it creates itself not through the dialectic of contrition
and redemption—he's too happy for that—but through the far more
subjective and impressionistic interpretation of visual cues and the
emotional reactions they elicit in him. The capacity for intuiting such
joy beneath the familiar surfaces of a church service is, in other words,
as forgiven as Rabbit ever gets. Equally typical is the movement of the
first sentence from world to self, communal redemption from eternal
death being construed as valuable primarily for annulling any possibility that "the wandering thread of his feelings leads nowhere." With
the exception of his unbaptized infant daughter, Becky, Rabbit's anxieties about personal extinction never extend to the fates of other
souls, either because Updike's Freudian presuppositions limit ultimate concern to self-concern, or because Rabbit can never visualize
an afterlife but can only feel immortality, in the abstract, as his personal desert.[5]

The "substance and respectabilty" that portly men in suits lend
Rabbit's "furtive sensations of the invisible" are, given his habitual
indifference to issues of respectability, clearly of secondary importance, and women claimed by other men contribute nothing more

than the artificial flowers on their hats to the materialization of his
belief. It's their daughters who embody "whole flowers" to Rabbit,
manifesting "blooms of faith"; they "release him from fear" by
"glowing with beauty, the beauty of belief." (Similarly, the God that
eighteen-year-old Jill Pendleton in *Rabbit Redux* describes experiencing while on drugs, her account briefly rekindling Rabbit's dwindled
faith, appears to her as a lily [391].) The fact that Rabbit's floral epiphany is soon to culminate in his lusting for the minister's wife, Lucy
Eccles, seated in the pew in front of him, activates the latent sexuality
of Rabbit's attentions to these parishioners "petaled in gauze and
frills" whose youthful flowering is so central to their appeal.[6] Even at
twenty-six, Rabbit is already mourning his own lost youth, and he
constantly seeks emanations of it in the ripeness of others. "The fullness ends," the novel's narrator explains, "when we give Nature her
ransom, when we make children for her. Then she is through with us
and we become, first inside, then outside, junk. Flower stalks" (194).
At the same time, the flower imagery here echoes the scene dramatizing Rabbit's joy in tending Mrs. Smith's garden, for which she attributes to him "the gift of life": "It's a strange gift and I don't know
how we're supposed to use it but I know it's the only gift we get and
it's a good one" (192). What he enjoys about gardening is burying
seeds that will generate flowers: "Sealed, they cease to be his. The
simplicity. Getting rid of something by giving it to itself. God himself
folded into the tiny adamant structure, Self-destined to a succession
of explosions, the great slow gathering out of water and air and sili-
cone: this is felt without words in the turn of the round hoe-handle
in his palms" (117). Updike's apology for writing over his protagonist's head notwithstanding, this passage effectively serves at least
three different purposes: it evokes how closely aligned to a sense of
natural beauty and fruitfulness is Rabbit's religiosity, laminates his
perception of young girls as flowers and inducements to belief, and
prefigures the horror he experiences at the hospital that Janice will die
in childbirth as a judgment upon the seeds he has more promiscu-
ously buried, as punishment for the "succession of explosions" com-
prising the sex life so integral to his self-conception. "He feels
underwater,"[7] we're told as, later in the novel, Rabbit waits in the hospital waiting room, feeling "caught in chains of transparent slime,
ghosts of the urgent ejaculations he has spat into the mild bodies of
women" (170). Like his "gift of life"—which in the course of the
novel produces a beautiful garden and two ill-fated pregnancies culminating in Ruth's condemnation of him as "Mr. Death himself"
(260)—Rabbit's faith is a complex psychic dynamic born of his best

and worst impulses, a belief system formed out of itself and its own negations and contradictions.

Largely because of the complex admixture of perceptions, intuitions and emotions that it is for him, belief as a constant condition proves difficult for Rabbit to maintain; his faith requires more than static visual cues for external corroboration of the existence of the "unseen world."[8] Accordingly, Rabbit has two experiences in *Rabbit, Run* that constitute intuitive validations of his belief, neither of which the novel's traditional Christians who witness them are completely willing to recognize as authentic religious revelations. Because these two spiritual epiphanies form the foundation for what religious faith Rabbit can be said to sustain through the tetralogy, and because they represent loci of both theme and metaphor from which most of the novel's dramatic tensions flow, I've chosen Rabbit's two mystical experiences of the sky as the twin foci of my discussion of *Rabbit, Run*.

In "Intercession," a story published while Updike was writing *Rabbit, Run,* the narrator, commenting upon the golf game, which provides the narrative's plot, offers a spatial/spiritual context for the first of Rabbit's religious experiences: "If miracles, in this age of faint faith, could enter anywhere, it would be here, where the causal fabric was thinnest, in the quick collisions and abrupt deflections of a game."[9] Golf, Updike argued in a 1972 review of Michael Murphy's book on the sport, "is of games the most mysterious, the least earthbound, the one wherein the wall between us and the supernatural is rubbed thinnest."[10] Throughout the tetralogy, Rabbit will share this conception, continuing to think of golf courses as his closest approximation to a replacement for that lost ground of potential miracles, the basketball court,[11] largely because of the shot he makes in a game with the Episcopal minister, Eccles, whose theological hectoring provokes it.

Eccles has exploited their shared interest in sport to lure Rabbit onto the golf course as "a way of getting to know him," his plan ill concealing the minister's agenda of keeping tabs on this fugitive husband of his parish in the hope of ultimately reuniting Harry with Janice. (Harry witnesses a quarrel between the minister and his wife, Lucy, before he and Eccles leave for the golf course in which Eccles reminds her that her want of faith had been no obstacle to their marriage "as long as [her] heart remained open for grace"; their argument establishes the conflictual terrain that is religious belief in Eccles's home, while introducing allegorically one of the many tensions of the novel in which Rabbit occupies a conflicted middle ground—between Eccles's Christianity and his wife's Freudian psychology.) As they tee off beneath accumulating storm clouds, Eccles takes the opportunity to goad Rabbit into articulating his reasons for deserting Janice. "I told ja," Rabbit heatedly responds, "there was this thing that wasn't there." When Eccles wants to know, "What thing? Have you seen it? Are you sure it exists?" Rabbit replies, "Well, if you're not sure it exists, don't ask me. It's right up your alley. If you don't know nobody does."

Part of Harry's spiritual education in the course of *Rabbit, Run* consists in learning to trust "his furtive sensations of the invisible" over the authority of institutional mentors like Eccles and Marty Tothero, his high school basketball coach, both of whom, as we'll see, prove to be more ethically and spiritually confused than he is; what the golf course scene dramatizes is how much more real faith is to Rabbit than to Eccles, who subsequently will surreptitiously feed off the belief Rabbit exudes while publicly repudiating and condemning the antisocial actions it inspires.

When Eccles offers him a definition of the human condition ("What we live in you might call . . . inner darkness") that is more abstract but nonetheless compatible with Rabbit's own perception, he confesses, " 'Well, I don't know all this about theology, but I'll tell you I *do* feel, I guess, that somewhere behind all this'—he gestures outward at the scenery; they are passing the housing development this side of the golf course, half-wood half-brick one-and-a-half stories in little flat bulldozed yards containing tricycles and spindly three-year-old trees, the un-grandest landscape in the world—there's something that wants me to find it' " (110). Nowhere in the Rabbit novels does Rabbit more explicitly define the feeling that constitutes his faith, a belief composed in roughly equal parts of distaste for middle-class American life an economic rung above his own, egotism (the assumption that "something" thinks he deserves better than the aura of sameness, familial predictability and present-day rootlessness,[12] which this development exudes no less palpably than does his apartment), and a passionately experienced impulse of ultimate concern. It is Updike's task in writing the golf course scene to give more than mere testimonial force to Rabbit's declaration of faith, to dramatically substantiate that he is sensible to and capable of what the novel's epigraph from Pascal terms "motions of grace."

Aggravated by his poor beginner's play, by Eccles's patronizing attitude toward it, and the minister's smug moralism, Rabbit decides that "underneath all this I-know-more-about-it-than-you heresies-of-the-early-church business, [Eccles] really wants to be told about it, wants to be told that it is there, wants to be told that he's not lying to those people every Sunday." Eccles then delivers the accusation that resonates through the tetralogy as a not-unjustifiable reading of Rabbit's character, a conception of him the validity of which even Rabbit occasionally entertains: "You don't care about right and wrong. You worship nothing but your own worst instincts." As happens elsewhere in the tetralogy, forthright, unambiguous accusation inspires in Rabbit the contradictory behavior, Eccles's ceremony of blaming inciting him to rise to the achievement of what I'll call his "perfect shot":

> In avoiding looking at Eccles he looks at the ball, which sits high on the tee and already seems free of the ground. Very simply he brings the clubhead around his shoulder into it. The sound has a hollowness, a singleness he hasn't heard before. His arms force his head up and his ball is hung way out lunarly pale against the beautiful black blue of storm clouds, his grandfather's color stretched dense across the north.[13]

Earlier in the scene, Rabbit had viewed the golf ball as "the hard irreducible pellet that is not really himself yet in a way is; just the way it sits there white and number one in the center of everything."[14] In its demonstration of his ability to read external objects as extensions of himself, the blurring of self and other implicit in Rabbit's identification with the ball exemplifies what the narrator later characterizes as Rabbit's "transactions with the unseen world"; it can also be construed as simple narcissism, invoking Rabbit's incapacity to perceive as significant anything beyond the confines of the self—"everything seems unreal that is outside of his sensations" (169), as the narrator at one point describes Rabbit's reflexes. As Rabbit hits the ball, which isn't himself yet is, he precipitates a parabolic/parodic vision of his soul on its journey through death toward salvation.

That the ball "already seems free of the ground" excites this ex-basketball player for whom both freedom and the sky represent incarnations of the sacred, and the simplicity with which he brings the clubhead around recalls the "effortlessness" and "repose of grace which is beyond willing" characteristic of authentic manifestations of the spiritual in "Packed Dirt." (Here, as there, faith must resurrect itself against a landscape of bulldozed earth.) The sound of Harry's figuratively driving himself into the sky has "a hollowness, a singleness" that ambivalently evoke the positive and negative poles of being a solitary individual: the "singleness" reflects his sense of his own unitary significance, of his soul's irreducibly individual value, while the "hollowness" prefigures his subsequent response to thoughts of death—"he pictures a vacant field of cinders and his heart goes hollow" (263). The fact that he drives/is driven into "the beautiful black blue of storm clouds" evokes something faintly deathly, which is immediately countered by the qualification, "his grandfather's color," the elaborate trope ultimately confirming visually Rabbit's sense of having a special death-evading destiny for which a personal protector on high is responsible.

Rabbit has explained to Eccles during their game that, when Rabbit was a child, his grandfather prevented him from becoming a "fosnacht." "I remember," he says, "one year I was the last downstairs and my parents or somebody teased me and I didn't like it and I guess I cried, I don't know. Anyway that's why the old man stayed up" (108). To Rabbit's thoroughly untheological mind, having a grandfather who waits upstairs in order that Harry not be the fosnacht is as close to an "our father who art in Heaven" as he can conceptualize; that the clouds bear his grandfather's colors reflects that he/He waits upstairs still, protecting Harry from being humilated, from being last.[15] (Rabbit's progressively deepening sexual involvement with Peggy Fosnacht in *Rabbit Redux* reflects how desperate is his need to be "led back," restored to health, in that novel.) The remainder of Rabbit's religious epiphany comprises elements no less intensely subjective and, considered in terms of conventional notions of spiritual ultimacy, trivial.

> [The ball] recedes along a line straight as a ruler edge. Stricken; sphere, star, speck. It hesitates, and Rabbit thinks it will die, but he's fooled, for the ball makes its hesitation the ground of a final leap: with a kind of visible sob takes a last bite of space before vanishing in falling. "That's it!" he cries, and turning to Eccles with a grin of aggrandizement, repeats, "That's it!" (115–16)

"Stricken; sphere, star, speck" reproduces approximately Rabbit's perception—one he will rearticulate repeatedly in the tetralogy—of the progressive dwindling his life has been since he starred on the basketball court, maturity for him being experienced as "the same thing as being dead." Rather than dying, however, the ball "makes its hesitation the ground of a final leap." Whether this vision embodies the regeneration of self that subsequently prompts Rabbit to tell Ruth, "If you have the guts to be yourself, other people'll pay the price," or of the soul's ascent to eternal life—a "leap of faith" in a more eschatological sense—is, of course, never specified; what *is* clear here is that the shot represents for Rabbit "visual proof of the unseen world," the "grin of aggrandizement" he shines upon Eccles his way of expressing that he has just answered the minister's question, "What *is* it? Is it hard or soft? Harry. Is it blue? Does it have polka dots?" As Edward P. Vargo argued, "Rabbit gains at this moment the exaltation, the sense of celebration, the sense of the transcendent which Eccles so desperately wants but is unable to attain."[16] It is Rabbit's version of what George Caldwell in *The Centaur* subjectively experiences in watching a dive that rates a ten from judges: "In fifteen years I've never seen the ten used before. It's like saying God has come down to earth."[17] Of such evanescent visual and sensual impressions is faith confirmed throughout Updike's fiction and in the Rabbit tetralogy.

If this golf shot executed in a Tuesday afternoon pickup game seems a remarkably slim reed on which to predicate the existence of universal order and personal salvation, its intermixing of the aesthetic, egocentric, and the spiritual replicates the fusion of psychic impulses that characterizes David Kern's religious epiphany in "Pigeon Feathers," while reasserting that revelation's dramatization of the irrational, highly intuitive and subjective bases of religious faith.[18] To the skeptic, this "perfect shot" scene might be said to enact the genesis of the gods/God as Freud describes it in *The Future of an Illusion*: "And thus a store of ideas is created, born from man's need to make his helplessness tolerable and built up from the material of memories of the helplessness of his own childhood and the childhood of the human race."[19] Far from repudiating such a view, Updike's fiction consistently insists on the childlike helplessness underlying religious faith, diverging from Freud's formulation only in holding open the possibility that the "store of ideas" is not a human creation but a human discovery. Simultaneously and contradictorily, this vision of the ball's/Rabbit's "final leap" prefigures Rabbit's second religious experience in the novel, one that conforms insufficiently to the set of moralistic dictates the others around him understand as Christianity for them to view it as authentic spiritual revelation. (Eccles is not completely mistaken in his accusation that "you don't care about right and wrong," so little is Rabbit's faith predicated upon biblical injunctions to act righteously.) As prelude to discussing that climactic scene, however, it's necessary to look briefly at the moralistically centered Christianity of Mt. Judge which, as much as Janice and the empty old-fashioned glasses she scatters around their apartment, provides a central impetus for Rabbit's flights.

A product of traditional provincial American Sunday schools, Rabbit nominally shares with other Mt. Judge Christians the assumption that religion and morality are inseparable. For both him and Janice, the mere invocation of God's name on *The Mickey Mouse Club* is sufficient to induce guilt, and when Janice is delivering Becky, Rabbit, summoned from Ruth's bed by Eccles, sits in the hospital waiting room in an agony of guilt, "certain that as a consequence of his sin

Janice or the baby will die. His sin a conglomerate of flight, cruelty, obscenity and conceit; a black clot embodied in the entrails of the birth" (169). The "straight road" that he manages to negotiate for a few days following the baby's birth is a thoroughfare of conscience regeneration cleaving through the moral wilderness that was his life with Ruth: "I was sort of in the bushes," he describes living with her to Lucy Eccles, "and it didn't matter which way I went" (180). As the name of his town, with its suggestions of judgment from on high implies, Rabbit and the Christians of Mt. Judge have submitted to the process described in Freud's characterization of the development of religions: "the more autonomous nature became, and the more the gods withdrew from it, the more earnestly were all expectations directed to the third function of the god—the more did morality become their true domain."[20] Consequently, throughout their relationship Rabbit expects Eccles to sit in judgment on him, and when the minister fails to do so, Rabbit concludes that, "he doesn't know his job." Accordingly, Rabbit is surprised by Eccles's confession immediately after they first meet, "Now if *I* were to leave my wife . . . I'd get into the car and drive a thousand miles" (92), not expecting a minister to acknowledge impulses in himself toward freedom similar to those animating Rabbit. He may never completely understand, following the "perfect shot," how thoroughly Eccles is living vicariously through Rabbit's intuitive, instinctive belief, one far more intense than Eccles's own ineffectual attempts to serve not the Father but the faith of his father, also a minister. When Eccles launches into his "you worship nothing but your own worst instincts" indictment, he is acting out the clerical role of moral arbiter Rabbit expects of him, the candid accusation freeing Rabbit to execute the physical act that constitutes his only justification for the selfishness of his actions. This small ritual of moral condemnation culminating in religious epiphany and radical self-affirmation prefigures the dramatically protracted, climactic ceremony of blame imposition, which is the Christian community's response to the death of Harry and Janice's baby, and to which Rabbit reacts in a parallel, albeit more violent, way.

The comings and goings at the Springer home following the baby's drowning basically represent a serial ritual of blame and forgiveness, a highly humanistic ceremony of visitors' condescension to the tragedy-stricken inflected by a religious vocabulary and concluding in the bestowal of forgiveness. The claustrophobia-inducing quality of this ritual for Rabbit is anticipated in the novel's opening scene: Janice's request that he buy her cigarettes while he's out retrieving Nelson and their car means "everything was forgiven, everything was the same"

(12), that implicit concurrence in culpability and consequent restoration of marital sameness constituting "a trap," which is a major provocation for his flight south. When Rabbit arrives at the Springer house following Eccles's informing him of the baby's death, Janice's father tells him, "I won't say I don't blame you, because of course I do. But you're not the only one to blame" (234), he adds, placing some of the responsibility for Janice's drinking on himself and his wife for their failure to make her feel secure. Other visitors from what Rabbit thinks of as "the world of the blameless" arrive: Tothero's wife brings him by for a visit, Rabbit's old coach reminding him that, back when he slept in Tothero's cot in the Sunshine Athletic Club, Tothero "begged him" to go back to Janice and "to avoid suffering," the old man regretting that "You young people . . . tend to forget" (238). In fact, it's Tothero who has forgotten: although that morning he promises Harry they will discuss "this crisis in your marriage" later in the day, by evening he is too full of the plans he's made with Brewer "queens" Margaret and Ruth to worry about "poor little Janice Springer" or to offer Harry a single word of admonition about suffering. As one of Rabbit's spiritual mentors, Tothero (whose name, as George W. Hunt noticed, reflects the ambiguity of Rabbit's relationship to his own past, combining child hero with dead hero, and whose "half-paralyzed" face symbolizes his confusedly contradictory guidance[21]) is the dispenser of distinctly ambiguous counsel: "run, run, run—you can never run enough," and "avoid suffering." Only through undertaking a regimen of jogging in *Rabbit is Rich* is Harry briefly able effectively to reconcile his coach's two precepts; otherwise, he's unable effectively to resolve in the tetralogy the conflict New Hampshirite Alf Clayton's variation on his state's motto in Updike's *Memories of the Ford Administration* limns: "Live free or go home."

Eccles appears at the house of mourning too, and when Rabbit invokes "the thing behind everything" in which he believes, Eccles responds, "you know I don't think that thing exists in the way you think it does." Eccles has nonetheless fed off this "thing" when its energy brought "a desperate gaiety" to games of golf; otherwise, he perceives it, ironically, as "the thing which makes Harry unsteady, that makes him unable to repeat his beautiful effortless swing every time," as "the thing at the root of all the problems that he has created" (144–45). Beating Harry decisively on the golf course, Eccles imagines, will enable him to "get on top of this weakness," which is Rabbit's "beautiful effortless" faith, "and hence solve the problems." "Harry, it's not for me to forgive you. You've done nothing for me *to* forgive," Eccles continues during his visit to the Springer home, differentiating himself from those who have assumed that dispensing blame and offering the reward of forgiveness is what these visitations with Harry are all about. The remainder of his counsel is, however, more characteristic and complicated: "I'm equal with you in guilt. We must work for forgiveness; we must *earn* the right to see the thing behind everything. Harry, I know that people are brought to Christ, I've seen it with my eyes and tasted it with my mouth. And I do think this. I think marriage is a sacrament, and that this tragedy, terrible as it is, has at last united you and Janice in a sacred way"[22] (241).

For Eccles seriously to maintain that he is equal with Rabbit in guilt is either to make an exaggerated and untrue claim about his culpability in the infant's death or to relegate to babbling relativism any conception of guilt. Even if, in the traditional Christian formulation, no one is without sin in the eyes of the Lord, the man whose absence from home was contributory to his child's death *feels* guiltier than the minister attempting to console him, and that sense of guilt, Updike seems to be suggesting, deserves not to be neutralized in clerical melodramatics. (Lucy Eccles has already dismissed as "neurotic" Eccles's suggestion that the baby's death was his fault.) Eccles's assertion that "we must work for forgiveness . . . [and] earn the right to see that thing behind everything" leaves ambiguous the source of that forgiveness, while invoking the works vs. faith controversy that underlies Fritz Kruppenbach's theological chiding of Eccles earlier in the novel. Eccles's insistence that he's "seen people brought to Christ" with his own eyes seems to affirm faith over works and sounds sincere, but there's far more evidence in the novel that he's too busy ministering to his flock's personal problems to see, much less facilitate, any such outcome. As for "tasting with his mouth" such conversions, the only taste with which he's thematically associated is that of the ice cream sodas he enjoys sipping at the soda fountain while he discusses "how far you can 'go' on dates and still love Jesus" with the teenagers he adores because "their belief is so real to them and sits so light" (163).

"You say role," Kruppenbach scolds him in a passage Updike critics have all but unanimously construed as articulating something bordering on an Updike ex cathedra pronouncement, "I say you don't know what your role is or you'd be home locked in prayer. *There* is your role: to make yourself an exemplar of faith. *There* is where comfort comes from; faith, not what little finagling a body can do here and there, stirring the bucket. In running back and forth you run from the duty given to you by God, to make your faith powerful, so when the call comes you can go out and tell them, 'Yes, he is dead, but you will see him again in Heaven'" (146–47). Kruppenbach's individual-oriented, otherworldly directed Lutheran theology[23] counters the dilution of the absolute primacy of faith by humanist and moralist agendas he finds in Eccles's notion of ministering—the communally interpersonal emphases implicit in Eccles's credo, "With my church, I believe that we are all responsible beings, responsible for ourselves and for each other" (132). It is the clerical "finagling" and marriage counseling therapeutics of Eccles's ministry that outrage Kruppenbach and make Eccles an ambiguous mentor for Rabbit, a spiritual advisor no less confused than is his advisee about the interfusion of moral imperatives and spiritual impulses that constitutes authentic faith.[24] Eccles enacts this confusion primarily by being titillated by the very manifestations of belief he seeks to crush in Rabbit, and thus it is from his contradictory counsel that Rabbit, at the cemetery, must ultimately run. Although he never encounters Kruppenbach in the novel, it is, ironically, Rabbit's experiencing of the truth of the Lutheran minister's salvationist theology—with "he/him" changed to "she/her" in the assertion "he is dead, but you will see him again in Heaven"—that sends Rabbit fleeing from Eccles and the other unseeing Christian mourners at Becky's funeral.[25]

Offended by the way in which carrying out the routine tasks of life continues as the family prepares for the funeral in spite of the pervasiveness of grief, Rabbit snaps at Janice, for which transgression "Mrs. Springer revokes the small measure of pardon she had extended him. The house again fills with the unspoken thought that he is a murderer. He accepts the thought gratefully; it's true, he is, he is, and hate suits him better than forgiveness" (245). Accordingly, when Janice's father returns from the police station with the news that no charges will be brought in the baby's death, the narrator summarizes Rabbit's response: "It disgusts him to feel the net of law slither from him. They just won't do it for you, they just won't take you off the hook" (246). The "hook," clearly, consists in being assumed guilty but never explicitly charged, the indeterminacy of that state allowing others to act as if he's guilty without troubling ever to have to validate their tacit charge. It is frequently from the "traps" the imposition of such moral ambiguities spins that Rabbit runs. Convinced by the "unspoken thought that he is a murderer," which pervades the Springer household, Rabbit accompanies Janice and the Springers to the funeral parlor, where his mother greets him with the question, "Hassy, what have they done to you?" His initial thought is that "they have done nothing to Harry, what has been done has been done to them," but this assumption gradually fades as the funeral begins. "All under him he feels these humans knit together" in their tacit agreement of the merely ceremonial significance of Eccles's recitation of the "I am the

resurrection and the life, saith the Lord" passage of the funeral service. Whereas "The angular words walk in Harry's head like clumsy
blackbirds; he feels their possibility. Eccles doesn't; his face is humor-
less and tired. His voice is false. All these people are false: except for
his daughter, the white box with gold trim" (251). For a moment at
the graveside, Rabbit's sense of solitude lifts, and he "feels them all
one, all one with the grass, with the hothouse flowers . . . all gathered
into one here to give his unbaptized baby force to leap to heaven"—
the same force that propelled the golf ball/Rabbit's soul from death
("he thinks that it will die") into renewed life ("it makes its hesitation
the ground of a final leap"). His second religious experience, then, is
the consequence of this certainty: "Rabbit's chest vibrates with excitement and strength; he is sure his girl has ascended to heaven"
(252). Eccles completes the service and

> closes his book. Harry's father and Janice's, standing side by side, look up
> and blink. The undertaker's men begin to be busy with their equipment,
> retrieving straps from the hole. Mourners move into the sunshine. *Casting*
> *every care on thee*[26] . . . The sky greets him. A strange strength sinks down
> into him. It is as if he has been crawling in a cave and now at last beyond
> the dark recession of crowding rocks he has seen a patch of light; he turns,
> and Janice's face, dumb with grief, blocks the light. "Don't look at *me*,"
> he says. "I didn't kill her." (253).

This scene assumes not only the "perfect shot" sequence as clarifying context, but has as defining touchstone as well the psychological
dynamic of an earlier incident that I cited in the first chapter in which
Rabbit and Ruth on a Sunday walk climb Mt. Judge and look down
on the city of Brewer. Rabbit's religious sensibility expresses itself in
his errant thought that "if there is this floor there is a ceiling, that the
true space in which we live is upward space," but that idea prompts
another: "In this great stretch of brick someone is dying." Imagining
that he is watching the soul of a dying man "mount through the blue
like a monkey on a string," Rabbit suffers a momentary, suffocating
awareness of death, the ultimacy of the experience prompting him to
ask Ruth to put her arm around him. Reassured by her embrace, Rabbit perceives Brewer spread beneath them as "the mother of a hundred thousand, shelter of love, ingenious and luminous artifact. So it
is in a return of security that he asks, voicing like a loved child a teasing doubt, 'Were you really a hooer?'" (99). This tactless insistence
on veracity born of the same experience of sudden existential security
is what underlies his ostensibly cruel graveside declaration to Janice:
having himself experienced a profound truth, he demands an answer-

ing commitment to the truth in his companion. Ironically, in this scene as well as at the burial, Rabbit is acting in corroboration of Eccles's assertion about truth earlier in the novel: "The truth shouldn't be able to hurt us," he tells Lucy. The narrator glosses Eccles's comment: "These words are a shadow of his idea that if faith is true, then nothing that is true is in conflict with faith" (229). *Rabbit, Run*'s largely satirical depiction of Eccles's theological humanism notwithstanding, this idea, so reminiscent of Updike's previously cited assertion "that the truth, what is actual, must be faced and is somehow holy," emanates validity and provides the best—and perhaps only—justification for Harry's confrontation of Janice at the funeral.[27]

The complex of associations that have been accreting around the sky in the novel coalesce in the sentence that follows his assertion, "I didn't kill her": "The sky greets him." To oversimplify an issue that I'll discuss in greater detail in addressing the heavens—"upward space," as he thinks of it with Ruth—as a spur to unbelief in *Rabbit Redux* and as a source of mortal terror in *Rabbit at Rest*, the sky in this passage calls up two opposed clusters of images. The context of the "sky which greets him" may be provided by "the blank sky" he sees through his windshield early in the novel, which he associates with "Ruth's blue-eyed nothing, the nothing she told him she did, the nothing she believes in. Your heart lifts forever through that blank sky" (84). That relativistically empty sky is invoked again in Tothero's assurance to Rabbit when he pays his mourning call that "right and wrong don't fall from the sky. We make them" (240). Rabbit's unexpressed objection to Tothero's assertion articulates both his childlike belief and the impression of sky, which more significantly colors his experience at Becky's interment: "He wants to believe in the sky as the source of all dictates."[28] Harry's conviction that Becky has ascended to heaven in fulfillment of the promises of his faith takes the form of "a strange strength" that sinks into him from that sky whose color approximates Becky's eyes and echoes a neighbor's earlier assertion to him that "Palm Sunday is always blue" (87). In order to further emphasize the significance of this moment, Updike likens Rabbit's epiphany to the most familiar conceptualization of truth's revelation in Western literature as a form of subtextual confirmation of the reality of Rabbit's subjective experience.

The cave he has been crawling in, Rabbit wouldn't comprehend, invokes that in which Plato's prisoners suffer the shadows of illusion as actuality because these apprehensions are the total reality to which their chains have limited their perspectives. The illusion to which Rabbit has been shackled, clearly, is the notion fiercely embraced by Eccles and the Mt. Judge Christians to whom he ministers: that the

only meaning Becky's death can have is contained in the humanly de-
vised, moralistic ritual of allocating responsibility, assigning blame,
and offering forgiveness, which has been the underlying purpose of
the human interactions in the Springer house since the baby's drowning. For the other mourners, clearly, the words of the Christian burial
service are without weight or consolation, "*Casting every care on
thee* ..." being beyond their Christian capacities; for Harry, the religious ritual has been efficacious, his perception of his daughter's leap
to heaven having prepared him for his liberation from the cave of illusion.[29] Consequently, Rabbit (whose "eyes turn toward the light
however it catches his retinas" [203]) glimpses "a patch of light" beyond the cave of their collective visions, one that, to him, bears the
truth of revelation.[30] When Janice's face—"dumb with grief" because
she has not believed Eccles's scriptural solace any more than its artic-
ulator has—blocks that light, Rabbit reacts by articulating the truth
which constitutes for him the light's correlative: "Don't look at *me*,"
he says. "I didn't kill her."

Although the next few paragraphs continue to reflect the third-
person limited narration embedded in Rabbit's angle of vision characteristic of the majority of the novel and the tetralogy as a whole,
there's a conviction and unequivocality to the assertions of the narrator in the remainder of the graveside scene that suggest a concurrence
with Rabbit's impressions nearly comparable to that on which the
novel closes. "They misunderstand," we're told. "He just wants this
straight. He explains to the heads, 'You all keep acting as if *I* did it. I
wasn't anywhere near. *She's* the one.'" Recognizing how callous this
sounds, Rabbit seeks to mitigate it by telling her, "It's okay. . . . You
didn't mean to." But Janice remains obdurate in her response of personal offense, prompting the narrator's gloss, "Forgiveness had been
big in his heart and now it's hate. He hates his wife's face. She doesn't
see. She had a chance to join him in truth, just the simplest factual
truth, and she turned away." Rather than, as Eccles predicted it
would, "having at last united [Rabbit] and Janice in a sacred way,"
this tragedy has crystallized the spiritual incompatibility of their marriage, Janice's willed blindness imposing the same on her husband: "A
suffocating sense of injustice blinds him. He turns and runs" (253).

In one sense, Rabbit *is* articulating "the simple factual truth" at
Becky's grave: he wasn't anywhere near, and he is only attempting to
act in conformity with his Mt. Judge religious tradition in assigning
blame—"*She's* the one"—and then forgiving the guilty party.[31] The
experience he has had of his daughter's ascension to heaven, however,
arguably translates his act into a different sphere of ethical justification.

Updike has candidly discussed how important the theology of Soren Kierkegaard (who "got me through the two years [1955–57] in New York"[32]) was to him during the period of religious doubt he suffered in his late twenties, the crisis of faith given fictional dramatization in the stories "The Blessed Man of Boston" and "Packed Dirt." In his interview with Jan Nunley, Updike acknowledged that the fiction he wrote in his twenties and thirties was his most "Barthian or Kierkegaardian" work, characterizing *Rabbit, Run* as "a fairly deliberate attempt to examine the human predicament from a theological standpoint. I'm not trying to force a message on the reader, but I am trying to give human behavior theological scrutiny as it's seen from above."[33] One idea that links the work of Barth and Kierkegaard is that of the absolute distinction between time and eternity, the positing of an otherness to the eternal that is irreconcilable with and incommensurate to the human. "Suffering," Updike quotes Kierkegaard from his journals in a *New Yorker* review, "depends on the fact that God and man are qualitatively different, and that the clash of time and eternity in time is bound to cause suffering."[34] Rabbit's less theological pass at this idea in *Redux* is "I think God is everything that isn't people" (360). That one way of interpreting Rabbit's experience at Becky's funeral is to see it as an enactment of precisely this disparity between temporal and religious experience is an argument a few of the novel's critics have made, citing Barth and Kierkegaard texts in support of their interpretations. As Ralph C. Wood suggested, "the risk of faith is always wagered, in Updike's fiction, upon such drastic egoistic stakes. Anything less than everlasting gratification is too small a reward for so great a hazard as belief in God."[35] At the risk of freighting Rabbit Angstrom with theological baggage apparently at odds with his intuitive understanding of things, I want to argue that Kierkegaard's *Fear and Trembling* represents a central explanatory text for Rabbit's experience of the eternal in *Rabbit, Run*, and that, although Rabbit never actually becomes the knight of faith Kierkegaard describes, that knight's condition of unmediatable paradox and human unintelligibility helpfully illuminates Updike's protagonist's situation.

In his *New Yorker* review of Kierkegaard's *The Last Years: Journals 1853–55*, Updike summarized the Danish theologian's major achievement: "By giving metaphysical dignity to 'the subjective,' by showing faith to be not intellectual development but a movement of the will, by holding out for existential duality against the tide of all the monisms, materialist, mystical or political, that would absorb the individual consciousness, Kierkegaard has given Christianity new life, a handhold, the 'Archimedian point.'"[36] When Rabbit returns from church having been "jazzed up" by Lucy Eccles's flirtatiousness and wanting to make love to Janice, she asks that he imagine how she, who has just given birth to Becky, feels; he can imagine it, he replies, "I can but I don't want to, it's not the thing, the thing is how I feel. And I feel like getting out" (213). Rabbit would never refer to this act as an expression of "the subjective," nor would he perceive what he's doing as upholding existential dualism, even if he *can* react against attempts to absorb his individual consciousness into communal forms of belief. Nor would he be able to make much sense of Kierkegaard's argument charting the movement from infinite resignation to faith or the distinctions the Danish theologian draws among aesthetic and tragic heroes and the knight of faith. Nonetheless, Kierkegaard's description in *Fear and Trembling* of Abraham's circumstance following God's demand that he sacrifice his son offers one possible gloss for Rabbit's actions at Becky's funeral.

> How then did Abraham exist? He believed. This is the paradox which keeps him on the sheer edge and which he cannot make clear to any other man, for the paradox is that he as the individual puts himself in absolute relation to the absolute. Is he justifed in doing this? His justification is once more the paradox: for if he is justified, it is not by virtue of anything universal, but by virtue of being the particular individual.[37]

Is Rabbit justified in putting himself "in absolute relation to the absolute"? Is he justified in acting as if his utterly subjective experience of Becky's ascendance to heaven vindicates his transcendence of the mourners' notion of the ethical ("the unspoken thought . . . is that he is a murderer") in favor of his spiritually inspired conception of absolute truth ("*She's* the one")? "I don't know any of these answers," Rabbit replies when Ruth poses questions to him about what he wants when he runs to her from the graveyard, "All I know is what feels right. You feel right to me. Sometimes Janice used to. Sometimes nothing does" (262). The raising of the individual above the universal constitutes the central paradox of faith in Kierkegaard's theology, one that keeps the believer in a constant tension of indeterminacy and anguish because "whether the individual is in temptation (Anfechtung) or is a Knight of Faith only the individual can decide" (89). Only the individual can decide, in other words, whether her/his willed transcendence of the ethical represents submission to egoistic temptation or faith. On the bus traveling toward the Springers' home after learning of Becky's death, Rabbit attempts to kill in himself the "something that held him back" from going home that day because "whatever it was murdered his daughter." "What held him back all day," the narrator subsequently explains, "was the feeling that somewhere there was something better for him than listening to babies cry and cheating people in used car lots, and it's this feeling he tries to kill, right there on the bus" (232). If the articulation of his belief in the existence of "something better" here doesn't qualify as religious reflex, the fact that it is his religious faith that he's attempting to squelch is confirmed by his praying only on buses in *Rabbit Redux*, as if only on those public vehicles where he sought to kill it is his belief recoverable. For Rabbit on this bus, his earlier articulated hope that he'd "find an opening" appears to him as murderous egotism, the oppositional character of his "something that wants me to find it" quest giving way to a need for forgiveness and self-effacement: "He feels he will never resist anything again" (233). Until his epiphany at the graveside, Rabbit remains convinced that "the wandering thread of his feelings" has led him only toward a share of guilt in his daughter's death; he hasn't the slightest notion of himself as being "higher than the universal."

Kierkegaard continues,

> Abraham acts by virtue of the absurd, for it is precisely absurd that he as the particular is higher than the universal. This paradox cannot be mediated; for as soon as he begins to do this he has to admit that he was in temptation (Anfechtung), and if such was the case, he never gets to the point of sacrificing Isaac, or, if he has sacrificed Isaac, he must turn back repentently to the universal. By virtue of the absurd, he gets Isaac again. Abraham is therefore at no instant a tragic hero, but something quite different, either a murderer or a believer. (62).

As if confirming the presence of the Kierkegaardian lexicon underlying his novel, Updike has his narrator comment on the character of Rabbit's faith while he listens to an Eccles sermon at the Episcopal Church: "Harry has no taste for the dark, tangled, visceral aspect of Christianity, the GOING THROUGH quality of it, the passage *into* death and suffering that redeems and inverts these things, like an umbrella blowing inside out. He lacks the mindful will to walk the straight line of a paradox" [38] (203). Lacking the capacity to walk the "straight line of a paradox" that creates faith out of the very subjectivity that at every moment threatens to reveal itself as mere egotism, Rabbit runs from the cemetery along the thin edge separating his being a believer from his being a conspirator in murder. The momentary certitude spawned by his epiphany of spiritual transcendence utterly vanished, it is in a state of desperate spiritual and moral irresolution that Rabbit runs through the final pages of the novel, becoming aware as he flees of the presence of a very different deity than the one who has upheld his sense of his own human value.

As he runs through the forest below the Pinnacle Hotel, Harry "feels lit by a great spark, the spark whereby the blind tumble of matter recognized itself, a spark struck in an encounter a terrible God willed" (256). That "blind spark" reemerges as a central preoccupation of his in *Rabbit at Rest*, Harry intuiting in the beginning of all things the inexorability of his personal ending. Consciousness of this spark in *Rabbit, Run* projects a similarly oppressive awareness of ultimacy, one clarified by an additional clause in earlier editions of the novel. The 1970 revision describes this spark as being "struck *in the collision of two opposed realms*, an encounter a terrible God willed" (original clause italicized). The "opposed realms" of this clause, I'd suggest, recall Rabbit's dream briefly following Becky's death in which two discs intersect and *"the cowslip swallows up the elder."*[39] He interprets this dream as "the explanation of death: lovely life eclipsed by lovely death" (242), and upon waking from it wants to "found a religion" based on its teaching. His unconscious mind's attempt to reconcile him to his daughter's death provides no basis for a religion, however, and when the dream's imagery of "a collision of opposed realms" recurs in Rabbit's flight, it is not "lovely life eclipsed by lovely death" that Rabbit experiences so much as the sense that in producing the spark creating all things, "a terrible God" had irremediably condemned him to death. Rabbit has discovered the deity Updike invokes in observing that "I've never understood theologies that would absolve God of earthquakes and typhoons, of children starving. A god who is not God the Creator is not very real to me, so that, yes, it certainly *is* God who throws the lightning bolt [in *Couples*] and this God is above the nice god, above the god we can worship and empathize with."[40]

It is an equally "terrible God" to whom Rabbit prays when he reaches Ruth's apartment. She reveals to him the pregnancy he'd "never looked outside his pretty skin" often enough while they were living together to notice, and he quickly understands how she may have responded to it once he'd abandoned her. "Did you get an abortion?" he asks her, and before she replies, "He closes his eyes . . . and prays, *God, dear God, not another, you have one, let this one go*" (261). The God whom he once conceived as being the "source of all things" Rabbit now views as one who "in all His strength did nothing" while Becky drowned: "Just that little rubber stopper to lift" (237). For Rabbit, God is now complicit with him in allowing children to die, perceived as a power who must be begged not to let another be sacrificed to Rabbit's transgressions. It is, consequently, largely because God's existence is so much implicated in the survival of Ruth's child in *Rabbit, Run* that Rabbit becomes so preoccupied with determining whether Ruth's daughter in *Rabbit is Rich* is his. If she is his daughter, God, in addition to refusing to deliver infants from death, also protects others and, through doing so, answers prayers ("*Let this one go*") of transgressors like Rabbit.

The most significant effect that Rabbit's revised, darkened conception of God has upon him is to consume his sense of self, the depletion of character he suffers sustaining itself through the conclusion of *Rabbit Redux*. Jill's exposition of the psychological baggage Rabbit has been carrying through the decade between *Rabbit, Run* and its sequel seems to me to describe the psychic ramifications of the earlier novel's final scenes quite accurately. "You carry an old God with you, and an angry old patriotism. And now an old wife," Jill explains to him in her final speech before withdrawing into the nowhere land of mescaline. "You accept these things as sacred not out of love or faith but fear; your thought is frozen because the first moments when your instincts failed, you raced to the conclusion that everything is nothing, that zero is the real answer" (465).

Jill's characterization of Rabbit's psychology is valuable particularly for its implication that for him the failure of instinct results in nihilism, thus corroborating the narrator's straightforward contention that Rabbit's "feeling that there is an unseen world is instinctive, and more of his actions than anyone suspects constitute transactions with it" (201). Because he experiences these transactions so subjectively and impressionistically, his changed perception of that "unseen world" has the consequence of altering his understanding of himself. As the nature and existence of the invisible world become increasingly problematical for him, his self-perception changes as well, culminating, in Jill's language, in the view that "everything is nothing, that zero is the real answer." It is in order to be "led back" from that nihilistic conviction that Rabbit suffers the bleak spiritual journey of *Rabbit Redux*.

As he, Janice, and Nelson walk to their apartment to get clothes for the funeral, Rabbit poses to himself questions that arise regularly in Updike's work, a form of self-interrogation he ascribes to Kierkegaard. "Why was he set down here?" Rabbit wonders, "why is this town, a dull suburb of a third-rate city, for him the center and index of a universe that contains immense prairies, mountains, deserts, forests, cities, seas?" The question to which this one inevitably leads, "Why am I me?" panics him, leading him to the conclusion that "he is no one; it is as if he stepped outside his own body and brain for a moment to watch the engine run and stepped into nothingness, for this 'he' had been merely a refraction, a vibration within the engine, and now he can't get back in" (243).What he has for personality is "the heavy knot of apprehension" that invaded him when he learned of Becky's death: it "remains in his chest, his own" (239); otherwise, the external world and his internal barometer alike accuse him of being no one at all. "You're not just nothing, you're worse than nothing," Ruth tells him when he seeks refuge with her after fleeing the cemetery. "You're not a rat, you don't stink, you're not enough to stink" (260). His instinctive connection with reality thus condemned by the woman who once praised him because "you haven't given up. In your stupid way you're still fighting" (80), Rabbit flees Ruth a second time. His final attempt to find solace in the world beyond the self evades him when the "underlying brightness" he seeks in a church window fails to appear, the window remaining, "because of church poverty or the late summer nights or just carelessness, unlit, a dark circle in a stone facade"—a far bleaker version, that is, of the single circle, pale and pure, which consummated his dream of "lovely life eclipsed by lovely death." This ultimate rejection by institutional religion catapults him into the solitude in which he relinquishes his last remaining vestiges of self.

"He feels his inside as very real suddenly," we're told in the novel's penultimate paragraph,

> a pure blank space in the middle of a dense net. *I don't know*, he kept telling Ruth; he doesn't know, what to do, where to go, what will happen, the thought that he doesn't know seems to make him infinitely small and impossible to capture. Its smallness fills him like a vastness. It's like when they heard you were great and put two men on you and no matter which way you turned you bumped into one of them and the only thing to do was pass. So you passed and the ball belonged to the others and your hands were empty and the men on you looked foolish because in effect there was nobody there. (264)

The "two men" they put on you correspond to the opposites— "Janice and Ruth, Eccles and his mother, the right way and the good way"—Rabbit contemplates as he leaves Ruth's apartment, his neutralization between these contraries convincing him that "those things he was trying to balance have no weight." Passing the ball recalls his reverie while driving south in which he imagined himself taking a shot: "but he feels he's on a cliff, there is an abyss he will fall into when the ball leaves his hands" (23). He is figuratively propelling himself into this abyss by relinquishing the ball (the possession of which is the point of the entire game) to "the others," the new paradox delineated by the ending becoming that burrowing deeper into the self culminates in the self's repudiation.

Liberated from the moral choices that defined and constrained that self, Rabbit becomes a body in motion, occasionally submitting to older impulses (his desire to travel to the "next patch of snow" recalling his first night with Ruth, "her pushed up slip a north of snow" [71]), but generally indulging himself in a sense of pure present, the aliveness of the steps and window sills he glimpses reinforcing his intuition that movement is all.[41] The panic he is suffering is sweet as he runs heedlessly off the page and out of the book, the narrator's complete identification with his flight signaled by his immersion of himself into Rabbit's sensual experience of the moment: "he runs. Ah, runs. Runs" (264).

In his introduction to *Rabbit Redux* in the Everyman's Library *Rabbit Angstrom*, Updike recalled his discomfort with the cultural dissonances of 1960s' America, using a phrase that seems particularly illuminating of the paradox that is the ending of *Rabbit, Run*. "Civil disobedience," he explained, "was antithetical to my Fifties education, which had inculcated, on the professional level, an impassioned but cool aestheticism, and implied, on the private, salvation through sensibility, which included an ironical detachment from the social values fashionable in the Thirties."[42] Given that the "thing behind everything" upon which Rabbit predicated his intuitive faith in *Rabbit, Run* has been transformed in his eyes into, at best, an inducement to alienation from other human beings, and, at worst, a murderer of children, what he is left with as he sprints out of the novel is an anxiety-plagued, highly tenuous belief in "salvation through sensibility." His self has dwindled to a sequence of disavowals of human accountability—he doesn't know, he can't choose; what remains is pure sensibility, existence registering manifestations of itself in the outside world and seeking to take direction from them. All but completely severed from any supernatural sanction, the "wandering thread of his feelings" is debased coin, the only resource Harry has, and, consequently, he can make no response whatever to the conclusive, completely unanswerable question Ruth puts to him when he tells her, "All I know is what feels right."

"Who cares? That's the thing," she replies, unconsciously echoing Harry's earlier assertion to Janice, "it's not the thing, the thing is how I feel": "Who cares *what* you feel?" (262), Ruth wants to know.

One reason for Updike's having been able to spin three more novels out of the material of *Rabbit, Run*, I think, is that he felt compelled to continue trying to answer Ruth's question. For Updike, of course, that question translated itself into a spiritual/aesthetic one: what evidence is there for the existence of "salvation through sensibility"? For *Rabbit, Run* is nothing if not an attempt to assert "salvation through sensibility"—Rabbit's and, more complexly and covertly, Updike's. To put the question another way, if, as *Rabbit, Run* implies, the existence of a God to whom the writer can direct his "songs of praise" is deeply problematical, then what purpose is his art serving? If the "wandering thread" of Updike's endlessly evocative, highly sensual prose "goes nowhere," why write at all?

The question returns us to the question of Updike's with which this chapter began: "Why write about people if they're just bundles of neurons and cartilege and going to live and die just like the other chickens in the yard?" The answer, we recall, evokes the same uncertainty I've been arguing that *Rabbit, Run* ultimately and so effectively dramatizes: that "the truth, what is actual, must be faced and is somehow holy" (Becky's leap to heaven inspires Rabbit to assert absolute truth) or "there is some virtue in trying to get things down exactly as they are," which invokes a more ethical/aesthetic/secular scheme of values. Updike feels empowered, in other words, as Rabbit does at the cemetery, to tell people what he believes to be God's truth. "I try to adhere to the testable, the verifiable, the undeniable little thing," Updike told Jeff Campbell in a 1976 interview, "Somehow, I hope the pattern in the art will emerge, and I guess I must have some such hope cosmically."[43] By the end of *Rabbit, Run*, Harry's hope that the pattern of his life delineates a more than merely individual, egocentric value and significance has all but vanished, and, as a result, it's often difficult in *Rabbit Redux* to distinguish Harry's mood of utter demoralization from the baleful atmosphere, which is his—and Updike's—perception of the radically secularized American 1960s. Jill is right: the protagonist Updike follows through three subsequent novels is one who never forgets the experience of moving from his identification with a golf ball—"Number 1 in the center of everything"—to the conviction that "everything is nothing, that zero is the real answer."

Never again in the tetralogy does Rabbit experience the intensity of religious epiphany that is the catalyst for his flight from Becky's burial ceremony, the existential—and plot—extremities of *Run* being generated largely by the disparity between Rabbit's theistic intuitions and the confused moralism of the Christian community from which he repeatedly flees. From *Redux* with its depictions of Harry's covert prayers on public transportation forward, his surviving faith seems increasingly a desperate and often belligerently egotistical attempt to sustain the childhood belief that his soul is "central and important and invisibly cherished" (743) in an America progressively skeptical about and even indifferent to the existence of anything invisible, one that seems incontestably to cherish him less and less. In his essay on Walt Whitman, Updike approvingly cites the poet's "Song of Myself" assertion that "And nothing, not God, is greater to one than one's-self is," before offering a significant qualification of Whitman's judgment: "—but incessant creative recourse to one's self ends, as youthful illusions of infinite capacity fade, in an arid emptiness and a desperate lunge over the frontier of sanity."[44] The conclusion of *Rabbit, Run* dramatizes its protagonist making that desperate lunge; *Rabbit Redux* dramatizes Harry's hideously corrupt effort to live on the other side of that frontier.

4

Desolate Openness:
Rabbit Redux

"Who cares what you feel?"

—Ruth to Rabbit in *Rabbit, Run*

In THE CLIMAX OF *RABBIT, RUN*, HARRY ANGSTROM IS FACED WITH A choice between two alternatives: he can, as he's promised Ruth, go to the delicatessen and return to her apartment with food as he did on the Palm Sunday he moved in with her. Or, he can go the other way, down Summer Street to where the city stops: "He tries to picture how it will end, with an empty baseball field, a dark factory, and over a brook into a dirt road, he doesn't know. He pictures a huge vacant field of cinders and his heart goes hollow" (263). As I've shown, his vision of the end of the city fuses Brewer geography with Harry's *"cowslip follows the elder"* dream envisioning death, the novel concluding with Harry heedlessly dashing off toward "the unseen end of Summer Street" in a paroxysm of release from the complexity of options and futures knitting before him, the narrator offering ecstatic encouragement as Rabbit runs off the final page of the book.[1]

The novel's ending is, in its way, highly romantic, the quester after meaning having abandoned that pursuit in favor of indulging his instincts by dismissing thought and acting out of pure feeling. The publication of *Rabbit Redux* constituted a literary deflation of that romantic culmination by validating the physical law that an object in motion cannot stay in motion forever—by dramatizing the sourly demythologizing notion that once you've reached the end of the city, you're somewhere else and have to begin making choices necessitated by having arrived there. For the reader exhilarated by Rabbit's impulsive flight from the nets the world has set for him, his return home documented by the opening of *Redux* is the same experience Janice describes in characterizing her husband's postflight homecoming: it's an "anticlimax."

90

As if seeking to reprise that anticlimax at the end of the second novel, Updike has Harry once again moving toward "the unseen end of Summer Street," but this time he is driving with Janice at his side, the couple on the verge of reunion. Ten years have passed since the day of Becky's funeral on which Harry sprinted desperately toward the empty unknown he imagined awaiting him, and he fails to anticipate the changed world he is to encounter in negotiating the same geography: "At the end of Summer Street he thinks there will be a brook and then a dirt road and open pastures; but instead the city street broadens into a highway lined with hamburger diners, and drive-in sub shops, and a miniature golf course with big plaster dinosaurs, and food stamp stores and motels and gas stations that are changing their names, Humble to Getty, Atlantic to Arco. He has been there before" (611).

We have all been there before. It is, of course, in part from such twentieth-century American mercantile secularism that Rabbit originally runs, Updike reinforcing the point that there is no "territory" for Rabbit to run (or drive) to by invoking Huckleberry Finn's ringing repudiation of civilization—"I been there before"—in dramatizing the impossibility of Rabbit's ever fleeing it and its most dispiriting commercial materializations. (Harry and Janice's choice of a motel along this spirit-numbing commercial strip in the closing scene of *Rabbit Redux* for their reconciliatory bedding down heightens the ambiguities of the novel's resolution.) In *Rabbit is Rich*, manifestations of American capitalism are often portrayed as part of the brave new world of prosperity, which the Toyota lot Janice inherits from her father affords Harry; in *Rabbit Redux*, the omnipresence of commodities and pop culture contributes to the novel's pervasive aura of oppressively banal, soulless materialism.[2] The mood of the ending's Summer Street passage with its patient detailing of urban atrocities typifies the tonality of *Rabbit Redux* as a whole, the novel's style incessantly evoking the exhaustion and sour urban demoralization introduced in the book's opening three sentences:

Men emerge pale from the little printing plant at four sharp, ghosts for an instant, blinking, until the outdoor light overcomes the look of constant indoor light clinging to them. In winter, Pine Street at this hour is dark, darkness presses down early from the mountain that hangs above the stagnant city of Brewer; but now in summer the granite curbs starred with mica and the row houses differentiated by speckled bastard sidings and the hopeful small porches with their jigsaw brackets and gray milk-bottle boxes and the sooty gingko trees and the baking curbside cars wince beneath a brilliance like a frozen explosion. The city, attempting to revive

its dying downtown, has torn away blocks of buildings to create parking
lots, so that a desolate openness, weedy and rubbled, spills through the
once-packed streets, exposing church facades never seen from a distance
and generating new perspectives of rear entryways and half alleys and intensifying the cruel breadth of the light. (269)

"His eyes turn toward the light however it glances into his retina,"
we're told in *Rabbit, Run*, but the "cruel breadth of light" here bears
little relation to that tropism and still less to the "patch of light" that
sparks Rabbit's hopes of Becky's resurrection at her burial. The pervasiveness of merciless glare, grime, and stupor characterizing the
"stagnant city of Brewer" in each of these opening sentences communicates a revulsion as precisely evoked as it is unrelenting. The "new
perspectives" of this world "expose church facades" as nothing but
facades and replace them with "rear entryways and half alleys," the
reader's eye, in anticipation of the novel's overall spiritual ethos,
being repeatedly drawn to what is no longer here and to the sensory
distress precipitated by its absence. Whereas erotically tinged nostalgia for his youth ("It was here, beneath the town in these smells and
voices, forever behind him" [194]) leaven Harry's perceptions of his
Mt. Judge home throughout *Rabbit, Run*, the primary environs of
Rabbit Redux—Penn Villas, the Angstroms' residential development
of identical ranch houses, and downtown Brewer where Harry and
his father work—are consistently visualized as terrains in which everything is out in the open, blanched by the sun and completely lacking in shadow, in resonance. As Robert Alter wrote of the closing
image's evocation of "a moment in social history," "the final observation about people turning yellow instead of tanning hovers somewhere between plausible fact and literary conceit but serves as a
firmly cinching summary of the feel of existence in this life-forsaken
town."[3] The aesthetic/spiritual ulteriority of *Run* that culminates in
Becky's leap to heaven is nowhere to be found in *Redux*, since, as
Harry blithely asserts of the familial religious practices, "We've kind
of let all that go" (388). If there were "something that wants me to
find it" for Harry in 1969 Brewer, Pennsylvania, it would have nowhere to hide.[4]

For my purposes, the key phrase in Updike's opening passage is
"desolate openness" because it so aptly characterizes the harshly
heightened discursiveness of *Redux*, an increased narrative diffuseness
which, by illuminating more human reality in even more graphic
terms than did the first novel, exposes greater human desolation. Admittedly, both *Rabbit, Run* and *Rabbit Redux*, in their present-tense
intensity, depict an oppressively barren, naturalistically rendered en-

vironment in unsparing and anything but inspiring terms. And yet, whereas *Rabbit, Run* dramatizes countercurrents to the prevailing spiritual stupefaction in the ecstatic moments of the perfect shot or in Rabbit's subjective experience of Becky's leap to heaven, there are no similarly ecstatic moments in *Rabbit Redux*. That novel's climactic, exclusively human relational epiphanies provide the only contestation to the "desolate openness" that characterizes both the landscape of *Redux* and the behavior of its characters in their emulation of the temper of moral release of 1960s America. The injunction to give praise, which Updike cites as a primary motivation for his career as a writer of fiction seems to have been displaced in *Redux* by an aesthetic translation of Eccles's—and Updike's—notion that whatever is true cannot be at odds with faith. But Harry's invocation of that ethic when Nelson begs that he be forced to listen to no more of Skeeter's Vietnam horror stories omits faith in favor of a grudging affirmation of full disclosure: "It happened, Nelson . . . If it didn't happen, I wouldn't want you to be bothered with it. But it happened, so we got to take it in. We all got to deal with it somehow"[5] (493).

Rabbit Redux seems, I'm suggesting, a markedly bleaker book than its predecessor, and at the risk of oversimplifying the sources of that difference, I want to suggest three primary explanations for it: 1) because Updike despised the political/moral ethos of the mid-late 1960s; 2) because, in reflection of that ethos, the book is pervaded by images of the decay of traditional sources of belief and the nation's consequent spiritual vacancy; and 3) because *Redux*'s major embodiment of religious belief is simultaneously its central negation of faith, the single spokesman of ultimate concern proving to be the advocate of a grotesque, self-serving, and murderous theology. The fact that Harry Angstrom is so completely incapacitated by all of this, necessitating—as Peter Prescott's *Newsweek* review suggested—"extreme authorial plot maneuvers finally to get him successfully led back,"[6] reflects, I'll argue, the novel's central symbol and symptom of Updike's experience of profound dislocation and spiritual disaffection at the end of the 1960s.

Updike has made no secret of how entirely dismaying he found the cultural milieu of the '60's, a period he characterized as "the most dissentious American decade since the Civil War."[7] As if seeking to dramatize how contentious the period was for him, he devotes much of a chapter of *Self-Consciousness* to revisiting and redefending his putative declaration of support for the Vietnam War in the pages of the *New York Times*. The distasteful consequences of that uncharacteristic act of political advocacy—primarily the negative ramifications of his being designated (inaccurately, in fact) as the only American

writer surveyed who expressed even minimal support for the war effort—color every judgment he makes about the period in his memoir
chapter. Nonetheless, it is clearly not only the Vietnam War obsession
of the decade that he recalls so sourly.[8]

"I had left heavily trafficked literary turfs to others, and stayed in
my corner of New England to give its domestic news," Updike explained with a mixture of modesty, self-effacing humor, and defen-
siveness. "Now along came this movement wanting to gouge us all
out of our corners, to force us into the open and make us stare at
our bloody hands and confront the rapacious motives underneath the
tricolor slogans and question our favored-nation status under God"
(S-C, 143). One might well term the "openness" Updike evokes
Americans confronting as "desolate," I think, given the guilt-riddled,
conflict-proliferating America it exposed underneath the jingoistic
self-congratulation of the late fifties and early sixties. Like the country whose central icon he will portray in a Fourth of July parade in
Rabbit at Rest by dressing up as Uncle Sam, Rabbit throughout
Redux is suffering a corresponding loss of his sense of "favored nation
status under God," one analogous to Updike's bruised feelings of revoked authorial privilege. *Self-Consciousness* supplies additional evidence that the author whose memoirs identify a favorite phrase of his
grandfather's, "out of harm's way," as central to his own psychological orientation toward the world didn't in the least enjoy being
"gouged out" of his corner of New England.

In his memoirs, Updike was candid in acknowledging that the
1960s' cultural disruptions and sociopolitical imperatives accorded
badly with his personal situation and agendas, since the "sixties were,
professionally, a balmy time for me." His relentless satire of Jack Eccles's communally inspired do-gooding in *Rabbit, Run* reflects how
little sympathy he had with secular humanist values even before the
dawning of the '60's; his remarkable literary success throughout the
decade—culminating in the publication of the 1968 best seller, *Couples*, and a *Time Magazine* cover story trumpeting the novel's commercial ascendancy—ill-disposed him further to embrace a cultural
ethic of communality, social accountability and bitter national debate.[9] Updike has confessed that there were other subjective influences affecting his responses to the 1960s and a penchant for
defending America not completely unlike Harry's in *Redux*: the be-
leaguered Lyndon Johnson reminded him of his maternal grandfather,
thus eliciting an extrapolitical sympathy in him, and he felt obliged to
be loyal to "a country that had kept its hackneyed promises—life,
liberty, the pursuit of happiness—to me" (S-C, 137). As a result, the
conflict between that national loyalty and the Left's anti-American

advocacy made the Vietnam era "no sunny picnic for me; I remember it as a sticky, strident, conflicting time, a time with a bloody televised background of shame. . . . My disposition to take contrary positions and to seek for nuances within the normal ill-suited me for the national debate; I found the country so distressing in its civil fury that I took my family to London for the school year 1968–9" (146).

For Updike, the privileged site of American critique had shifted from an individual author's scrutinizing, in the pages of novels and stories, "nuances of the normal" for signs of tension and spiritual corruption to a national, widely televised debate over American flaws. The "movement" had, arguably, become competition for his self-appointed literary office of "'showing' people, of 'rubbing their noses' in our sad human facts" (*S-C*, 149), political debate displacing him and fiction in general as dominant diagnostician of the nation's sick character. Just as Rabbit is happier carrying out his covert lustful forays in a 1950s' world pervaded by sexual inhibition and reticence, in a culture whose repression of the facts of human carnality affords him greater room libidinally to maneuver, so, I'm suggesting, Updike had preferred writing in an era in which it was the vocation of individual writers working in seclusion—not mass media–disseminated politics—to expose the ills of the American soul, to reveal to us the secret truths of the nation's covert immorality and soullessness. Arguably, Updike's resentment at his writer's displacement by other media is indirectly expressed in *Redux* through Harry's abhorrence for the demotion in self-image his Verity Press printer's job has imposed on him,[10] the protagonist's eventual firing attesting to a public indifference to the truth he has been producing parallel to that which Updike was suffering.[11] Harry and Updike were sharing, I'm suggesting, a depreciation of the value of their acts of witness, a mutual experience of cultural silencing epitomized by Ruth's question to Harry in *Run*, "Who cares what you feel?," and by Updike's feeling that his Harvard-inspired belief in "salvation by sensibility"[12] was being undermined by a cultural affirmation of political and social action over quality of soul. In response, Updike chose exile in England, while Harry opts for a more psychological form of expatriation in his living room.

Similarly, the era's ethos of sexual frankness and experimentation—to which *Couples* was, certainly, a significant contributor—must have seemed yet another appropriation by mass culture of territory to which Updike's fiction had laid special claims, and Harry (who contends in *Rabbit, Run* that "if you have the guts to be yourself, others'll pay the price") pays the price as his formerly repressed wife, acting in conformity with the sexual liberatory ethic of the decade, shacks up with her fellow Springer Motors employee, Charlie Stavros. Neither Harry nor his creator is an enthusiast of the cultural ethos of the 1960s, then, and the exhaustive and exhausted realism of *Redux* conveys emphatically, through stylistic imitation, Updike's repugnance for the "desolate openness"—the spirit of political contentiousness and sexual candor—of the era.

The negativity of Updike's perception of the decade permeates the novel, but it is particularly conspicuous in the dramatization of the country's displacement of spiritual ideals by secular objectives. The era's antispiritualism is embodied most consistently in *Redux* by the national preoccupation with technology—with the *Eagle* and its landing on the moon.[13] In the novel's opening scene, Harry and his father stop on their way home from the print shop at the Phoenix bar, its television repeatedly rerunning the *Eagle*'s takeoff: "For the twentieth time that day, the rocket blasts off, the numbers pouring backwards in tenths of seconds faster than the eye until zero is reached: then the white boiling beneath the tall kettle, the lifting so slow it seems certain to tip, the swift diminishment into a retreating speck, a jiggling star." Updike's depiction of this liftoff evokes ironically the religious vision of redemption from *Rabbit, Run* in which Rabbit fears that the golf ball, an externalization of his soul, he has hit will die—"Stricken; sphere, star, speck"—but is fooled because it makes its hesitation "the ground of a final leap . . . before vanishing in falling." The rocket's ignition, the narrator insists, has no correspondingly transcendent effect upon those witnessing it, eliciting nothing approaching Harry's ecstatic "That's *it*!" golf course response: "The men dark along the bar murmur among themselves. They have not been lifted, they are left here" (272).

As he and his father pay for their drinks, Harry notices that their currency has been similarly devalued. The coins they leave, in Pop's nostalgic perception, "are real silver . . . instead of just cut-copper sandwich coins that ring flat on the bar top." Much of what Harry experiences in the novel will "ring flat" in much the same way that these cheapened coins do, prompting him to mourn the passing of "Old values. The Depression when money was money. Never be sacred again, not even dimes are silver now. Kennedy's face killed half-dollars, took them out of circulation and they've never come back. The metal got sent to the moon" (275). In *Rabbit is Rich*, the "sacred" quality of coins is resurrected through the krugerrands in which Harry and Janice invest and which they joyfully roll around in while naked once they've brought them home; in *Redux* the human sphere is constantly debased in the name of supporting the government's technological objectives in space. "Uncle Sam is on the moon!" Earl

Angstrom exults upon *Eagle*'s landing, but his wife, her speech impaired by Parkinson's disease, is less impressed: "That's just. The place for him," she replies" (347).

For Harry's father, the nation's social security system is inseparable from its space program, Harry perceiving him from his vantage point on a bus as one of the country's "little men": "Pop stands whittled by the great American glare, squinting in the manna of blessings which come down from the government, shuffling from side to side in nervous happiness that his day's work is done, that a beer is inside him, that Armstrong is above him, that the U.S. is the crown and stupefaction of human history. Like a piece of grit in the launching pad, he has done his part" (276). His patriotic reflexes notwithstanding, Harry sees the new frontier to which so much American substance is being consecrated as nothing but "emptiness": "Columbus flew blind and hit something," he decides: "these guys see exactly where they're aiming and it's a big round nothing"[14] (285).

Contributing further to the sky's degeneration from the site of a faith-validating perfect shot to the backdrop for a "big round nothing" is Rabbit's mother's fatal illness. At the funeral home scene in *Rabbit, Run*, Harry imagines that her hug and the words she speaks express his mother's desire to "carry him back to the sky from which they have fallen" (250). His impression recalls the earlier-established fact that "he wants to see the sky as the source of all things," his mother being elided into the inchoate realm of origins he projects. By the beginning of *Redux*, however, Parkinson's disease has severely withered that source: "He can't bear to see [his mother] like this is the secret of his seldom visiting, not Janice. The source of his life staring wasted there while she gropes for the words to greet him" (276). In *Rabbit, Run*, it is Harry's most intense experience of "upward space"—"The sky greets him"—that precipitates his epiphany of Becky's leap to heaven; in *Redux* the source of his life whom he has so often associated with the sky struggles for language with which to welcome him. Throughout the second novel of the tetralogy, the "upward space" beneath the "great big nothing" of the moon is "a sky poisoned by radio waves," "television aerials raking the same four-o'clock garbage from the sky" (440).

Because *Redux*—like the entire tetralogy—is narrated in third person limited narration, Rabbit's conviction that he is moving through a devalued world is necessarily part social commentary, part self-projection. "Let's face it," he tells his mother late in the novel, "as a human being I'm about C minus. As a husband I'm about zilch. When Verity folds, I'll fold with it and have to go on welfare. Some life" (350). Mrs. Smith, an elderly woman whose garden he tends in

Rabbit, Run, assures him, "That's what you have, Harry: life. It's a strange gift and I don't know how we're supposed to use it, but I know it's the only gift we get and it's a good one" (192); in the decade capped by *Redux*, Janice's experience of living with him has been the growing awareness that "you were a beautiful brainless guy and I've had to watch that guy die day by day." His spritual inertia has provoked her to replace him with Charlie, someone who "loves life. He really does, Harry" (329). The emotional effects of these ego diminutions are well established in Harry by the novel's opening; Janice's leaving him for Charlie at the end of the first chapter, "Pop/Mom/Moon," allows Updike to confound Harry's sense of personal betrayal with the prodigy of humanity walking on the moon. As Harry, his parents, and Nelson watch television coverage of the *Eagle*'s landing and Neil Armstrong's descent to the lunar surface, Harry confides to his mother, "I know it's happened, but I don't feel anything yet" (352). The ambiguity of Harry's "it's"—which could refer to Armstrong's feat or to Janice's moving in with Charlie—elides into a pronoun the strangeness of the new world Harry and his culture have entered upon, one that precipitates in both, Updike implies, a moral and spiritual paralysis.

Harry is permitted flashes of rebellion against the counterculture world he inhabits: he wonders "where has the side of right gone" (286) and habitually defends America as "the face of God" because in doing so he "is defending something infinitely tender, the star lit with his birth" (307). After Becky's drowning in *Rabbit, Run*, however, Harry "feels he will never resist anything again" (233), and ten years' worth of habituation to this frame of mind has produced the Harry Angstrom of *Rabbit Redux*. Reprising his moralistic reversal following his initial desertion of Janice in *Rabbit, Run*, he decides early in *Redux* that "the world is quicksand. Find the straight road and stick to it" (294), and while the rest of his culture indulges itself in offroad experimentation, Harry spiritlessly plods his moral highway. For Janice, Harry's desertion and post–*Rabbit, Run* return is a sad story: "The angelic cold strength of his leaving her, the anticlimax of his coming back and clinging: something in the combination that she cannot forgive, that justifies her" (296) in her affair with Charlie.[15] While she indulges herself in the sexual freedom of the age, Harry stays home, inheriting the burden of Becky's death because "women and nature forget." He feels a "faceless unknown in their lives, a fourth member of the family" reminiscent of the phantasmal third person Janice imagined in their apartment just before Becky's drowning. The kink in his chest that settles in when Eccles in *Run* informs him of Becky's death is still associated by Harry in *Redux* with a punishing

God, and since he was riding a bus when he tried to quash that impulse in himself because "whatever it was, it had killed his daughter," he prays only on buses in *Redux*, the site of his forswearing of his God.[16] When not bus riding, consequently, Harry, like the culture he deplores and epitomizes, experiences "no belief in an afterlife, no hope for it" (355). Late in the novel, his unbelief plumbs its bleakest depth: "Rising, working, there is no reason any more, no reason for anything, no reason why not, nothing to breathe but a sour gas bottled in empty churches, nothing to rise by" (513).

The buses on which Harry intermittently prays have, however, accrued a contesting association: early in the novel, Nelson says his father likes riding the bus, to which Harry responds, "I hate it! . . . It stinks of *Negroes*" (296). Appropriately, it is a "Negro" who subsequently ministers to the gaping wound of Harry's faithlessness, the militant's absolutist credo speaking compellingly to Harry's dependency upon transcendent values to give his life meaning. Two of the reviewers of *Redux* found Skeeter the most interesting character in the novel, Guy Davenport arguing that "the young black revolutionary (or criminal, or con man) who enters and confuses Harry's already discombobulated life is a character of powerful interest and dramatic force. He embodies the world that Angstrom isn't ever going to understand, and he may be the emblem of the world's future."[17] If Skeeter represents America's post-Christian future, Brom Weber expressed more anxiety about it, contending that "the mesmeric Skeeter becomes a brilliant rendition of the evolution of rational protest and revolt in megalomaniacal anarchy; a Satanic being believing he is Christ destined to rule, he precipitates holocaust."[18] I'll be arguing that both reviewers' characterizations of Skeeter have real validity, that Skeeter represents the best of the American 1960s in his defiant questioning of all socioreligious principles and structures, and that he constitutes simultaneously Updike's principal, most powerful dramatization of the fatal misguidedness of the age's attempt to supplant faith with psychohistory, politics, and drugs.

Given Harry's general incapacity to be much interested in anything or anyone unrelated to sexuality, bringing him and Skeeter together necessitates a female intermediary. Jill Pendleton, a teenage fugitive from American prosperity and counterculture sexual adventurer,[19] is passed into Harry's care by blacks in Jimbo's bar who recognize that police scrutiny of them will be heightened as long as a white girl is living among them. Save for one characteristic, Jill is clearly an embodiment of hippie cultural relativism and moral indeterminacy, Updike's narrator explicitly remarking that "in rejecting instruction and inventing her own way of moving through the world, [Jill] has lost any vivid idea of what to be looking for" (377). Lacking anything else to affirm, she affirms pleasure: "The point is ecstasy. Anything that is good is in ecstasy. The world is what God made and it doesn't stink of money, it's never tired, too much or too little. . . . Everywhere is play" (402). Consequently, she raises no objection to going home with Harry, forthrightly offering him sex for rent. (Jill's ethic is summed up in her explanation to Harry that "whatever men ask of me, I must give, I'm not interested in holding anything for myself. It all melts together anyway, you see"[453].) Arriving at his Penn Villas house, she reveals to him the one trait of hers that runs counter to her prevailing cultural relativism, a capacity that, because of its vulnerability to exploitation by others, eventually proves fatal to her. She has fled from her Stonington, Connecticut, home to escape a lover who provoked her to become addicted to "heavy drugs" because while stoned she saw God, the lover, Freddy, predatorily feeding off her descriptions of Him. Updike invokes the era's characteristic confusion of scatology with eschatology as Harry asks her for a description: Jill responds with a detailed portrait of Freddy. But it's God that Harry, like Jill's lover before him and Skeeter after, yearns to hear described, the scientism and secularism of the age combined with his own faltering belief engendering his curiosity in a deity even if He may be only a teenager's drug-induced phantasm. "You're nice . . . not to lose faith," Harry replies after she depicts "the inside of a big lily, only magnified a thousand times, a sort of glossy shining funnel that went down and down. I can't talk about it" (391). What she *has* talked about in characterizing her lover is the inability of addicts to concentrate on anything but their addiction: "You think they're talking to you or making love or whatever, and then you realize they're looking over your shoulder for the next fix. You realize you're nothing" (391). As if intent upon substantiating this judgment, which will come to have increasing relevance to her own position in the commune Harry is too passive to prevent forming in his house, Jill brings home Skeeter.

Terrified by the fact that Skeeter needs to hide out with them because he has jumped bail, and remembering the hostile, blatantly racist things the ex-Vietnam veteran said to him at Jimbo's bar the night Harry acquired Jill, Harry, believing he's protecting Nelson and Jill, welcomes the black visitor with violence. He gradually comes, however, to find in Skeeter a kindred spirit, a visionary every bit as single-mindedly and inconsistently committed to his self-generated absolutist creed as Harry is to his own religious quest in *Rabbit, Run*. Robert Alter's characterization of Harry's fascination with Skeeter effectively conveys the psychic power the Vietnam vet exercises over him:

"the conventional Angstrom is hypnotized into a trance of passivity by the black man's sheer *outrance*, compelled to a dazed attentiveness quite unlike his ordinary mental habits by the psychological and rhetorical contortions of the utterly alien black."[20]

In effect, Harry lives a double life while Skeeter resides with him: he goes off to Verity Press every day like a diligent bourgeois breadwinner, then returns home to smoke grass, debate black history and radical politics, and participate in the acting out of perversely racialized sexual scenarios with Jill and Skeeter. In the short run, Harry's neighbors ultimately terminate his culturally schizophrenic life by setting fire to the split-level site of what they perceive as an interracial ménage à trois; their terrorism, in turn, precipitates the long-term, tetralogy-spanning consequence of Nelson's never forgiving his father for Jill's death in the conflagration. The outcome of Skeeter's brief Penn Villas tenancy is so unambiguously negative, then, as to eclipse the positive traits and ideas Updike has attributed to him.

Harry's reflexive racism is tempered by Skeeter's tutelage, the nightly readings in black history allowing him to defy the neighbors who threaten him with dire consequences for bringing a black man and white girl together in their Penn Villas neighborhood. Nonetheless, a passage from Frederick Douglass's autobiography Skeeter has him read aloud sums up Harry's behavior toward Skeeter's occupation of his home and his human weight throughout the novel: *"A man without force . . . is without the essential dignity of humanity. Human nature is so constituted that it cannot honor a helpless man, though it can pity him, and even this it cannot do long if signs of power do not arise"*[21] (511). Harry's instinctual response to the texts Skeeter brings with him is to reject "history, Marx, economics," because they are all "stuff that makes Harry feel sick, as when he thinks about what surgeons do, or all the plumbing and gas lines there are under the street" (463). That antipathy for infrastructural systems—especially those supporting his life—deepens in *Rest* when Harry is obliged to view on a monitor the angioplasty he's undergoing, but a few weeks' immersion in Skeeter's Marxist ideology sensitizes Harry to his socially dictated exploitation by American capitalism, inspiring him to admit how much he hates the rich of Penn Park, the wealthier section of his Brewer neighborhood. (His firing by Verity Press within days of his house's immolation confirms Skeeter's view of the callousness of American business, but Harry has clearly come to disregard Skeeter's teachings by the end of *Rabbit is Rich*, when he and Janice buy a Penn Park house.) There is validity, too, in Skeeter's claim that what he is doing for Harry is teaching him how to die. Skeeter explains to Nelson, who has expressed the desire to grow up "average and ordinary," like his father, "You still want to live, they got you. You're still a slave. Let go, let go, boy. Don't be a slave. Even him, your Daddychuck, is learning. He's learning how to die. He's a slow learner, but he takes it one day at a time, right?" (494). This is a considerable compliment from Skeeter, who is invoking through it another Douglass passage he will subsequently have Harry read. *"It was a resurrection from the dark and pestiferous tomb of slavery,"* Douglass writes, recalling his rebellion against the tyrannical slavemaster, Covey, *"to the heaven of comparative freedom. I was no longer a servile coward, trembling under the frown of a brother worm of the dust, but my long-cowed spirit was roused to an attitude of independence. I had reached a point at which I was not afraid to die"* (512). Harry's reaching that same point is what *Rabbit at Rest*—if not the entire tetralogy—essentially dramatizes.[22]

Harry is so delighted to realize that he and Skeeter support the war in Vietnam that he never fully comprehends how different their positions are. Harry supports the war effort largely out of nationalistic loyalty, remaining true to America as to "the face of God. Wherever America is, there is freedom, and wherever America is not, madness rules with chains, darkness strangles millions" (307). (Rabbit's Vietnam stance, clearly, is a hyperbolic version of Updike's, both of them incorporating highly subjective, deeply personal imagery as a major component of their largely patriotic positions.) Skeeter endorses the war as the incarnation of a differently conceived form of freedom: Vietnam, he insists, "is where the world is redoing itself. . . . It is where God is pushing through. . . . Chaos is His holy face" (494). What Harry's and Skeeter's Vietnam stands have in common is the notion that in its chaos lies possibility, deliverance from the ordinary: "Chaos is God's body," as Skeeter insists, "Order is the Devil's chains"[23] (505). "Well now what could be nicer than Vietnam?" Skeeter asks the three whites he seeks to proselytize, "We is keepin' that coast open. Man, what is we all about if it ain't keepin' things open? How can money and jizz make their way if we don't keep a few cunts like that open?" (495). Even after the fire has routed Skeeter from Penn Villas, Harry's continuing defense of the Vietnam war echoes him. "It's a, it's a kind of head fake," he tells his sister, Mim, at novel's end. "To keep the other guy off balance. The world the way it is, you got to do something like that once in a while, to keep your options, to keep a little space around you. Otherwise, he gets so he can read your every move and you're dead." When she objects that the war may simply be the attempt of "a lot of little guys trying to get more space than the system they're under lets them have," Harry recalls with distaste the doctor who blithely sentenced his mother to death, replying, "Sure there are these little guys, billions of them . . . but then there's this big guy trying to put them all in a big black bag. He's crazy, so must we be, a little" (576–77). *Rabbit Redux* dramatically authenticates this late '60s' vision of the fundamental irrationality of institutions, apparently validating Guy Davenport's view of Skeeter as an "emblem of the world's future" and accounting, as well, for Updike's provocative interview speculation that Skeeter might, just as he says he is, *be* Jesus.[24] Problematizing the we/he polarity that Harry, clearly inspired by Skeeter's ideology, projects here, however, is the fact that the drugs primarily responsible for Jill's death are concealed by Skeeter in a large black bag.

Skeeter's most significant source of fascination for Harry, of course, is his embodiment of the spirituality that Harry sought to kill in himself after Becky's death, the moral of his *Rabbit, Run* flights seeming to him to have been that "freedom means murder. Rebirth means death" (175). The religious tropism—"his eyes seek the light however it strikes his retinas"—remains strong in Harry, however, and it is because of Skeeter's powerful and unrelenting advocacy of an absolutist spiritual creed that Harry suffers in silence the moral chaos the black militant precipitates in the Angstrom house. Joyce B. Markle sympathized with Harry's perception, arguing that "Skeeter is the only one with beliefs deep enough and a vision of America strong enough to be a priest and life-giver."[25] Skeeter's aura of religiosity is based partly in his having been in Vietnam, the experience having liberated him from the stabilizing fixities of the American mentality such as common sense, racial difference and the belief in a white God. Harry initially objects to Skeeter's making "something religious out of [Vietnam] just because you happened to have been there," but Skeeter has already persuaded him to acknowledge that "you want to have been there because that is where it was at, right?" (487). In trying to communicate his Vietnam experience to Nelson, Jill, and Harry, Skeeter feels he is "selling it short. The holy quality is hardest to get."

> "The thing about Charlie is," he says, "he's everywhere. In Nam, it's all Charlies, right? Every gook's a Charlie, it got so you didn't mind greasing an old lady, a little kid, they might be the ones planted punji stakes at night, they might not, it didn't matter. A lot of things didn't matter. Nam must be the only place in Uncle Sam's world where black-white doesn't matter. Truly. I had white boys die for me. The Army treats a black man truly swell, black body can stop a bullet as well as any other, they put us right up there and don't think we're not grateful, we are indeed, we hustle to stop those bullets, we're so happy to die alongside Whitey." (492)

The "holy quality" of Vietnam that Skeeter's monologue so effectively evokes is partly a product of the war's violent eradication of
distinctions and ethics, a circumstance that Harry experienced on a
more personal, subjective scale in *Rabbit, Run* in feeling, while initially living with Ruth, that "it was like I was in the bushes and it
didn't make any difference which way I went" (180). Whereas Harry
could find his way out of that morass by taking the "straight road"
of moral responsibility, Skeeter's experience of chaos leaves him associating racial equality with unimaginable human brutality. Equally
contributory to that "holy quality" of Vietnam Skeeter wants to express, consequently, is his victim's obsession with race.

Harry asks Skeeter how he got through his year in Vietnam without being hurt, which provokes memories of Skeeter's made accessible to the reader through interior monologue: "These white faces.
These holes punched in the perfection of his anger. God is pouring
through the white holes of their faces; he cannot staunch the gushing.
It gets to his eyes. They had been wicked, when he was a child, to
teach him God was a white man. 'I *was* hurt,' Skeeter says" (496).

Rabbit Redux makes clear how completely Skeeter's psychic condition is the product of his having been "hurt" by being raised in a
world that insists God is white, racism and its suspension in the killing fields of Vietnam having made him who he is; the novel also
clearly dramatizes that this war veteran—who will subsequently have
a white girl die for him—is dangerously psychotic. Having suffered
so sorely in response to bigotry, Skeeter has come to perceive himself
as Christ hanging on the cross of American racism, his elision of the
spiritual with the political exemplifying in extreme form the 1960s'
confusion of these realms. Skeeter has suffered a spiritual wound that
he has transformed into a political stance; this is, in Updike's view,
a central error of the 1960s—the conflation of the spiritual with the
political. As Skeeter's horrific image of the white God effectively conveys, the merging of the experience of social oppression with his religious sensibility seems a natural and thoroughly understandable
psychic dynamic; nonetheless, its product is a psychotic and magalo-
maniacal delusion. "I am the Christ of the New Dark Age," he explains, "or if not me, someone exactly like me, whom later ages will
suppose to have been me. Do you believe?" High on the marijuana he
has gotten in the habit of smoking every night and desperate for any
creed offering redemption from the spiritual vacancy of the world he
moves through, Harry responds, "I do believe" (507).[26]

It is less Harry's belief that Skeeter seeks to gain than Jill's, and in
order to win that, he has to ply her with more serious narcotics than
grass. On the day he arrives at Penn Villas, Skeeter gives Jill a potent

form of cannabis, which makes her sick, prompting her to plead with Harry, "Get him out of here, Harry, don't let him stay, he's no good for me, he's no good for any of us" (471). Harry's thoroughly passive response is, "You brought him here," this refusal to act recalling his reaction to Janice's confession of her affair with Charlie: "see him if you want to. Just as long as *I* don't have to see the bastard" (336). Later that week, Harry returns to find Jill behaving peculiarly, and asks her, "Has Skeeter been feeding you anything?" She protests that he hasn't, but over the dinner she has badly undercooked, Skeeter implies otherwise in revealing his designs on her: "Hey you cunt, look me in the eye. What do you see? . . . You see Him, right?" (490). Unlike her former lover, who demanded that she describe the God her highs gave her access to, Skeeter insists that the deity she visualize actually be him in order to confirm that he is the "Christ of the New Dark Age." In this scene, Jill denies him, replying to his promptings, "Skeeter, He's not there" (490). Days later, however, his third-person limited interior monologue reveals the progress of Skeeter's Jill-exploitation project: "This afternoon he got her to drop some mescaline. If she'll eat mesc, she'll snort smack. If she'll snort, she'll shoot." The line that follows may come closer to invoking pure villainy than any sentence Updike has published outside of Darryl Van Horne's dialogue in *The Witches of Eastwick*: "He has her"[27] (496).

From this point of the novel on, consequently, Jill proves progressively incapable of defying Skeeter, retreating as a character as Skeeter's drugs hook her back into addiction,[28] her deepening habit largely annulling her as anything but the incarnation of the white female in the black man's acting out of perverse religious/racial scenarios. Although Skeeter objects to the tendency of whites to perceive blacks as symbols (477), throughout the scenes in Harry's living room, he constantly treats Jill as a representative of white womanhood. He tells Harry early on that he "can't be a man" unless he kisses her as Harry watches, and thereafter he deliberately augments his sexual violations of her in front of his host in order to prove his "God is chaos" willingness to transgress moral boundaries and also to test to what level of debasement he needs to descend to provoke Harry into intervening to defend her. As Nelson hysterically and repeatedly objects, Harry's unflagging passivity facilitates Jill's victimization and intensifying addiction, his father rationalizing his inertia with a trademark '60s' "do-your-own-thing" banality: "We can't live Jill's life for her."

On a subsequent night, Skeeter delights in turning Harry into a "lovely nigger" by having him read from Frederick Douglass and then masturbating in response to Harry's recitation of Douglass's rebellion against Covey. Escaping upstairs from what he perceives as a

threateningly tempting invitation to homosexual sex, Harry crawls in
bed with Jill, who desperately begs that he hold her to prevent her
from "crashing through." He feels she wants to be fucked as an antidote to the free-falling of her high, "but he cannot pierce the fright,
the disgust between them. She is a mermaid gesturing beneath the skin
of the water. He is floating rigid to keep himself from sinking in terror" (513). Seeking deliverance from the excesses and terror of this
evening, Harry the next morning calls Peggy Fosnacht—a touchstone
of sexual normalcy and ordinary life for him throughout the novel—
to accept her invitation for dinner and more for Saturday night. While
he is "cashing her check" in Peggy's bed, his absence from home
allows the immolation of his house and the death of Jill. Before she
dies, however, Skeeter gets what he wants from her.

> "Who's your Lord Jesus, Jill honey?" he asks her the night before the fire.
> "You are."
> "I am, right?"
> "Right."
> ". . . What do you see when you look at me? . . . You see a giant lily,
>   right?"
> "Right. You promised."
> "Love my cock? . . . Love my jism, Sweet Jill? Love it in your veins?"
> "Right. You promised. . . . Please shoot me. You promised."
> "I your Savior, right? Right?"
> "You promised. You must, Skeeter."
> "O.K. Tell me I'm your Savior."
> "You are. Hurry, you did promise."
> "O.K." Skeeter explains hurriedly, "I'll fix her up. You go upstairs,
>   Chuck. I don't want you to see this."
> "I want to see it." (526–27)

The purpose of this horrific scene, clearly, is to expose unequivocally the basis of Skeeter's claims to godhead. In order for him to be
affirmed as the messiah he fancies himself, his worshipper must be in
a state of such pitiful addictive dependency that she will agree to any
stipulation he posits to gain her the shooting up she craves. Skeeter
has convinced himself that the drug he is about to inject in her is his
semen, and that it is his holy jism to which she has become addicted.
He is acting upon paranoiac delusions; her conceding the point is a
response purely chemical. Skeeter's psychotic confusion of sex and
religion, political power and spirituality, are, I'm convinced, what
Updike is dramatizing in this grotesque dialogue, the remarkably un-
Updikean excess of it expressing the hostility which the 1960s' notion of a God accessible exclusively through drugs inspired in him.

Having, by his own account, said "no, in *Couples*, to a religious community founded on physical and psychical interpenetration,"[29] Updike in *Rabbit Redux* says no to religious experience provoked by narcotics.[30] Trailing in the wake of that fundamental negation of dope-induced faith is an excoriation of the pervasive interpenetration of values of the age that allows Skeeter to become such an overwhelming presence in the Angstrom household. What makes him such a powerful orator is his completely justified sense of personal injury—"I *was* hurt"—inflicted by American racism; what renders him criminally psychotic is his injury-induced belief that his individual suffering elevates him spiritually above both those who have injured him and his fellow victims as well. Like so many messages of that ideologically charged era, Skeeter's is egocentrism masquerading as objective political/spiritual critique. Few of Skeeter's diagnoses of American political realities seem utterly without historical validity or intellectual persuasiveness, this fact explaining why readers such as Guy Davenport and Joyce B. Markle, among others, could have offered such compelling apologias for him; the act of perverse human cruelty these ideas liberate Skeeter to commit seems to me to invalidate him completely as a genuine alternative to the banal secularism of late-sixties America. Instead of countering the "why not?" ethic that permeates the culture and epitomizes its moral drift throughout the novel, Skeeter's exploitation of Jill's vulnerability to addiction proves him to be that ethic's most shameless practitioner.

"The gospel that Skeeter preaches," Edward P. Vargo argued, "is not a gospel of power or common sense or love, but a gospel of death, of confusion and sameness and salvation only through the acceptance of himself."[31] What Skeeter's spiritual/political stance never acknowledges is how little faith he has in anyone or anything but himself—other militant blacks he dismisses as "Toms," and he gives hardly a thought to the Jimbo's crowd that had befriended and protected him before he found shelter at Harry's. The vapidity of the communal ideals of the 1960s is effectively conveyed through *Redux*'s portrayal of a would-be messiah who talks nothing but politics, but who finally cares about nothing but his own ego. "Everybody stuck inside his own skin" is his valedictory pronouncement to Harry, one that Updike deleted from the *Rabbit Angstrom* edition, "might as well make himself at home there, right?" (335).[32] Skeeter is, accordingly, the perfect redeemer in whom the self-preoccupied Rabbit Angstrom can place his absolute belief. If that redeemer exemplifies, in Davenport's words, "the world that Angstrom isn't ever going to understand, and he may be the emblem of the world's future," that future is one distinctly imperiled by this hatred-crazed messiah with his black bag of believe-in-me smack. For Jill, at any rate, Skeeter's incarnation of an agent of liberating chaos culminates only in the deliverance of death-by-immolation.

Early on during Skeeter's stay, Jill tells Harry that she's "scared of you and him together" (484), her comment clearly echoing the William Lloyd Garrison antislavery passage Nelson reads culminating in the assertion, *"If the American Union cannot be maintained, except by immolating*—what's that?" the boy interrupts himself. "Sacrificing," Jill responds, and Harry says, "I thought it meant burn" (479). The American Union is maintained in the novel through the "sacrificing" of Jill, and Harry is clearly complicit with Skeeter in her death. ("Him and Skeeter did it," Nelson proclaims solemnly to an investigator at the fire scene.) Harry never goes so far as to dismiss her death as callously as Skeeter does when Harry finds him sleeping in Peggy Fosnacht's car at dawn following the fire: "Tell [Nelson]," Skeeter urges the boy's father, "there's a ton of cunt in the world" (558). And, because it was clearly his reactionary neighbors who started the fire, there is some justification for Harry's immediate response, also omitted from *Rabbit Angstrom*: "I don't *feel* guilty" (1971, 335). Nonetheless, the sustained lack of affect in his reaction to her death in the novel's last eighty pages has puzzled numerous critics of the novel, leading at least one of them to wonder whether his apparent indifference isn't a reflection of Updike's nonengagement with the character.[33]

In his most extensive comment on the novel, Updike remarked that "tolerant curiosity and reluctant education seemed to me the parable that nobody else, in those shrill years, was offering. America and Harry suffered, marvelled, listened and endured. Not without cost, of course. The cost of the disruption of the social fabric was paid, as in the earlier novel, by a girl. Iphigenia is sacrificed and the fleet sails on, with its quarreling crew. If Harry seems hard-hearted, hardness of heart was what his original epigraph was about."[34] As Updike's comment suggests, Jill's death is a thematic inevitability in *Redux* in that it balances out Becky's drowning in *Run*, thus putting Harry on an even plane with Janice as terminators of young females ("Her trip drowns babies," Harry thinks, "his burns girls"), symbolically facilitating their reunion. For a writer who has expressly acknowledged his reluctance to kill off characters because of what their creation has cost him and come to mean to him, Updike's sacrificing Jill to the dictates of a symbolic design seems no less hard-hearted than he describes Harry as being. Two critics, in fact, have found far more than hardheartedness in Jill's fate and in Harry's incapacity to mourn her, Mary Gordon construing the death as the epitome of Updike's fiction's sustained hatred of women, Mary Allen contending that Updike "allows his bias in favor of stupid women to determine that a thinking woman must be killed off."[35]

Misogyny may figure in this plotting decision, but Updike's distaste for the ethos of the 1960s seems a far more significant factor. Jill and Skeeter are the novel's central symbols of that ethos, and in order for the novel to achieve its ultimate destination—the reconciliation of Harry and Janice, emblematizing the restoration of private life and the domesticity that the '60s' counterculture sought to subvert—both Jill and Skeeter have to be banished from the narrative. Skeeter, of course, appears to escape it much more comfortably, Harry driving him out into the country and leaving him there: "In the rearview mirror, Skeeter looks oddly right, blends right in, even with the dark glasses and goatee, hanging empty-handed between fields of stubble where crows settle and shift, gleaning" (559). In an important sense, however, Jill's and Skeeter's fates are the same: Skeeter survives the fire and flees Brewer, but, as Harry learns from a news article anonymously mailed to him between *Redux* and *Rich*, Skeeter too meets a violent death. Skeeter's role in readdicting Jill to narcotics is avenged through his own death in a shoot-out with Philadelphia police, one he allegedly precipitates in an effort to defend his "Messiah Now Freedom Family."

Insofar as their fates dramatize a moral judgment Updike is making on their values and actions—and I'm reluctant to think the novel functions in such one-dimensionally moralistic terms—Jill is the victim of her belief that "anything that is good is in ecstasy" working in complicity with Skeeter's megalomaniac need to make the world mirror his paranoid visions of himself as black messiah. It seems an unavoidable conclusion: one way that authors have of asserting their lack of agreement with characters is to banish them while those whose viewpoints they prefer remain, and Updike's refusal to endorse Jill's mystical pleasure-seeking or Skeeter's self-worshipping ideotheology is to have their choices ultimately expel them from the novel's stage. The temptation is strong to interpret them in such culturally allegorical terms because, in addition to being symbols of the late-1960s' ethos Updike detests, Jill and Skeeter might also be said to be symptoms of it.

As my brief sampling of the Davenport and Weber reviews indicates, the untypicality of Skeeter in Updike's canon was much remarked upon in reviews of *Redux*, and in a letter in response to George Hunt's questioning of Jill and Skeeter's believability, Updike seemed to be attempting to account for that discrepancy: "This was an era when we lived by television," he explained, "and those two just

came in off the set into Harry's lap."³⁶ In an interview, he reasserted
the point: "The television set invades the guy's life," Updike told Jeff
Campbell. "That is, these are sort of headline figures that come upon
him, and I think it was true of a lot of us in the late sixties that all
the things that we preferred not to think about became unavoidable."
Harry, then, became "the middle-class man whose living room becomes the scene of atrocities and teach-ins and all those things."³⁷
That Updike could to this extent perceive Jill and Skeeter as projections of mass media disputation is significant, because it suggests how
thoroughly the novel's plot is imbued with the very value system it
seeks to criticize.

Throughout *Redux*, the reader becomes aware of metaphors invoking ideological debates of the age: Harry tells the tendentiously
named Charlie Stavros he wants no part of any "coalition government" with him, and Skeeter calls Harry "Chuck," a variation on
Charlie, American soldiers' nickname for the Vietcong. Jill's green
eyes are likened to "a microscopic forest [Harry] wants to bomb,"
his attempt to protect her proving as efficacious as the United States's
efforts to protect South Vietnam, which—as a contemporary military
apologia insisted—had similarly to be immolated to be "saved." This
allegory is perpetuated by Skeeter's response to the burning of Harry's house: "the war has come home." Unlike *Rabbit, Run*, in which
the dense net of subtextual meanings provides structural reinforce-
ment of Harry's "furtive wordless hopes that at moments made the
ground firm," the system of political allegories in *Redux* in which Jill
and Skeeter are so pervasively involved seems a symptom of Harry's
disorientation and his culture's misdirection; they are, in effect, what
Rabbit has to be "led back" from. Rather than contesting the "desolate openness" of the late 1960s, the novel's Vietnam allegories reflect
a national preoccupation with the political, which is ultimately redeemed through Harry's ultimate restoration to the spirit-nurturing
security of domesticity. Working from his Christian/Freudian position, Updike has two basic objections to the political-centeredness of
the American 1960s: politics doesn't address individual desires, but
posits a communality in which he doesn't believe; and, they seek to
find solutions to spiritual conflicts in society rather than locating
them in the individual human soul/heart. Hard-hearted or not, the
fable of *Rabbit Redux* suggests that Jill and Skeeter combine to constitute a form of amorality and egocentric irreligion from which
America needs deliverance, and which the nation must repudiate.
Harry is let off the hook by the withdrawal of these two characters,
but despite his reunion with Janice that is his deliverance's consum-

mation, he's anything but in the clear. Jill and Skeeter leave behind a substantial and extremely vocal legacy of Rabbit rebuke: Nelson.

"You fucking asshole, you've let her die," Nelson screams at Harry at the fire scene, "I'll kill you. I'll kill *you*" (544). In neither *Rich* nor *Redux* does Nelson literally make good his threat, but he remains the incarnation of Oedipal opposition to practically every source of pleasure or self-satisfaction Harry experiences in the later novels, his son repeatedly and bitterly reminding him of the actual and figurative sisters he insists his father has cost him. Nelson's unrelenting defiance of his father will prove its own source of grief in the ensuing novels, then, becoming an increasingly substantial unit in his education in dying, but even in *Redux* the boy's very existence is in itself an enduring castigation. As morning dawns following the fire, Harry looks to the sky, that medium which he once sought to believe in as "the source of all things": "The freshening sky above Mt. Judge is Becky, the child that died, and the sullen sky to the west, the color of a storm sky but flawed by stars, is Nelson, the child that lives. And he, he is the man in the middle" (552). Whereas at the end of *Rabbit, Run* Harry perceives Nelson's existence as "a hardness he must carry with him" (263), the boy has become in the close of *Redux* a sullen and storm-colored hardness with whose antagonism Harry will spend the remainder of his life contending. (Unlike the storm clouds against which Harry's "perfect shot" is executed in *Run*, this cloud formation exemplifies not grandfatherly concern that Harry not be last [114] but Oedipal rivalry contesting Harry's patriarchal prerogative of being first.) Nelson's defiance is all the more galling for Harry because he continues to associate Becky with new beginnings and spiritual rebirth, while "the child that lives" is the product of his father's dwindling faith. Harry asks Nelson, "'Blame me, huh? . . . You don't think [the fire] was just bad luck?' And though the boy hardly bothers to shrug, Harry understands his answer: luck and God are both up there and he has not been raised to believe in anything higher than his father's head. Blame stops for him in the human world, it has nowhere else to go" (548).

By incessantly subverting his father's *Rich* and *Rest* efforts to insulate himself in upper-middle-class equanimity, Nelson will be simultaneously commemorating the young woman who provided him with an education in antiauthoritarianism while complying with Skeeter's plea: "Don't keep the Good Lord out, Nellie. . . . Put your hand on my head and promise you won't keep the Good Lord out. Let him come. Do that for Skeeter, he's been hurtin' so long" (494). Without ever again explicitly invoking his savior's name as a consciously embraced mentor, Nelson remains a devotee of Jill's and Skeeter's anti-middle-class conformity creed, though one whose want of personal charisma and authority doom him to merely petulant modes of cultural resistance. Although the net of law slips by Harry yet again as *Redux* concludes, the police exonerating him of culpability in Jill's death, Harry is sentenced nonetheless to a lifetime—two novels' worth of one, at any rate—of reminders of his late-1960s' passivity and to incessant reproaches from a son whom he has taught to blame for the hardness of the world no one but his father.

In order for that familial ritual of blaming to establish itself, the Angstrom family must be reconstituted, a process requiring three basic steps in the concluding chapter, "Mim." The arrival in Brewer of Harry's younger sister is the first of these. George Hunt's characterization of Mim's entrance into the novel as "a *deus ex machina*" introduced "to straighten out all the tangled relations"[38] appears to me highly persuasive: Mim argues that Harry needs Janice's hardness to shore up his softness, her primary contribution to reconciling them being sleeping with Charlie Stavros as a way of weaning him away from Janice.[39]

The other two steps necessary to the restoration of the Angstrom household consist in parallel epiphanies experienced by Harry and Janice. Lying in his childhood bedroom at his parents' Jackson Road home once the fire has decimated his Penn Villas house, Harry dreams that Jill has touched him, and he wakes to confront for the first time her death, images of her becoming "the body of his memory." "Pensive moments of her face return to hurt him," the narrator affirms, Harry then recalling guiltily that he had rejected the girl's "daughterly attentiveness" because he had "retreated into deadness and did not wish her to call him out. He was not ready," the narrator adds: "he had been hurt." Whether these sentences account sufficiently for Harry's inertia throughout the novel is, perhaps, debatable; what seems certain is that the very distinct echo they contain of Skeeter's response to his Vietnam experience—"I *was* hurt"—is metaphorically eliding them. Accordingly, Skeeter is immediately and more explicitly invoked: "Let Black Jesus have her, he [Harry] had been converted to a hardness of heart, a billion cunts and only one him." This passage of indirect interior monologue provides what seems to me the only possible rationale for Harry's desertion of Jill: resentful at Skeeter's drugs' successful seduction of her away from him, he abandoned her in a response of sullen, jealous anger. Updike leaves it to the reader to intuit that Harry knows that in abandoning her as he did, he left Jill at the mercy of what he elsewhere terms the "religious-craziness" of Skeeter, and that his final protracted thoughts of her in the novel involve both guilt and pain:

She breathes upon him again as he lies in his boyhood bed and this time
he does not make the mistake of turning his face, he very carefully brings
his hand up from his side to touch the ends of her hair where it must hang.
Waking to find his hand in empty mid-air, he cries; grief rises in him out
of a parched stomach, a sore throat, singed eyes; remembering her daughterly blind grass-green looking to him for more than shelter, he blinds
himself, leaves stains on the linen that need not be wiped, they will be
invisible in the morning. Yet she had been here, her very breath and presence. He must tell Nelson in the morning. On this dreamlike resolve he
relaxes, lets his room, with hallucinatory shuddering, be coupled to an
engine and tugged westward toward the desert, where Mim is now. (596)

In "Pigeon Feathers," David Kern lies in bed, praying that Christ
will touch his upraised hands to assure him of His existence, the boy
remaining uncertain whether his prayer has been answered because
"would not Christ's touch be infinitely gentle?" (128). Harry's experience is clearly the antithesis of David's, the absence of Jill's touch
briefly releasing the grief he has been too deadened since she died to
express. His regression to childhood masturbation upon returning
home to help him sleep has made him conscious of staining sheets,
but the tears he sheds here, though invisible by morning, are more
indelible because they are so much more generous than the ejaculations of his late '60s' self-indulgent despair. In mourning Jill in this
scene, he foresees his mortality in hers, perceiving falling asleep as
being borne toward the desert, the place of sun-blanched hardness
where there is no grass and nothing is green—the place that Mim has
described as America's future. As part of his process of learning how
to die, Harry in losing Jill has relinquished his link to "grass-green"
youthfulness and has—like Gabriel Conroy at the end of Joyce's
"The Dead"—begun "his journey westward."[40]
If Harry's epiphany brings him closer to death, Janice's is all about
life. Charlie's heart condition worsens one night when he and Janice
are in bed together, and when she fails to locate the nitroglycerin pills
he needs, she resorts to her own improvised form of physical therapy
to keep him alive. Once his seizure is past, he toys lovingly "with the
ends of her hair as it twitches on his shoulder," the touch of it on
his fingers contrasting with the emptiness Harry experiences when
he reaches up to caress Jill's hair. In "bringing [Charlie] back from
nowhere," Janice has simultaneously faced up to the third person in
the room when Becky died and erased "the mark upon her as a giver
of death," which Harry ascribed to her, her two adversaries being exposed as one and the same: a male presence who insists upon her female inadequacy and irresponsibility. Aware that her sexual healing
miracle may kill Charlie the next time, she terminates their affair,

thereby renouncing the one imperfection in "the vast volume of her love": "its object" (603). She is free, consequently, to take over the role Mim relinquished to her in returning west and which her new-found sense of her own capability as redeemer of men qualifies her to undertake—that of leading Harry back to health.

Like two space modules docking, Harry and Janice set their ren-dezvous in Penn Villas, before their burned-out house.⁴¹ Ideological graffiti left on the walls still standing of their former home offer the novel's consummate judgment on the climate of political contentious-ness the ruins now incarnate: "It all adds up no better than the cluster of commercials TV stations squeeze into the chinks between pro-grams" (609). The author for whom "out of harm's way" constitutes such a pivotal phrase directs his characters to the "Safe Haven" motel on Summer Street, where they consummate their reconciliation by—literally—sleeping together amid the rankest commercial weeds of Brewer. They don't make love because Harry's *Redux* experience has briefly changed his attitude toward his once favorite activity: "All this fucking, everybody fucking, it just seemed too sad. It's what makes everything so hard to run. There must be something else" (611). If there is, it's not to be found in the pages of *Redux*, a novel whose climactic scene generates a terminally interrogatory, "O.K.?"

Most obviously, the closing question echoes the epigraph of the "Mim" chapter in which Buzz Aldrin is coaching Neil Armstrong as he attempts to complete the docking of the module, the successful docking of Harry and Janice remaining in some doubt. The closing "O.K.?" also sets off a complex sequence of other intertextual echoes: Harry asks it of Jill after Skeeter has given her the potent cannabis, Jill responding that she is "scared of you and him together" (484), and a version of it is the last thing Harry ever says to her—"You O.K. with this crazyman?" (530). Contrastingly, Charlie signals Janice that his heart seizure has passed by saying "O.K." (601). For Janice, the "why not?" ethos of the '60s, which *Redux* telescopes, has provided her with a recess from the oppressive ordinary, liberation resulting in growth. For Harry, the era represents a respite from responsibility culminating in regret, grief, and a deepened sense of the world and his interaction with it as absence. The closing line reflects as well that the 1960s condition emblematized by Harry's amorality and passivity has not been lifted, for as the narrator characterizes it early in the novel, "In his frightened, hypnotized condition, Rabbit can only, it seems, ask questions" (349). Can such disparate experiences of the 1960s that Harry and Janice undergo culminate in a marriage that is "O.K.?" Updike devoted himself in *Rabbit is Rich* to responding to that ques-

tion. There is, however, a more profound question that *Redux* is raising in posing its final "O.K.?"

When Janice asks him who he thinks he has become in their months
apart, he replies, "Nobody," an Odyssean self-perception Updike has
elaborated earlier in the novel. Sitting in his mother's bedroom, Harry
thinks that

> there was a time when this homely street . . . excited Rabbit with the magic
> of his own existence. These mundane surfaces had given witness to his life;
> this cup had held his blood; here the universe had centered, each downtw-
> irling maple seed of more account than galaxies. No more. Jackson Road
> seems an ordinary street anywhere. Millions of such American streets
> hold millions of lives, and let them sift through, and neither notice nor
> mourn, and fall into decay, and do not even mourn their own passing but
> instead grimace at the wrecking ball with the same gaunt facades that have
> outweathered all their winters. However steadily Mom communes with
> these maples, the branches' misty snake-shapes as inflexibly fixed in these
> two windows as the leading of stained glass, they will not hold back her
> fate by the space of a breath; nor, if they are cut down tomorrow to widen
> Jackson Road at last, will her staring, that planted them within herself, halt
> their vanishing. And the wash of new light will extinguish even her mem-
> ory of them. Time is our element, not a mistaken invader. (590–591)

This passage summarizes the pessimism that is Harry's basic mood at
the end of *Rabbit Redux*, the "desolate openness" of the exterior
world depicted in the opening having become his interior landscape
in the end. Like the neighborhood that was the magical universe of
his childhood, he perceives himself as similarly depleted into ordinariness, the specialness with which his faith had imbued his life feeling
revoked. Ralph C. Woods effectively characterized the existential de-
spondency that often surfaces in Updike's work, and which is dramatically incarnated in Harry's ethical inertia throughout *Redux*.
"This celebrated incident [the church burning in *Couples*] points up
the moral passivity of Updike's work," Wood argued, "his reluctance
to find fault and access blame, his conviction that our lives are shaped
by forces too vast for mere mortals to master. There is a deep tragic
pessimism pervading the entirety of his fiction. For Updike, as for
few contemporary writers, there are problems that admit of no solution, that must be patiently endured, and that have their ultimate
source in God as the primordial origin and end of life. . . ."[42] Harry
patiently endures in *Redux*, but in the end he tells Janice, "I'm still
pretty screwed up" (616), and early in *Rich* he will summarize his experience of God with bleak fatalism: "water, flames, the tongues of
God, a man is helpless" (714).

Given this conviction of the transience, rootlessness, and helplessness of human life, is it "O.K.?" to live purely in the present tense of domesticity? Is it "O.K.?" to find safe haven in the midst of what Jill and Skeeter inveighed against as a wasteland of commercialism and consumer exploitation? Is it "O.K.?" for Harry Angstrom, lapsed believer in what Wallace Stevens termed "imperishable bliss," to find substance enough in the passing pleasures of mortality to remain engaged in his life and the world? Once he has responded to what has become by the end of *Redux* the central existential question for Harry—Robert Frost's "What's to be made of a diminished thing?"[43]—will it be "O.K.?" It isn't too simplistic to suggest that, whereas *Rabbit is Rich* generally responds to such questions in the affirmative, *Rabbit at Rest* ultimately says "no."

5

Domestic Peace:
Rabbit is Rich

For a while Harry had kicked against
death, then he gave in and went to work.

—Rabbit is Rich

BY MOST STANDARDS, HARRY'S RELIGIOUS FAITH AT THE END OF *Rabbit Redux* seems dwindled to almost nothing. When he leaves Skeeter on the road to Galilee, Pennsylvania, the last question the black man asks is "[You're] just waiting for the word, right?" (558); on the phone with Janice immediately before their reconciliatory Safe Haven bedding down, Harry admits, "I don't know what I'm waiting for" (604). Although consoling and potentially restorative, his reunion with Janice does little to reverse his judgment that "rising, working, there is no reason any more, no reason for anything, no reason why not, nothing to breathe but a sour gas bottled in empty churches, nothing to rise by"[1] (513). Like so many sentences in the tetralogy, this one illustrates how thoroughly Harry's conviction of the presence of the transcendent in the world is determined by his internal barometer, by the extent to which he feels instinctively at one with and attuned to the world. Which is, of course, precisely what he never feels throughout *Redux*.

Harry's declaration of belief in Skeeter-as-Christ in *Redux* might resemble a restoration of faith, but it's only the residuum of waning religious impulses: were his "I do believe" a profound leap of faith and not merely symptomatic of late-60s' spiritual desperation, a lifting of Harry's novel-spanning catatonic state would result. As for the bar spectators watching *Eagle* soar into space, so for Harry's brief Skeeter worship: there is no lifting, he "is left here." "Don't expect much," he warns Janice in the last pages of the book, "I'm still pretty screwed up" (616). The close of *Redux* is permeated by Harry's insistence that he's "nobody" and that the once-sacred geography of his

117

and his mother's existences has reduced itself irrecoverably into utterly untranscendent, thoroughly spiritless and quotidian terrain of the Safe Haven Motel. That perception of his life and worth is the culmination of feelings that have been accumulating throughout the novel and that pervade the prose of *Redux*.

That prose style, as I've suggested, evokes Harry's prevailing mood, Updike's language absorbing the disheartened impassivity of his protagonist's disposition. In part, this is because practically everything Harry notices mirrors the exhaustion and demoralization he feels, and, consequently, the "desolate openness" the prose keeps exposing gradually seems to generate a reluctance to expose still more. This characteristic is discernible as well in the fact that the perspicacity of the controlling intelligence of *Rabbit, Run* seems dulled in *Redux*. Harry only infrequently manifests the energy to rise to being the epigrammatic social critic and wiseass savant he is in the earlier text, Mim's arrival in Brewer alone provoking from him something approaching his characteristic skeptic's punditry.[2] Whereas Updike fled the United States with his family for England, Rabbit stays home, sucking up with stoical sullenness the bad vibes of late '60s' America his fabricator had fled. It's difficult not to conclude that Updike's distaste for 1960s America expresses itself in *Redux* in ways he couldn't completely control, Rabbit's depression and want of spiritual energy conspiring with the era's invasive propensity to "gouge us all out of our corners" to produce a sometimes ideologically overdetermined novel less than perfectly harmonized with Updike's gifts for illuminating the nuances of domestic life. If so, *Rabbit is Rich* is Updike Redux.

"This is what he likes," Updike has his protagonist think as Harry sits reading *Consumer Reports* in his Barcalounger, thus expressing solidarity with a preference of the author's own: "domestic peace" (694). By 1979, the rancorous ideologizing of human conflicts of the late 1960s had subsided from the foreground of American experience, these debates' reabsorption into the fabric of the culture's private life having allowed Updike to return to exploring "nuances within the normal" through the depiction of the Angstroms' unremittingly domestic life. The relief Updike felt is conveyed most powerfully in the novel through Harry's prevailing late-1970s' equanimity. ("Skeeter thought that [the Vietnam War] was the doorway into utter confusion," Harry tells Janice at the end of *Redux*. "There would be this terrible period, of utter confusion, and then there would be this wonderful stretch of perfect calm" [618], which is enacted in *Rich*.) Looking in the mirror early in *Rich*, Harry acknowledges that "a chaos of wattles and slack cords blooms beneath his skin in a way that doesn't bear study. Still, life is sweet. That's what old people used to say and when he was young he wondered how they could mean it" (626). How the "still pretty screwed-up" guy of *Redux* gets transformed into an affirmer of the sweetness of life in *Rich* is the question.

> He feels he is floating on their youth, on his money, on the brightness of this June afternoon and its promise that tomorrow, a Sunday, will be fair for his golf game.

With Fred Springer's death, Harry has become "the man up front" at Springer Motors, and there is "an airiness to it for Harry, standing there [in the showroom] in his own skin, casting a shadow." He likes the "nod he gets from the community" in response to his professional stature and prosperity, he "loves this crowd, his crowd" of friends who gather for games, titillating gossip, and drinks at the Flying Eagle Tee and Racquet Club, and he has reached a semblance of marital truce with Janice at least partially predicated on his recognition that he owes to the Springer family's ownership of the Toyota franchise both the nod from the community and his beloved crowd. "She is," he acknowledges late in the novel, "his fortune" (970). Perhaps above all, "He likes having money to float in, a big bland good guy is how he sees himself, six three and around two fifteen by now. . . ." (625). "For the first time since childhood," Updike writes in a sentence inconceivable in *Run* or *Redux*, "Rabbit is happy, simply, to be alive" (629). Rabbit is happy, and Updike was happy for him: "I feel some sort of relief," he told *Time Magazine*'s Paul Grey, "when my characters become well off."[3]

The happiness Harry experiences early on in the novel comes with an intensified obligation, one he is both fully capable of and largely unaware of fulfilling. As Updike's favorite fictional center of consciousness, Rabbit is the author's preferred medium for the registering of sensations and perceptions, and the insularity of his prosperous middle-class existence combined with his improved attitude toward the world allows *Rabbit is Rich*, to a greater extent than the previous two novels do, to foreground rendering—the evocation of Harry's subjective impressions—by minimizing plot. Rabbit's anxiety that "the wandering thread of his feelings leads nowhere" consistently precipitates flights—that is, plot—in *Rabbit, Run*; the plotting extremities of *Redux* coupled with Harry's deepening depression and passivity in response to them limit, in some measure, what he is willing or able to register of the outside world. The economic prosperity that is Harry's in *Rich* allows him substantially more leisure to consider and articulate in detail the world around him. Rather like Stan-

ley Elkin's George Mills, Harry has entered a "state of grace . . . in
which nothing could ever happen to him," in which "he was past it—
anticipation and interest and concern and disappointment and injury—and glory too."[4] At forty-six, Harry is, as he characterizes his
condition, like "a ball at the top of its arc, still for a moment," and
thus well situated to chart the motion taking place around him. As
Michiko Kakutani argued in her review/essay on *Rich*,

> Instead of charting, as he did in the previous books, Rabbit's growth and
> his struggles against the temper of the times, Updike now seems more in-
> terested in delineating his character's state of mind. And in an odd way,
> this impulse is appropriate to Harry and his condition: middle age, after
> all, is a period of consolidation, of stock-taking, of stasis even, and its pe-
> culiar tone and texture are here subtly evoked.[5]

"When you feel better," is Harry's way of summarizing this notion,
inadvertently accounting for the novel's heightened perspectival rendering, "you see better" (866). Although much of what he sees in Diamond County whizzing by the windows of his Toyota Corona is
disheartening, it seldom punctures the bubble of "serenity of middle-
age" he has achieved or discourages him from continuing mentally
to record the reality he perceives. Although I'm not certain that the
argument works for the entire tetralogy, in *Rich* John Neary's description of the link between Updike's lyricism and the grace Harry
has achieved seems exactly right: "And even if Rabbit doesn't himself
realize it yet—and perhaps he never will entirely—this lyricism indicates something that the reader who stays with Rabbit for the entire
novel series will eventually realize: grace, in the world of these novels,
is a return of and to the ordinary."[6]

Because of its increased emphasis upon filtering the world through
Harry's perception of it, *Rich* is the least-plotted of the *Rabbit* tetralogy, the novel, as Thomas Edwards noticed, repeatedly "teasing us
into anticipating tragedies which never quite occur."[7] *Rich* is, consequently, the Rabbit novel most vulnerable to Norman Mailer's infa-
mous charge that "when action lapses, Updike cultivates his private
vice—he *writes*."[8] Outside of Rabbit's largely interior wonderings
about the paternity of Ruth's daughter, Nelson's unremitting attempts to subvert his father's hard-won equanimity, and a Caribbean
trip for wife-swapping, there's little action in the third of the Rabbit
novels *to* lapse—*Rich* is an act of protracted attentiveness toward the
material world from the point of view of Harry Angstrom, generally
complacent *homo economicus*.[9] Harry and Updike collaborate in the

creation of this literary medium of witness that—unfortunately for Harry, since he can't perceive this aspect of his being—constitutes the protagonist's most compelling raison d'etre.

Even amid the cultural squalor and spiritual demoralization of *Redux*, the one shred of heroism Updike vouchsafes Harry is what the author characterized as Rabbit's "tolerant curiosity and reluctant education"—his grudging willingness to remain attentive to the world around him, no matter how terrible the perceptions it imposes. Even the hypodermic fix that Skeeter owes Jill for affirming that he is the Lord elicits from Harry the assertion, "I want to see it." Harry defends this impulse in chastening Nelson's plea that they listen to no more Vietnam war horror stories from Skeeter: "It happened . . . so we've got to take it in," Harry affirms, "We got to deal with it somehow" (493). Throughout the tetralogy, Harry is Updike's writer-surrogate, one who shares his creator's "impatience with everything that clouds and clots our rapt witness to the world that surrounds and transcends us."[10]

This affirmation of Harry's, although less literarily phrased and theologically inflected, resembles Updike's description of the religious roots of his realist aesthetic, which I cited at the beginning of the *Rabbit, Run* chapter:

> One thing that's given me courage in writing has been the belief that the truth, what is actual, must be faced and is somehow holy. That is, what exists is holy and God knows what exists; He can't be shocked, and He can't be surprised. There is some act of virtue in trying to get things down exactly as they are: how people talk, how they act, how they smell. So I have felt empowered in some way to be as much of a realist as I could be, to really describe life as I see it.[11]

In his self-interview conducted by Henry Bech accompanying the *New York Times Book Review* review of *Rabbit is Rich*, Updike articulated a similar objective in emphasizing the importance of what he termed "naming":

> I cannot do justice to the bliss that attends getting even a single string of dialogue or the name of a weed right. Naming our weeds, in fact, seems to be exactly where it's at. I've been going out into my acre here . . . and trying to identify the wildflowers along the fringes with the aid of a book, and it's remarkably difficult to match reality and diagram. Reality keeps a pace or two ahead, scribble how we will.[12]

Reality's capacity to surpass the writer's attempts to linguistically encompass it remains for Updike an essentially religious fact, I'm convinced; as for Rabbit, a less devoted namer of flora, "He loves nature, though he can name almost nothing in it" (746). Lacking any diagram to match reality to, Rabbit must make of observation an end in itself. The nature to which he devotedly bears witness in *Rich* is not the animistic universe that Nelson's companion, Melanie, extols ("as long as there are growing things, there's still a world with endless possibilities") but his own more local and tangled sphere: "One big weed patch" (709), as Harry characterizes it. This Rabbit's willingness to observe precisely and grow in that garden into which he's been dropped earns him Melanie's—and Updike's—ultimate commendation: "You're still learning"[13] (735).

Robert Frost defined a poem as "a figure of the will braving alien entanglements";[14] I want to characterize Harry Angstrom as a figure of Updike's realist aesthetic braving contradictions to its own validity and integrity. ("He turns me on," Skeeter in *Redux* says of Harry, "he's so true to life" [477].) The disposition toward realism in art and life is, I'm reasserting, where Updike and his creature most significantly converge, their sharing of this creed providing a primary explanation for Updike's willingness to continue dramatizing with marked sympathy the "wandering thread of [Harry's] feelings" over four novels. What unites them is a respect for actuality: "the creative imagination, as I conceive it," Updike has suggested, "is wholly parasitic upon the real world—what used to be called Creation. Creative excitement, and a sense of useful work, has invariably and only come to me when I felt I was transferring, with a lively accuracy, some piece of experienced reality to the printed page."[15] Their shared realist impulse is not, of course, unrelated to their dwindling intimations of the transcendent through the tetralogy, their mutually held, doleful consciousness of inhabiting "what used to be called Creation."

Updike's "God can't be shocked" description of his realist aesthetic contains an equivocation which, I want to argue, is implicit in Harry's enactment of the aesthetic throughout the Rabbit novels. His initial assertion that "the truth is somehow holy" gravitates toward the more ethically oriented claim that "there is some act of virtue in trying to get things down exactly as they are." The transition signaled here from conceiving the representation of truth as serving a transcendent purpose to ascribing to it a more empirical value is, I'm contending, analogous to the journey Rabbit undertakes from faith to doubt, the protagonist coming decreasingly to perceive "the truth as somehow holy" and progressively to settle for finding "some act of virtue" in "facing things as they are." Skeeter tells Harry that "history won't happen any more" now that he, the "Christ of the New

Dark Age" has arrived, but for Harry quite the opposite is the case: history, and the material world whose events it records, come increasingly to fill the mental space where he once gathered proofs of the unseen world.

Harry and Updike seem in fairly close agreement throughout *Rich*: if it's not a "song of joy" they're harmonizing on, it's nonetheless the closest approximation to it that the evocation of a predominantly secular, all-but-exclusively material world can become. "I am not sorry," Updike approvingly quotes Howells as affirming, "for having wrought in common, crude material so much; that is the right American stuff . . . I was always, as I still am, trying to fashion a piece of literature out of the life next at hand." Updike's uncharacteristic coda to this citation at the end of his Howells essay resounds of resignation, if not disappointment: "It is hard to see, more than eight decades later, what else can be done."[16]

What else can be done, of course, is to invoke the central modernist elevation of artistic creation as faith's replacement, which David Kern seeks to do in the *Pigeon Feathers* stories I've discussed, and which are the objectives as well of Peter Caldwell in *The Centaur* and for the narrator of the crucially important Updike narrative, "Leaves." "In an age of disbelief," Updike quotes Wallace Stevens in his review of Holly Stevens's study of her father's youth, ". . . it is for the poet to supply the satisfactions of belief, in his measure and his style."[17] Is the writer's "measure and style" sufficient compensation for the loss of centering faith? Is the novelist's devotion to painstakingly "naming" the things of external reality spiritually sustaining for author or reader even if reality is always outdistancing her/his scribbling? If God has withdrawn from the world, is it worthwhile to emulate the Deists and settle for describing the mechanism once conceived as His Creation? On the level of plot, the epistemological/aesthetic question translates to something like this: if *Rich*'s evocation of middle-age serenity is the culmination and sequel of Harry and Janice's reunion at the end of *Redux*, does that mean that the answer to *Redux*'s closing question—"O.K.?"—is yes? Alternatively phrased, can "domestic peace" ever be enough in a universe from which "the peace that passeth human understanding" has vanished?

The relative eventlessness of *Rich* allows Updike to move those questions—questions of, on his level, the ultimate value of artistic rendering and, on Harry's, of facing the truth of the world—to the very center of *Rabbit is Rich*. How resonant, Updike's text asks, can a "song of joy" be that goes no higher than the characters' heads? How meaningful, Harry's self-interrogations wonder, can a life be predicated upon what he learned on summer trips as a child?—that his life is "a paltry thing, roughly duplicated by the millions in settings where houses and porches and trees mocking those in Mt. Judge fed the illusions of other little boys that their souls were central and dramatic and invisibly cherished" (743). What is being debated dramatically through the highly impressionistic and texture-impelled narrative of *Rabbit is Rich*, I'm suggesting, is whether it is possible for Harry Angstrom to live a meaningful life supported by nothing but the fleeting pleasures afforded by his having achieved a prosperous, cozy, and protected middle age. Rabbit's optimistic speculation while vacationing in the Poconos, "There must be a good way to live" (745), constitutes perhaps the central subject of interrogation in *Rich*. What gets debated on the linguistic/structural level of *Rich* is whether the generously supplied felicities of language and the dynamic interplay of motifs are sufficient to sustain a novel that has for dramatic closure the protagonist's attainment of two distinctly domestic conditions: Harry gains a home of his own and becomes a grandfather. Updike's education, we recall him explaining, "had inculcated, on the professional level, an impassioned but cool aestheticism, and implied, on the private, salvation through sensibility. . . ." Through its relentless evocation of Harry Angstrom's interior landscape, the question that *Rich* poses more pointedly than does any other Updike novel is whether, in the apparent absence of salvation through divine intervention, "salvation by sensibility" is achievable. At stake for Harry in *Rich* is whether the interior pleasures of an insularly private life can be sufficient compensation for the loss of the conviction that his soul is "central and dramatic and invisibly cherished"; at stake for Updike is the tension that has pervaded his work since the publication of "The Blessed Man of Boston": whether "his measure and his style" can provide the "satisfactions of belief" despite the fact that that literary instrument—as "Pigeon Feathers" dramatizes—evolved expressly to expose "the moist white wood of joy" underlying daily events, to give literary substance to "intimations of divine joy."

In illuminating *Rich*'s interrogation of "salvation by sensibility," I need to divide the projections of and forms of opposition to Harry's sensibility into more discrete components than the novel—which presents them in constant dynamic interaction and interpenetration with each other—ever does. First, I'll discuss the "daughter" who constitutes Harry's best hope of personal secular redemption; second, the "external circumstances" of Harry's transactions with the world around him; third, his surviving religious impulses; and, fourth, the son whose primary goal in life seems to be laying waste the tranquility of interior landscape, the "domestic peace" which is Harry's major, if highly tenuous, midlife achievement.

> *And is your mother's name Ruth?* Harry wants to ask but doesn't, lest he frighten her and destroy for himself the vibration of excitement, of possibility untested. (640)

Perhaps the clearest indication that "the serenity of middle age" is not meaningful enough is Harry's need to intensify his equanimity by allowing himself another, secret pleasure, which he and the reader must wait well beyond the novel's conclusion to see validated: a daughter. Harry decides the young woman who accompanies a teenager window-shopping Toyotas in the opening pages of the novel is his daughter by Ruth Leonard, whom he leaves pregnant at the end of *Run* and whose child would be roughly this girl's age. In secular terms, Harry uses his imagined paternity as a clandestine form of self-reinforcement and reassurance when it becomes clear that Janice is concealing from him information about why Nelson has come home, what Nelson's relationship is with Melanie, who has accompanied him to Brewer, and what it is that Nelson was running from in Colorado. Harry's desire that this girl be his daughter, of course, represents more than simply his fantasy of having a child more satisfactory and less refractory than Nelson.

"Ever since his girl baby drowned in *Rabbit, Run*, Harry has been looking for a daughter," Updike explained in one of his self-interviews "conducted" by Henry Bech in the *New York Times Book Review*: "It's the theme that has been pressing forward, without my willing it or understanding it exactly, through these novels."[18] In *Rich*, Harry recalls that "every time in his life he has made a move toward [the invisible] someone has gotten killed" (767), both of those someones, being, of course, literal (Becky) and figurative (Jill) daughters. Believing that this stranger is his daughter is Harry's complexly conflicted way of once again "moving toward the invisible" even as he acknowledges the hazards of that motion. The secret of her, he thinks, is "like seed: seed that goes into the ground invisible and if it takes hold cannot be stopped, it fulfills the shape it was programmed for, its destiny, sure as our death, and shapely" (641). If she is his daughter, in other words, she restores to him the destiny that he has felt to have been revoked ever since he became aware that "a stony truce seems to prevail between himself and God" (747).

Although he never explicitly contemplates this in *Rich*, his daughter's existence would also constitute confirmation of a prayer answered. At the end of *Run*, when Ruth reveals to him her pregnancy, deliberately equivocating about whether she's had an abortion, Harry silently prays, *"God, dear God, no, not another, you have one, let this one go"* (261). The extension of her existence down through the years, completely unsuspected by Harry until her appearance at Springer Motors, would corroborate David Kern's imagined response from God in "Pigeon Feathers" to one of his prayers: *"I answer your prayers in My way, in My time"* (120). Harry's daughter's existence would signify that, in other words, God had "let this one go." Accordingly, when Harry returns to the lot one day to find the car Jamie Nunemacher considered buying gone, he knows he will now be able to identify Ruth's daughter's home through this Toyota parked in front of it, and feels as if "God has kissed him out of space" (869).

Harry's "daughter" is a source of both sacred and secular mystery, "that mysterious branch of his past that has flourished without him, and where lost energy and meaning still flow" (722). More than merely the road not taken, she is proof that there has been for him another road stretching out in time and running parallel to the one he has traveled; consequently, Harry imaginatively ascribes to her a genetic superiority to the child he has incontestably fathered in order to further embellish the crowning touch to the wealth and sense of well-being that she represents for him. Like so much else in *Rich*, Harry's "daughter" is simultaneously indistinguishable from his pleasure in his material success and emblematic of his need to seek beyond it for something more spiritually fulfilling.[19]

Harry's quest to discover whether he is Ruth's daughter's father provides his life with an animating purpose and personal drama countering the domestic peace that simultaneously consoles, justifies, and suffocates him; that quest, of course, plays a similarly shaping role in Updike's novel. *Rich* opens on the afternoon the girl appears at Springer Motors, and closes within days of his conversation with Ruth about the child's paternity. Ruth's acknowledgment that he is her father would, Harry believes, give him a destiny, a fate alternative to and additive upon the *arriviste* middle-class life into which he has comfortably settled; the delayed discussion of the young woman's paternity provides *Rich* with its primary structural dynamic. Because *Rich* lacks the narrative percussiveness of Rabbit's flights in *Run* and the agon supplied by antagonists Jill and Skeeter in *Redux*, the third novel of the tetralogy functions according to a different dynamic, one Michiko Kakutani characterized as "a kind of willful circularity"[20] in which the contents of Harry's sensibility accrue associative complexity without ever achieving real resolution. The contradictions involved in Harry's perception of his "daughter" exemplify the point.

The interiority of the novel dictates that what is often being dramatized in the text is the complex interplay between Harry's impulses, impressions, and ideas: his perception of his "daughter," for instance, is gradually revealed to be a palimpsest of his contradictory attitudes toward the domesticity he's embraced, combined with his desire that he have a hitherto unsuspected, sexually generated destiny different from the one he has been living, one that counterpoints rural poverty with his prosperity and a life in nature against the comfily suburban existence he has enjoyed. Whereas the narrative dynamic of *Rabbit at Rest* is provided largely by the presence of death as antagonist, destiny, and end, the absence of any such teleology in *Rich* allows Updike, working within the confines of the daughter quest, the freedom to concentrate on the play of consciousness of his protagonist living, bearing witness to, and ceaselessly evaluating the potential for transcendence of his daily existence. Through its intense and protracted evocation of Harry Angstrom's subjectivity, Updike creates in *Rich* the tetralogy's most focused exploration of the profound satisfactions and spiritual insufficiency of private life—one substantially more compelling, as I'll argue, than that evoked in "Rabbit Remembered."

> It gives him pleasure, makes Rabbit feel rich, to contemplate
> the world's wasting, to know the earth is mortal too. (631)

Although Harry's mental reality is the narrative locus of *Rich*, this doesn't mean that the external world isn't constantly impinging on it with cultural oppositions to and familial intrusions upon his opening chapter equanimity. Ironically, Harry's happiness exists in spite of, rather than in congruence with, his culture's condition. "America is running out of gas," we're told in the novel's first paragraph, but it hasn't done so yet; like the prospect of personal extinction, it's a threat, but not one that seems urgent or imminent. (If *Rest*—in which Rabbit is running out of intestinal gas—deals with the patient's terminal disease, *Rich* depicts him in only slightly anxious remission.) Besides, Harry is actually benefiting from this threat: he co-owns with Janice and her mother an automobile dealership that sells fuel-efficient Toyotas. For the only time in his life, he feels himself to be on the right side of American cultural decline; for the first time since he starred on the Mt. Judge High School basketball team, his condition constitutes an improvement upon the status to which his birth apparently sentenced him. If not a benefactor of the American Dream of upward mobility, Harry in *Rich* is the next best thing: proof that in the United States of America one can advance economically and socially just as far as his wife's inheritance will take him.

Another face that the American cultural decline wears in the Carter

era, however, is inflation, and because Harry associates it with a much
more personal dwindling he has noted in himself of late, the ebbing
worth of the dollar constitutes a more substantial threat. "Somewhere
early in the Carter Administration," the narrator explains, "[Harry's]
interest, which had been pretty faithful, began to wobble, and by now
there is a real crisis of confidence." The interest invoked here is not
money accrued on dollars invested, but Harry's investment in sex
with Janice: "He blames it on money, on having enough at last, which
has made him satisfied all over; also the money itself, relaxed in the
bank, gets smaller in real value all the time, and this is on his mind,
what to do about it, along with everything else: the Phils and the dead
and golf" (665). It is typical of the conflicts in *Rich* that Harry's sur-
feit—"having enough [money] at last"—generates another deficiency,
his achievement of material satisfaction having eroded his characteristic preoccupation with sexual gratification.[21] Further vexing this situation is the fact that Harry's sexual substitute is replicating the
declining potency of his relationship with Janice. The palpably sexual
limning of inflation in the passage's language makes the "relaxed"
character of his money and its penchant for "getting smaller in real
value all the time" seem the very semblance of phallic flaccidity. For
this too, however, Harry has a solution in *Rich*.

He takes a cashier's check for more than $11,000 to a store recently
opened in Brewer called Fiscal Alternatives, emerging with two cylin-
ders of Krugerrands so heavy "they threaten to tear the pockets off
his coat." Anticipating surprising Janice with his bounty in their bedroom, he conceals his purchase from the rest of the family, hiding the
coins in a bedside table drawer. He worries about his stash during the
evening, anxious that "something so dense with preciousness would
broadcast signals bringing burglars like dogs to a bitch in heat" (815),
Harry's simile again evoking the sexual emanations of his treasure.
Once he has revealed his surprise to her, Janice asks him whether they
need a license to own the coins. "Just the bucks, just the fucking
bucks, Wonder Woman," he responds, the narrator characterizing
Harry's subsequent sensation: "Blind, he feels amid the pure strangeness of the gold his prick firming up and stretching the fabric of his
jockey shorts" (816).

The ensuing scene constitutes what is probably the most ecstatic
and guiltless sex Janice and Rabbit—or he and any other female—
experience in the tetralogy. Their childlike precoital delight in decor-
ating each other's naked bodies with the golden coins provides the
novel's most compelling emblem of the excitations of upward mobility, the scene achieving *Rich*'s most successful conflation of material
wealth with sexual fulfillment. En route to envisioning the basic phys-

ical relation between man and woman as Updike perceives it, the narrator continues: "Lording it over him, holding him captive, she grinds
her wet halves around him; self to self, bivalve to tuber, this is what it
comes to . . . Gods bedded among stars, he gasps in her ear, then she
in his" (819). The reader is never told what Janice and Harry gasp to
each other, but it seems certain that if it were "O.K." they are groan-
ing, neither would feel the slightest need to tack on a question mark,
so perfectly are the two united in their capacity to be sexually aroused
by this golden materialization of their shared wealth.

> "Hell, what I think about religion is—"
> All eyes are upon [Harry].
> "is without a little of it you'll sink." (800)

Perhaps the only ambiguity in the celebratory Krugerrands scene is
introduced through the number of coins Harry has bought—thirty.
(The quantity—the same number of dollars Harry gave Skeeter in
parting from him in *Redux*—is underscored in the close of the scene
as Janice and Rabbit rise from sexual satiety to seek the bedding for
the last—thirtieth—coin.) *Rich* is pervaded by implications that in
worshipping Mammon Harry is betraying spiritual commitments,
Harry's purchase consummating the point by suggesting that he has
in effect sold out Christianity for thirty pieces of gold. (He subsequently exchanges them—at a loss—for silver.) Before he can take Janice upstairs to reveal his surprise, Ma Springer is "drifting in some
world of her own where the Episcopal Church has presided since
Creation; but Harry felt above them all, a golden man waiting to take
his wife upstairs to show her their treasure" (815). Something of the
same association of gold with invulnerability informs Harry's musings about the improved dentistry that his prosperity has allowed
him. Now that the sensitive, poorly filled cavities he suffered as a
child have been replaced by gold crowns, he nibbles too much, food
having become a new pleasure because he is conscious of "no more
twinges, just everlasting gold" (763). Even his favorite dancer at a strip
joint the Flying Eagle couples visit bears the stage name "Gold
Cherry."

Other areas of his life that once carried reverberations of the transcendent have been similarly secularized. Golf, which he now has the
resources to play regularly, is in *Run* a game in which miracles like
the "perfect shot" can occur; in *Rich*, it has shrunk to a diversion capable of generating only "normal healthy happiness" (783). Running,
his means of obeying his sacred impulses and of keeping in touch
with the voice of his glory days coach, Tothero, and his admonition

"run, run, run. You can never run enough" (54), is analogously dis-
counted in *Rich*: the closing phrases of *Run* ("out of a kind of sweet
panic growing lighter and quicker and quieter, he runs. Ah, runs.
Runs") are reprised satirically in *Rich* in a description of Harry's
modest nightly jog. Although he has never been much for quoting the
Bible ("we've sort of let all that go," he explains at one point),[22] Harry
has adopted a new gospel: "Read *Consumer Reports*, April issue.
That's all he has to tell people when they come in Springer Motors"
(623). When he's not wangling for a position at the family Toyota
agency, Nelson often echoes Jill in excoriating Harry's materialism,
criticizing his father for acting as if his Toyota Corona were "some
divine chariot or something" and for caring about "nothing but
money and things" (728).

Harry's consumerist propensities notwithstanding, what is true in
Run remains only minimally less so in *Rich*: "His feeling that there is
an unseen world is instinctive, and more of his actions than anyone
suspects constitute transactions with it." Accordingly, Harry's internal conflict between the material and spiritual often takes an associative or parabolic form. As he stands in his Toyota showroom
contentedly surveying his realm, his eye is frequently drawn to a
patch of land the developers haven't gotten to yet:

> Beyond [the lot of the adjacent Chuck Wagon restaurant] littered with
> flattened takeout cartons a lone tree, a dusty maple, drinks from a stream
> that has become a mere ditch. Beneath its branches a picnic table rots un-
> used, too close to the overflowing dumpster the restaurant keeps by the
> kitchen door. The ditch marks the bound of a piece of farmland sold off
> but still awaiting its development. This shapely old maple from its distance
> seems always to be making to Harry an appeal he must ignore. (626)

Updike originally intended to title the third novel in the Rabbit series *Rural Rabbit*, and what remains of his initial conception of that
work as "a pastoral book, an eclogue,"[23] may be discernible, albeit
in negative form, in the "shapely old maple" passage. *Rich* gradually
became a novel predominantly dramatizing Harry's disregarding of
this stranded maple's appeal, his commitment to the commercial having aligned him with the flattened cartons of the Chuck Wagon
against the deserted picnic table the flight from whose familial communality his Toyotas have facilitated. That his severance from this
"farmland" causes Harry regret and guilt is clearly conveyed in this
passage, and if God is never explicitly identified in its palimpsest of
associations, the lack is supplied by Harry's identification of his
imagined daughter with nature and the rural setting of the biblically

named Galilee, where she lives with her mother. Having in *Redux* dropped off Skeeter, his previous incarnation of transcendent truth, in the cornfields of Galilee, it is only fitting that Harry find an ulti- mate concern substitute in the "daughter" residing there he so des- perately wants to believe is his own. Like her, this tree grew from "seed that goes into the ground invisible and if it takes hold cannot be stopped, it fulfills the shape it was programmed for, its destiny, sure as our death, and shapely," her endurance and the tree both earn- ing the transcendentally inflected modifier, "shapely." Harry ignores the maple tree's atavistically natural appeal, in other words, only to respond wholeheartedly to the appeal of that rural part of himself he has chosen to designate "daughter."

If the God in whom Harry professes faith seems more immanent than explicit in these scenes, it isn't solely through absence that He manifests Himself in the novel. Harry construes his good health (if not—like a good Puritan—his wealth) as evidence of God's prefer- ence; he rejects air conditioning in favor of "the air that God gave," and he enjoys rainfall as "the last proof left to him that God exists" (733).[24] But God has always been the source of fierce ambivalence for Harry, and the "stony truce" that he feels existing between them is at least partially a product of his recollection of God's two major emer- gences in his life: "Water, flames, the tongues of God, a man is help- less" (714). A Flying Eagle conversation's allusion to Mary Jo Kopechne's drowning a decade earlier provokes his initial reflection, but Harry is obviously segueing to his own experience by recalling the God who, "in all His strength, did nothing" to lift "that little rubber stopper" and prevent Becky's drowning (237), and who per- mitted the immolation of Harry's house, which killed Jill. "Think of all the blame God has to shoulder" (686), Harry has previously thought, the product of Kruppenbach's Lutheran Sunday school never for a moment denying His culpability in the meting out of human fates. Learning from Janice that Peggy Fosnacht has had a mastectomy, Harry imagines this "breast he had sucked . . . Flicked away by God's fingernail" (1039). Harry's intuition of God's respon- sibility for human fates is undergirded by a theological assumption of Updike's: "I've never understood theologies that would absolve God of earthquakes and typhoons, of children starving. A god who is not God the Creator is not very real to me, so that, yes, it certainly *is* God who throws the lightning bolt [in *Couples*] and this God is above the nice god, above the god we can worship and empathize with."[25] In Harry's more intuitive and personalistic theology, God is alternately a source of protection, vitality, self-esteem, and unmerited punish- ment, and in what constitutes a sort of tetralogy summa of the lifelong evolution of the protagonist's relationship with Him, Harry in *Rich* remembers that

> when Harry was little God used to spread in the dark above his bed like that and then when the bed became strange and the girl in the next aisle grew armpit hair He entered into blood and muscle and nerve as an odd command and now He had withdrawn, giving Harry the respect due from one well-off gentleman to another, but for a calling card left in the pit of the stomach, a bit of lead true as a plumb bob pulling Harry down toward all those leaden dead in the hollow earth below. (830)

Throughout *Redux* and *Rich* Harry is moving inexorably toward this summary evocation of God as Deus absconditus, as a power that incites his sexual urges and refuses to save him from death while constantly confronting him with its imminence. From *Rich* through *Rest*, Harry's religious sensibility consists largely in darkening variations on this characterization of God, spirituality for him coming to seem indistinguishable from and reducible to intimations of mortality. In *Run*, Harry's experience of God is that He "entered into blood and muscle and nerve as an odd command," one that fuses the protagonist's anticommunal impulses to his sexual drives. "Run," I assume, is the "odd command" that satisfies the first impulse while frustrating the second. The centrality of sexual appetite to that command both explains the fervor of Harry's tetralogy-encompassing libido and renders highly ambivalent his remaining experiences of desire: like his response to the external world in general, Harry's response to women from Jill onward is consistently imbued with a distancing nostalgia for intensities lost. Even Harry's wealth seems implicated in the withdrawal, God having given him "the respect due from one well-off gentleman to another" in removing Himself, thus seeming to confirm what Harry's actions often appear to dramatize: the idea that if you have enough money, the "unseen world"—like sexuality—becomes superfluous. These cumulative associations underlie and explain Harry's densely ambivalent early novel characterization of himself at forty-six: "He sees his life as just beginning, on a clear ground at last, now that he has a margin of resources, and the stifled terror that always made him restless has dulled down. He wants less. Freedom, that he always thought was outward motion, turns out to be this inner dwindling" (708).

Nelson and Janice are embracing. *Those little Springer hands.* (687)

Harry's delight in being "on clear ground at last" proves as short-lived as the ability of the passage that evokes it to sustain its aura of existential optimism. Relaxing at the Flying Eagle with his friends while indulging himself in sexual fantasies about Cindy Murkett, the youngest wife of the set of couples, Harry compares the dark suspiciousness that in childhood was his family's disposition toward outsiders with the "real sunlight people" who surround him: "Rabbit basks above that old remembered world, rich, at rest" (682). The juxtaposition of the modifiers of the last two tetralogy novel titles creates a contiguity between rich and at rest anticipating the incipient dissolution of his bliss, ominously conflating the pleasure of the former with the extremity of the latter. Janice has been called away from the pool to answer the phone, her return signaled by her summons, "Harry."

"He lowers his gaze at last out of glory and as his eyes adjust his forehead momentarily hurts, a small arterial pain: perhaps with such a negligible unexplained ache do men begin their deaths, some slow as being tumbled by a cat and some fast as being struck by a hawk. Cancer, coronary. 'What did Bessie want?'" he asks Janice. Updike's simile for slow death evokes the rabbit whose adversary is a hulking cat in the poem, which provides one of *Rich*'s two epigraphs, Wallace Stevens's "A Rabbit as King of the Ghosts":

> The difficulty to think at the end of the day,
> When the shapeless shadow covers the sun,
> And nothing is left but the light on your fur . . .[26]

Harry's death will take the form of a "slow tumble" through one-and-three-quarters' worth of novels, his descent seeming to be precipitated by Janice's reply: "She says Nelson's home. With this girl" (683).

As we've seen, Harry's most obvious reason for associating Nelson with death is the threat his son makes in *Redux* as they watch the remains of the Penn Villas house smolder after Jill's body has been removed: "You fucking asshole, you've let her die, I'll kill you. I'll kill *you*" (544). There is, I think, substantial textual evidence in the tetralogy that Updike doesn't share Nelson's conviction that Harry "let Jill die"—and that Nelson isn't certain, either. Harry's sister, Mim— whose Didionesque prediction that West Coast nihilism is overtaking America is arguably fulfilled in the tetralogy—objects when her brother claims responsibility for Jill's death that Jill "let herself die" (*Redux*, 579). Unknowingly echoing Mim's judgment on Jill's self-destructive tendencies, Nelson admits in one of his interior monologues to feelings of guilt for failing "to save Jill from the ruin she wanted" (755). His private acknowledgment of Jill's desire not to be saved to the contrary, Nelson hypocritically continues to invoke Jill's death as his father's ultimate trespass against him.

The last two novels of the tetralogy, for all their remarkable want of sympathy for Harry and Janice's only child, dramatically corroborate Nelson's accusation against his father to this extent: *Rich* and *Rest* consistently depict Nelson's character as being the product of Harry's harboring Jill and Skeeter in *Redux*. The primary obstacle to Harry's *Rich* notion that "he sees his life as just beginning, on clear ground at last" is Nelson, who not completely unintentionally conveys Skeeter's black bag of drugs and death from *Redux*'s bleak late '60s' miasma into Harry's sunny Flying Eagle equability in the late 1970s. (The first half of the club's name translates the cultural heroics of the late '60s—"the Eagle has landed"—into the private, domesticated pleasures at the inception of Reagan's America.) Nelson constitutes Harry's punishment for the faithlessness that is his primary legacy to his son; he is simultaneously the antagonist of Harry's hard-won equanimity in the novel, and an Oedipally motivated saboteur of Harry's hopes of "salvation by sensibility."

Evidence that Nelson personifies an era Harry would prefer to forget is plentiful in *Rich*. Although "Jill is a sacred name to the boy; he will never talk about" her or the fire (806), Harry recognizes that Pru, whom Nelson has impregnated and subsequently marries, "has some of Jill's hippie style" (867). Nelson tends to identify the two as well, complaining in a self-pitying moment of interior monologue that "he is nothing to [Pru] like he was nothing to Jill, a brat, a bug to be humored" (923). When he is most enraged by his father, Nelson reverts to Jill's favorite derisive term for Harry—"creep." Although Nelson is not in the least political, he has been enrolled for three years at that institution indelibly identified with countercultural protest, Kent State—which, ironically, he derides for being insufficiently "radical."[27] What he retains of his nightly ideological indoctrination by Jill and Skeeter is a generalized resentment against things as they are, one accompanied by the incapacity to locate the source of his discontent in anyone or anything other than his father. Through keeping the heat on Harry's middle-class equanimity, Nelson is honoring Skeeter's plea, "Don't keep the Good Lord out, Nellie," which, in Skeeter's view, would be the effect of his emulating his father's philistine values.

Harry seems markedly less conscious than is Updike of how committedly Nelson is carrying on the legacy of drug use introduced to him in his Penn Villas living room by Jill and Skeeter. Smoking too much marijuana at a party, Nelson thinks he may have pushed his new wife down a flight of stairs in response to her derisive question,

"When are you going to grow up?"[28] Nelson continues to deny that his use of drugs is anything more than recreational, but throughout *Rich* marijuana and cocaine use remains his chosen means of evading his troubles, and in *Rest* his cocaine addiction necessitates his institutionalization in a rehab center, his financing of the habit costing his parents the Toyota franchise Harry so dearly loves in the process. Consequently, Nelson's drug use constitutes a different, more threateningly environmental sense of "seed" than the spiritually inflected one in which Harry secretly wraps his "daughter": "like seed: seed that goes into the ground invisible and if it takes hold cannot be stopped, it fulfills the shape it was programmed for, its destiny, sure as our death, and shapely" (641). In terms of both moral dynamics and literary structure, Nelson incarnates a more paternally constructed destiny: "There is no getting away," Harry thinks early on in the novel, "our sins, our seed, coil back" (650).

"I don't know *why* you're such an unnatural father," Janice—who never explicitly makes the connection between Jill, Skeeter, and Nelson's adult drug use, either—taunts Harry as they drive home from the Flying Eagle to confront Nelson and Melanie's arrival. "I think one of the troubles between me and the kid," Harry later tells Thelma Harrison, wife of Rabbit's Mt. Judge basketball teammate, "is every time I had a little, you know, slip-up, he was there to see it. That's one of the reasons I don't like to have him around. The little twerp knows it, too" (777). Nelson's knowledge of Harry's "little, you know, slip-ups" translates to the son's awareness of his father's sexual adventuring, a point that Nelson insists upon in reminding Harry that he was "fucking Peggy Fosnacht" while their Penn Villas house was being torched. Sexual knowledge sits no more comfortably when it is borne by father about son.

Harry was content being a father when Nelson's interests were confined to baseball statistics and rock songs, the boy's presence in the house representing nothing more to his father than "the persistence of his own childhood in an annex of his brain; but when the stuff with hormones and girls and cars and beers began, Harry wanted out of fatherhood." This judgment is contextualized by two images Harry associates distastefully with "men descending from men": a remembered glimpse of his father's saggy buttocks, "limp and hairless, mute and helpless flesh that squeezed out shit once a day and otherwise hung there in the world like linen that hasn't been ironed," and the sight of adolescent Nelson's penis, "a man-sized prick, heavy and oval, unlike Rabbit's circumcised and perhaps because of this looking brutal, and big. Big" (813). As he perceived himself between Becky and Nelson in *Redux*, so is he positioned between his father and Nelson—"the man in the middle." His father's sexless, purely functional butt is what awaits Harry as he ages; his son's "man-sized prick" proves that Nelson has matured to the point at which he represents a sexual rival to his father. Lucy Eccles in *Run* calls Harry "a primitive father," implying his ignorance of the Freudian psychology ("it's like God—you make it true"), which dictates her understanding of her husband's relationship with his daughter; whether or not he would recognize "Oedipal" as the proper descriptor for the conflict he is experiencing in *Rich*, Harry knows enough to answer Janice's implied question about being an unnatural father by responding, "The kid's got it in for me" (685).

Harry's animus toward Nelson closely approximates that expressed by a character in Lisa Alther's *Kinflicks*: "I always saw the world as a stage. . . . And any child of mine would be a ballsy young actor wanting to run me off the stage altogether, watching and waiting to bury me, so that *he* could assume center stage."[29] Although the relationship between father and son in *Rich* often seems as formulaically and classically Oedipal as the perception of Alther's abstainer from parenthood configures it, Updike's novel complicates and humanizes the filial rivalry his novel protractedly depicts not only through showing how thoroughly Nelson's deficient socialization is the product of Harry's *Run* and *Redux* transgressions but also by delineating Nelson's mutual antipathy toward his father and by counterpointing their antagonism's evolution with dramatizations of how very similar the sexual disputants are. In an appropriately Freudian paradox, what problematizes the integrity of Harry's and Nelson's Oedipal conflict with each other is the extent to which each perceives the other in himself.

Nelson's reciprocation of Harry's antagonistic feelings are primarily expressed through three interior monologues that constitute the text's only divergences from Harry's third-person limited point of view. Nelson distastefully recalls his father "com[ing] in the room all big and fuzzy and sly when he's a killer, a body-count of two to his credit and his own son next if he can figure out how to do it without looking bad" (906). He wishes on Harry the same fate he imagines his father seeking for him: "Why can't Dad just die? People that age get diseases. Then he [Nelson] and Mom [would have Springer Motors to themselves]." That would allow Nelson, the "ballsy young actor," to assume center stage at the lot because, as his self-revelatory reflection concludes, "he knows he can manage [his] Mom" (914). Short of the unviable possibility of eliminating his father from competition, Nelson sets himself the goal of overcoming his own Oedipal fixation: "If I could just once make him see himself for the shit he is," he tells

Melanie, "I maybe could let it go" (908). Dramatizing Nelson's ultimate success in "letting it go" ten years after Harry's death is the primary purpose for Updike's return to Brewer for a final time in the
novella, "Rabbit Remembered."

Fully cognizant of the role that cars and their merchandising have
played in Harry's ascent in the world, Nelson hones in, unconsciously or not, on Toyotas as his primary means of avenging himself on his father. Shortly after returning to Brewer, Nelson reunites
with Billy Fosnacht, whose involvement in the decade-past conflagration night—as Harry and Nelson leave the Fosnacht apartment
for home, Billy accuses his mother of being a "whore" for sleeping
with Harry—makes him other than Harry's favorite companion for
his son. Taking Billy for a Sunday drive in Harry's 1978 Luxury Edition liftback five-door Corona, Nelson manages to collide with a telephone pole, the accident necessitating Harry's prize Toyota's weeks-
long incapacitation in the Springer Motors body shop and Harry's
status-life demotion to driving a markedly less prestigious loaner Corolla.

Harry's sense of personal violation and professional diminution are
evoked as he examines the damage to the Corona: "The urethane
bumper, so mat and black and trim, that gave Harry a small sensuous
sensation whenever he touched the car home against the concrete
parking-space divider on the place on the lot stencilled ANG-
STROM, was pulled out from the frame." If Nelson's smashing of the
car's rear doesn't quite constitute crucifixion, it falls only a little
short: Harry "feels his own side has taken a wound." For all his feelings of victimization, however, Harry is too honest not to recognize
his complicity in this act of Oedipal sabotage: "He feels he is witnessing in evil light a crime in which he has collaborated" (717). Having
earlier acknowledged to himself that the lettuce in his garden—the
literal leafy vegetable, but also, in Harry's vernacular, money—is
more real to him than his son (663), Harry cannot help but sympa-
thize with Nelson's repeated assaults upon the incarnations of his
father's prosperity—his "divine chariots." Once again, Nelson is inadvertently chastening his father's attempt to replace transcendent belief with material objects. Throughout the remainder of *Rich* and *Rest*,
Harry will oscillate between resenting Nelson's rebellions against
him, identifying with them as reminders of his own postadolescent
revolts against the repressiveness and monotony of civilized life, and
guiltily intuiting in them a rebuke of his abandoned spirituality.

Nelson's subsequent act of automotive retaliation is a gesture manifesting similar psychic ambivalence. While replacing his father, who
is vacationing with Janice and Ma Springer in the Poconos, on the

Springer Motors sales floor, Nelson, ignoring the low gas mileage figures, which make them difficult sales in an era of escalating fuel prices, buys or takes as trade-ins three early-1970s convertibles. Intent upon demonstrating to his father his auto trader's savvy, Nelson proudly escorts him to the lot on a Sunday afternoon to flaunt his bargaining coup. Explaining that these cars represent an alternative to the diminished vehicular expectations exemplified by Toyotas, Nelson assures his father that this sidelight specialty will boost Springer Motors' sales overall. For Harry, of course, Toyotas are inseparable from the diminished expectations of his middle age and represent as well his single form of financial leverage in a time of economic decline. The last thing he wants taking up space at Springer Motors are these throwbacks to an age of automotive ostentation and self-indulgence, dismaying reminders that for other males, cars remain manifestations of individual freedom, projections of personal attractions, and facilitators of sexual conquest.[30] In a scene reminiscent of Adam Trask's rejection of his son Cal's gift of war-profiteering crop money in *East of Eden*, Harry harshly rebuffs Nelson's desperate appeal for praise. The contention between them builds to a climax as Nelson defends his transactions by attacking Harry's substitute source of devotion and transcendence: "People don't *care* about money that much anymore, it's all shit anyway," Nelson angrily tells his father, "Money is shit" (773). When Nelson promises to buy no more convertibles, Harry responds, "You'll promise me nothing. You'll promise me to keep your nose out of my car business and get your ass back to Ohio. I hate to be the one telling you this, Nelson, but you're a disaster. You gotta get yourself straightened out, and it isn't going to happen here."

Rather than, as Harry expects him to, expressing his rage against the deliverer of this heartless judgment, Nelson takes it out on his beloved convertibles, simultaneously decimating both his hopes for paternal approbation and two units of Harry's inventory. As Nelson weeps behind the wheel of one of the cars he has totaled, Updike describes Harry watching his son's grieving: "These strange awkward blobs of joy bobbing in Harry's chest. Oh what a feeling" (774). The invocation of Toyota's new motto here conveys not only the extremity of Harry's response to Nelson's eruption, but perhaps invokes as well the even more appropriate corporate motto this one replaced: "You asked for it, you got it." That Harry asked for precisely this reaction from Nelson is confirmed, in an effectively suspended revelation, when Harry later in the novel recalls this pivotal confrontation with his son. Escaping into his car from a collie guarding Ruth Byer's farm the second time he ventures to Galilee in search of confirmation that her daughter is his, Harry "pops the clutch and digs out, the thing inside his chest feeling fragile and iridescent like a big soap bubble. Let it pop. He hasn't felt so close to breaking out of his rut since Nelson smashed those convertibles" (876).

The "thing inside his chest" is a version of the kink that gathers there in response to Becky's death in *Run*, a symptom of guilt resultant upon the expression of his instinct for freedom. "What held him back all day," the narrator of *Run* explains, "was the feeling that somewhere there was something better for him than listening to babies cry and cheating people in used-car lots, and it's this feeling he tries to kill, right here on the bus" (252). The intuition that there is "something better for him" has, as we've seen, dwindles considerably through *Redux* and *Rich*, but this impulse resurrects itself fitfully in the latter novel. Right before Harry lights into Nelson about the convertibles, he experiences a flashback sensation that encourages him to let loose:

> He hears his voice straining, feels that good excited roll of anger building in him, like in a basketball game when you're down ten points and less than five minutes left on the clock and you've just taken one too many elbows in the ribs and all the muscles go loose suddenly and something begins lifting you and you know nothing is impossible, with faith. He tries to hold himself back, this is a fragile kid and his son. Still, this has been his lot. (770)

The closing pun effectively makes the double-edged point: Springer Motors has been Harry's franchise, but it has also been his "lot" occasionally to experience "something lifting in him" inspiring extreme action which, however antisocial or destructive to others, is nonetheless an expression of his intuitively grasped belief that "nothing is impossible, with faith." "The world the way it is," Harry explains to Mim in *Redux*, defending both his pro-Vietnam stand and his harboring of Jill and Skeeter, "you got to do something like that once in a while to keep your options open, to keep a little space around you" (576). Harry's *Rich* prosperity contents him sufficiently that his primary revolt involves the rather modest pursuit of his "daughter"; at the lot with Nelson, however, atavistic urges declare themselves, prompting Harry to briefly renounce his accustomed good behavior in the name of achieving momentary deliverance from the domestic peace into which his life has settled. Instinctively, he bears down on Nelson as if feeling his way toward the catharsis he is reminded of in his flight from Ruth's collie: "He hasn't felt so close to breaking out of his rut since Nelson smashed those convertibles." "[H]is rut" remains comfortable enough in *Rich* as to dissuade him from ever fully repudiating it, the novel's conclusion contenting itself with clarifying the ambivalences implicit in that state; Harry's escalating awareness of impending death in *Rest* restores him to one whose "lot" it is to burst through his quiescence and assert his impulses at the cost of a violent rending of the social and familial fabric knit around him.[31]

It is, of course, Nelson's heedless self-assertion in the convertible-smashing scene with which Harry so intensely identifies. Nelson has suddenly come to seem not the hapless pursuant of the trap that is his father's life, but the embodiment of Harry's own order-subverting, role-repudiating tendencies. Harry perceives this rebellion against himself, the lot, his money, and his patriarchal power as exactly the sort of attempt he often made in his own postadolescence to spring himself free from the "rut" his life has become; it is, he understands, Nelson's way of affirming the existence of "something better for him than listening to babies cry and cheating people in used-car lots," the intuiting of which reality represents Harry's own barometer of the transcendent. The "thing in his chest" simultaneously registers the excitement of transgressions against ordinary bourgeois life and warns of the punishments such deviations inevitably bring; but the heart is, at the same time, the organ which, worn out by this ineluctable and irresolvable tension between civilization and the discontent it inexorably engenders, gives out in *Rabbit at Rest*.

The "Springer Motors massacre" (as the body shop crew comes to characterize the convertibles apocalypse) culminates in a not completely reconciliatory moment, Nelson weeping tears of frustration and rage on his father's shoulder. From this scene on, the ambivalence Harry feels toward Nelson increasingly dominates his relationship with him, father seeing son alternately as "my enemy" and the image of his lost vitality and irreconcilability, as "all Springer" and "too much me." It's a manifestation of the latter, empathetic attitude that prompts Harry to discourage Nelson from marrying Pru and to offer to bankroll his son's flight from Brewer on the ground that he would be making the same error Harry made of being trapped into marriage by Janice's pregnancy with Nelson. Rejecting Harry's narcissistic projections on him, Nelson insists that "I'm not you and I'm not caught." Nelson then proceeds to prove Harry's apprehensions accurate by telling him he doesn't want his father's flight money, but wants him instead to "stop making it so hard for me to fit in at the lot" (809). Nelson remains very much the boy who, in *Redux*, insists that, "I want to grow up like *him*"—his father, Harry, the room's big man—"average and ordinary" (494), and it is precisely this imitative ambition that Harry can't countenance. Accordingly, he ignores this appeal: "Stonily Rabbit says nothing" (810). The adverb Updike chooses here recalls the God between Harry and whom "a stony truce seems to prevail," the convergence invoking Freud's illumination of the psychic conflation of father and Father implicit in Melanie's admonition to Nelson that "your father's not God" (741). That linguistic convergence also invites the reader to recall whose responsibility it is that Harry's son "has not been raised to believe in anything higher than his father's head" (*Redux*, 548).

What Harry finds most unforgivable in Nelson is his constant enactment of the faithlessness that is Harry's major legacy to his son: "When you're dead, you're dead" (799) expresses the sum of Nelson's religious concern. It is not excessively simplistic, in fact, to describe Nelson as a young Harry whose most significant lack is the spirituality that inspires his father's best moments and the charisma that faith engendered in him. ("I'm a mystic. I give people faith," Harry, jocularly quoting Eccles, declares in *Run*; Ruth, Mrs. Smith, Eccles, Peggy Fosnacht, Thelma Harrison, Pru, and others in the tetralogy dramatize Updike's only partly equivocal corroboration of his self-assessment, one that Harry reprises for Thelma at the end of *Rich*: "He dares to confide to Thelma, because she has let him fuck her up the ass in proof of love, his sense of miracle at being himself, himself instead of somebody else, and his old inkling, now fading in the energy crunch, that there was something that wanted him to find it, that he was here on earth on a kind of assignment" [1001]). Nelson is referring to this capacity of his father's to open himself to mystical experience in his self-indictment, at a party, of his own reluctance to dance. Dancing requires "letting the devil of the music enter you, which takes more faith than he's got. . . . Dad would do it if he were here, just like when Jill was there he gave himself to Skeeter and never looked back even when the worst had happened, such a fool he really believes there is a God he is the apple of the eye of."[32] Too buzzed to follow this thought further, Nelson confirms the limits of vision his father has imposed upon him in deciding that it is "the dots on the ceiling" that prevent his taking "this glimpse higher than this." Watching Pru's complete self-abandonment in dancing, Nelson "hates for a second that in himself which cannot do it, just as he could not join in the flickering mind play of computer science and college generally and could not be the floating easy athlete his father had been." Whether Harry's deficient fathering is directly responsible for Nelson's inability to immerse himself in life's stream is never completely settled by the novel; that this dark second is "dissolved by the certainty that someday he will have revenge on them all" (915) suggests how bitterly the differences between himself and his father plague Nelson and also how much maturation Updike must intro-

duce into his character to make him a credible hero in "Rabbit Remembered."

The double-edged irony of Nelson's threat consists in that the form
"the revenge he will have on them all" in *Rest* ultimately takes requires his own institutionalization, and in that his father—who at this
stage in *Rich* harbors motives of revenge against no one, desiring only
an insular home of his own—blunders in *Rest* on a far more devastating form of "revenge on them all" than his son can even imagine, an
irremediable, ultimately antifamilial means of "keeping his options
open and keeping a little space around himself." Nonetheless, for all
the differences between them that *Rich* documents, Updike devotes a
significant number of motifs in the novel to establishing the similarities between father and son.

Often, those similarities are indistinguishable from parent-child influence. "Sometimes at the lot, standing in the showroom with no
customers in sight," we're told in one of his interior monologues,
"[Nelson] feels return to him from childhood the old fear of being in
the wrong place, of life being run by rules nobody would share with
him" (921). "Everybody else has a life they try to fence in with some
rules," Mim tells Harry during her *Redux* visit. "You just do what
you feel like and then when it blows up or runs down you sit there
and pout" (587). Lacking his father's now-declining faith in his instincts, Nelson has developed two strategies for dealing with his sense
of exclusion from the secure realm of rules: he "sits there and pouts,"
often smoking a joint, or he reverts to the tactic he employs as a three-
year-old getting beaten up by Billy Fosnacht in *Run*: he complains
"It's not fair!" to whatever woman-in-authority—his grandmother or
mother, primarily—happens to be present. Harry taunts this penchant in Nelson by claiming that his own generation never got "so
scared that we kept running back to Mamma. And Grandmama"
(809), but Nelson is quick to see his father implicated in this jibe.
There is substantial irony, then, in his answer to Harry's question
with its assertion of equivalence between them. "What're you gonna
do when you run out of women to tell you what to do?" Harry asks
him; Nelson responds, "Same thing you'll do. Drop dead" (809). In
terms of the tetralogy, the irony here, is that Nelson has just predicted
precisely the circumstances dramatized in *Rest* of his father's death.

Even in assailing Harry's religious sympathies, Nelson resorts to
arguments his father should find familiar. Offended by Nelson's
mocking of church communion ceremonies, Harry objects that such
rituals make Ma Springer feel good: "Who does this Amityville horror make feel better?" he wants to know about the book Nelson has
been reading. "It's not supposed to," Nelson replies, echoing his

father's, "It happened . . . so we've got to take it in" defense of Skeeter's Vietnam horror stories: "it's just something that happened. The
people in the house didn't want it to happen either, it just did" (767).
Such events, in fact, should command Harry's particular attention because, as the narrator suggests, "Rabbit's feeling about things has
been that if it doesn't happen by itself it's not worth making happen"
(990).

Both men perceive themselves to be martyrs for truth: Harry flees
the cemetery in *Run* because the other mourners refuse to join him in
the truth he has felt and forthrightly expressed; "you try to speak the
truth," Nelson insists, "and all you get is grief" (947). They share an
intuitive prejudice in favor of coordination as well. For Harry "unco-
ordination is the source of all evil as he feels it, for without coordination, there can be no order, no connecting" (665); as he is leaving the
party with Pru, Nelson notices that she "is unsteady, pulled out of
the music, and this further angers him, his wife getting tipsy. . . . Her
brittle imbalance makes him want to smash her completely" (921).
When Nelson confesses to a worry that he deliberately pushed Pru
down the stairs that night, Harry asks why he would do that. "Because I'm as crazy as you," Nelson replies. In these and many more
details, *Rich* confirms Harry's judgment on his relationship with Nelson: "For all that is wrong between them, there are moments when
his heart and Nelson's might be opposite ends of a single steel bar, he
knows so exactly what the kid is feeling" (972).

The consummate similarity between father and son emerges in
Rich's culmination of the Harry-Nelson conflict: Nelson runs, abandoning his pregnant wife much as his father once did his.[33] Whether
Nelson is actually taking his father's advice in fleeing Brewer isn't
clear, although the fact that he absconds in Harry's repaired Toyota
Corona suggests that he has cashed in his father's offer of financial
backing for his escape. What he gets no opportunity to savor is the
significant Oedipal triumph his escape occasions: Nelson never learns
that his flight costs Harry a night in bed with Cindy Murkett, the
object of his sexual fantasies throughout the novel, because Harry and
Janice are called back a day early from the Caribbean by Ma Springer
to help her deal with Nelson's disappearance and Pru's birthing of the
baby. The novel's father-son conflict is suspended rather than resolved, consequently, the possibility of Nelson's returning to Kent
State to complete his degree[34] allowing a cessation of Oedipal hostilit-
ies until the stakes are higher and the antipathy is stoked by anxieties
of existential ultimacy in *Rabbit at Rest*. Besides, in the end of the
novel Harry feels he has created for himself a refuge from his son:
"The kid was no threat to him for now. Harry was king of the castle"

(1036). The Penn Park home Janice and Harry have bought represents the consummation of the prevailing ethos of *Rich*, a catharsis of security attained and insularity achieved. The Super Bowl, the apotheosis of American middle-class spectatorship, provides the media backdrop for the coda of *Rich*, the arrival of Nelson's daughter alone intruding on the middle-class ideal of retreat and seclusion which Harry has earned for himself.[35] The "king of the castle" is safe for the moment, then—safe until *Rest*, when Nelson returns via a death-associated plane flight to launch additional incursions upon Harry's lot.

The suspended chord on which the Oedipal tension of *Rich* closes resounds as well in the novel's resolution of the issue of Harry's "daughter." His third trip to Galilee results in a confrontation with Ruth and the discussion of her daughter's paternity, Ruth initially claiming that she underwent the abortion she tells him, in last pages of *Run*, she doesn't want. As their conversation evolves, however, her certitude ("Rabbit," she declares, "Believe me. She's not yours") gives way to unmistakable equivocation. "I wouldn't give you the satisfaction of that girl being yours," she subsequently acknowledges, "if there was a million dollars at stake. I raised her. She and I put in a lot of time together here and where the fuck were you? . . . I've known where you were all these years and you didn't give a simple shit what had happened to me, or my kid, or anything" (1027). Disgusted by his sudden appearance at her farm to claim his daughter, Ruth insists that thinking of Annabelle as his daughter is like "rubbing her all over with shit," her simile recalling Nelson's likening of Harry's other sacred object—money—to excrement,[36] but she soon reverts to her equivocation: "Suppose she *was* yours. At this stage it'd just confuse her."

Similarly confused—by his feelings of pity and nostalgic desire for Ruth and by the human responsibility he has come to this poverty-stricken farm in conflicted quest of burdening himself with—Harry "longs to be out that double door into the winter air, where nothing is growing." He momentarily longs, in other words, to have annulled that "secret message carried by genes all that way through all these comings and goings all these years, the bloody tunnel of growing and living, of staying alive" (651). He leaves Ruth's farm simultaneously wondering whether he should have asked Ruth to see Annabelle's birth certificate and resigning himself to the idea that "God doesn't want him to have a daughter" (1030).

The publication of "Rabbit Remembered" in 2000 annulled this judgment of Harry's, the novella confirming what neither *Rich* nor *Rest* explicitly does—that Annabelle is Ruth's and Harry's daughter.

While the two novels, like Joyce's *Exiles*, affirm the irresolvability of the ultimate human mystery of fatherhood, there is one scene in *Rich* that can be construed as making a largely subtextual case for Nelson and Annabelle being half-siblings.

The two meet one night at a Brewer party, their encounter constituting one of the potential calamities Thomas Edwards noted as looming in the novel but never eventuating. Nelson never learns Ruth's daughter's name: like the Caribbean island—Harry's other almost-paradise—the Flying Eagle couples travel to, the girl remains unnamed throughout the novel, Ruth identifying her as Annabelle only in the final twenty pages. Updike hints that these two are the children of that couple who made love in Ruth's apartment twenty years before by depicting Nelson—much as his father does with Ruth in their first meeting—assuring Annabelle that she's "not fat, just nice." Nelson complains about his father, Annabelle speaks lovingly of her mother; he gripes about "the chick in green"—Pru—who got "knocked up," obliging him to marry her, while she speaks fondly of Jamie, who accompanied her to Springer Motors where she met the man she doesn't know is her conversation partner's father and to this party, and their conversation ends. Nelson later uses the bathroom and finds there an album of "posters and photographs from the Nazi days in Germany" to which he responds homophobically: "Having this here is some kind of swish thing like those tinselled cards showing women so ugly and there seems no protection against all the ugliness that is in the world, no protection for that girl asleep or him" (926). "[T]hat girl asleep" is Ruth's daughter, and Nelson's grass-induced plaint recalls his earlier musings about the lack of protection in the world, the juxtaposition of passages implying that this is an indictment of his, or his and the girl's, father. In his earlier ponderings, Nelson thinks that he chose Pru because "they agreed on things, basic things. They knew at bottom the world was brutal, no father protected you, you were left alone in a way not appreciated by those kids horsing around on jock teams or playing at being radicals. . . ." (907). Although Nelson's penchant for self-pity regularly undermines the validity of his perceptions, this judgment holds up. Throughout *Redux*, Harry fails to protect Nelson against the "ugliness" of Skeeter's abuse of Jill, and, as Ruth insists when they meet in *Rich*, he has completely disregarded, until the beginning of that novel, the possibility that he might have another child living within a few miles of his home whom Ruth is carrying when he abandons her in *Run*, one whom, we learn in "Rabbit Remembered," was in even greater need of protection against ugliness.

This implicit indictment of Harry woven by this juxtaposition is obliquely reinforced in *Rich* by the fact that Harry too experiences a significant epiphany via the medium of an analogously obscene set of photos: Polaroid shots he discovers in the drawer of their bedside table of Webb and Cindy Murkett having sex before the camera. In addition to confirming Harry's earlier acknowledgment that "the trouble with consumerism is that the guy next door is always doing better than you are" (995), these photographs constitute visual proof of an unseen world different from the one he seeks in *Run*: they are visual proof that in the privacy of their bedrooms, others are as sex-crazed as he is.[37] Although Harry conducts himself with remarkable seemliness throughout *Rich*, the interrelationship of these scenes indirectly confirms one of Nelson's central accusations against his father's past behavior: Harry's failure to protect his children from the ugliness of the world has often been a consequence of his single-minded, egocentric pursuit of and preoccupation with sex.[38] Harry worries late in the novel about the possibility that he is responsible for having "fucked up"—pun surely intended—a child as badly as Nelson is "fucked up," but *Rich* contains an even more serious potential indictment against him. That one of these two children may be the product of his carnal obsession's heedlessness and want of concern for others is the ultimate, implicit charge the tetralogy tentatively registers against Harry Angstrom. The tentativeness with which that indictment is delivered is perhaps the most characteristic element of the end—if not the totality—of *Rabbit is Rich*.

"Harry suddenly hates people who seem to know," we are told late in the novel: "they would keep us blind to the fact that there is nothing to know. We are each of us filled with a perfect blackness" (1007). Harry's dismal judgment is colored by his having just learned that Nelson's disappearance back home is costing him his Caribbean night with Cindy Murkett, but the overall skepticism toward certainty and absolute knowledge articulated here is characteristic of both Updike's fiction and his attitude toward creating it. When asked by *Time Magazine* in 1960 how he felt about Harry's flights in *Run*, Updike offered an intentional equivocation:

> What I feel or felt in this novel as well as in the previous one [*The Poorhouse Fair*] is that there are irreconcilable forces operating in our lives; there are opposite arguments, neither of which are answerable, there are opposite courses of action, both of which are justified. You try, by seeing both sides, to find a sort of pitch. . . . There is a certain necessary ambiguity. I don't want my fiction to be any clearer than life seems to be.[39]

The dense texture of images and themes of *Rich*, a small portion of which I have tried to illuminate, constitutes the novel's attempt to imitate what Updike elsewhere calls the "terribly tight knit of reality," the novel's deliberate and multilayered irresolution constituting its primary means of emulating the actual. The tension between Harry and Nelson is suspended, not resolved. Nelson flees Brewer convinced that everything wrong with him is his father's responsibility: "It *is*. . . . Everything's his fault . . . and he enjoys it, the way he looks at me sometimes you can tell that he's really eating it up, that I'm fucked up" (742). Whether Harry's parental shortcomings are completely responsible for generating the unattractively graceless and querulous man Nelson grows into is left to the reader's judgment, though Janice's reassurance to Harry at the end of *Redux*—"Relax. Not everything is your fault" (619)—provides a necessary corrective to the all-encompassingness of Nelson's condemnation. Harry concludes following the interview with Ruth that "God doesn't want him to have a daughter" (1030), but he continues to wish he had demanded that she show him Annabelle's birth certificate, and he wonders whether the tears in Ruth's eyes as he left weren't proof of what he remembered about her from years before: that her eyes water when she is lying. The relative eventlessness of middle age allowed Updike in *Rich*, even more than in *Run* and *Redux*, to write a novel evocative of "a certain necessary ambiguity," one that turns out to be "no clearer than life seems to be." Insightfully comparing the film *As Good as It Gets* to Updike's representation of Harry's perceptions, James Yerkes argued that "we experience life with the wildly vacillating sentiments of minimalist pessimism and maximalist optimism. At certain moments we stoically accept life's deliverances as the most we can expect and at other times as the best we could possibly imagine— precisely Updike's fictional world."[40]

If there is no clear resolution to *Rich*, there *are* clarifications and developments—many of them prefiguring the darker world of *Rest* lying ahead. Harry and Janice's new Penn Park residence represents a refuge from both family (Ma Springer and Nelson are offended by this defection from the Springer family home) and friends: Janice has decided that the wife-swapping in the Caribbean proved the Flying Eagle crowd evil, her determination to have nothing further to do with them dictating that only one of "the gang" figures significantly in *Rest*. The revelation that it is Thelma Harrison—the Flying Eagle veteran who plays a substantial role in the closing novel—who the previous April sent the clipping announcing Skeeter's death reinforces the ending's evocation of Harry's isolation by establishing that he has no surviving tie to African American Brewer, no remaining link to a world of cultural difference and personal growth. Harry is speaking for himself and Janice as well as the nation in responding to the Super Bowl halftime show, "Who needs Khomeini and his oil? Who needs Afghanistan? Fuck the Russkis. Fuck the Japs for that matter. We'll go it alone, from sea to shining sea" (1044). *Homo economicus* has settled into the insularity that his long-desired home affords and epitomizes, and when he complains to Janice that waiting for the arrival of Ma Springer, Pru, and the baby is like "waiting for the other shoe to drop," Janice implicitly predicts that his newly consummated equanimity is good for the decade separating the close of *Rich* from the beginning of *Rest*: "I'd say that you've had enough shoes drop lately to last ten years" (1044).

Eventually, of course, Pru appears, "depositing in his lap what he has been waiting for" since the end of *Redux*. As Marshall Boswell noticed,[41] the description of Pru's baby as Harry perceives her replicates his perceptions of Becky when he first sees her at the hospital, right down to the phrase, "she knows she's good" (187, 1045). The infant, consequently, fulfills the quest for a daughter Updike acknowledged as a significant motivation behind the tetralogy, but does so with a substantial equivocation—this "daughter" is not Harry's, but Nelson's. It is in acknowledgment of Nelson's Oedipal triumph, then, that Harry's ultimate response to this "little visitor" is that she is "another nail in his coffin. His." The characteristic narcissism of Harry's reaction to his granddaughter anticipates the fact that this child, at age ten, will witness his first heart attack as they share a Sunfish ride in Florida. Implicit in this scene as well, however, is what she and Becky do not have in common. "Oblong cocooned little visitor," we read in *Rich*'s closing paragraph,

> the baby shows her profile blindly in the shuddering flashes of color jerking from the Sony, the tiny stitchless seam of the closed eyelid aslant, lips bubbled forward beneath the whorled nose as if in delicate disdain, she knows she's good. You can feel in the curve of the cranium she's feminine, that shows from the first day. Through all this she has pushed to be here, in his lap, his hands, a real presence hardly weighing anything but alive. Fortune's hostage, heart's desire, a granddaughter. (1045)

The Rabbit's-eye view description of Becky in *Run* contains a highly significant difference:

> The baby is held by the nurse so her profile is sharp red against the buttoned white busom of the uniform. The folds around the nostril, worked out on such a small scale, seem miraculously precise; the tiny stitchless seam of the closed eyelid runs diagonally a great length, as if the eye, when it is opened, will be huge. In the suggestion of pressure behind the tranquil lid and in the tilt of the protruding upper lip he reads a delightful hint

of disdain. She knows she's good. What he never expected, he can feel she's feminine, feels something both delicate and enduring in the arc of the long pink cranium. . . . (187)

Profiled not against the virginal white of a nurse's bosom but bombarded instead by jerking lights emanating from the Super Bowl broadcast, Judy's very real beauty is testimony to life bursting through, of her having survived "the bloody tunnel of growing and living" (651). There is, however, no implied creator—compare David Kern's perception of dead pigeons in "Pigeon Feathers"—responsible for the precision of her nostril's whorls whose precision is never characterized as "miraculous," nor is there anything "enduring" in the feminine curves of her cranium she'll bear from first day to last. What Judy lacks is precisely what keeps this warmly domestic scene from constituting a happy ending and what her grandfather has gradually been losing over the course of the three novels of the tetralogy: a soul.

In *Rabbit at Rest*, Harry's intuitive grasp of some diminution between his daughter and granddaughter comes home: he has to come to terms with being nothing more than a body.

If this chapter succeeds in illuminating the dense webs of plot connections and metaphoric convergences underlying *Rabbit is Rich*, it has performed one of its objectives. Discussing *Rabbit, Run* and *Rabbit Redux*, though, I tried to demonstrate that, in addition to providing each text with a "hidden poem of consistent metaphor" (*Museums*, p. 178) of the kind he and his Harvard classmates liked to extrapolate from literary works, Updike had a subtextual strategy dictated by the thematic trajectory of each novel. The most markedly eschatological of the novels, *Run* is the work most reflective of Harry's sense of "interactions with the invisible world," that novel's subtext coming closest to fulfilling Updike's statement, "I hope the pattern in the art will emerge, and I guess I have some such hope cosmically" (*Conversations*, p. 99). *Redux*'s subtext imitates the political ethos of the late '60s, the characters often allegorized as lunar explorers or Vietnam disputants. That these Brewerites are in part determined by their political prototypes suggests the cultural ethos of the period, while implying sour authorial concurrence in the idea that sociopolitical definitions of self are the only ones available to them in this era of "desolate openness." The density of texture of *Rich* si little less secular, but its subtextual underpinnings are permeated by nexus-impelled convergences and human conjunctions: one motival pattern validates the psychological similarities between feuding father and son, another hints that Annabelle *is* Harry's daughter, while a third generates the familial closure of the arrival of Nelson and Pru's daughter, further completing the "search for a daughter theme" Updike discovered was at the thematic center of the Rabbit series. In general, the subtext of *Rich* is pervaded by human concords and consummations, a trajectory Updike seems to be invoking in suggesting that Harry "feels love for each phenomenon [of nature] and, not for the first time in his life seeks to bring himself into harmony with the intertwining simplicities that uphold him, that were woven into him." The familial vexations of *Rich* notwithstanding, the subtext reinforces Harry's hopeful assertion: "There must be a good way to live" (745). If the motifs of *Rich* are centripetal, then, those of *Rest* are centrifugal, tending toward individuation, separation, disconnection and disjunction: following Judy's admission that he hadn't saved her from drowning, Harry tells his granddaughter that he and Janice will always take care of her, while he ponders his conviction that, "We are each of us like our own little blue planet, hung in black space, upheld by nothing but our mutual assurances, our loving lies" (p. 1290).

6

Nothing is Sacred: *Rabbit at Rest*

"I don't *not* believe."

—Rabbit to Thelma in *Rabbit at Rest*

IN THE TETRALOGY'S BEGINNING IS ITS END: HARRY'S FLIGHT OPENING *Rabbit, Run* has numerous provocations. The pickup basketball he plays with neighborhood kids resurrects adulthood's dulled athletic intensities while reviving his feeling of performing in the world in a way that isn't "second rate"; the image of Nelson being fed in Harry's parents' home confirms that the boy is happier here than in his own home;[1] and the recognition that the quarrel he has just had with a cocktail-sodden Janice has run its course, ensuring that "everything is forgiven, everything is the same" (15). Jumping into his car, Harry has no more coherent or realistic goal than driving south with the goal of "fall[ing] asleep by the Gulf of Mexico" (23). But the map he uses to navigate his flight becomes "a net he is somewhere caught in" (33), what was supposed to be a highway becomes a dead-end lovers' lane emblematizing the futility of his erotic quest, and Harry finally turns back toward Pennsylvania, having penetrated no farther south than West Virginia. Harry's quest for "something better for him" than busted toys, crying children, and old-fashioned glasses becomes, then, the great suspended chord of the Rabbit tetralogy.

It is one of the major culminatory elements of the last novel of the quartet that in *Rabbit at Rest* Harry manages to complete this truncated journey. The flight he embarks upon precipitating the climax of the tetralogy's final volume mirrors the flight that inaugurated the four novels, both in the sense of reprising it and in the sense of reversing its sequence. If in *Run* a game of basketball inspires the Rabbit to run for his life, in *Rest*, playing the same game affords him release from the incessantly conflicted impulse to run.[2]

The ostensible catalyst for Harry's second solitary journey south is Pru's revelation to Janice that on the night of the day that Nelson entered a rehabilitation center for cocaine addiction treatment and

151

Harry was released from the hospital following angioplasty, she and Harry slept together. Calling Harry at their house, Janice insists that Harry drive from Penn Park to her childhood home where Nelson and Pru have been living in order that the four of them begin to "process" what Janice characterizes as "the worst thing you've ever done, ever, ever. . . . Now you've done something truly unforgivable . . . I will never forgive you. Never" (1443). As Janice explains how Pru offered her confession, Harry is aware that his wife has shifted into the shared language of the couple's thirty-three years of marriage, and he "feels relieved, beginning already to be forgiven, and faintly disappointed." Squeezed by the "everything is forgiven, everything is the same" prospect, Harry hangs up the phone, and, rather than heading over to Brewer to begin penitential family therapy, he packs a bag and heads off to consummate his Gulf of Mexico quest of thirty years earlier. As Marshall Boswell noticed, in order to signal the intertextual convergence, Updike employs the same phrase— "His acts take on a decisive haste" (21, 1445)—with which he characterized Harry's resolve as he walks away from his parents' house in *Run* to describe the deliberateness with which Harry prepares for his drive to Florida in *Rest*.[3]

His car radio provides musical companionship as it had in 1959, but it's now "All the good old [tunes]. All show tunes . . . from decades when Americans moved within the American dream, laughing at it, starving on it, but living it, humming it, the national anthem everywhere" (*Redux*, 372) that he seeks out rather than late-'50s pop hits, and the farther he drives, the more obvious becomes the difference the intervening thirty years have made in the character and gravity of his parallel flights. In beginning my discussion of *Rest* by focusing upon the darkened perspectives of Harry's valedictory flight, I want to show not only how deliberately Updike has orchestrated the tetralogy's beginning and end, but to demonstrate as well how thoroughly the stunningly dismal dramatization of Harry's final days reflects Updike's experience of a personal loss coincident with the novel's writing.

"Deciding to wrap up the [Rabbit] series," Updike commented shortly after the novel appeared, "was a kind of death for me."[4] *Rabbit at Rest*, I want to show, constitutes a culmination of the protracted crisis of faith, which the tetralogy dramatizes, the shared experience of spiritual extremity of author and protagonist getting expressed in Updike's other summary judgment on *Rest*: that it is "a depressed book about a depressed man written by a depressed man."[5] In this final novel of the tetralogy, Updike dramatically confronts the probability that the "wandering thread of [Harry's] feelings leads nowhere," and thus, as Mikhail Bakhtin argued, "In the individual sealed-off consciousness, . . . death is only an end, and as such is deprived of any real productive associations."[6] That would mean that Harry's perceptions of the world over four volumes have failed to confirm what Updike hoped they would: "And so in writing," he told Jeff Campbell, "I try to adhere to the verifiable, the undeniable little thing. Somehow, I hope the pattern will emerge, and I guess I have some such hope cosmically."[7] In another interview conducted upon the publication of *Rest*, Updike suggested that "It might be that the will to believe is an aspect of our vitality, and as vitality ebbs, so does faith. I was somewhat dispirited when I wrote the book—I had chest pains, and my mother was crumbling in Pennsylvania."[8] A critical case has been made that *Rest* attempts to, in Updike's words, "show a happy death, at least a man content in some ways to die . . . an arrival has been reached;"[9] I'll be arguing here that Rabbit's arrival is to a place relentlessly condemnatory of the spiritlessly materialistic America we are fortunate enough to survive him in, and that, if there is contentment in his dying, it reflects the relinquishment of the religious hopes that sustained his life.[10] Updike's fiction is notoriously ambiguous on spiritual issues, and I won't suggest that the ending of *Rest* clearly dramatizes either Rabbit's redemption or merely depicts his mortal end; I *will* suggest that this novel, along with *In the Beauty of the Lilies*, constitutes Updike's most profound literary enactment of his own spiritual doubts, *Rabbit at Rest* constantly invoking the absence Updike invoked in his conversation with the *Boston Globe*'s Gail Caldwell: ". . . you don't want to make God into another character, you know, like George Burns. And since God's voice seems to be mostly silence, I think a novel has the responsibility to represent that silence. And the silence has become kind of loud in *Rabbit at Rest*."[11]

It is, obviously, a deeply depressed man who drives from Penn Park to Florida at the end of *Rest*. Harry's literal destination in 1989 is much more certain than it was in 1959: it's "this mass-produced paradise where Janice's money has taken him" (1089), the Angstroms having bought a condominium in Deleon from which they could initially glimpse the Gulf of Mexico before subsequent construction blocked their view of that objective of Harry's initial flight. In *Run*, Harry justifies to Eccles that flight as a response to "this thing that wasn't there" in his marriage, as a quest for "something that wants me to find it," and consequently that act of self-liberation seems a bolt for freedom, an affirmation of the life that he feels has been crushed in him by a foundering marriage and the door-to-door merchandising of vegetable peelers. Although his completion of that journey in *Rest* has a clearer goal, its self-affirmative character is shadowed by the sequence of defeats Harry has suffered and farewells he has offered, these experiences constituting much of the novel's narrative and representing the dramatic correlatives of the bleak spirit in which Updike composed the novel.

Harry's sole act of seemingly indisputable heroism—saving Nelson's daughter, Judy, from drowning when the Sunfish they are sailing on capsizes, Harry suffering a heart attack in the process—is only a game that Judy, an experienced swimmer, plays with him by hiding under the sail. That he initially believes this action to have evened the score for his role in Becky's death—"Maybe he was happy to have saved this one" is how Nelson summarizes it (1197)—makes its negation more painful still, the incident ultimately reinforcing the truth he learns at Jungle Gardens earlier in the novel: that his life is "a silly thing he'll be relieved to toss off" (1143). Harry's attempts to feed the inner man starved by American materialism have left him overweight and prone to myocardial infarction, the heart attack compelling him to "see the light" of his tenuous condition.[12] Like "some eyeless worm you find wriggling out of an apple where you just bit" (1294), the angioplasty catheter that he watches invading him instills the terrible knowledge that "The Rabbit Angstrom Show" he sees on an operating room monitor is a purely physical phenomenon: "The mechanically precise dark ghost of the catheter is the worm of death within him, Godless technology is fucking the pulsing wet tubes we inherited from the squid, the boneless sea-cunts" (1298). Consequently, "Harry has trouble believing how his life is tied to all this mechanics—that the *me* that talks inside him all the time scuttles like a water-striding bug above this pond of body fluids and their slippery conduits. How could the flame of him ever have ignited in such wet straw?"[13] (1295). He tries to pray while the procedure is in progress, but "it feels like the wrong occasion, there is too much crowding in of the actual material world. No old wispy Biblical God would dare to interfere" (1295).

He associates the "insult" of the catheter's invasion with another affront to his self-perception, the presence of the male advisers with whom Janice's preparations for a realtor's license surround her seeming to Harry an incursion "as devious as that televised catheter nudging forward into his shadowy webbed heart" (1357). Springer Motors, the source of Harry's equanimity in *Rich* as well as the site of his primary interaction with and professional involvement in the world,[14] has, at Janice's instigation, become Nelson's domain, their son using the agency as a cover for the purchasing of drugs to feed his cocaine addiction. (Harry clearly continues to "pay the price" for introducing Nelson to Jill, who introduced him to drugs.) The debt Nelson runs up culminates in the Toyota corporation's withdrawal of the franchise, prompting Janice and Nelson to develop schemes for "restructuring" the massive debt, reassessing the family real estate holdings, and transforming Springer Motors, all of which Harry construes as their therapeutically inclined conspiracy to ignore the moral ramifications of Nelson's actions. Janice forthrightly explains to Harry that the primary reason for selling the Penn Park house he loves is that it will help defray the debt Nelson incurred as well as accomplishing what both she and Pru want, "a happy and healthy Nelson" (1440), their collective objective utterly displacing Harry. (That Nelson has, during his and Pru's residence in the Springer family home, removed the beechnut tree outside what is Harry and Janice's bedroom window in *Rich* is another reason for Harry's reluctance to move back there: the sound of rain in its branches had been his solitary confirmation that God still exists.) Harry's one Brewer distraction from Janice's and Nelson's machinations, his lover, Thelma Harrison, dies of lupus; his last fantasy passion from *Rich*, Cindy Murkett, has been divorced by Webb, but her potential availability is undermined by the fact that she, like Harry, has gotten fat. There is, clearly, nothing to keep Harry in Diamond County, Pennsylvania, and, provoked by Janice's outraged call, he drives south, heedlessly indulging at every stop the very appetite that affirms his sustained purchase on life while simultaneously ensuring that life's imminent extinction.

These reversals, compounded by his escalating disaffection with the America that has nurtured him as well as his declining interest in life, culminate in his suicidal basketball game with a black teenager. As Matthew Wilson has argued, *Rabbit at Rest* "could be seen as a long suicide on [Harry's] part."[15] If *Rabbit at Rest* works dramatically, the reader approaches the last pages emotionally prepared to acquiesce in Harry's doctor's diagnosis of his patient's condition after he's suffered a second myocardial infarction during the game with Tiger: "Sometimes it's time."

The parallels between Harry's two journeys link the beginning and end of the tetralogy and, in their suggestion that the "something that wants me to find it" has become indistinguishable from Harry's death ("I mean, it's not kidding," he tells the AIDS-stricken Lyle in *Rest*, "it wants it all" [1248]), they constitute the bleak judgment the latter novel offers on the protagonist's 1950s radically and romantically self-affirming impulses. As I will demonstrate, the "kink in his chest," which Harry in *Run* initially associates with his impulses toward freedom before redefining it as a cause of his daughter's death, carries the same ambiguity in *Rest*, the operating room monitor informing him that what he's witnessing in watching his heart beat is anger—"the anger is his life, his soul, mind over matter, electricity over muscle." His flight south is his penultimate expression of that anger, the last one before the act in which the anger of self turns angrily upon itself in a fatal game of one-on-one. Having run south to evade the chastisement to which Janice has sentenced him, Harry is on the verge of inadvertently fulfilling Nelson's *Rabbit is Rich* prophecy about both of them. "What're you gonna do when you run out of women to tell you what to do?" Harry asks him. "Same thing you'll do," Nelson responds. "Drop dead" (809).

I've made a good deal of the convergence between Harry's opening and culminating flights not only because of its tetralogy-synthesizing consonance, but also because in a series of novels in which God comes increasingly to define Himself through His absence, Harry's inchoate tropisms toward freedom become the sole remaining repositories of religious feeling—or, viewed from a more conventionally moralistic Christian standpoint, the confirmation of their cultural bankruptcy. Much has changed in the three decades intervening between Harry's journeys south, clearly, but something that hasn't is Updike's reluctance to take a clearly defined stance on ultimate questions. No less than the earlier three novels, *Rest* ends on chords of artfully calculated ambiguity: Harry tells Nelson "all I can tell you is, it isn't so bad," the antecedent of his "it" remaining undefined. "Rabbit thinks he should maybe say more," is the novel's closing line, "the kid looks wildly expectant, but enough. Maybe. Enough" (1516). But then, Updike is Updike, and even that judgment is subject to reconfiguration and revision. These final lines are crosslit by a passage earlier in the novel: just before setting out on the Sunfish with Judy, Harry is inspired by the vista of "water and sand and air and sun's fire, substances lavished in giant amounts yet still far from filling the limitless space." In his exhilaration, he feels "reawaken in him the old animal recklessness. His heart, his skin, can never have enough" (1163).

In discussing *Rabbit at Rest*, a novel so thematically focused upon human ultimacy as to seem to defy the impulse toward equivocation of even the most extreme devotee of ambiguity, I intend to illuminate the spiritual ambivalences Updike has insisted are an essential element of his fiction, and to demonstrate that the epigraph of this chapter— "I don't *not* believe"—is about as definitive an affirmation of Harry's religious belief as the novel affords. Reviewing a Graham Greene biography, Updike offered a highly characteristic formulation of the ideal relationship between faith and the novelist's responsibility in depicting it through narrative. "Fiction concerns dramatized tensions, not settled conclusions," Updike suggested. "Greene's value as a religious novelist," he continued, "lies not in embodied homilies but in his agonized sense of faith's shaky ground in the unhappy human condition."[16] As my less-than-exhaustive catalogue of Harry's *Rest* reversals and disaffections suggests, this culminating novel confronts the protagonist with precious little evidence to support his tetralogy-spanning conviction that—as Nelson pejoratively phrases it in *Rich*— "there is a God he is the apple of the eye of." Nonetheless, *Rabbit at Rest* is no less adamant than its protagonist is in its insistence that there can be no positive alternative to seeing Rabbit Angstrom as he desperately seeks to perceive himself—as "[a] God-made one-of-a-kind with an immortal soul breathed in. A vehicle of grace. A battlefield of good and evil. An apprentice angel. All those things they tried to teach you in Sunday school, or really didn't try very hard to teach you, just let them drift in and out of the pamphlets, back there in that church basement buried deeper in his mind than an air-raid shelter" (1265). As I will illustrate through considering Harry's conflicting religious associations with the sky in *Rest*, Updike puts Harry's faith to its severest test in this novel, battering his beliefs simultaneously with apparent supernatural repudiations of their grounds while confronting him as well with repeated demonstrations of the undeservingness of human beings—Harry included—to the promises of Christian faith. The sky's refusal unambiguously to confirm the existence of mercy from on high throws Harry back upon himself and the inner impulses, which have simultaneously been the most dependable and most antisocial corroboration of his religious hopes, his "furtive sensations of the invisible" (201-2) continuing to be the only evidence of it he has. In *Rest*, as I will attempt to show, Harry's intuitions of the "unseen world" become so inextricably interfused with his assertions of himself as a "God-made one-of-a-kind with an immortal soul breathed in" that his experience of God becomes indistinguishable from solipsism, the "battlefield of good and evil" which is himself mixing impartibly impulses toward self-affirmation and self-destruction. If Updike is finally unwilling to weigh in on whether, beyond "Maybe. Enough," there is spiritual redemption for Rabbit Angstrom, his final Rabbit novel is thoroughly unambiguous in its dramatization of the irresolvable enigma of faith that confronts the believer like Harry—or Updike himself—at the end of the twentieth century, and is even more decisive in his remarkably negative depiction of the two major human antagonists of faith in the narrative: Nelson and Janice.

Before proceeding to elucidate a few of the assaults upon his faith that the sky rains down on Harry in the novel, however, I need to attempt to make good on the promise that explication in *Rabbit (Un)Redeemed* will always be presented in the service of the illumination of the personal struggle between faith and doubt underlying the prose in these novels. Updike's characterization of *Rest* as "a depressed book about a depressed man written by a depressed man" suggests an identification with Rabbit that I've emphasized frequently because that convergence tends to focus the issues of faith Rabbit helps Updike confront in the tetralogy. Harry's invocation of the impact of Sunday school upon his intuitions of his soul's ultimate value, it's worth pointing out, are clearly anticipated in *Self-Consciousness*, published the year before *Rest* appeared. In defending his pro-Vietnam position in the "On Not Being a Dove" chapter, Updike asserted that, "My undovishness, like my battered and vestigial but unsurrendered Christianity, constituted a refusal to give up, to deny and disown, my deepest and most fruitful self, my Shillington self—dimes for war stamps, nickels for the Sunday school collection, and grown-ups maintaining order so that I might be free to play with my cartoons and Big Little Books" (141). Later in *Self-Consciousness*, Updike returns to this source of the inspiration of his life and work: "What I felt, in that basement Sunday school of Grace Lutheran Church in Shillington, was a clumsy attempt to extend a Yes, a blessing, and I accepted the blessing, offering in return only a nickel a week and my art, my poor little art" (231).

I want to suggest that, more than its predecessor fictions, *Rabbit at Rest*, in the bleakness of its depiction of the human condition, constitutes a quintessential literary enactment of Updike's unremitting commitment to the affirmation of that Shillington self whose "fruitfulness" has been such a source of pride to him even as it seemed insufficient gratitude—"my poor little art"—to the benediction and inspiration that was his childhood. Even more than the fact that Updike never played basketball and departed from Pennsylvania to prosper, the most significant difference between author and protagonist is that Harry never had "my cartoons and Little Big Books" to serve as an apprenticeship for a literary career, no "poor little art" to offer up as inadequate recompense for his withered self-perception as a "God-made one-of-a-kind with an immortal soul breathed in." What he lacks, Updike proliferatingly has: "The papery self-magnification and immortality of printed reproduction—a mode of production which leaves the cowardly perpetrator hidden and out of harm's way" (*S-C*, 108). For Harry, the recognition that he will never again be the teenager who made love to Mary Ann in his car exemplifies his attitude toward time—its passage is nothing but a source of betrayal: "Though the stars recycle themselves and remake all the heavy atoms creation needs, Harry will never be that person again, that boy with that girl, his fingertips grazing the soft insides of her thighs, a few atoms rubbing off, a few molecules" (1447).

As I suggested in earlier chapters, Harry serves Updike as a medium of praise, as a fictional projection of the author's deepest-held conviction about writing, which he articulates in *Self-Consciousness* immediately following his apology for "my poor little art": "Imitation is praise," he insisted. "Description expresses love" (231). *Rest*, like its predecessor novel, *Rabbit is Rich*, imbues its protagonist with a nonliterary version of this tropism: "there's a grace of sorts," Harry thinks, in the solar system "that chimes with the excessive beauty of this crystalline late-summer day. He needs to praise" (1423). This convergence notwithstanding, *Self-Consciousness* serves as the perfect countertext to *Rest* because its prevailing affirmation of Updike's life is so inextricably linked to his life's work of praising reality through literary imitation of it, of expressing love for actuality through description. "I early arrived at these self-justifying inklings," Updike continued in his memoirs,

> Having accepted that old Shillington blessing, I felt free to describe life as accurately as I could, with especial attention to human erosions and betrayals. What small faith I have has given me what artistic courage I have. My theory was that God already knows everything and cannot be shocked. And only truth is useful. Only truth can be built upon. From a higher, inhuman point of view, only truth, however harsh, is holy. The fabricated truth of poetry and fiction makes a shelter in which I feel safe, sheltered, within interlaced plausibilities in the image of a real world for which I am not to blame. Such writing is in essence pure. Out of soiled and restless life, I have refined my books. (231)

On the evidence of this distinctly modernist account, the central paradox of Updike's literary career is that a thoroughly nurturing, morally centered, and stable childhood is responsible for the courage required to make a career of enacting what he learned from Kierkegaard and Karl Barth: "to say the worst about our earthly condition" (149) in literature. (As we shall see, the inspiration for Alma Wilmot's tragic movie performances in *In the Beauty of the Lilies* derive, similarly, from the everyday experiences of small-town life.) Ironically, depicting "the worst" in fiction conferred upon Updike precisely the "sense of shelter" that Harry in *Rest* associates with the long-lost, irrecoverable experience of mental air raid shelter with which Sunday school had provided him. As I demonstrated in the *Rabbit, Run* chapter, Harry's affirmation of truth ("I'm not the one. She did it") at Becky's burial is—in Kierkegaardian terms, at any rate—an act of intelligible heroism, fulfilling Updike's insistence that "from a higher, inhuman point of view, only truth, however harsh, is holy." Consequently, this exhilarating self-liberatory experience prompts Harry, until the consequences of his act begin ramifying, to want to reassure Jack Eccles, *"I'm on the way"* (257). Not until his trip to Deleon in the last pages of *Rest* does Harry once again act so immediately upon impulse or so completely isolate himself from others. Once again, it is the truth—Pru's confession to Janice of the truth of Pru's and Harry's lovemaking—that has set him free: free to confront the fate with which Pru has been associated from her first appearance in the novel. Bessie Springer's phone call announcing Pru's arrival in Brewer with Nelson coincides with the eruption of "a small arterial pain" behind Harry's eyes, the narrator speculating that "perhaps with such a negligible unexplained ache do men begin their deaths, some slow as being tumbled by a cat and some fast as being struck by a hawk" (683). Thus Pru's arrival in *Rich* is metaphorically figured as the onset of Harry's death, and although her providing him with "soul food" through sex is dramatized through highly positive and resonant metaphors invoking naturalness and innocence, Pru's confession sparks this climactic southward flight in which Harry is "on the way" to deliverance from the condition of incessant conflict that has been his life.

It is Harry's capacity to act in such unreflective and impulsive ways, I think, that makes him Updike's most engaging protagonist, the absence of the insulations of modernist aesthetics rendering him more vulnerable and threatened than so many of Updike's other point-of-view characters who, if not writers themselves, are selfconsciously submitting their lives to paper in an attempt to make literary sense of them.[17] More than those protagonists who possess that "curious trick, possibly useless" of literary rendering, which the narrator of "Leaves" claims for himself,[18] Harry forces Updike to confront the issue frontally: what is life worth for those whose acts of praise waste themselves meaninglessly in the self-annulling, onrushing flow of consciousness? What is life for those for whom the registering of bleak human truths generates no "shelter in which I can feel safe" but only a sense of heightened vulnerability and human fragility? Even more significantly, Harry incarnates Updike's doubt that, however praiseworthy the world might be, there is anyone or anything to praise for it, and his anxiety that if "description expresses love," this is ultimately a manifestation of nothing other than the describer's love of the self's capacity for describing. These are not new concerns for Updike, of course—we found the very same worry surfacing in the David Kern stories in the ambiguity as to whether David in "Pigeon Feathers" has recovered God or simply discovered an artistic vocation in registering the exquisite design of a pigeon's wings, and in the unresolved question as to whether the narrator of "My Grandmother's Thimble" has generated through his narrative a "song of joy" or merely a family memoir.

What makes *Rest*'s addressing of these issues more urgent and bleak than their dramatization in the previous Rabbit novels is the fact that Harry's decline is so pervasively imbued with the death of Linda Grace Hoyer Updike, the author's mother. The details of her heart disintegration, Updike acknowledged, inform the highly clinical descriptions of Harry's enlarged heart in the novel, and because her death effectively terminated his familial ties to Pennsylvania, Updike was as much saying good-bye to his childhood home in *Rest* as Harry unknowingly is when he makes his final drive to the Gulf of Mexico. His mother died, Updike explained, "ten days after I finished the first draft [of *Rest*],"[19] and so closely was Updike synchronizing his narrative to the present in which he was writing that Rabbit ended up losing his life within weeks of Mrs. Updike's October 1989 death. As is suggested by his dedication to *The Coup* ("To My Mother: *fellow writer and lover of far lands*"[20]), Updike very much associated his "Shillington self" and the writer he evolved into with his mother and her literary inspiration. Her death—the desolation of which pervades the narratives in Updike's 1994 *The Afterlife* short story collection, "A Sandstone Farmhouse" in particular—is not the only source of *Rest*'s omnipresent gloom, certainly, but it incontestably deepened the predilection of author, and, therefore, protagonist, unrelentingly to behold in the world little but emblems of loss and emotional devastation. In a number of senses, then, "deciding to wrap up the [Rabbit] series was a kind of death for [Updike]."[21] For both protagonist and author, the equivocal messages of the sky are a central source of that depression, one summarized in Updike's poem, "On Becoming a Senior Citizen":

> We hug those first years and their guardians
> so close to spite the years that took away
> the days of trolley cars, coal furnaces,
> leaf fires, knickers, and love from above.[22]

When Harry first sees *his* mother at Becky's funeral in *Run*, it occurs to him that her hug seeks to "carry him back to the sky from which they have fallen" (250). This is but one of many positive associations Harry makes with the sky in the first novel, some of which I discussed in the *Run* chapter. Early in the novel he perceives the sky optimistically as "a blank scoreboard of a long game about to begin"

(36), the optimism of this vision carrying over to his early associations with Ruth: "Now the noon of another day has burned away the clouds, and the sky in the windshield is blank and cold, and he feels nothing ahead of him, Ruth's blue-eyed nothing, the nothing she told him she did, the nothing she believes in. Your heart lifts forever through that blank sky" (84). Although Harry often projects upon the sky this blankness of possibility and freedom, he more often finds written there an empyrean concern for himself. His perfect shot on the golf course takes place against "the black blue of storm clouds, his grandfather's color stretched dense across the north" (115), the color recalling the old man's remaining upstairs so that young Harry won't be a fosnacht. Perhaps his other most important projection of the sky is the fact that he "wants to believe in the sky as the source of all dictates" (241) in contradiction of his coach, Marty Tothero, who assures him that "right and wrong don't fall from the sky. We. We make them" (240). Obviously, the sky is a medium upon which Harry repeatedly projects the condition of his soul at the moment he looks up at it, this "upward space" alternating between seeming a source of intentionality and concern for Harry and a corroboration of his human freedom. The sky that "greets him" at Becky's funeral clearly interfuses these two impressions, validating Christian promises while provoking him into flight. Harry continues this tendency of viewing the sky as an emblem of his being throughout the tetralogy, the sky becoming a progressively ambivalent reality.

In *Redux*, the American preoccupation with the moon shot stokes Harry's feelings of personal worthlessness, while his disillusionment with the information glut of the late '60s prompts him to perceive the "upward space" beneath the "great big nothing" of the moon as "a sky poisoned by radio waves," "television aerials raking the same four o'clock garbage from the sky" (440). In *Rich*, however, Harry experiences the takeoff of the 747 flying him, Janice, and the Flying Eagle Country Club couples to the Caribbean as a resurgence of belief: "God, having shrunk in Harry's middle years to the size of a raisin under the car seat, is suddenly great again, everywhere like the radiant wind. Free: the dead and the living alike have been left five miles below in the haze that has annulled the earth like breath on a mirror" (975). The return flight to Pennsylvania deflates this exhilaration by restoring Harry to a sense of his limitations. As the plane passes over Delaware, the rich DuPont women who were the subjects of his sexual fantasies during his initial flight in *Run* recur to him, compelling the acknowledgment that "he has risen as high as he can, the possibility of such women is falling from him, falling with so many possibilities

as he descends" (1009). The ultimate implications of that descent are
protractedly epiphanized throughout the final novel of the tetralogy.

At the beginning of *Rest*, Harry is not on an aircraft, but waits for
one to arrive:

> Standing amid the tan, excited post-Christmas crowd at the Southwest
> Florida regional airport, Rabbit Angstrom has a funny sudden feeling that
> what he has come to meet, what's floating in unseen about to land, is not
> his son Nelson and daughter-in-law Pru and their two children but some-
> thing more ominous and intimately his: his own death, shaped vaguely
> like an airplane. (1051)

That Nelson is associated with this skybound avatar of death perpetu-
ates the tetralogy's insistent Oedipal theme, and if the son never literally carries out his *Redux* threat to kill his father as vengeance for Jill's
death, his addict's squandering of Harry's beloved Toyota franchise
is, because it constitutes a betrayal of his father's primary God-substi-
tute, Mr. Shimada,[23] certainly contributory to Harry's self-destruction. The airplane that Nelson's has put him in mind of, clearly, is the
one that preoccupies him throughout the novel: "How about death?"
he asks his fellow golfers, ". . . How about that Pan Am jet?" (1111).

Harry and his Deleon golfing partners discuss the explosion of Pan
Am Flight 103 in the skies over Lockerbie, Scotland, before the
Christmas holidays, the players debating whether it was an act of terrorism. For Harry, the element of the incident that becomes obsessive
is the violent suddenness with which a meal served on an uneventful
airplane flight was transformed into a horrific confrontation with annihilation. Accordingly, as his preoccupation with mortality deepens,
his every thought of death is accompanied by images of the Flight 103
passengers tumbling out of the sky. When Nelson visits Harry in the
hospital following his heart attack, he brings a newspaper containing
official speculations about the type of bomb used to bring down the
plane, the convergence of Flight 103 with Harry's antagonistic son
(who, Harry notices, is still "bathed in the artificial light of the world
that hasn't broken through into death yet") inspiring in him a vision
of personal extinction surpassing the terrible mortality intimations of
David Kern in Updike's Olinger stories. Envisioning the tranquil seconds on Flight 103 leading up to the instantaneous holocaust, Harry
suffers the realization that

> even now as he lies here in this antiseptic white fog tangled in tubes and
> ties of blood and marriage he is just like the people he felt so sorry for,
> falling from the burst-open airplane: he too is falling, helplessly falling,
> toward death. The fate awaiting him behind this veil of medical attention

is as absolute as that which greeted those bodies fallen smack upon the boggy Scottish earth like garbage bags full of water. *Smack, splat,* bodies bursting across the golf courses and heathery lanes of Lockerbie drenched in night.

Not even the flickering image of a golf course, Harry's sole remaining emblem of the possibility of human perfectability, can leaven this scene of horror for him or lessen its epitomization of the ephemerality of ordinary life which—especially in *Rich*—has been one of primary stabilities in his existence. Like one concurring in his creator's belief that "only truth, however harsh, is holy," Harry forces himself to imagine the horror in punishing detail:

> Reality broke upon these passengers as they sat carving their airline chicken with the unwrapped silver or dozing with tubes piping Barry Manilow into their ears and that same icy black reality has broken upon him; death is not a domesticated pet of life but a beast that swallowed baby Amber [an infant in the news who died for want of a liver transplant] and baby Becky and all those Syracuse students and returning soldiers and will swallow him, it is truly there under him, vast as a planet at night, gigantic and totally his. His death. His purely own. (1209)

By comparison, Harry's closing *Rich* epiphany echoed in this passage—the new grandfather perceiving Judy, his grandaughter, as "His. Another nail in his coffin. His" (1045)—seems abstract, casual, even complacent; in his Florida hospital, the protagonist who in *Run* declared to Ruth that "if you have the guts to be yourself, other people'll pay the price" is undergoing the terrifying experience of confronting the ultimate price of selfhood. "Every plane had a bomb ticking away in its belly," Harry subsequently concludes, likening the human body to doomed aircraft: "We can explode any second" (1499).

Harry's allusion to baby Becky's death implies the existential protest underlying his Flight 103 fixation often overwhelmed by fear or self-pity. In *Run*, when Harry returns to the Wilbur Street apartment following Becky's drowning, he pulls the plug of the fatal bathtub, draining the water that asphyxiated her. "He thinks how easy it was" to complete this mechanical act, "yet in all His strength God did nothing. Just that little rubber stopper to lift" (237). God's indifference to humanity's—or, more precisely, to Harry's—well-being is a recurrent theme in the Rabbit novels, but only in *Rest* does Harry consistently indict the skies he so closely associates with God: after dinner at Valhala Village's Mead Hall, he looks up to the "teeming sky" and thinks "*There is no mercy*" (1126). Scotland Yard's documentation of Flight 103's having been detonated by a plastic explosive called Semtex reinforces Harry's horror at the universe's permitting such a deed: "Harry can hardly bear to read about it, the thought of all those conscious bodies with nothing all around them, freezing, *Ber-nie, Ber-nie*, and Lockerbie a faint spatter of stars below, everything upside down and void of mercy and meaning" (1132).

Harry here is not so much denying the existence of God as accusing Him of creating a universe "void of mercy and meaning."[24] The odd *"Ber-nie, Ber-nie"* reference is Harry's associative means of ascribing blame for the freezing world turned "upside down," which Flight 103 victims suffered as their final experience. When Harry's golfing partner, Bernie, emerged from anesthesia following quadruple bypass surgery, the first thing he registered were the words of his Pakastani anesthetist. Bernie tells Harry, " 'Ber-nie, Ber-nie,' this voice says, so honest to God I think maybe it's the voice of God, 'oper-ation a success!' " That the "voice of God" is capable of saluting human beings in markedly more maledictory terms is Harry's point in eliding the "Ber-nie, Ber-nie" epiphany with the horror of Flight 103, for Bernie's subsequent description of "the voice" characterizes it as if "it came out of the clouds to Abraham, to go cut Isaac's throat" (1106).

As we've seen, in Kierkegaard's reading of the Abraham and Isaac story, it is precisely Abraham's ability to retain belief in a God who would command that he cut his son's throat that qualifies him as a knight of faith; as Harry has aged, however, he has proved no more adept than he is in *Run* at achieving "the mindful will to walk the straight line of a paradox" (203) that Christianity—in Updike's Kierkegaard-imbued theology—demands. Consequently, God becomes for Harry an adversary. As Harry struggles with the post-heart attack pain in his chest while seeking to steer the Sunfish back to shore, the narrator explains, "There is satisfaction, in his skyey enemy's at last having found him. The sense of doom hovering above him these past few days has condensed into reality, as clouds condense into needed rain" (1175). The manifestations of God's presence in Harry's universe remain remarkably consistent: this "skyey enemy" gathering "as clouds condense into needed rain" differs only in intent from the God whose rain in the beechnut tree outside Harry's bedroom window confirms His existence. After this incident, consequently, the sky's meaning has inalterably changed for Harry: "the balmy blue air of the Gulf of Mexico changed for him, as if a filter had been slipped over his eyes, when the Sunfish tipped over" (1258).

For the remainder of the novel, then, Harry's positive associations with the sky are predominantly nostalgic, including his memory that "as a little kid he couldn't tell what God did from what people did; it all came from above somehow" (1469). His alternative means for finding a source of reassurance in the heavens is to associate them with a human agent. The mercilessness he earlier ascribed to the sky is briefly redeemed as he lies on the beach waiting for an ambulance following his heart attack: "The sky is a blank redness out of which Pru's factual Ohio voice falls with a concerned intonation" (1177).

Nonetheless, the sky in *Rest* remains for Harry preeminently a reminder of personal extinction, the disappearance of a French airliner on its way from Paris to Chad, the Vincennes' downing of an Iranian civil airliner, its passengers falling from sky to hit "the dark, hard water" (1465), and the *Challenger* disaster (Harry has read that the victims may have been alive for as long as many as three minutes as they fell [1466]) providing additional evidence of the heavens' mercilessness. As Harry's quota of days dwindles, the newspapers are full of reports of the airborne approach of Hugo, and he "scans the sky for hurricane signs, for clouds God's finger might write, and reads none" (1494). If "hope reads a word where in fact only a scribble exists" ("Pigeon Feathers," 120), despair reads nothing even where fatal convergences are there to be discerned.

Playing basketball for the penultimate time—a game of "Three misses, you out" with black Deleon teenagers—Harry tries a backward trick shot, his perspective forcing him to view the world in the same frighteningly inverted way the Flight 103 passengers did: "Seen upside down, how blue and stony gray the cloudy sky appears—an abyss, a swallowing, upheaving kind of earth" (1498). In addition to eliminating any distinction between heaven and earth, this description reinvokes the approach of Hugo, a skyborne disaster so closely associated with Harry's death that in talking to his dying father in the hospital, Nelson seems to be "shouting into a fierce wind blowing from his father's direction" (1516). The threat of the hurricane may explain why it is that on the morning of his fatal game, Harry thinks that "it may be his imagination, but the sky seems clean of airplanes" (1506). Symbolically, of course, it *is* his imagination—the absence of aircraft signals that Harry's determination to push his heart condition by playing basketball (he's worn Bermuda shorts in case he can scare up a game on the court where he played "Three" the previous day) has removed the descending, bombed planes from his vision. As for David Kern's father in "Packed Dirt," another victim of an enlarged heart, "death has been advancing under cover," and Harry has similarly resolved to "engage the enemy and defeat it," his resolution ensuring that he can be tormented no longer by its airborne avatars. If

Harry can't defeat death, he at least outscores Tiger, 20–19, before his second myocardial infarction levels him and halts the contest. Those who hear the ambulance approaching to convey the stricken athlete to the hospital mistake the siren for a hurricane alert, mistakenly believing that Hugo has wheeled around in its devastating airborne path to South Carolina and imperils them once again. As Tiger flees the scene of the white man's sudden collapse, the sky prefigures Harry's demise: "An airplane goes over, lowering on a slow diagonal." Meanwhile, Harry lies beneath the basket into which he stuffed his go-ahead point, "as alone on the court as the sun in the sky, in its arena of clouds" (1511). What takes the self-sacrificing George Caldwell of *Rabbit, Run*'s counternarrative, *The Centaur*, a single volume to accomplish—"Zeus had loved his old friend, and lifted him up, and set him among the stars as the constellation Sagittarius"[25]—costs the narcissist Rabbit Angstrom four novels of exhilaration and misery to achieve. He has become part of the sky with which his desperate ambivalences about the meaning of existence have been so complexly and inextricably woven.

What, then, does the complex matrix of sky motifs in *Rest* lead the reader to conclude about the human relationship to the divine? One provisional answer is suggested by Harry's comparison of God to Ronald Reagan: he decides that Reagan had that "dream distance," so "you never knew how much he knew, nothing or anything, he was like God that way, you had to do a lot of it yourself" (1318). Perhaps the central theological paradox of Updike's oeuvre is its conflicting dramatization of the inseparability of God from the self suggested by Harry's Reagan analogy, and its contradictory insistence—derived from Karl Barth—upon the absolute otherness of God. If the best Harry can do in trying to describe his experience of this conflict is to invoke contesting impressions of the U.S. president, the disputants in *Roger's Version* (1986) are distinctly more adept at articulating their theological premises, the contention between them closely approximating the opposed intuitions Harry dies without ever expressing or resolving.

Anticipating Harry's realization while watching his heartbeat on the monitor that "the anger is his life, his soul," Dale Kohler introduces God into this epiphany: "That sort of thing can be said and maybe *should* be said; I mean, it's God speaking within us, this indignation. . . . But . . . what I framed one night to say to you is this: you should realize that our loyalty to God will not go away, because it is basically loyalty to ourselves. . . ." The kink in Harry's chest that sets him running in *Run* is precisely this intuition of God-as-loyalty-to-himself, which similarly underlies his certainty that Becky has leaped to heaven, freeing him to speak the absolute truth he experiences at the cemetery. It dictates also Harry's lifelong loyalty to the self shaped by the Sunday school classes of childhood, and figures as well in Updike's loyalty to the "Shillington self," which provides him warrant to write the harshest of truths about humanity. Consequently, the mystery of God's existence throughout Updike's work proves inseparable from the question that pervades the author's oeuvre and Rabbit's wonderings: "The mystery that more puzzled me as a child," Updike wrote in "The Dogwood Tree: A Boyhood," "was the incarnation of my ego—that omniverous and somehow pre-existent 'I'—in a speck so specifically situated amid the billions of history. Why was I I? The arbitrariness of it astounded me; in comparison, nothing was too marvellous."[26]

As Updike has often acknowledged, this most ultimate of existential questions ("the excitement of being . . . himself," as Harry thinks in Rest, "Harold C. Angstrom, called Hassy in those days never to be relived" [1486]) is one he learned from Kierkegaard, and Roger's Version's Roger Lambert, whose theological leanings favor Barth, objects that Kohler's position "sounds awfully close to humanism to me," his comment invoking a consistent adversary in Updike's fiction, but one from which his fiction often seems indistinguishable. "There has to be an Other," Lambert insists, that Other quickly coming to resemble Harry's "skyey enemy." "And once you get the Other," Lambert continues, "He turns out to be a monster, full of terrible heat and cold and breeding maggots out of the dung and so forth."[27] If God is Other, his majesty is necessarily coalescent with the cruelty that allows Becky innocently to suffer death and the Challenger victims to consider their terrible fates for minutes as they fall; if God is inherent, our own subjectivity and transgressions corrupt and minimize Him, dwindling Him until He is no larger than "a raisin under the car seat." The impartibility of the human and the humanly projected divine is, I think, Rest's most resonant and dramatically achieved ambiguity, and the source of Harry's most ennobling conflict. He is intellectually incapable of turning his intuition into the paradoxical theological solace Roger Lambert and his mistress find in the depth of their fall, and yet such ideas do, I'm convinced, underlie Updike's conviction of Harry's ultimate human worthiness: "We wanted to be rid of each other, to destroy the evidence," Lambert explains in Roger's Version:

> yet [we] perversely clung, lovers, miles below the ceiling, our comfort being that we had no further to fall. Lying there with Verna, gazing upward, I saw how much majesty resides in our continuing to love and

honor God even as He inflicts blows upon us—as much as resides in the silence He maintains so that we might enjoy and explore our human freedom. This was my proof of His existence, I saw—the distance to the impalpable ceiling, the immense distance measuring our abasement. So great a fall proves great heights. (281)

Harry, who believes that "without God to lift us up and make us angels, we're all trash" (1362), can only fruitlessly scan the distance between earth and heaven on the golf course, gaining no reassurance when he looks up to the sky "where your eyes can usually find relief," because it is "dirtied by jet trails that spread and wander until they are indistinguishable from God's pure clouds" (1109). To perceive that "So great a fall proves great heights" requires the capacity to "walk the straight line of a paradox," which Harry lacks; characteristically, he has to stumble through deeds into knowing the "comfort that [h]e had no further to fall."

Harry's identification of himself with God's substance—his perception of himself as "[a] God-made one-of-a-kind with an immortal soul breathed in"—more frequently suffers the "universal devaluation" that permeates the world he sees, his novel-pervading impulse toward solipsism as a result becoming a progressively distasteful experience. In their last conversation, Thelma counsels him, "Harry, you're not actually the center of the universe, it only feels that way to you"[28] (Knopf, 201). Nonetheless, "Brewer and all the world beyond feel like frills on himself, like the lace around a fat satin valentine, himself the heart of the universe, like the Dalai Lama"[29] (1317), and he acknowledges "some limitation within him really, a failure or refusal to love any substance but his own" (1348). Although Updike's Freudian presuppositions prevent his fiction from ever seriously questioning narcissism as an ineradicable human trait, Harry's ability to "love his own substance" declines precipitously following his and Janice's ushering of their grandchildren through Thomas Alva Edison's home and Jungle Gardens theme park. Edison's estate abounds with grotesque plants, odd "tricks" that God created "off by Himself in the Amazon jungle," which are now offered by the museum as spectacular prodigies for jaded Florida tourists to gawk at. The climactic incident of the Jungle Gardens visit is Harry's eating of nuts intended for the park's exotic birds, his error seeming to Judy "the dumbest thing I ever saw anybody do!"; her description of the seed as "little brown things like rabbit turds" suggests that what Rabbit has eaten is his own defecation. (In *Rich*, Ruth transforms his pride in the daughter he imagines she and he parented into excremental ugliness by saying that his claim to being Annabelle's father is like "rub-

bing her all over with shit" [1313], and Harry expresses his revulsion
at kissing Thelma good-bye after she had performed fellatio on him
and tasting himself on her lips. Clearly, what Harry is increasingly
sickened by, as Mary O'Connell has suggested, is himself and his ex-
cretions.) The heart attack he suffers on the Sunfish Harry later attributes to "that birdfood I ate" (1178), the entire day of grandparenting
conveying one message to him: "It's hell, to be a creature. You are
trapped in yourself, the genetic instructions, more strictly than in a
cage" (1144).

Harry's progressively dispiriting self-confrontation in *Rest* culminates in an uncharacteristically political assessment recalling his
marching as Uncle Sam in a Brewer Fourth of July parade, his rumina-
tions expanding upon the notion of being "trapped in yourself" while
offering the clearest illumination of the Rabbit/Harry distinction the
tetralogy offers:

> Harry catches a sudden reflection of himself and is startled by how big he
> is, by how much space he is taking up on the planet. Stepping out on the
> empty roadway as Uncle Sam last month he had felt so eerily tall, as if his
> head were a giant balloon floating above the marching music. Though his
> inner sense of himself is of an innocuous passive spirit, a steady small
> voice, that doesn't want to do any harm, get trapped anywhere, or ever
> die, there is this other self seen from the outside, a six-foot-three ex-
> athlete weighing two-thirty at the least, an apparition wearing a sleek grey
> summer suit shining all over as if waxed and a big head . . . a fearsome
> bulk with eyes that see and hands that grab and teeth that bite, a body
> eating enough at one meal to feed three Ethiopians for a day, a shameless
> consumer of gasoline, electricity, newspapers, hydrocarbons, carbohy-
> drates. A boss, in a shiny suit. His recent heart troubles have become, like
> his painfully and expensively crowned back teeth, part of his respectabili-
> ty's full-blown equipage. (1395–96)

As so often happens throughout the tetralogy, inner and outer
selves, body and spirit, get insolubly intermixed here, the protagonist
who once affirmed that "goodness lies inside, there is nothing outside" (264) having now discovered that his heart's disintegration is as
much depletion of the outer man as his "shiny suit" incarnates his
soul. The same ambiguity plays itself out in the carnal/spiritual ambivalences of Harry's self-indulgent eating.

One of the two epigraphs of *Rest*, from Frederick Douglass, suggests that "Food to the indolent is poison, not sustenance." This passage, which Harry reads aloud in his Penn Villas living room during
the racial consciousness-raising sessions with Skeeter and Jill in
Redux, is juxtaposed on the epigraph page with a sentence from *Rich*:

"Rabbit basks above that old remembered world, rich, at rest" (1050). What in *Rich* constitutes immobile tranquility propagated by wealth is reconfigured in *Rest* as an "indolence" that turns sustenance into poison, the implications of "at rest" undergoing an analogously ominous transformation.[30] Harry often acknowledges that he is an excessive consumer of the world's resources, "eating enough at one meal to feed three Ethiopians for a day," and incessantly nibbling on top of that. His doctor warns him against the dangers to his heart in his junk food snacking habit, but he is ultimately unable to quit for two conflicting reasons: because he so closely associates eating with self-affirmation indistinguishable from religious impulses and because he impulsively responds to manifestations of his fear of death through self-celebratory eating. His favorite nibbles are nuts, a source of pleasure in which he is already indulging himself in *Rich*, and which carry a complex weave of largely positive associations for him.

At his condominium's golf course bar, Harry, disregarding Bernie's admonition that "that crap's loaded with sodium," devours a bowl of nuts: "Yeah, but it's good for the soul," Harry says, [which is] "about as religious a remark as he dares put forth" (1112). He is reluctant to make "religious" remarks with his Jewish golfing partners because he fears they would look contemptuously upon his Christian hopes for his soul, the three men in Harry's view having "gotten on top of sex and death so they don't bother" them (1113), as sex and death continue to plague him. Nonetheless, his defense of nuts as "soul food" is, by his estimation, a "religious remark," and, as usual, his perception of the religious trails sexuality in its wake. Having been warned by his doctor as well that "nuts are poison," Harry finishes off two bowls at his lover Thelma Harrison's house, associating her providing of them with the other beneficence she has so generously offered him: she is, he thinks fondly, "the one person who for these last ten years has given him what he needed. Sex. Soul food"[31] (1229). His association of nuts with carnal pleasure is reinforced as he savors the macadamia nuts in his salad, feeling the texture of the cracked nut in his teeth as "miraculously smooth, like a young woman's body" (1268), and in his recollection of performing cunnilingus on Thelma, his memory of loving "it when she would clamp his face between her damp thighs like a nut in a nutcracker and come" (1228–29). Harry's hedonistic delight in nuts and snacking, like his preoccupation with sexuality, carries with it an elemental theological rationalization: "If God didn't want us to eat salt and fat," he asks Nelson after his first heart attack, "why did He make them taste so good?" (1210).

Harry's love of nuts traces its inception to his childhood. He is

pleased to recognize in *Rest* that a Brewer store he patronized on Saturday mornings in his youth continues to sell "the best peanuts in
town." He recalls walking around downtown Brewer "as a kid not
much older than Judy is now . . . with a dime bag of peanuts still warm
from the roaster" in his hand; he would "walk all around cracking
them and letting the shells fall where they would on the sidewalks of
Weiser Square" (1274). The memory of the joyful freedom and sense
of belonging he felt perambulating among the adults of Brewer, the
town's "civic conscience" epitomized by an "old bum" who chas-
tised Harry for littering, is contrasted with the Brewer ethos circa
1989, the old downtown now seeming deserted: a landscape "ghostly,
and hollow in lunar colors" (1273). Closer to home still, Harry's second protracted sexual relationship was initiated at a nut counter, Janice and he having met at Kroll's department store where he worked
in shipping and she, wearing a smock with "Jan" stenciled on it, had
a job "selling cashews and candy" (13). Her Kroll's job seems memorialized in *Rest* in Harry's repeated perception that she has a "brown
little stubborn nut of a face" (1303). At the end of *Rich*, Janice brings
Harry a jar of salted nuts to snack on during the Superbowl, but in
Rest she turns Harry in to Dr. Olman by characterizing him as "a
terrible nibbler," "courting" the physician and "betraying her husband" by acknowledging that "he loves nuts."

"Worst thing for him, absolutely the worst," is the doctor's response, because they are "full of fat, not to mention sodium, and cashews, macadamia nuts, they're the worst, macadamia nuts, but it's all
bad, bad" (1204). (As I've indicated, for Harry the epitome of good
is the sound of beechnuts in the tree outside his window "popping
like little firecrackers" [1277] and reassuring him of God's presence.)
What a young Janice lovingly dispensed at Kroll's is now a "poison"
that she must deny him, and consequently eating nuts and other junk
food becomes a form of rebellion against moderation and self-control
he can undertake, a means of asserting his human freedom. Harry's
depressed elision of the dissolution of youthful eroticism with his
forfeiture of professional stature is epitomized by a dismal reflection
of his that turns suddenly (and characteristically) eschatological:
"Now Springer Motors is *kaput*, *finito*. Down the tubes just like
Kroll's. Nothing is sacred" (1472).

Harry's dwindled *Rest* ego notwithstanding, the impulse toward
resistance remains strong in him: "he sometimes says a thing to try it
out," the narrator comments, evoking Harry's basketball past, "like
a head fake, to open up a little space" (1147). This is necessary, Harry
decides in *Rich*, because "you got to do something like that once in a
while to keep your options open, to keep a little space around you"

(576). Accordingly, on the beach before he and Judy set out on the Sunfish, Harry feels a reawakening of the "old animal recklessness. His heart, his skin, can never have enough" (1163). Like the revolt of nut-devouring and junk food-bingeing, the "old animal recklessness" that prompts the Sunfish incident is ultimately self-destructive. Harry defends his need for defiance as self-defense: "If there's anything that makes me hypertense, . . . it's women telling me all the time what to eat" (1098). Beset by admonitions and prohibitions, Harry's existence is gradually reduced to a stale vigilance over its own perpetuation: he tells Pru, "Me, all they need to do is nail down the coffin lid. I can't run, I can't fuck, I can't eat anything I like, I know damn well they're going to talk me into a bypass" (1363).

The spiritual creed Harry evolves in *Rest* as a response to these prohibitions is a form of hedonistic oppositionality granted ultimacy by his awareness that in gratifying the self he is simultaneously condemning it to death. Finishing off Judy's dessert at the condominium restaurant, Harry thinks, "In a way, gluttony is an athletic feat, a stretching exercise. *Makes your stomach say 'howdy'*" (1125). Gluttony, then, is the conflux of two positives for Harry: its capacity to be construed as an athletic achievement dovetails with its association with an advertising jingle celebrating eating that his beloved sister, Mim, sang as a child.[32] Add the potential for perceiving gluttony as a form of resistance to what he imagines women demanding of him, and it comes to seem, in Harry's eyes, an absolute good, even if it carries with it a portion of self-hatred. After finishing off a bag of Keystone Corn Chips, Harry acknowledges this, thinking that "he has wrapped himself around all 6¼ oz. of sheer poison, pure sludge in his arteries, an oily aftertaste in his throat and between his teeth. He hates himself with a certain relish" (1348). For a man with no more quests to undertake, eating becomes a masochistic diversion as well as a form of transgression and insubordination against the women who, no longer offering themselves to him to devour, now presume to tell him what to eat instead. Janice, of course, is primary among these women.

The marital concord that characterizes the Angstrom marriage throughout much of *Rich*, one founded upon both spouses' shared commitment to American materialism epitomized by their Krugerrands-sparked sexual romp together, is largely unraveling at the opening of *Rest*. Notwithstanding Harry's musing, "What was there about Janice? It must be religious, their tie, it made so little other sense" (1235), the lot which Janice grew up thinking of as "the source of all things" remains the central bond between them, but Harry's accumulating medical problems have increasingly turned his thoughts to mortality and his eyes to the skies, which have ever been his preferred "source of all things."[33] Janice's conviction that his grandfather would have wanted Nelson to have a place in the franchise has gradually resulted in Nelson's displacing his father there, exacerbating the raw Oedipal tensions between them left unresolved by *Rich*. In addition, the success of Springer Motors has fueled Janice's interest in the world beyond the realms of home and the Flying Eagle tennis courts, and the family outing viewing of *Working Girl* at a Florida mall further reinforces her desire for a career. Unlike Harry, with his protracted postadolescent decline, Janice embodies the energy described by the narrator of Updike's story, "The Afterlife": "Women had the passion of conspirators, the energy of any underground, supplied by hope of seizing power."[34]

Harry is thoroughly cognizant of the shift in status that over the years has taken place between them, complaining to Thelma that "without her, I'm shit. I'm unemployable. I'm too old. All I can be from here on is her husband" (1237). Harry perceives Janice's efforts to earn a realtor's license as her means of preparing to support herself in widowhood, and as she becomes increasingly preoccupied with real estate law, she struggles against mentally validating his unvoiced accusation: "Maybe being a widow won't be so very bad is the thought she keeps trying not to think" (1331). Like the protagonist of Updike's "The Poker Night" whose husband has been diagnosed with cancer, Janice "[is] considering what she had been dealt; she [is] thinking how to play her cards."[35]

Janice's growth in independence wins grudging respect, Harry seeming to echo Ruth's most positive judgment on himself in *Run*—"in your stupid way you're still fighting" (80)—in the ultimate compliment Harry pays Janice: "She won't give up," he tells Thelma, "She never really figured out how the world is put together but she's still working at it" (1231). More often, however, his acknowledgments of her growth are imbued with condescension and resentment, his feelings of abandonment resonating through his reflection that he has come to admire her "as you admire children you have raised whose very success pulls them away, into the world's workings, into distance and estrangement" (1304). The want of activity retirement has imposed on Harry exacerbates his feelings of Janice's withdrawal, certainly, but there is external corroboration that she has become inattentive to him. Even before she begins real estate training, Janice has begun routinely to ignore his moods, a point which Nelson implies in asserting that "he seems depressed. Have you noticed?"

"I can't notice everything at once," Janice responds, "What I do notice about you, Nelson, is that you're not at all yourself" (1186).

When Janice has evolved her plan for paying off the massive Springer

Motors debt Nelson's drug use has incurred, she will justify its disruption of Harry's life in terms that similarly subordinate his needs to those of their son: Pru will agree to Harry's and Janice's moving back into the Springer homestead with her, Nelson, and the children, Janice explains to Harry, because "we both want the same thing—a happy and healthy Nelson" (1440). It is not only because her plan favors Nelson over himself that Harry resolves to make this scheme the final actuality he will ever deliberately resist; in fact, he may never fully comprehend how thoroughly his characteristically priapic transgression constitutes a subversion of Janice's professional/familial strategy.

Notwithstanding his sudden epiphany of Judy as "another nail in his coffin" at the end of *Rich*, the preceding scenes depicting Harry settling into his new Penn Park home are largely positive, corroborating his earlier premonition that no longer sharing a house with others will allow him to "breathe his own air" (655). "You have to step down into the den," Updike's narrator explains as Harry surveys the unaccustomed dimensions of his new home: "one step down from the hardwood floor of the living room, and this small difference in plane hints to him of many reforms and consolidations now possible in his life, like new shoots on a tree cropped back" (1033). As Updike's simile implies, the new house demands accommodation and sublimation: the *Penthouses* and *Playboys* Harry discovers in a closet with their pictorial survey of the progressively graphic exposure of women's genitals excite him not at all, and, bemusedly registering the cavalcades of cunt, he disposes of the magazines without regret. In recompense for this sublimation of desire, the house offers him immunity from his Oedipal antagonist: "The kid was no threat to him for now. Harry was king of the castle" (1036). Consequently, when in *Rest* Janice unveils her plan for relocating herself and Harry back into her childhood home with Nelson and family and selling the Penn Park house she and Harry have owned for a decade for the commission it will bring her and the running start it will provide her real estate career, Harry responds like one being dethroned: "I love that house." Were there any doubt that Updike's attitude toward Janice's relocation plan is highly critical, we need only recognize that she is attempting to replicate the one act for which Updike could never completely forgive his mother: that of moving her family back to her childhood home against their wishes.

Despite the fact that her scheme is certain to restore a circumstance she abhors—"I'm tired of you and Nelson fighting your old wars through me," she complains (1276)—Janice pushes ahead righteously with her Nelson redemption cause. Recognizing his heart attack victim's dependency upon her, Harry is reluctant forthrightly to oppose the strategy, having previously acknowledged to Thelma "without her, I'm shit." For Harry to be restored briefly to emotional/spiritual health, he must, as he notices Janice has done, learn to reject defining himself through his relationship to others. He wants no more to be merely her husband than she wants to be "Harry's wife, Springer's daughter, a famous coke addict's mother" (1410), and if his climactic and self-regenerative rebellion against the idea that "all I can be from here on is her husband" is largely precipitated by another's revolt, it is nonetheless thoroughly characteristic of Harry in that sexuality is its medium.

Updike has admitted that in writing each successive Rabbit novel, he committed himself to outdistancing the previous one in terms of Harry's sexual adventurings: fellatio with Ruth in *Run* is outstripped by Harry's taking an adolescent mistress in *Redux* and his near-involvement in a ménage à trois with Jill and Skeeter, which in turn are exceeded by his performing sodomy on Thelma in *Rich*.[36] By committing incest with his daughter-in-law in *Rest*, Harry would appear to have surpassed his previous sexual excesses. There is, however, remarkably little evidence in the scene invoking moral transgression or taboo violation.

When Harry places Pru's hand on his erection, the "gesture has the pre-sexual quality of one child sharing with another an interesting discovery—a stone that moves, or a remarkably thick-bodied butter-fly" (1364). Aware that what he is on the verge of doing is a trespass (he is "watchful of his heart, his accomplice in sin"), Harry experiences no rebuke in Pru's kiss, which tastes pleasingly of the dinner "she so nicely prepared, its lemons and chives, and of asparagus." (Janice has been too preoccupied recently with her real estate studies to cook.) A flash of lightning illuminates the room, and "[a]s if in over-flow of this natural heedlessness, Pru says 'Shit,'" and strips off her robe and nightie, offering herself to her father-in-law. The lightning flash reprises Harry's meandering thoughts a few pages earlier about rain spattering the window of his room and a PBS show he's seen: "Like the origins of life in one of those educational television shows he watches: molecules collecting and collecting at random and then twitched into life by lightning" (1359). The "natural heedlessness," which is the sex act's catalyst and its conflation with the origins of life, metaphorically render Harry and Pru's coitus the blameless product of natural forces no less accidental than the genesis of life. If blame for this union is to be assigned, in fact, it might better be as-cribed to Janice, whose focusing upon a real estate exam allows her to leave her infamously priapic husband, a man convinced that "he can't run or fuck" because of his heart attack and its attendant medications, alone in a house with a woman for months deprived of sex out of fear that her husband would infect her with diseases picked up from his "coke whores." (As Janice's parents agree in *Redux*, "she makes bad decisions" [493].) As Pru straddles Harry, "Her tall, pale wide-hipped nakedness in the dimmed room is lovely as those pear trees in blossom along the block in Brewer last month were lovely, all his it had seemed, a piece of paradise blundered upon, incredible" (1364). The comparison of her nakedness to the Bradford pear trees he saw in Brewer amplifies the naturalness of this act while implying that Pru, like these urban trees, withstands malaise like the one beseiging Harry, since their beautiful blossoms have proven impervious to the poisons of city life (1220). Looking back on the incident days later, Harry recalls that he went along with the condom Pru produced from her robe pocket because "it was her show" (1368), one mercifully distracting him from fixating on the terrifying "Rabbit Angstrom Show" he watched on the radiograph screen during his angioplasty. Once characterized by Mrs. Smith, for whom he gardened, as a man whose ability to make her rhodies bloom proved him possessed of "the gift of life," Harry has come to perceive "the *me* that talks inside him all the time scuttl[ing] like a water-striding bug above this pond of body fluids and their slippery conduits"; consequently, he is terrifically vulnerable to the ministrations of a younger woman whose beauty evokes that of paradisical Bradford pear trees and whose touch restores him to that manifestation of nature—the one contained within his loins—he has always best understood. Visiting him at the hospital in the novel's final pages, Janice tells Harry that she forgives him, but he isn't sure what for, and, far from depicting the sex between in-laws as a moral horror, *Rest* projects the consequences and ramifications of Pru and Harry's lovemaking as being unequivocally beneficial, the final incarnation of Harry's "gift of life."

Late in *Rest*, one of Harry's major resentments concerns Janice's refusal to punish Nelson for allowing his cocaine addiction to cost them the Toyota franchise. From Harry's perspective, Nelson's irresponsibility merits more penalty than Janice's therapeutic New Age banalities that son and father have both been sick, and that both are now "in recovery." Had Nelson not been taken off that morning to a rehabilitation center for treatment of his addiction, Harry and Pru would never have had the opportunity—created completely by Janice's real estate classes schedule—to be in a house alone together. Somewhat unpurposefully, then, Harry has ensured that Nelson's addiction not go unpenalized. In retrospect, in fact, he seems to have ascribed intentionality to the act: remembering Pru's expostulation,

"Shit," he recalls, "her voice relaxing into their basic relation, cock to cunt, doing Nelson in" (1457).

The more significant repercussion of Harry and Pru's lovemaking is no more completely calculated than Harry's impulse toward gaining revenge upon Nelson. Pru confesses to the act only because Janice is so intent upon selling the Penn Park house and moving herself and Harry back into the Springer homestead that Pru must resort to extreme measures to convince her mother-in-law why the cohabiting of the two families is impossible.[37] Too physically weakened to defend the house that emblematized his *Rich* feelings of cultural arrival and redemption, and too financially dependent on his wife effectually to oppose Janice's various real estate machinations, Harry has inadvertently conspired with Pru to commit the one action the exposure of which subverts all of his wife's familial, territorial, and careerist plotting. At one point in *Redux*, Harry feels "paralyzed, by the rain, by thunder, by his curiosity, by his hope for a break in the combination, for catastrophe and deliverance" (485), which is precisely what Pru's revelation precipitates, liberating him into a final flight. Weeks later, in Florida, Harry looks back on his inadvertent revolution and finds it good: "he's shown [Janice] he still has kick" (1476).

Pru's disclosure of Harry's fornication-precipitated triumphs over Nelson and Janice set him running south for a final time, that flight constituting both a dramatization of the isolation he has chosen (he has, in his terms, "set himself adrift") and an unstinting depiction of its personal cost. That isolation is, I think, all that Harry—who has concluded that "nothing is sacred"—has left of belief, and accounts for the necessity of his unforgivable revolt against Nelson and Janice before he leaves. From *The Poorhouse Fair* onward, Updike has sustained a remarkably unambiguous attitude toward one philosophic position: secular humanism. Hook in that first novel excoriates Connor's secular position by insisting that "there is no goodness, without belief, there is nothing but busyness. And if you have not believed, at the end of your life you shall know you have buried your talent in the ground of this world and have nothing saved, to take on to the next."[38] Reverend Kruppenbach in *Run* echoes Hook in mercilessly rebuking Eccles's humanistic family counseling model of ministry: "There is nothing but Christ for us. All the rest, all this decency and busyness, is nothing. It is Devil's work" (147). That Eccles has transformed himself into a '60s therapeutic meddler, when Harry meets him on a bus in the one substantial scene Updike added to *Redux* in the *Rabbit Angstrom* revision, extends the tetralogy's humanist critique. Having admitted that he no longer believes in God, Eccles tells Harry, "I believed [then] in certain kinds of human interrelation. I still do. If people want to call what happens in certain relationships Christ, I raise no objection. But it's not the word I choose to use anymore." The grafting onto *Redux* of Eccles—who, unlike Harry or Updike, believes "that [the late 1960s] are marvelous times to be alive in"—facilitated the final Oedipal irony of the tetralogy (438).

As a result of his stay in a rehabilitation center in *Rest*, Nelson emerges as an Eccles clone, incessantly mouthing the platitudes of New Age therapeutics derivative of the '60s humanism Eccles in *Redux* finds so exhilarating. At the welcome home dinner Pru puts on for Nelson, he offers a self-consciously secular grace—"Peace. Health. Sanity. Love"—and when Harry ridicules his son's newly adopted sanctimoniousness, Nelson responds with an Eccleslike semantic equivocation, insisting that he still doesn't acknowledge God "in the form that orthodox religion presents it in. All you have to do is believe in a power greater than ourselves—God as we understand Him" (1415). During their phone conversation late in the novel, Nelson confesses to his father his ambition to become—as Eccles briefly had been—a social worker, in order to "help other people instead of myself for a change" (1488). Assaying his nascent creed, Nelson attempts to one-up the father whom he once described as believing in "a God he was the apple of the eye of" with Narcotics Anonymous–inspired communal agendas: "Like they say, you give your life over to a higher power," Nelson affirms, "You ought to try it, Dad."

"I'm working on it" (1486), Harry responds, invoking the death he feels approaching or the God-haunted silence and isolation of his Deleon condo habitation, which he intuits as his extinction's necessary preliminary. (Nelson enters a drug rehabilitation center the same day Harry is admitted to Brewer Hospital for angioplasty; Nelson emerges endorsing a "higher power," while Harry returns with his faith destroyed by "Godless technology.") Harry remains remarkably consistent in his attitude, which he doesn't recognize as Barthian, never contradicting his *Redux* objection to Peggy Fosnacht's suggestion that "God is people": "No, I think God is everything that isn't people" (360). Although the closing hospital scene dramatizes a modest reconciliation between father and son, to which we'll return, Updike saved the ultimate reconciliation between Harry and Nelson for "Rabbit Remembered."

There is, of course, no parallel reconciliation with Janice in *Rest*: "You didn't *talk* to her, Dad" is Nelson's complaint when he follows his mother into Harry's ICU. The absence of any such rapprochement, I think, reflects the fact that the ending of *Rest* reprises Harry and Janice's last interaction in *Run* with Janice's and Harry's positions reversed. At Becky's funeral, Harry briefly experiences a communal

impression that the mourners are "all gathered into one here to give
his unbaptized baby force to leap to heaven" (252). Eccles's words,
"*Casting every care on thee. . . ,*" reverberate in Harry's ear, early
versions of the novel adding the sentence, "He has done that; he feels
full of strength" (1960 ed., 293), in needless authorial advocacy of
what he is about to do. His cruel rebuke of Janice—"Don't look at
me . . . I didn't kill her"—prompts a mitigating "Hey, it's okay . . .
you didn't mean to," but the mourners' expressions of incomprehen-
sion and horror fill him with "a suffocating sense of injustice" inciting him to run because "forgiveness had been big in his heart, and
now it's hate" (253). He felt forgiving of Janice, as I've tried to show,
not only for drowning their daughter but also for failing to experience
the central spiritual miracle of their faith: Becky's ascent to heaven.

   In *Rest*, Harry experiences a similarly brief and equally delusional
moment of communal affirmation following the phone call from Nelson: "Talking to his family has exhilarated him; he feels them safely
behind him" (1503) in the vigil of solitude to which his final flight
south has sentenced him. This intuition of familial solidarity is no
more trustworthy than Harry's conviction in the *Run* cemetery scene
that he and the mourners are "all gathered into one here to give his
unbaptized baby force to leap to Heaven" (252); Nelson has called
primarily because he and Janice are still angling for Harry's approval
to sell the Penn Park house. Inspired by the phone conversation,
Harry launches into a prodigious bout of gluttony, putting into practice his single theological credo—"If God didn't want us to eat salt
and fat, why did He make them taste so good?" (1210)—by downing
a two-person serving of frozen lasagna before heading down to the
condominium Mead Hall for a second humongous and suicidally fat-
laden meal. His basketball game with Tiger the next morning con-
summates the defiantly self-affirmative and self-destructive quest that
comprises the narrative of *Rest*, and when Janice visits Harry at the
hospital, forgiveness is big in her heart: "He sees her, his wife here,
little and dark-complected and stubborn in her forehead and mouth,
blubbering like a waterfall and talking about forgiveness. 'I forgive
you,' she keeps saying, but he can't remember for what" (1515). Her
forgiving him for committing incest with Pru proves as effectual as
his forgiving her for drowning their baby and for failing to register
the truth of the promises of their Christian faith.

   The strikingly unsympathetic portrait of Janice in the conclusion
of *Rabbit at Rest* is, in part, a consequence of the fact that whereas
Nelson talks to Harry about putting himself in God's hands, Janice's
pitifully ineffectual monologue with God dramatizes how completely
prosaic is her conception of "casting every care on thee." "Janice

thinks she should pray for Harry's recovery, a miracle," the narrator explains,

> but when she closes her eyes to do it she encounters a blank dead wall. From what Dr. Olman said, [Harry] would never be alive the way he was, and as Dr. Morris said, sometimes it's time. He had come to bloom early and by the time she got to know him at Kroll's he was already drifting downhill, though things did look up when the money from the lot began to be theirs. With him gone, she can sell the Penn Park house. *Dear God, dear God*, she prays, *do what You think best.* (1514)

Still no believer in divine miracles, Janice, clearly, is casting Harry's most ultimate cares on thee in full recognition that if there is no recovery, she can begin her real estate career in earnest. ("Maybe being a widow won't be so very bad," the narrative has her musing earlier in the text, "is the thought she keeps trying not to think.") Janice's *"do what You think best"* is less a prayer than her disavowal of any further personal responsibility for Harry's fate, and seems consistent with her unwillingness to acknowledge any accountability for the fact that the man to whom she had been married for thirty-three years had begun "drifting downhill" at the very beginning of their marriage, a decline that, in her eyes, was only interrupted by her coming into her inheritance.

To her credit, Janice does admit responsibility for Harry's circumstance; for good measure, she is judged culpable as well by Updike's narrative. When she arrives at the Deleon hospital, Janice acknowledges that in the last months Dr. Morris had paid more attention to Harry than she had (1513), and although she doesn't meditate long upon Morris's comment that Harry is "too young for retirement," the reader is aware that the Deleon condo and Harry's early retirement have been above all else Janice's means of providing space for Nelson at Springer Toyota. Admittedly, her weeks of vindictive indifference receive a severe chastening when she first sees Harry "as white as his sheets with these tubes and wires going in and out of him . . . an emotion so strong she fears for a second she might vomit hit her from behind, a crushing wave of sorrow and terrified awareness of utter sense of loss like nothing ever in her life since the time she accidentally drowned her own dear baby" (1514). Her sincere experience of loss in this moment, however, doesn't alter the final sentence's implication that she may be as responsible for the second tragedy as she was for the first. (That Harry, a firm believer in the notion that "every plane had a bomb ticking away in its belly. We can explode any second" [1499], unconsciously suspected his wife of being capable of terrorist murder has been established by his noticing that she carries a "purse packed like a bomb" [1306].) The advice Harry wants to give Philadelphia Phillies third baseman Mike Schmidt—"quit, when you've had it. Take your medicine, don't prolong the agony with all these lawyers" (1373)—not only presages one of Harry's own motivations for quitting, but also associates the world he'd have Schmidt repudiate with Janice's new career. "Thinks she's so hot," he later thinks, "running everybody's lives with these accountants and lawyers Charlie [Stavros] put her on to" (1476).

The ultimate indictment of Janice's privileging of profession over marital loyalty, however, comes not from Harry but, rather obliquely, from Updike. When police in Florida try to contact Janice in Brewer about Harry's second myocardial infarction, she can't be reached because she's out showing a property—a sandstone farmhouse in rural Oriole, one sounding very like the Plowville home in which Updike spent his adolescence and his mother lived until her death in 1989. Perhaps his recent experience with realtors seeking financially to capitalize on others' losses accounts for the negative take that Updike—who ultimately sold the Plowville property to his cousin[39]—offers of real estate in the novel. Or perhaps Updike's distaste for real estate brokers dates back to his grandfather's fateful choice of that profession once he had abandoned his Indiana Presbyterian ministry, trading the hope of heaven for merchandizing the soil of this world (*S-C*, 180). For whatever reason, real estate is depicted in *Rest* as a projection of Janice's most secular tendencies, her capacity for translating things of the spirit into matters fiduciary. It is appropriate, then, that the gas station where Rabbit is given the highly instrumental, antimystical advice in *Run*, "The only way to get somewhere, you know, is to figure out where you're going before you go there" (26) has, by his 1989 drive south, become a real estate office.

Condemning Nelson and Janice for falling short of Harry's standards for "transactions with the unseen world" seems particularly unjust in a narrative dramatizing Harry's own religious impulses having apparently dwindled nearly to nonexistence. Nonetheless, in one of his few explicit comments about issues of faith in *Rest*, Updike cautioned an audience at the University of Pittsburgh against overemphasizing the absence of references to the transcendent in the novel. "So although Harry is less specifically theological than [in] the last novel," Updike remarked, "in some way it's the most peaceful theologically because he's almost got beyond the vocabulary of theology and is acting out a religious event which is his own demise."[40] The most explicit passage invoking Harry's relationship with God in the novel's last hundred pages offers corroboration of Updike's characterization. "Funny about Harry and religion," the narrator muses:

> [w]hen God hadn't a friend in the world back there in the Sixties, [Harry] couldn't let go of Him, and now when the preachers are all praying through bullhorns he can't get it up for Him. He is like a friend you've had so long you've forgotten what you liked about Him. You'd think after that heart scare, but in a way the closer you get the less you think about it, like you're in His hand already. Like you're out on the court instead of on the bench swallowing down butterflies and trying to remember the plays. (1459)

Throughout the last third of *Rabbit at Rest*, Harry has been gradually realizing he's already on the court, playing the game that costs him his life while perhaps redeeming it.

The concluding irony of *Rest*—that the game that brought Harry his only moment of notoriety and sense of accomplishment in life becomes his chosen means of self-annihilation—is obvious, manifesting Updike's characteristic interlading of the secular and the religious, of Harry's conflicting psychic tropisms towards life and death. The kink in his chest, which is the central repository of that antinomy and Harry's internal barometer of extremity in *Run*, reemerges in *Rich*. Playing golf one afternoon, Harry worries that he's supposed to be elsewhere, that he has an appointment he's forgotten, which he compares to the fatal moment in which Skeeter "decided to pull his gun out and get blasted" (782). As Harry drives home, summoned by Janice's phone call, he contemplates the grim reality that "your life is your own and nobody else's," and feels as if "a loop is rising in his chest as in a rope when you keep twisting" (785). Waiting at home to meet him for the first time is Pru, whose confession to Janice ten years later will figure so centrally in launching Harry toward his self-liberatory voyage of death to Florida.

In *Rest*, of course, that kink has become his heart, "tired and stiff and full of crud," as Dr. Olman characterizes it, ". . . a typical American heart, for his age and economic status et cetera" (1201). Once he arrives in Florida, Harry describes the tightness he feels in his chest to Dr. Morris, and is told that he should "get interested in something outside yourself, and your heart will stop talking to you." Harry undertakes the regimen of exercise Morris recommends, but his commitment to it is equivocal because, as is the case with the gas station attendant in West Virginia in *Run*, "The smell of good advice always makes Rabbit want to run the other way" (1483), and because "getting interested in something outside himself" has always provided an insuperable challenge for him. In addition, it is "nature's way," he privately believes, "that you are interested in less and less" in the world, and if "life from here on is apt to be insulting," fraught with "pacemakers, crutches, wheelchairs. Impotence" (1482), the inducement to choose life over death dwindles.

Harry's fateful decision is made no more consciously than is Edna Pontellier's similarly self-destructive determination in *The Awakening*, and its enactment carries imagery that, again as in Kate Chopin's novella's depiction of justifiable suicide, confers a measure of benediction upon the deed. The Deleon condominium has become baleful in its emptiness—"The well-sealed hollow place that greeted his arrival seventeen days ago now does brim with fear"—which Harry seeks to disperse by devouring the frozen pizza he'd picked up in an excess of joy stemming from his basketball game of "Three" with local teenagers. While eating, he watches network news reports of the approach of Hugo as the hurricane smashes its way through the Caribbean. The pizza tastes like napalm, conjuring up Charlie Stavros, who is always associated with the Vietnam War and who must (Harry assumedly worries) have free access to Janice with Harry down in Florida. Harry finishes the entire two-person helping, inspired to gluttony by the images of destruction he's seeing on the tube. He channel surfs back and forth between Jennings and Brokaw reports in the way that he told Judy Janice was mad at him for doing, seeing "wild wet wind screaming through rooms just like this one, knocking out entire glass doors and skimming them around like pie plates." What he's experiencing here is a mix of terror and exhilaration: terror because of the devastation, but exhilaration because "everything flies loose, the world is crashing, nothing in life can be tied down." This moment corresponds to that in *Run*'s climactic scene in which Harry decides that "those things he was trying to balance have no weight" (264) and can surrender himself to pure impulse, to the intense promptings of nature. It is difficult not to hear something both celebratory and desolate in his one word judgment on this realization: "Terrific" (1499). This is, of course, the moment in which Harry has made his decision: he'll open himself to this natural force because nothing can be tied down anyway, though he hasn't yet consciously decided how he'll place himself in the path of this disaster that reopens possibility and reanimates the world. Having made this resolution, he feels a sudden need, like a man on diuretics needs suddenly to urinate, to call his grandchildren—to say good-bye.

Consequently, the following morning when Harry challenges a young African American wearing a tank top displaying a tiger's head to a game of basketball, he is symbolically confronting the two reali-

ties that throughout his life have been a source of obsession and terror. Skeeter, the other significant black man in the tetralogy, tells
Nelson, "You still want to live, they got you. You're still a slave. Let
go, let go, boy. Don't be a slave. Even him, your Daddychuck, is
learning. He's learning how to die. He's a slow learner, but he takes
it one day at a time, right?" (494). Harry in *Rich* clearly admires the
terms in which Skeeter confronts his own death, compelling police
officers to kill him by firing on them without provocation, and he is
clearly emulating his black tutor—"this hostile stranger descended
like an angel" (649) whom he never ceases revering and fearing—in
the death he chooses for himself. For all of Harry's reverence for
Skeeter, however, he never completely abandons his initial wonder-
ment at having "invited this danger" to live in his house or his racist
attitudes toward him: "Wait, wait. He is poison, he is murder, he is
black" (451).

Tiger not only reprises Skeeter's embodiment of the whites' projection of their fear of death upon "the other"—upon African Americans.[41] At the beginning of *Redux*, Harry thinks that Becky's death
has made sex with Janice seem too dark, too much associated with
death; accordingly, "he had fled her cunt like a tiger's mouth" (289).
"You want sumpin'?" the teenager asks, his "light, level, unsmiling
voice" seeming "to come out of the tiger's snarling violet mouth"
(1507). In challenging a black teenager to a game of Twenty-One, he is
deliberately courting that fear, confronting that death Janice's vagina
embodied for him following Becky's drowning. Deep into the game,
Tiger asks Harry if he wants to quit because "you puffin' pretty bad."
Unconsciously imitating the parataxic speech of his Parkinson's-
suffering mother in *Redux*, Harry answers, "You wait. Till you're my
age," and then insists, "Let's keep our bargain. Play to twenty-one."
After Becky's death in *Run*, Janice's father tells Harry, "Life must go
on. We must go ahead with what we have left" (235). Harry replies,
"I promise to keep my end of the bargain," the narrator remarking
upon the strangeness of Harry's choice of words. The bargain Harry
is striking with Tiger, clearly, is to continue playing until life stops
going on.

Given the centrality of racial issues in *Redux* and Harry's association of his own deathly premonitions with Skeeter's decision to die
in *Rich*, the race of Harry's fatal opponent is not incidental. After the
two have played to an eighteen-all tie, the narrator affirms Harry's
delight in defying his adversary by transforming his honky's characteristics into sources of intimidation: "He is enjoying scaring Tiger
with his big red face, his heaving cheesecake bulk, his berserk icy blue
eyes." In one of the culminating ironies of Harry's demise, his death

epiphanizes the "white man's burden" concept of which even Skeeter was unable to disabuse him: Harry "takes a slam of a dribble, carrying his foe on his side like a bumping sack of coal, and leaps up for the peeper." The layup he scores ("The hoop fills his circle of vision, it descends to kiss his lips, he can't miss") represents the go-ahead point, the intentness with which Harry is competing conveyed by Tiger's feeling "a body bump against him as if in purposeful foul" as Harry's heart attack levels him, ending the game. Only in a contest with stakes this high does Harry play so aggressively for, as Tothero recalled his high school style of play, "you never fouled." Before abandoning the stricken white man whose collapse he is certain to be held responsible for, Tiger repeats his black man's benediction upon a superannuated honky's two-handed way of shooting the basketball: "Pure horseshit." In the basketball shooting competition called "H.O.R.S.E.," the accumulating of the word's five letters/five misses means you're out.

And so Harry lies unconscious beneath the basket, "as alone on the court as the sun in the sky." He may, as I suggested earlier, have equaled George Caldwell of *The Centaur* in having been metaphorically lifted up to the skies, or the dirt on his face may signal his fulfillment of a different fate. "Adhesive dust of fine clay clings to one cheek of the unconscious flushed face like a shadow," the narrator explains, "like half of a clown's mask of paint" (1511). In the opening pages of *Run*, Harry notices beneath the steps of his Wilbur Street apartment building "a plastic clown. He's seen it there all winter, but he always thought some kid would be coming back for it" (8). Fifteen hundred and eight pages later, Harry has become the clown no kid comes back for.

Rabbit at Rest, I have been attempting to demonstrate, is as unambiguous about Harry's end-of-novel intentions as it is equivocal about his act's connection to anything transcending his egotistical impulses. Just as Pru's encouragement that he and she repeat their lovemaking (and that she has condoms in her robe's pocket) repudiates any notion of the act's being motivated by uncontrollable desire, so Harry's insistence that he and Tiger carry through on their "bargain" of playing to twenty-one resolves any doubt as to his self-destructive intent. Unconsciously or otherwise, Harry is enacting his concurrence in Dr. Morris's judgment: "Sometimes it's time."

Their sparring over higher powers notwithstanding, Harry and Nelson come to something of a reconciliation as *Rest* ends. At the hospital following Harry's first heart attack, Nelson insists that he's "too young not to have a father" (1210), and after the second one, he begs Harry not to die. His father's stoic response is that Nelson doesn't understand that by dying, he is doing his son a favor, just as Harry's own parents did for him: "The dead make room," is how he characterizes in *Rich* the inevitable parental withdrawal. It's in this spirit of Oedipal resignation and equivocal paternal reconciliation that Harry attempts to answer the "unaskable question" that tweaks the hairs of Nelson's eyebrow by responding, "Well, Nelson . . . all I can tell you, is it isn't so bad" (1516). If his "answer" seems too typically Updikeanly ambiguous, it may be because the question at stake is really the one Harry invokes earlier in the text: "the unanswerable question that surrounds his rustling upright stalk of warm blood" (1499).

That question invoking the meaning and value of the individual human being's existence is ultimately unanswerable, Updike insists throughout his fiction, and the unanswerability of that question constitutes the basic ambiguity at the center of his work, one upon which practically all of his critics agree. To cite once again what seems to me the most concise articulation of that inescapable ambiguity in Updike's fiction from "Leaves," "we stand at the intersection of two kingdoms, and there is no advance and no retreat, only a sharpening of the edge where we stand."[42]

"The religious faith that a useful truth will be imprinted by a perfect artistic submission underlies the Rabbit novels" (xiii), Updike wrote in his introduction to the *Rabbit Angstrom* volume, and I want to use that assertion to make a closing brief for my conviction that, although I acknowledge *Rest*'s unwillingness to answer ultimate questions, my reading of the novel finds a "useful"—if dark—"truth" there, an existential assertion that manages not to be relegated to ambiguity by self-canceling ironies. In an early draft of the novel, Updike composed a paragraph that he subsequently cut, which points in the direction of the thematic trajectory of the Rabbit narrative that survives the spiritual irresolution of Harry's death. "Our lives reduce us in the living," Updike wrote: "[Harry] never quite grew into, though born in the area, and his mother a Renninger, the local restfulness, the ability to accept reduction gracefully. Something in him, the pronged syllables of his Swedish name, or the black-Irish mother his father had, or a perverse streak he inherited from his own outspoken mother, held him some inches off the earth, where those around him seemed content to have their feet."[43] I suppose that Updike deleted this passage because it celebrates excessively Harry's idealism while too baldly explicating what I have been reading as a central dramatic tension of the Rabbit tetralogy: the individual ego's need to affirm and perpetuate itself in the face of the inevitability of the fact that "our lives reduce us in the living." That reduction is, as I've tried to demonstrate in these pages, a crucial aspect of the "useful truth" dramatized throughout the Rabbit tetralogy, one so closely associated for Updike with Linda Grace Hoyer Updike's death that it is no surprise to find a poignant readdressing of it surfacing in "A Sandstone Farmhouse." Joey's mother, the story's narrator explains, "saved in separate sections of the [kitchen] floor, the empty cans, and the plastic bags the supermarket bagged her groceries in, and slippery stacks of mail-order catalogues, and string and twine snarled in a galvanized bucket. Joey recognized in this accumulation a superstition he had to fight within himself—the belief that everything has value. The birds in the trees, the sunflower at the edge of the orchard, the clumsily-pasted-up Valentine received years ago from a distant grandchild—all have a worth which might, at any moment, be called into account. It was a way of advertising that one's life was infinitely precious" (114–15).

Harry Angstrom's single theological tenet, I've been suggesting, is that his "life was infinitely precious," and that a central dramatic dynamic of *Rest* charts his desolating relinquishment of that belief. In the aftermath of his mother's death, Joey, cleaning out the farmhouse so that it can be sold, "stacked the magazines and catalogues and Christmas cards and tied them with baling twine from the bucket and carried them to the barn to be trucked by a Mennonite neighbor to a landfill. The Boy Scouts no longer collected paper and bottles: nothing was precious any more, there was too much of everything. As his family assembled, Joey impressed them with his efficiency, portioning out the furniture and heirlooms among his children, his ex-wives, the local auctioneer, the junkman" (125).

For Joey, as for Rabbit, the reduction of the material world's value—"nothing was precious any more"—is indistinguishable from the depletion of the self's value. "A Sandstone Farmhouse" and Rabbit tetralogy dramatize their protagonists' confrontation with the grim truth that the belief that "everything has value" is only "a superstition" as a significant component in the process which Skeeter, via Frederick Douglass, calls "learning to die." That process, I am arguing, is the most profound and unambiguous "useful truth" of the tetralogy, which is, as Updike once suggested, "about, and not only in the last book, a man's relationship with his coming death."[44] Even as he mercilessly depicts the inexorable process of reduction to which late middle age and an increasingly materialistic world subject Harry, Updike clearly signals that what he admires most in his protagonist is Harry's refusal to "accept reduction gracefully." This tension, I think, prevents the tetralogy from being neutralized by its own spiritual uncertainties, the four novels offering a compellingly protracted agon between the inexorable forces that reduce a human life and erode the individual's savoring of the living of it, and the opposition he poses to that reduction—as Ruth puts it to Harry in *Run*, "In your stupid way you're still fighting." That fighting—"the hardness of the heart"—constitutes Updike's "yea"; the precisely documented, fully dramatized, and deeply moving "external circumstances" of existence's heedless reduction of the individual are his "nay"—one enacting the devotion to truth-telling impartibly uniting Rabbit Angstrom and John Updike, which may, or may not, constitute "the motions of grace."

7

Room for Belief:
In the Beauty of the Lilies

"Things change is world's sad secret."
—Mr. Shimada's final word to Harry before
divesting him of his Toyota franchise

IN *RABBIT REDUX*, HARRY'S FIRST REACTION TO THE EVENING READ-
ings from Black history that Jill, Skeeter, Nelson, and he undertake
in order to educate him in American racial politics is that he's being
confronted with "a vision of bottomless squalor, of dead generations,
of buried tortures and lost reasons" (513). The works from which this
nonnuclear family reads—*The Selected Writings of W. E. B. DuBois,
The Wretched of the Earth, Soul on Ice, Life and Times of Frederick
Douglass*—and "others, history, Marx, economics" are "stuff that
makes Rabbit feel sick, as when he thinks about what surgeons do, or
all the plumbing and gas lines there are under the street" (463). He
continues to distrust and resist most infrastructural explanations of
reality, disliking particularly recalling the angioplasty procedure the
findings of which transform his personal history of nutritional self-
indulgence into a virtual death sentence. In *Redux*, Skeeter tells him
that "history won't happen any more" now that he, the "Christ of
the New Dark Age" has arrived (507), but for Harry quite the opposite becomes the case: one manifestation of his growth in *Rest* is the
fact that a sense of the past has been born in his mind—he's reading
history.

Barbara Tuchman's *The First Salute* is the volume he has chosen in
Rest, and although "it knocks Rabbit out, . . . he'll finish it if it kills
him" (673). (He doesn't; it didn't.) Harry isn't a completely enthusi-
astic convert, clearly, partly because Tuchman's death the previous
year has "put a blight on the book"; nonetheless, history "has always
vaguely interested him, that sinister mulch of facts our little lives
grow out of before joining the mulch themselves, the fragile brown

190

rotting layers of previous deaths, layers that if deep enough and squeezed hard enough make coal as in Pennsylvania" (1088). The possibility that that geologic pressure will generate a substance that can ultimately generate light and heat from layers of death is Harry's tacit hope, and consequently his interest in the subject, as in another educational pursuit, is characteristically spiritual and teleological: "Along with history, Harry has a superstitious interest in Astronomy. Our Father, who art in Heaven . . ." (1204). Like David Kern, whose encounter in "Pigeon Feathers" with H. G. Wells's agnostic *The Outline of History* precipitates an adolescent crisis of faith, Harry seeks in history not illumination of sociopolitical evolutions but signs of God's governing, all-determining presence in the passage of time, without which the procession of his hours of life, he is convinced, adds up to nothing. It doesn't always work. "Just thinking about those old days lately depresses him," Updike describes Harry thinking in an antihistorical funk in *Rest*, "it makes him face life's constant depreciation . . . he feels a stifling uselessness in things, a kind of atomic decay whereby the precious glowing present turns, with each tick of the clock, into the leaden slag of history" (1431–32). Harry reads history, then, for one of two reasons that are never more distinguishable than are Updike's purposes in writing fiction: to seek confirmation that the passage of time has a *telos*, a divine intentionality that ensures him perpetuation beyond death, and/or because it offers him, as Frank Kermode explained, "a fictive substitute for authority and tradition, a maker of concords between past, present, and future, a provider of significance to mere chronicity."[1]

One of my fundamental arguments in *Rabbit (Un)Redeemed* is that Harry Angstrom's conflicts are oblique dramatizations of Updike's more intellectual and aestheticized concerns; it follows, then, that Harry's unexpected late-middle-age interest in reading history in *Rest* would be reprised in some form in Updike's subsequent fiction—in a more extensive literary attempt to discover/create meaning through a carefully reconstructed historical narrative. As its patient, highly particularized evocation of eight decades of American material reality and its lengthy acknowledgments of historical sources confirms, *In the Beauty of the Lilies* is Updike's most historical novel, one that seeks to present a century of American spiritual history through tracking four generations of the Wilmot family.[2]

Reviewing Joyce Carol Oates's 1987 novel, *You Must Remember This*, Updike somewhat slightingly called "a historical novel of sorts, centered in the mid-fifties, with traces of research in its passing references to Adlai Stevenson, Senator McCarthy, the Korean War, the Rosenberg executions, bomb shelters, and the popular songs and prizefights and automobiles of the time." His own historical novel, with its patient evocation of the American silk industry strike of the early nineteen hundreds, its depiction of a Delaware town's survival of the Depression, its reproduction of the evolution and decline of the Hollywood studio system, and fictionalization of the David Koresh/Branch-Davidian holocaust incorporates far more than "traces of research." Nonetheless, Updike praised Oates's novel for its capacity to animate the past she recreates with a compelling emotional authority: "the background events of the period are by and large feelingly translated into subjective experience, by an author who was there."[3] Updike wasn't "there" for much of the period covered in Lilies, and therefore had to translate history into "subjective experience" by working from material bearing significant familial resonances for him, the Wilmot lineage, as I'll show, shadowing that of the Updike family's progress through the twentieth century.

If Rabbit's late-life interest in reading history enacts his confused effort to discover transcendent meaning in time or to find in chronological reconstructions of the past compensation for his abandoned sense of the past's spiritual significance, then Updike's complexly layered historical novel poses the question whether the preoccupation of In the Beauty of the Lilies with precise historical rendering is undertaken as a literary reproduction of the "Providence that shapes our ends," or is, instead, being offered as a literary surrogate necessitated by the loss of belief in a transcendent understanding of history. My purpose in this chapter, then, is to attempt to answer the question whether In the Beauty of the Lilies dramatizes an understanding of history as kairos (which Frank Kermode defined as "the coming of God's time") or chronos—"passing time."[4] Implicit in that question is this one: is Lilies a fabricated narrative revealing an image of God's plan, or an artifact like the newel post in Clarence Wilmot's rectory, whose creation was "guided by the benighted, hopeless mentality which seeks ornament as a distraction from the intolerable severity of the universe"[5] (12).

I've previously cited Updike's comment that "I try to adhere to the testable, the verifiable, the undeniable little thing . . . Somehow, I hope the pattern in the art will emerge, and I guess I must have some such hope cosmically;"[6] the fact that Lilies opens with the most profoundly harrowing dramatization of the loss of faith Updike has composed since his early David Kern stories invites the reader to wonder whether that cosmic hope of Updike's has dwindled in this 1996 novel even beyond Rabbit Angstrom's faint faith. But then, Updike's own comments about his purposes in writing the novel suggest that an atheistic reading of Lilies omits a significant factor: ". . . I was

trying through this throng of identities," Updike wrote in an introduction to *Lilies*, "to tell a continuous story, of which God was the
hero. I invited Him in, to be a character in my tale, and if He declined,
with characteristic modern modesty, to make His presence felt unambiguously, at least there is a space in this chronicle plainly reserved
for him, a pocket in human nature that nothing else will fill."[7]

That a "space in this chronicle" might be "plainly reserved for
God" is an idea that Alf Clayton, the narrator of *Memories of the Ford
Administration* and Updike's most closely self-identified persona in
his 1990s' meditations upon the value of history, would find unexpected and perhaps even admirable. "Modern fiction thrives only in
showing what is *not* there," Clayton argues in *Memories*: "God is not
there, nor damnation and redemption, nor solemn vows and the sense
of one's life as a matter to be judged and refigured in a later recounting, a trial held on the farthest, brightest quasar. The sense of eternal
scale is quite gone, and the empowerment, possessed by Adam and
Eve and their early descendents, to dispose of one's life by a single,
defiant decision. Of course, those old fabulations *are* there, as ghosts
that bedevil our thinking" (296). These "ghosts that bedevil our
thinking" make Clayton want to reduce the complexity of James Buchanan's life to a single, decisive choice: as he argues in a passage that
seems so evocative of Updike's anxieties about his literary efforts to
bear repeating:

> My attempt to bestow upon Buchanan *the award of posterity* collapsed
> when I, having imagined an eagle's-eye view that would make of his life a
> single fatal moment, found myself merely writing more history, and with-
> out the pre-postmodernist confidence of Nevins and Nichols and Catton,
> yarn-spinners of the old narrative school. My opus ground to a halt of
> its own growing weight, all that comparing of subtly disparate secondary
> versions of the facts, and seeking out of old newspapers and primary doc-
> uments, and sinking deeper and deeper into an exfoliating quiddity that
> offers no deliverance from itself, only a final vibrant indeterminacy, infi-
> nitely detailed and yet ambiguous—as unsettled, these dead facts, as if
> alive. (360)

Clayton is invoking two conflicting notions of historiography here,
the antinomy in more theoretical terms paralleling Harry's conflicted
perceptions of history. It seems clear that Clayton believes that his
biography's failure to validate the "eagle's-eye view" methodology
has sentenced him to the failure he experienced symptomized by his
settling for the "exfoliating quiddity" model of historical reconstruction. The religio/moral methodology that Clayton's researches failed
to generate assumes that a human life can be conceptualized in terms

of "a single fatal moment" in which the subject with "one defiant decision" dispenses with her/his life. If human existence is morally centered, what Adam and Eve do after they eat of the forbidden fruit
doesn't matter much; their story counts because of a single, significant moral choice that has major ramifications for humankind. Because Clayton's researches fail to locate any similarly decisive
moment in Buchanan's life, his biography of the fifteenth president
sank "deeper and deeper into an exfoliating quiddity that offers no
deliverance from itself": biographical detail accumulated without
clarifying the meaning of Buchanan's life or adducing a moral principle the mass of detail could be shown to delineate.[8] The only meaning
such a biography could be said to have, Clayton acknowledges, consists in its contesting the findings of previous Buchanan biographies,
and therefore it contributes to a closed system referring only to its
own conventions of biographical reconstruction and the assumptions
within that discourse—the "real Buchanan" whose life the biogra-
phers seek to illuminate has escaped. "At some point, history becomes like topography," Clayton complains, "there is no *why* to it,
only a *here* and a *there*"[9] (269).

   That poststructuralist conclusion is not one that Clayton—who
rejects deconstruction methodologies on the ground that "*Deconstruction despises art, stripping away all its pretenses*" (175) while it
"flatten[s] everything eloquent, beautiful and awesome to propaganda
baled for the trashman" (201)—nor Updike would ever affirm, as the
odd equivocation at the end of Clayton's credo implies. The reader
never expects that "exfoliating quiddity" to turn into anything positive, but then "a final vibrant indeterminacy, infinitely detailed and
yet ambiguous—as unsettled, these dead facts, as if alive" resonates
vitality and possibility rather than what Harry's "leaden slag of history" embodies, as does the "unsettledness" of "these dead facts."
The reason, arguably, that Clayton's confession of professional failure takes an unanticipated upturn, is that in having Clayton address
the problem of making history live in prose, Updike found himself
rearticulating a secular construction of his goals for his own work.
What could better characterize the outcome of four volumes of Rabbit novels than that they achieve "a final vibrant indeterminacy, infinitely detailed and yet ambiguous"? The "infinitely detailed"
representation gives substance to the indeterminacy of Harry's fate
rather than resolving it—the meaning of the dramatization of Rabbit's thirty years of life remains, quite deliberately, "ambiguous," and
the "question that surrounds his upright rustling stalk of warm
blood" remains, similarly, "unanswerable" (1499).

   Similarly secular construings of the artist's mission arise regularly in Updike's essays, reviews, and interviews: typical is his assertion that "the world, so balky and resistant, and humiliating, can in the act of mimesis be rectified, adjusted, chastened, purified. Fantasies defeated in reality can be indulged; tendencies deflected in the cramp of circumstance can be followed to an end."[10] In *Lilies*, however, charismatic Christian Jesse Smith dismisses secular art forms such as Hollywood films as "devil's work," and, as we've seen, writerly craftsmanship—products of the artist as God-surrogate creator—ultimately isn't sufficient response to the existential dilemma for Updike, whose "own concern gravitates to the intimate, where the human intersects with something inhuman, something dark and involuntary and unsubmissive to man-created order. After all that Kierkegaard and Barth that I once consumed, it is hard for me to be reverential about the purely human."[11] The life Updike seeks "to feel engendering itself beneath his hands" through artistic creation strives toward the eschatological, aspiring to generate the morally intelligible realm he finds in Graham Greene's fiction: "Out of whatever depravities he needed, out of whatever depressions he overcame, Greene managed in his best novels to locate modern men and women in the old Christian space, giving them souls and the urgency that the concepts of sin and damnation bestowed upon human decisions."[12] Without the "urgency that the concepts of sin and damnation bestowed upon human decisions," fiction is no more illuminating, substantial, or fructifying than the movies Clarence Wilmot ritualistically attends in *Lilies* to distract him from the excruciating truth of his spiritual collapse. The "old Christian space" is precisely the one that Clayton—a more postmodern skeptic than Updike—claims is irretrievably lost to us: "The sense of eternal scale is quite gone," he insists, "and the empowerment, possessed by Adam and Eve and their early descendents, to dispose of one's life by a single, defiant decision." Whether Updike's fictions "locate men and women in the old Christian space" in which history is inescapably moral and human choices are irreversible, fatal, and dramatic in the most existential sense, or whether his stories and novels delineate no *"why"* but manage to evoke only a *"here"* and a *there"* of random human migrations is, of course, the basic antinomy of Updike's fiction I've been seeking to illuminate throughout these chapters; *In the Beauty of the Lilies* provides a less ambiguous response to this question, I'll contend, than the Rabbit tetralogy does, the novel suggesting, on its lower levels, that there is a *why* to human history, an intelligibility and *telos* to it, even if humanity exhibits a striking capacity to misread, minimize, or completely ignore these consonances. God may have declined Updike's invitation to appear in *Lilies* in any very concrete or palpable form, but the patterns underlying this text nonetheless affirm a causality and coherence to history transcending human intentions, a *kairos* the characters involuntarily enact while misconstruing their lives as adumbrating a random and meaningless *chronos*.

The "single, defiant decision" upon which *Lilies* opens seems, initially, less a decision than a defining religious experience: "At the moment when Mary Pickford fainted [on the Paterson, New Jersey set of *The Call to Arms*], the Reverend Clarence Arthur Wilmot, down in the rectory of the Fourth Presbyterian Church at the corner of Straight Street and Broadway, felt the last particles of his faith leave him. The sensation was distinct—a visceral surrender, a set of sparkling bubbles escaping upward."[13] Updike's particularization of Clarence's condition of disbelief immediately aligns it with naturalism and with a devastating epistemological dislocation. "Life's sounds all rang with a curious lightness and flatness," the narrator explains, "as if a resonating base beneath them had been removed. They told Clarence Wilmot what he had long suspected, that the universe was utterly indifferent to his states of mind and as empty of divine content as a corroded kettle. All its metaphysical content had leaked away, but for cruelty and death, which without the hypothesis of a God, became unmetaphysical; they became simply facts, which oblivion would in time obliviously erase. Oblivion became a singular comforter" (7).

Clarence's withering conviction of the universe's spiritual vacancy renders his ministry fraudulent, and it simultaneously inspired Updike to write two of the most compelling dramatic dialogues his fiction contains. The day following his "visceral surrender" of faith, Clarence is obliged to pay a call on a parishioner in the hospital in Paterson, where Clarence serves as Presbyterian minister. The clergyman attempts to reassure Mr. Orr, an unmarried laborer and devoted attendee of Clarence's church services, that his condition isn't so perilous as the patient believes. The proximity of death having dissolved his characteristic deference toward his minister, Orr rejects these blandishments and offers a blistering critique of Clarence's ministry. Orr complains that he never heard enough about damnation emanating from Clarence's pulpit, and he insists that this staple Calvinist tenet be their theme in this meeting that, he insists, his condition dictates will be their last. A minister whose theological stance emphasizes works over faith, Clarence has always been unable to endorse Orr's creedal belief in election, and Clarence's newly experienced faithlessness further vexes his interaction with this terminally ill patient. Orr wants assurance from the minister that salvation may await him, but, failing that, he needs to hear an affirmation that the universe is underpinned by the Calvinist principle of election, even if he won't be a beneficiary of that law. Because the universe has come to seem to Clarence "as empty of divine content as a corroded kettle," the minister has existential as well as theological reasons for not being able to provide the dying man the reassurance he craves. By minimizing damnation in favor of the significance of works and goodness of soul in his visit with Orr, Clarence is unintentionally undermining Orr's faith, one founded on his family's Calvinist belief in the existence of eternal damnation. ("Take away damnation, in my opinion," Orr pointedly informs Clarence, "a man might as well be an atheist. A God that can't damn anybody to an eternal Hell can't lift a body up out of the grave either" [47].) Orr's family's faith has construed American democracy as a Manichean system in which there are many losers and only a few predestined winners, and Orr dismisses Clarence, whom he clearly believes has failed him at this terrible moment, from the hospital with the angry protestation that "There have to be losers, or there can't be winners" (48), a position that resonates throughout this novel with its procession of—in American sociocultural terms, at any rate—unambiguous human failures and successes.[14]

Clarence's attempt to assuage the shame he feels over how badly this interview has gone ironically replicates Orr's winners/losers dichotomy while consigning the dying man to annihilation: Clarence guiltily theorizes that the universal machinery of salvation and damnation would never have been created for a figure as minor and unimportant as Orr (45). This cruel estimation of one of "the least of these" in God's kingdom reflects the bad faith Clarence enacted in concluding their interview: by lying to Orr about seeing the "light of election" shining in his eyes, Clarence has demonstrated to himself how necessary it is for him to leave the ministry lest his own unbelief continue to eviscerate others' faith.

After Orr has died, Clarence seeks to allay his bad conscience over their final meeting by addressing his parishioner's concerns in a sermon to his congregation. Skirting the notions of the absolute otherness and potency of the God Orr insistently invoked, Clarence suggests that, through Christ, God resolved to "descend to our condition, and to speak to men in metaphors drawn from their daily lives" (51). Clarence's inability to complete this sermon—his throat becomes so constricted in delivering it that his wife, Stella, has to conclude the service for him—persuades him that secularizing his Christian message can't redeem his ministry, and his conscience-driven effort to renounce his vocation precipitates *In the Beauty of the Lilies'* second great spiritual debate.

Whereas Orr brings more faith to their conversation than does Clarence, playing, in effect, Fritz Kruppenbach to Clarence's Jack Eccles,[15] the moderator of the presbytery to whom Clarence takes his desire to relinquish his congregation is nearly without belief. Thomas Dreaver (whose surname comes as close to "either" as Updike's "Dreaver/Orr" wordplay would apparently allow) offers arguments for Clarence's remaining in the pulpit reminiscent of those with which the Reverend Dobson so ineffectually addresses David Kern's anxieties about immortality in "Pigeon Feathers." Dreaver's hyper-liberal training at Union Theological Seminary taught him "not to be afraid of science, not to fear admitting that the Holy Book is embedded in history—that it contains the best wisdom of its time, but that time is not our time. Relativity is the word we must live by now. Everything is relative and what matters is," he continues, invoking Jack Eccles's Christian humanism, "how we, the human creatures, relate to each other" (75–76). His argument about the decisive event of Christian history dilutes it as completely as Clayton's biographical researches deny any such moral/dramatic center to the life of James Buchanan: whether there was a resurrection cannot be known, he contends, but it is nonetheless indisputable "that the Jesus movement resurrected itself in the months and years after the Crucifixion. . . . If there was no Resurrection, something happened just as inspiring and transformative. Here's a crux, actually, where history helps the believer, and puts the burden of explanation on the skeptics" (77–78). For Dreaver, clearly, history constitutes an acceptable—if not preferable—substitute for revelation, largely because it is a thoroughly human construction. "We don't any more merely investigate reality— Lilliputians crawling over some huge dark Gulliver sleeping there," Dreaver argues, recalling David Kern's mother's delighted reassurance to her son of the human contribution to God's being: "We make it, make it with our minds and wills. We make God, you could say" (79).

What makes this dialogue between a lapsed Presbyterian minister and his relativism-spouting superior such a stunning literary performance is that, having provided Dreaver with a number of positions with which he has expressed no sympathy at all ("We make God, you could say"), Updike allows this doubting Thomas to conclude his interview with Clarence by articulating theological arguments approximating Updike's own. "The soul needs something *extra*, a place outside matter where it can stand," Dreaver argues. (Updike told an audience at the University of Pittsburgh, "We all have some religious need . . . we all need to orient ourselves in terms of something bigger."[16] "The impalpable self cries out to [God] and wonders if it detects an answer," Updike wrote in *Self-Consciousness*: ". . . The need for our 'I' to have its 'Thou,' something other than ourselves yet sharing our subjectivity, something amplifying it indeed to the outer rim of creation, survives all embarrassments, all silence, all refusals on either side" [229].) Dreaver continues, "The Bible—think of it as the primer of language whereby we can talk to one another about what matters to us most. It is our starting point, not the end point" (79). There is, it seems to me, a similar discounting of the revelatory authority of scripture in Updike's "The Future of Faith" description of Christian iconography: the checkpoints of the Christian story represented in paint and sculpture by Renaissance artists in Italy "began to seem opaque, inconsequent, a repetition like that of certain maddening television commercials, this ancient Christian story, this cosmic anthropocentricity, that had provoked oceans of words and served a hundred generations as a paradigm to live and die by, and whose details in hasty summary I professed assent to every time I attended church. How much more mileage could be squeezed from these darkened, crumbling images?"[18] As he would do with Jesse Smith's evangelical absolutism in *Lilies'* fourth chapter, Updike here leavens the novel's implicit critique of Dreaver by lending his skepticism a subjective compellingness evocative of the author's own moments of doubt.[17]

Aware that their interview is coming to a end, Clarence seeks closure:

> "You're saying," Clarence said hesitantly, "that within the general indeterminacy—"
> "There is room for belief," Thomas Dreaver finished, sinking back in his wooden swivel chair so emphatically that the spring hinge beneath the seat squeaked in surprise." (79)

Through that squeaking chair, Updike may be expressing his own surprise that, amid all its relativistic indirections, Dreaver's credo still has "room for belief," but the Presbyterian moderator's position is really the inversion of Updike's "Future of Faith" assertion that "faith is not so much a binary pole as a quantum state, which tends to indeterminacy when closely examined" (86).

In creating spiritually disoriented Clarence Wilmot's dramatic confrontations with Orr and Dreaver, Updike dramatized as effectively as his fiction ever does his conflict between affirming a highly authoritarian, otherworldly faith and embracing a markedly more tentative religious creed invoking a greater reverence toward material reality. Updike obliquely summarized this spiritual antinomy in himself while describing the Lutheranism in which he grew up: "Lutheranism is comparatively world-accepting; it's a little closer to Catholicism than Calvinism. I don't feel much affinity with the New England Pu-

ritan ethos insofar as it still exists. No, I would call myself a Lutheran
by upbringing, and my work contains some of the ambiguities of the
Lutheran position, which would have a certain radical otherworldly
emphasis and yet an odd retention of a lot of Catholic forms and a
rather rich ambivalence toward the world itself."[19] That Clarence offers substantial rejoinders to neither the Calvinist zealot nor the liberal Presbyterian suggests, I think, not only the protagonist's spiritual
dislocation, but reflects Updike's attraction to elements of the antino-
mies while portraying as well how uneasily he occupies his medial
position between these two theological antipodes.

The remainder of Clarence's narrative adumbrates in grim detail
the personal cost of the eschatological crisis he has experienced, its
dying fall trajectory seeming dramatically to validate his perception
that "the metaphysical content [of the universe] had leaked away, but
for cruelty and death, which without the hypothesis of a God, became unmetaphysical; they became simply facts, which oblivion
would in time obliviously erase." As James Schiff described Clarence's postfaith condition, "Without God, Clarence is empty and
lacks those characteristics—will, energy, confidence, ambition, hope,
even voice—which once filled him. God is associated with vitality and
drive, and without him one simply stops trying."[20] Before he becomes
one of the facts obliviously erased by history's oblivious progression,
the ex-minister takes the only job he can find in Paterson in the early
'teens: that of peddling a repository of the facts to which the world as
he perceives it has been reduced. At a time of great financial instability
exacerbated by a silk industry strike that practically incapacitates the
city, Clarence takes to the Paterson streets, attempting to sell the *Popular Encyclopedia*, which his promotional spiel characterizes this way:
"For the twentieth century, these books are what the Bible was for
. . . times long ago" (93). History, in other words, is being presented
as compensation for the loss of revelation. An encyclopedia, he explains to a prospective customer who once served as a domestic in his
rectory, "is a blasphemy—a commercially-inspired attempt to play
God by creating a print replica of Creation" (101). Once the expectation of revelation has been dispensed with, all an encyclopedia need
concern itself with are facts—"there is no *why* to it," as Alf Clayton
describes his failed project, "only a *here* and a *there*." "Facts," Clarence asserts in pushing his wares to highly resistant potential customers, "—the *Popular Encyclopedia* contains nothing but facts, the facts
of the world, clearly and straightforwardly presented." In merchandising this proletarian-oriented encyclopedia, Clarence has sentenced
himself to a mendacious advocacy no more supportable than were his
faithless sermons, the "facts" patter he has contracted to reproduce

for prospective customers prompting him to think, "Saying this, he seemed to be sunk in a deep well of facts, all of which spelled the walled-in dismal hopelessness of human life. The world's books were boxes of flesh-eating worms, crawling sentences that had eaten the universe hollow"[21] (94). Ralph C. Wood's description of Updike's fragile faith characterizes equally well, I think, the passivity of belief of the ex-minister and encyclopedia salesman in *Lilies*: "[*Couples*] reveals how fully Updike is inclined to an ethical quietism. It derives, I believe, from an overly transcendent sense of God's otherness. Having so little sense of God as incarnate in either Christ or the church, Updike takes refuge in an abstract monotheism that makes him ambivalent about every moral reality. . . ."[22]

Clarence's only compensation for the emergence of a Wordless world "gutted by God's withdrawal" is the technological innovation that, Updike's novel suggests, provided for many Americans suffering religious erosion compensatory images of transcendent wonder—the movies. Clarence sees the movie house as a church, "with its mysteries looming brilliantly, undeniably, above the expectant rows" as the projectionist and piano player manipulate their mediums to channel the audience's emotional responses in much the same way that a preacher modulates tone and rhetoric to lead the congregation toward homiletic epiphany. Rather than inculcating spiritual guilt in its congregation, this substitute church liberates Clarence from it: "Within the movie theatre," *Lilies'* narrator explains, "amid the other scarcely seen slumped bodies, [Clarence] felt released from accusation. The moving pictures' flutter of agitation and gesticulated emotion from women of a luminous and ideal pallor licked at his fevered brain soothingly. Images of other shadows in peril and torment lifted his soul out of him on curious wings, wings of self-forgetfulness . . ." (104–5).

That the silver screen can engender a five-cent ascendance lifting "his soul out of him on curious wings" is dubious enough; that the lifting facilitates "self-forgetting" indicates how much the movies constitute a falsifying and alienating self-transcendence. In addition, the movies' ability to "transport the audience to everywhere but to workaday places like Paterson" (105) reinforces the idea that this very American medium is one intended to facilitate diversion, distraction, and escapism.[23] The technological and artistic growth of the medium is not lost on Clarence, who recognizes that "from year to year the camera had grown in cunning and flexibility, finding its vocabulary of cut, dissolve, close-up, and dolly shot. Eyes had never before seen in this manner; impossibilities of connection and disjunction formed a magic, glittering sequence that left real time and its three dimensions

202   RABBIT (UN)REDEEMED

behind" (106). Film creates a new way of seeing, understanding, and
constructing the world, then, which is also—like the *Popular Encyclopedia*—a means of substituting an alternative world for it; film's
innovative connections and disjunctions can, however, provide no
compensatory meaning for one whose eyes once saw the world
through the hope of heaven. Although movies provide solace to the
soul-afflicted Clarence ("He felt himself fading away, but for the hour
when these incandescent power of the manufactured visions filled
him" [107]), they constitute a merely visual substitute for the spiritual
vision he once knew. (For his granddaughter, Essie, born a decade
after his death, the silver screen constitutes the only human transcendence she can imagine, and her ascendancy to movie stardom briefly
seems to the Wilmot family to redeem Clarence's descent into faithlessness and film escapism from which the ex-minister is never delivered.) At the end of the "Clarence" chapter of *Lilies*, the narrator
abandons the protagonist of the first quarter of the novel with this
doleful summary: "Though he still walked erect, with a touch of the
Wilmot panache, his sandy mustache was so whitened as to scarcely
show in his face—the drained face of an addict [of movies] enduring
his days for the one hour in which he could forget, in a trance as infal-
lible as opium's, his fall, his failure, his disgrace, his immediate responsibilities, his ultimate nullity." The narrator then offers a closing
benediction on Clarence—"Have mercy" (108)—although to whom
it is addressed is never clarified.

    In a very significant human sense, Clarence's loss of faith in 1910
and his subsequent withdrawal from his Presbyterian ministry is the
precipitating cause in the courses of the lives taken by three subsequent generations of Wilmots: in both financial and emotional terms,
the experiences of Teddy, Essie, and Clark are shaped by Clarence's
spiritual descent. Before moving on to more briefly consider the more
secular narratives of Teddy, Essie, and Clark, however, it's important
to understand why Clarence views his loss of faith in the terms that
the narrator characterizes it—as "his fall, his failure, his disgrace."
Early in the novel, Clarence characterizes his faith as something
highly fragile—"Not an invalid, perhaps, so much as an infant he
must tenderly nurture and indulge and take care not to harm" (14–
15). Updike admitted to a similar anxiety about the condition of his
belief in committing to paper a characterization of his "feeble faith"
in his revelatory *New Yorker* essay, "The Future of Faith," as if writing about it might dissolve what belief he had left;[24] a still more significant parallel between Clarence's and Updike's positions is the idea
that human beings are stewards of their belief and personally responsible for its perpetuation or dissolution.

Before his voice gives out on him during his sermon responding to the late Mr. Orr, Clarence reconstructs the notion of election with which his parishioner was preoccupied as a choice rather than as an externally imposed fate. "Those who are condemned to damnation," he struggles to tell his congregation through his afflicted throat, "have already *condemned themselves to non-existence*, as understood in the light of the miraculously full existence which Christ's coming and His redemption has made possible. . . . We must bring something to the new covenant. The mountain has come to us, but we must climb it. He who stands at the base of a mountain and refuses to climb it stands in an abyss. That abyss of non-attainment is Hell" (53). By transforming hell from Orr's punitive pit of nonelection to a bourn of deprivation for those who fail to choose the path of belief, Clarence makes of belief something voluntary, a state that human beings must actively nurture in themselves.

"Election is not a few winners and many losers, as we see about us in this fallen, merciless world," Clarence's sermon continues. "'Election,' he mouthed, 'is winners and non-players. Those who do not accept Christ's great gift of Himself waste away. They become nothing. Election . . . is *choice*. . . . If we cannot feel God's hand gripping ours, it is because'—and now his throat felt catastrophically closed, his breath reduced to a trickle, a wheeze—'we have not reached up, not truly'" (54). The throat affliction that nearly silences him here is, in medical terms, the first stage of the tuberculosis that will kill Clarence ten years later, in 1920; more symbolically, it suggests his spiritual doubts and unbelief seeking to gag his affirmations of faith.[25] Clarence's sermon explicates an early perception he entertains about his loss of belief, one that, like Rabbit's similar experience, is perceived as a loss of manhood: "the failure was his own, an effeminate yielding where virile strength was required. Faith is a force of will whereby a Christian defines himself against the temptations of an age" (18). At the end of the service whose sermon he cannot complete, Clarence wants nothing but to "be alone with his miserable miracle, his glaringly clarified condition" (55). Reversing and redeeming that "glaringly clarified condition" of unbelief is the dramatic burden of the last three chapters of *In the Beauty of the Lilies*.

In writing Clarence's sermonic rejoinder to Orr, Updike created for his minister a theology much closer to his own overall position than those of Orr and Dreaver. "No religion is apt to be founded on cold reason," Updike wrote in "The Future of Faith": "It takes faith out of the equation. Belief, like love, must be voluntary" (90); in *Self-Consciousness*, he suggested that, "When you move toward Christianity it disappeared, as fog solidly opaque in the distance thins to transparency when you walk into it. I decided I, nevertheless, WOULD believe" (230). The notion that faith is a "reaching up," which one can fail to do, is a recurrent element in Updike's work,[26] but as early as the middle 1960s he was already admonishing against the risk of validation failure embedded in that test of faith: "The real God, the God men do not invent, is *Totaliter aliter*—Wholly Other," Updike wrote in a review of Karl Barth's *Anselm: Fides Quaerens Intellectum*: "We cannot reach Him; only He can reach us."[27] Nonetheless, Updike's fiction has been consistently critical of those who never attempt the spiritual reaching out that Clarence advocates: Orson, in "The Christian Roommates," whose envy of his roommate Hub's more intense and intuitive spirituality prompts him, after leaving Harvard, to abandon belief; Piet Hanema in *Couples*, who condemns himself by choosing a creature of the earth—Foxy—over one of the heavens—Angela; Dale Kohler, of *Roger's Version*, who intellectualizes his longing for God to exist by attempting to prove His creation of heaven and earth through computer technology. Citing the book of Matthew in his sermon, Clarence argues that the weeds and fruitless fig tree be pitied, but that "men are not plants, they have minds and souls and free wills, they are responsible for their deeds and the eternal consequences of those deeds. They have *made* themselves chaff if they are so judged when the great farmer comes with his winnowing fan. The tree has made itself fruitless, the weeds . . . have grown where they were not wanted, and have elected themselves to be uprooted and cast away" (51). Clarence's self-condemnation from his own pulpit constitutes one of Updike's fiction's most profound and thoroughly earned dramatic moments, the scene seeming to me to all but single-handedly refute James Wood's argument that "Updike's tranquil aestheticism" renders Clarence's crisis of faith insufficiently evocative of "God's terrible absence from a life."[28]

Updike has consistently argued that "the creative imagination, as I conceive it, is wholly parasitic upon the real world,"[29] and if Clarence's religious crisis is as compelling spiritual drama as I've suggested, its familial, historical source provides partial explanation. In 1896, Updike's paternal grandfather, Hartley Updike, abandoned his ministry in Livonia, Indiana, as a consequence, his 1923 obituary explained, of a throat infection. Updike's treatment of Clarence's throat affliction contains some of the same ambiguity in regard to cause and effect embedded in his description of his grandfather's ailment in *Self-Consciousness*: Updike family lore maintained that Hartley's self-silencing was prompted by a parishioner he overheard saying that his wife would be a better minister than he, and when Clarence fails to make it through a sermon because of a throat constriction produced, clearly, by his sense of lost vocation, his wife takes over for him, winning praise from the congregation she continues to shepherd during Clarence's impairment. Although Updike never suggests that his grandfather abandoned his vocation because of a religious crisis—Hartley Updike's wife ascribed the loss of his parish to the fact that "so much work and worry is attached to the ministry" (S-C, 176)—he nonetheless acknowledges that this event "was a strange little shadow on the religiosity of our family"—one analogous to that suffered by the Wilmots after Clarence's fall. Updike's father, Wesley, was particularly affected: "My father was haunted, I think, by his own father's failure to uphold the faith somehow."[30] Consequently, "a lurid quality attached to my father's memory of his own boyhood . . . ," and he developed "a miserable, helpless pity for his failing father" (S-C, 183).

"I imagined [Hartley Updike's unsuccessful postministerial career in real estate[31]] as a kind of abyss, howling with sadness," Updike acknowledged in Self-Consciousness; "his three children each set themselves to climbing out of the abyss, to 'making good' out of so total a ruin that, in my father's case, it was a two-step process that left it to me to establish, on the platform of his doggedly held place in Shillington, a redemptive prosperity equivalent to [that achieved by Wesley Updike's brother and sister]. Within the kinship network, I am helping carry Hartley to the boat" (S-C, 183).

Eight years intervened between Updike's description of this family history and the publication of Lilies—a period in which his thinking about the familial repercussions of Hartley Updike's relinquishment of his ministry might have undergone significant change. In addition, Lilies is a work of fiction in which Updike was free to transmute family materials for the purposes of drama and theme, and clearly did. Nevertheless, the juxtaposition of these autobiographical and fictional narratives invites the reader to draw highly tentative generational connections between the Updike and Wilmot families, which I'll want to return to while discussing the chapters devoted to the next three generations of Wilmots—Teddy, Essie/Alma, and Clark/Esau/Slick. By this very rough calculus, Wesley Updike corresponds to Teddy Wilmot, the least successful of Clarence's children, whose lack of aspiration is traceable to his having been the Wilmot most traumatized by his father's forswearing of his church and by "the terrible defeated hush of the house after Father's death" (125). For my purposes, the Teddy/Wesley Updike convergence ends there: Updike's portraits of his father in nonfiction (Self-Consciousness) and fiction ("Pigeon Feathers," "Packed Dirt," The Centaur, and "My Father on the Verge of Disgrace" in particular) reflect little of Teddy's extreme diffidence or the qualities that his brother, Jared, ascribes to him: he's like his father, Clarence—"scared of life, happy to die" (150). Teddy's life, clearly, is less a life than a symptom of abreaction to his father's fate. As his wife, Emily tells their daughter, Essie, "I wonder how much [Clarence's] death left your dad able to love anybody else, ever. . . . It's as if after whatever it was that happened he just wants to get through this vale of tears . . . with minimal damage. It's as if he won't give God any satisfaction" (269). In his last days, Clarence cautions his wife, Stella, "Don't let the children fall away [from belief]. Especially Teddy; he's the one that needs it most. He's such a sensitive, fearful child" (152). Teddy exemplifies secularism without poetry; he confronted Updike with the difficult Howellsian challenge of making a thoroughly average American unbeliever a compelling character. In high school, Teddy perceives himself as a "harmless cog, doing his assignments, taking his place at the desk assigned" (114). Once he has graduated, he resolves "to leave the aspiring to others because that should make things easy" (140); his primary strategy for living assumes that it's contribution enough "if you don't make anything worse" (143). He seeks release from the competition and anxiety of his job in a bottle cap factory by going to the movies, though not as his father had. Clarence seeks in the movie palace to lift himself up out of the deep pit into which his life had fallen; Teddy is more menaced by what he sees on the screen, the "garish profusion of life troubling him." Movies, in Teddy's view, "embrace the chaos that sensible men and women in their ordinary life sought to avoid"; "always these films were trying to get you to look over the edge, at something you would rather not see—poverty, war, murder, the thing men and women did when they were alone together" (147). Movies validate his naturalistic conclusion that "we are like a swarm of mosquitoes, crazy with thirst and doomed to be swatted. Life was endlessly cruel, and there was nobody above to grieve—Father had proved that" (147). Hollywood's products, then, fail to divert Teddy, who realizes that "these bright projections were trying to distract him from the leaden reality beneath his seat, underneath the theatre floor. Death and oblivion were down there, waiting for the movie to be over"[32] (148). Teddy's summarized philosophy of life could have provided an epigraph for *Rabbit at Rest*: "Life basically had to be endured. Nature fought for you until it turned against you" (162). Insofar as Teddy constitutes a projection of Updike characteristics, he dramatizes the self Updike describes in *Self-Consciousness*, whose primary goal in life is to stay "out of harm's way." Teddy is the quintessential nonplayer invoked in Clarence's sermon ("'Election,' he mouthed, 'is winners and non-players'"), and it is the reader's sad task to watch this decent, caring, agnostic man fulfill the rest of Clarence's prophecy: "Those who do not accept Christ's great gift of Himself waste away . . ." (54).

When Teddy's mother, aunt, and sister run out of ideas for what their utterly ambitionless relative can do for a living after the factory proves impossible for him to tolerate, the opening of a government position resolves their dilemma: whereas his father delivered spiritual messages, Teddy delivers the mail. Ironically, it is the former postman's two letters to Clark in the final chapter that briefly provide his grandson with a sanely proletarian alternative to the perfervid evangelism of the Temple of True and Actual Faith, but not one compelling enough to save him from the Temple's fate.

For all the bruised agnosticism he carries, Teddy's life is not without its transcendent moments. His love for Emily Sifford, an unlovely woman afflicted with a clubfoot, inspires his first spiritual epiphany: his sudden realization that she is his future leads him to understand that "seeing Emily at the end of a straight road of his life was the closest thing to a religious experience Teddy ever hoped to have" (198). His brother, Jared, cruelly affirms their compatibility by suggesting that Emily and Teddy are both cripples, Teddy, in his estimation, having been one ever since their father's collapse. On their honeymoon, Emily corroborates Jared's characterization of the couple, comparing them to a museum under construction—"a rubble of lumber, worked stone, scaffolding, and ungrassed frozen earth." "It's like us . . . at the beginning," Emily says of the museum. She then pleads with her new husband, "I want to see something complete and perfect" (210). Teddy responds by taking her to the Philadelphia Academy of Fine Arts, but her desire won't be fully gratified until she gives birth, in 1930, to Esther Wilmot. Teddy walks in on Emily shortly after the child is born, finding Emily clutching the baby's feet: "Softly, greedily squeezing, Emily had been taken unawares by her husband; her eyes, with their big movie-star whites, rolled upward to him in a glance of guilty surprise swiftly replaced by a watery plea that he ignore in her worship the something shameful. 'She's perfect,' she said apologetically" (226).[33]

Given how little Essie/Alma's silver screen apotheosis resembles Updike's literary career, the most intriguing life/art conjunction implied by Updike's *Self-Consciousness* comments prefiguring the narrative of *Lilies* is the one that implicitly identifies him with Essie. According to the "two-step process of familial redemption" Updike's memoir delineates, he corresponds to Essie/Alma, who is dramatized in *Lilies* "establish[ing] a redemptive prosperity" through becoming a Hollywood star by himself similarly having ascended from the

American lower middle class to become a nationally known, thoroughly prosperous professional. In concluding my discussion of *Lilies*, I'll argue that, its Calvinist credentials notwithstanding, "redemptive prosperity" is the salvation of neither the Wilmot nor Updike family, but first I need to establish the way in which the "Essie/Alma" chapter encourages the reader to misconstrue Essie/Alma's earthly success as redemption for Clarence's fall.

Teddy's anger at the effect that faith had on his father prompts his utter neglect of spirituality in raising Essie, and the child compensates for this lack by attributing her sense of wonder in her existence to the only God she can imagine: her "dead, unearthly grandfather"—Clarence. "In his unreality," the narrator explains, "he held a promise of lifting her up toward the heavenly realm where movie stars flickered and glowed and from which radio shows, with movie stars as guests, emanated. When Essie prayed to God, she felt she was broadcasting a beam a pleading upward to a brown cathedral-shaped radio and her grandfather was sitting in a chair beside it listening. She would make his sadness up to him" (270–71). Once Essie has become the star she longed to be and has, at her studio's insistence, changed her name to Alma DeMott,[34] Clarence's wife, Essie's grandmother, confirms that Alma has fulfilled the goal of familial redemption she had set for herself. She tells her granddaughter that,

> "When Clarence—when he fell, it was so sudden and uncalled-for, there
>   had to be something to . . ."
> Alma prompts her, "There had to be something to—"
> ". . . To make it come right in the end," Clarence's widow responds.
> "Like in the movies," Alma smiled. (350)

As Updike explained to Dwight Garner, "the hero of *Lilies* is female. She's the one who really reverses the family's destinies and gets to the stars, or as close as you can get to the stars in this life."[35]

As *Lilies* so often dramatizes in its inventory of American spirituality over the course of the twentieth century, the loss of belief in universal order spawns in both Alma and her grandmother a compensatory worship of film images and the reconceiving of human fates in terms of the beginnings, middles, and ends of movies. In Updike's story "The Wallet," the protagonist, Fulham, touches on the same point in recalling those movies "that once had lifted him far out of himself and whose high moments had lingered in millions of brains like his in lieu of religious visions."[36] The process of secularization implicit in the shift of worship from biblical figures to cinematic ones so central to the unfolding narrative of *Lilies* is not without its eschatological retentions: Alma is too oblivious to theology to know that she's enacting a distinctly Calvinist idea in her relationship with a God who exists for her largely as the source of her thoroughly deserved success in the world—like Rabbit, but to a greater extreme, her conviction of God's existence is indistinguishable from the magnitude of self-esteem she's feeling at the moment. For her, God is He who gives Essie what she wants, whose universal plan it is to reinforce her specialness and superiority by rewarding her with ever greater success, and her early career as a model—and later in the movies—reinforces this sense: "She had known as a child she was the center of the universe and now the proof was accumulating, click by click" (280). When she fleetingly worries about God's reaction to the sexual experimentation she precociously enters into with boys, she immediately dismisses the concern by reassuring herself that, "God understood. He made us all" (267)—which offers the same theological argument underlying Rabbit's question, "If God didn't want us to eat salt and fat, why did He make them taste so good?" (1210). Neither of these Christians, clearly, is at all interested in a God who exacts self-denial. Accordingly, making movies, by Essie's lights, is a religious experience, because it reminds her of "when she was a child and God watched over her, recording every prayer and yearning." The movie camera, like God, misses nothing—because, to Alma, everything is surface, everything is material. Criticized for appearing in ads in the back of *Esquire* magazine, Essie's response is, "what's to hide? It's me" (313)—which suggests that "me" is thoroughly a surface manifestation, a body that can be photographed. The first photographer who takes an interest in her encourages this tendency to think of herself as contentlessly photogenic, instructing her at their first photo shoot, "sometimes it's best when you think of nothing" (278). There is, nonetheless, an art to her ultimate craft that impinges on the transcendent: one of her acting coaches tells her that "the audience must know exactly what she is doing—there can be no room for uncertainty or the ambiguous actions we make all the time in life. This clarity makes a refuge for audience and actors alike, lifting them up from everyday reality to a reality more keen and efficient but not less true" (335). Essie's acting coach, obviously, brings a modernist sensibility to his celebration of film, invoking "high moments [that] had lingered in millions of brains . . . in lieu of religious visions."

The one imperfection that Essie admits to having seems an inheritance of her grandfather's life-ending vocal incapacity while replicating an infirmity Updike acknowledges suffering in the "Getting the Words Out" chapter of *Self-Consciousness*: she stutters. The first movie she's allowed to attend by herself, *One Hundred Men and a*

Girl, deals with a singer who saves her band by her singing, art re-deeming life in a way that inspires the pattern Essie chooses for her life to take. The film convinces her that every dream of Deanna Dur-bin's will come true through the power of her pure singing, and she resolves to ask her mother to get her singing lessons so she can save others through having such an icy pure sound—not a stutter—emerge from her face (246). Although she takes singing lessons, they don't eliminate her vocal flaw, which, from her perspective, uncomfortably manifests the existence of a self within herself different from the per-fection of her physical being. Like Updike's stutter (*S-C*, 84–85), hers occurs when she feels herself to be in the wrong, the discomfiture causing her to forget to breathe with her belly. Acting is, once again, the solution: "Painted and oiled and every hair lacquered as firm as the fibres in a hat, Essie felt armored in pretense, formless and safe behind her face, like the filling of a stiff chocolate" (291). She never stuttered with Mr. Bear—her first audience—and "she knew she would never stutter in this painted armor of beauty with which she faced the invisible audience gathering behind those remorseless lights" (291). By the time she's changed her name and become a star, "Alma almost never stutters except when she remembers she is Essie" (324). Acting for Essie corresponds to writing for Updike as he de-scribes it in "Getting the Words Out": they are professional disguises that generate "the freedom conferred by masks," or "*maskenfreiheit*" (*S-C*, 87), artistic facades actress and author can secrete themselves behind through which they never stutter.

When she's a child, Essie's "favorite pictures are the ones in which women"—Sonja Hennie and Ginger Rogers are the actresses she's imagining—"just skim along over everything" (246–47), and she re-mains consistent into her late fifties to this acclaiming of the superfi-cial, drawing inspiration for the enactment of scenes of cinematic tragedy not from her own emotional traumas but from the daily re-versals and existential disappointments of her family and acquain-tances in Basingstoke, Delaware, where she grows up. (The most potent memory she recalls on the set to provoke violent weeping in herself is that of dust-covered Mr. Bear in her Basingstoke attic wait-ing in vain for her to come back, "wondering why that little girl never comes to play with him" [334].) Another irony of the genesis of her stardom is that it is the product of her compelling dramatizations of how trapped Americans are in a reality completely unlike Holly-wood's glamor; Alma tends to be typecast as a woman who dreams big and has paid her dues, someone carrying a "weary, wounded pes-simism." The stardom these cinematic portraits creates raises her above the starmakers' condition, each movie she appears in being a "well-lit spaceship carrying her and the other actors into an immortal safety, beyond change and harm" (335). For her, playing movie roles is a means of staying "out of harm's way." (The Updike parallel again functions: "The fabricated truth of poetry and fiction," Updike wrote in *Self-Consciousness*, "makes a shelter in which I feel safe, sheltered within interlaced plausibilities in the image of a real world for which I am not to blame. Such writing is in essence pure" [231].) Occasionally, Alma has no control over the process that generates her liftoff, and she must depend on her amorphously defined God to make the magic happen. "Sometimes, when she couldn't locate through a tedious succession of takes what the director wanted," the narrator comments, "she would shut down her memories and think of nothing, and something from God would flow into her face from behind, and Zinneman or Wilder or Walter Lang would cry out from the darkness around her, 'That's it! You've knocked it, Alma. Print!'" (336).

It is probably coincidental that the directors' phrase of radiant, ecstatic closure—"that's it!"—is the same one Rabbit uses on the golf course with Eccles in *Run* in exultantly assuring him that he's just witnessed the visualization of the "something that wants me to find it." Nonetheless, there is something of the same theophanic quality to both moments, and these religious instants have another highly significant element in common: the faith they materialize is impossible to pass down to the believers' children. The subjective, intuitive, and markedly egocentric beliefs of Rabbit and Alma—both of whom experience God most intensely through rainstorms—are too self-focused to communicate to others, and therefore both Nelson Angstrom and Alma's only son, Clark, grow up in a godless world. Nelson "has not been raised to believe in anything higher than his father's head" (*Redux*, 548), and Clark's complete lack of mothering (Alma is too busy cultivating her dimming stardom to be a parent to him) includes a complete spiritual dereliction. Jesse Smith, the novel's evangelical radical, has a good sense of Alma's relationship with her God: "Your mother was perhaps jealous of her God and did not wish to share him with the world, even with her son" (383). Nelson, as we've seen, becomes an unconscious Oedipal avenger of the choice that Harry makes following Becky's death that "we've kind of let all that"—Christianity—"go": the form his self-destructive revenge for Jill's drug-induced death takes, ironically, is his becoming himself a cocaine addict, his habit costing Harry the Toyota franchise, which has been the source of his midlife prosperity and equanimity. Until "Rabbit Remembered," so confused is Nelson by his directionless, value-lacking upbringing that he doesn't even fully understand how

completely the meaning of his life is summarized in a phrase his father
intimates to his mother: "The kid has it in for me" (685). Clark's
wounds from the parental vacancy he experienced go deeper still as
he unconsciously works his way toward replicating Nelson's role of
the redemptive avenging son—though he, hardly knowing his father,
will avenge himself on a father not his own.

In describing his largely absent mother, Clark is consistently item-
izing qualities he doesn't share with her: her face could "look homely
or tired, but she never lacked life, a kind of hungriness he could never
blame her for, it was so simple and innocent" (363). He lacks both her
energy and her hunger, and in his sense that human possibilities have
been exhausted before he had a chance to define himself, recalls Updike's recounting of his relationship with his parents in *Midpoint*:

> My parents, my impression was,
> had acted out all parts on my behalf;
>
> their shouting and their silences
> in the hissing bedroom dark
> scorched the shadows; a ring of ashes
>
> expanded with each smoldering remark
> and left no underbrush of fuel
> of passion for my intimidated spark. (8)

Clark's self-effacement and passivity thus reminds his uncle, Jared, of
Teddy—"always fearful and feeling sorry for everyone, himself foremost."[37] Like his grandfather, Clark is harmless looking, bland (414),
and therefore has ever felt himself out of place in the Hollywood in
which he grew up, where surface beauty is everything. Never having
heard about Teddy, Jesse Smith will describe Clark as the first person
in history without a powerful story to tell, "the first soul that God
left totally empty of eternal possibilities" (378). The narrator sums up
Clark's complete spiritual dislocation as an epitome of secularism, of
spirituality reduced to mere morbidity: "He didn't know what to believe—he only knew he was going to die someday" (408). Clark is
very much the spiritual "empty shack" that the false Christ drifter,
Jesse Smith, will find so easy to inhabit.

Clark's adolescence-spanning disaffection reaches a literal climax
following an evening of glimmertown indulgence in 1984: he has
downed four vodka and orange cocktails and done some cocaine lines
in the men's room in a club populated by "these identical fascist
surfer types with great tans and studded leather vests and close-
cropped blond hair standing around like bit parts from *Blade Runner*,

zombies invading from the super-queer cool future" (429). Demoralized by his evening, Clark returns home, exchanges testy words with his mother and a business connection she's attempting to seduce to further her career, and retires to his room, where he lights a joint and masturbates to a generic "French maid" pornographic video. After ejaculating on himself, he decides, "God, people are disgusting," and resolves to get out of Los Angeles, out of reach of the fucking movies (434). Hollywood has taught him that women "are a trap—like drugs, like booze, like fame," and he consequently leaves the West Coast for the "God's country [that] people called Colorado" (365).

Clark's two-decade immersion in the egocentricity and corruptness of the movie capital has primed him to embrace—albeit somewhat numbly—the first embodiment of antisecularism he encounters, Jesse Smith. Updike's fictionalization of David Koresh and the Branch Davidian holocaust continues *Lilies'* reproduction of American history, while allowing him to reproduce the dramatic situation he created between Rabbit and Skeeter in *Redux*—the juxtapositon of the desire for spirituality encountering a crazed embodiment of it. "Clark could not remember when he decided to believe in Jesse," the narrator comments, invoking Clarence's view that belief is a decision: "the big man had just stepped into him like a drifter taking over an empty shack. In Jesse's presence he felt possessed of a value he possessed nowhere else—not in the presence of his mother, to whom motherhood had been an interruption of her real life, nor of any of those to whom he was, foremost, his mother's son. . . . He could not project for himself the moment of conversion; in one frame he was on the outside . . . and in the next he was inside, unable to leave, tied by gravity to this savior's unpredictable orbit" (399).

Alma's indifference to Clark, clearly, has left him "an empty shack" the charismatic drifter can move into; that Clark's conversion experience is likened to a film in which the decisive moment has been edited out suggests how very little control he has over his spiritual life. Clark's bitterness toward the Hollywood that deprived him of a mother makes him particularly vulnerable to Smith's argument that the movies are a Mephisthophelean secular expropriation of God's kingdom: "The color was overwhelmingly glorious, and such a wealth of attention was paid to every detail that you thought you were looking upon reality itself. The devil's work is lovingly done—give Satan his due" (380). Clark turns out to be an extremely passive Jesse Smith follower, never explicitly affirming the community's evangelical creed to the satisfaction of other adherents, who dub him Esau, meaning "rube," and gaining a place among the Lower Branch faithful largely by serving them in a public relations capacity for which briefly held jobs in Hollywood have prepared him. His neophyte's name isn't completely derogatory, however, for, as the narrator remarks of the millennialists who preceded Jesse's followers, "rubes are accustomed to disappointment, and the Millerite sect trickled on without Miller, twisting and splitting and arriving in one of its rivulets at the sensation in Jesse Smith's balding head that God was about to act through him" (398). Significantly, Clark proves incapable of joining the Temple faithful when they engage in glossolalia: "Esau tried to let the voices in him speak, but something watchful in his head, that little motionless sardonic spectator, though shrunk to the size of a computer chip, prevented it" (452). That sardonic spectator, a remnant of his Hollywood cynicism that typically distances Clark from his experiences by making them all seem like scenes from an interior movie running in his head, becomes, ironically, responsible for Clark's two religious experiences in the novel.

The first of these occurs in the incident corresponding to the "search and arrest" assault of the Bureau of Alcohol, Tobacco, and Firearms against the Branch Davidians on February 28, 1993. As he watches one of the policemen who has entered the compound, "Not only was Clark's head suddenly as clear as an adjusted TV screen, but his eyesight too: he could see the buckle on the cop's belt and the shine on his boots and the duller black gloss of his empty holster. Esau held the bead [of the Ruger he is gripping] steady just above that holster and squeezed off a round" (446). The comparison of Clark's clear-sightedness to a TV screen invokes his American middle-class media-inflected past; the fact that Esau fires at a state patrolman suggests how strongly Jesse's evangelicism has affected him. But Jesse has already warned Clark that the clearest and most compelling visions of reality can be clever illusions—"devil's work"—and in his second religious experience of "hyperclarity," Clark will redeem this error.

Clark's willingness to murder Gog's agents for the True and Only Faith notwithstanding, the community's suspiciousness toward his commitment to them increases when his decision to let the Lower Branch children attend a secular school culminates in one of the children returning to the encampment with a class handout endorsing Darwinism. The most substantial sermon Updike writes for Jesse attacks those who seek a middle way—as Clark sought to do in accommodating Colorado education statutes—and affirms the power of faith in much the same terms that Kruppenbach does in *Run*, though Jesse's reasons for affirming it suddenly turn deeply sinister: "Christ said it, faith as small as a grain of mustard seed will see you through, but only faith. Oh my faithful friends, when that cup comes, drink ye all of it. Though it be hot as molten lead, you wash it right down" (477). The faith Jesse is invoking here is faith in himself—faith in his insistence that the believers of the True and Actual Faith ingest poison in imitation of him in order to escape Gog—his version of the government that Koresh termed "Babylon." More than Koresh ever seems to have been, Jesse is committed to precipitating the "day of wrath" which will winnow the chosen down to 144,000, and thus he is the clear instigator of the holocaust that levels his compound. Jesse's escalating Christ complex derives from Koresh's final days' self-identification as the Lamb of God, but it differs in that Updike has, in his depiction of Jesse, omitted significant characteristics of Koresh that make him such an ambiguous figure, and has also underplayed the issues of the FBI's handling of the Branch Davidian episode by presenting it from the perspective of one inside the compound. Koresh's claim that, in the last days before the April 19 holocaust, he was waiting for a message from God before bringing the Branch Davidians out isn't included in Updike's version, which translates Jesse into an armament-obsessed psychotic whose clear goal is to make certain that the members of the True and Only Temple not survive the confrontation with Gog. The ambiguity of whether the BTFA or Branch Davidians ignited the fatal fire at Mt. Carmel is similarly eliminated in *Lilies*: it is part of Jesse's plan that the buildings of the compound be torched as soon as the federal agents arrive. Once the fire is set according to Jesse's plan, Clark attempts to lead a group of women and children to their deaths, and as he does so, he "could not get it out of his head that the insulting, billowing, insinuant, ubiquitous smoke was a person, a malevolent soul with a mind" (481). That malevolent soul is Jesse, whose final Bible study session with his flock gets cut short when his voice gives out. The silencing of Clarence is about to be avenged and redeemed through Clark's extermination of the voice of this unambiguously "malevolent soul."[38]

As Clark leads the Temple's women and children through the smoke, he decides that "in a few minutes they would all be out of this into the icy-cool clarity of Heaven," but his ensuing description of their celestial destination shows how impossible it is for him to separate heaven from Hollywood: paradise would be "gold and blue and jasper, with marble stairs and still lakes and the women drifting about in tiaras and silken gowns falling in parallel folds like Elizabeth Taylor in a movie whose name he had forgotten" (482). The remainder of Clark's brief time on earth continues this hapless intermixing of the eschatological and the cinematic: the point here is that we can't imagine eternal bliss that isn't embedded with corny scenes from movies' version of perfection. Tinseltown static notwithstanding, Clark undergoes his second, Hollywood-inflected but nonetheless genuine religious experience.

Clark's religious epiphany is precipitated by Mehetebel, a new member of the commune, fainting from the smoke. "A flock of sparkling dark immaterial bubbles descended into Esau," the narrator explains, recalling the "sparkling bubbles escaping upward" (3) that heralded Clarence's loss of belief, "and he knew what to do. He felt his physical body existing within that hyperclarity that for years had come and gone in his head." Although Clark's hyperclarity enters him thoroughly imbued with movie imagery, its outcome in action is one that Updike's novel unambiguously affirms. Mehetebel's faint recalls Mary Pickford's swoon at the opening of the novel, the implication being that, just as Pickford's faint was simultaneous with Clarence's loss of faith in God, Mehetebel's faint is coincident with the moment of hyperclarity in which Clark relinquishes his faith in Jesse. When Jesse sees Clark take another believer's gun from him, he encourages him to use the weapon on the believers: "Take 'em to Heaven, Slick! Big Daddy needs his girls!" Repudiating the second nickname Jesse had given him in acknowledgment of his PR skills, Clark responds, "'Slick . . . you fucker, I'll give you Slick,' and shot the false prophet twice . . ." (484).

There is no attempt made by the narrator to mitigate the judgment that Jesse is a "false prophet," the novel having increasingly dramatized how much his ministry has been about elevating himself to the position of messianic figure and how little concern he has shown for his followers save insofar as they can serve him as objects of proselytizing or sexually as wives. Lest the reader miss the point of Clark's tergiversatory epiphany, Updike reinforces it once Jesse lies dead at Clark's feet: "He yelled at the women, 'For God's sake, you idiotic bitches, get out! It's over. Git! Git!' He cried with his inspired certainty, 'Can't you see there's nothing here any more? Those people outside are your friends!'" (485). Updike is equally explicit about the reality of Clark's recognition that he is about to die and the religious certainty that accompanies that recognition: "There was nothing for him on the outside now, just hassle, and embarrassment for Mother. Whoremongers, sorcerers, the whole pack of supercilious shits. He wasn't worried; the living God had laid hold of him, the present tense God beyond betting on" (486). This is as unambiguously religious a moment as Updike's fiction contains, following as it does on the invocation of a pattern in history involving two faintings, and two parallel and compensatory moments of faith relinquished. Clearly, Clark isn't aware that God declined Updike's invitation to appear in *Lilies*: nowhere else in Updike's fiction does an otherworldly sanction of perceived truth seem so absolute and unequivocal.

Clark is, however, too much a man of his time and place to sustain such eschatological certainty through to the moment of his death, and when Jack, a convert from American postmodern secularism whose faith in Jesse has always been as fragile as Clark's, approaches him through the smoke with his rifle drawn, Clark imagines he hears a "cup settling on a saucer," suggesting that the "bitter cup" of which Jesse spoke so often has come around to him, or which might be the sound of the bolt of a rifle being stealthily slipped back. Clark's final thought as he awaits the bullet derives from the movies: *"Go ahead and shoot,"* he recalls Humphey Bogart telling Ingrid Bergman in *Casablanca, "You'll be doing me a favor."*

Despite the inevitable intrusion of Hollywood scripts upon such sacred moments, *In the Beauty of the Lilies,* I'm arguing, affirms the existence of religious epiphany:[39] the novel reinforces the idea we've seen in Updike's work numerous times that truth is the closest that human beings can come to knowing God, and suggests that Clark's response to his experience of truth—that of killing the "false prophet"—is an act of redemptive violence. (Seventy-four people died on April 19 at Waco;[40] in Updike's fictionalizing of that event, Clark manages to save all but one of the unarmed believers before dying himself. Fiction, in this case, is much less lethal and distinctly more unambiguous than fact.) Clark's subjective religious experience is not, however, where *Lilies* ends.

Alma has appeared in Colorado during the weeks of the standoff, largely because the media circus attending the event gives her endless opportunities to be interviewed about her son's situation but also about her film stardom and Hollywood. She has reached sixty and no longer maintains her youthful belief in celluloid's capacity to render her deathless: "what had once seemed to her absolute immortality turned out to be a slow dissolution within a confused mass of perishing images like a colorful mountain of compressed rotting garbage" (465). She still maintains her belief in the God who made her a star, however, and is convinced that He is still favoring her in resolving the Lower Branch saga the way He does. During the standoff, she prays to Him, *"Do the impossible, Lord, for him, as you have done for me. Rescue [Clark] from that terrible house. Reach down, so that none but I can see. I will not tell. Let me love You again"* (468). (Alma's notion of prayer here is clearly modeled on her star's negotiations with a studio head like Harry Cohn: she demands special considerations based on their past relationship, then promises favors for the mogul's agreement to the deal's terms.) Once she learns of Clark's death in the conflagration, Alma becomes certain that God has answered her prayer so that none but she can see by writing her a Hollywood ending only a thoroughly unloving mother could love. She has to look in the mirror to determine whether the tears she forces from her eyes are sincere or not, and then, "Tears achingly welled from beneath her closed lids. While her eyelids were still shut she prayed in the blood-tinged darkness they made, *Thank you, Lord, for letting my son be a hero in the end*" (488). Clark's martyrdom will help her stalled career—that is why she is grateful.

In Basingstock, Delaware, where Clark as a child sometimes visited his grandfather, there is no more awareness of God's intercession in Clark's life than there is in Alma's self-serving take on the Long Branch consummation. Teddy, Clark's grandfather, is watching the evening news, and "it shook him up, too, a Wilmot shot to death and charred to cinders out in some Godforsaken nowhere out west" (489). He has talked to Alma, feeling sad for her when she sobbed as she hadn't since she lost the Miss Delaware Peach contest, and he is clearly moved by Clark's death as well. But Teddy is in his eighties, and what he sees on television, not all of which penetrates his increasing deafness, doesn't make complete sense to him. "Some nights he gets to watching the comedies, one after another" the narrator points out; "they run together as he bobs in and out of sleep." Sitting next to him in his wife Emily's chair on this evening is his cleaning woman, Farrah, and "it's as if Em [who died by 1988] is sitting right there, if he doesn't make a mistake and look" (490–91). In a letter to Clark written during the early days of the standoff, Teddy summed up his life with this benediction: "I didn't expect anything of dying, but then I never expected too much of life. That way, you can't be too disappointed. I got more than I expected, it turned out. Em and the Postal Department were mighty good to me" (418). By the end of the novel, this remarkably clear-sighted man who had once believed that "we are like a swarm of mosquitoes, crazy with thirst and doomed to be swatted" (147) is able sincerely to affirm his life, but his affirmation is indistinguishable from the mental disorientation that makes it difficult for him to completely grasp that the reason he is so saddened by what he sees is because it is his family's history that he is watching come to an end on Tom Brokaw's *NBC News*.[41]

The generic heroism that the broadcast has ascribed to Clark, and that Teddy seems vaguely to comprehend, contains no hint of the spiritual epiphany that precipitated it: from the *NBC News* audience's perspective, all that happened on this day is that a mad religious zealot died at the hands of one of his followers, who saved others of the faith through an act of self-sacrifice. Clark has eliminated the "false prophet," but has left behind no trace of the existence of "the living God [who] had laid hold of him, the present-tense God beyond betting on" (486). The transforming element of the event, in other words, is precisely what history fails to record; falsehood, embodied in Jesse

Smith, has been destroyed, but spiritual truth has slipped away. History will remain silent on the transcendent event that is Clark's sacrificial death, because only Clark feels the "inspired certainty" with which he acted, and which dies with him. The alternative spiritual reading of this incident—that Clark has silenced the devil that silenced his grandfather—is an interpretation of Lower Branch's outcome only Clarence's son, with his knowledge of his father's fall, might generate, and Teddy is too mentally befuddled by age and senility to make the connection. History records "only a *here* and a *there*," in Alf Clayton's terms; what it leaves out is what we most desperately seek to know: whether or not "there is a *why* to it."

Teddy's affectless conflations of his life and the images of television comprise *In the Beauty of the Lilies'* final comment on history: history, the conclusion of the novel dramatizes, is no more enduring than the perspicacity of its perceiver, and *Lilies* closes in the point of view of a mournful man at the end of his life for whom his past, commercials, and the death of his grandson are mulched together into something like what Alma understands her film career to have constituted—"a confused mass of perishing images like a colorful mountain of compressed rotting garbage." As the dust jacket copy of the novel suggests, *Lilies* ends "in Lower Branch, Colorado, and on television." "What does our Lamb Jesus Christ say in Gethsemane?" Jesse Smith asks in his final scripture study session. "He says, 'My soul is exceeding sorrowful, even unto death: tarry ye here, and watch with me'" (476). *In the Beauty of the Lilies* is as pervaded by that sorrowfulness as is *Rabbit at Rest*, but surpasses it in desolation because the novel so profoundly dramatizes how unlikely we are to recognize religious epiphany when we see it—in life or on television.

8

A Contentious Spirit: "Rabbit Remembered"

> As one supernatural connection after another fails, the chain of
> ancestors and descendants—the transcendent entity of family—
> offers to solace us. But the dissolution of ego, which family de-
> mands, is just what we fight.
>
> —Ben Turnbull in *Toward the End of Time*

THE DISTANCE BETWEEN *RABBIT, RUN* AND "RABBIT REMEMBERED"
might best be summarized through the contrast of the epigraph of the
first novel and the sentence cited in the novella that might have served
well as an epigraph for it. The Pascal fragment prefacing *Rabbit,
Run*—"The motions of grace, the hardness of the heart; external circumstances"—invokes unresolved tensions, spiritual dissonances: it
isn't even clear whether the central "hardness of the heart" refers to
spiritual perseverance or insensitivity to others, both of which can be
ascribed to Harry Angstrom in the novel. It is clear that the realities
on either side of the "hardness of the heart" are at odds with each
other, requiring that "hardness" to even bring them into the remote
relationship with each other projected here. The Pascal epigraph, Updike told Jeff Campbell, "in its darting, fragmentary, zigzaggy form
fits the book, which also has a kind of zigzaggy shape, settles on no
fixed point. . . ."[1] "Rabbit Remembered" bears no epigraph, but a
book that Nelson's stepfather, Ronnie Harrison, gives Nelson for a
Christmas present contains a sentence that Nelson cites approvingly
to Annabelle at the narrative's close and that effectively telescopes the
dramatic dynamic of Updike's "Sequel" to the Rabbit novels. The
book is *The Art of Happiness*, by the Dalai Lama; the sentence is "The
very motion of our life is toward happiness."

It's difficult to imagine a less apposite prefatory sentence to a
"Rabbit" work than this assurance of the Dalai Lama's, but "Rabbit
Remembered" is, even more than *Rich*, the sunniest of the Rabbit series—so upbeat, in fact, that the novella occasionally runs the risk of
overachieving plot consonances and of thereby trivializing the tetral-

ogy it sequelizes. Typical of the novella's will-to-closure and its intention to tie up "Rabbit" ends is the tacit aptness of Ronnie Harrison's gift to Nelson.

Relations between stepfather and stepson are strained because, on Thanksgiving, Nelson walks out of the home he has shared with Janice and Ronnie since his separation from Pru because of Ronnie's abusive behavior toward Nelson's stepsister, Annabelle Byer, whom Nelson wants to include in his family and whom Ronnie prefers to exclude because she is Rabbit's daughter by Ruth. Ronnie's Dalai Lama present, consequently, is an obvious chastening of Nelson's disdain for Christianity, Ronnie's way of prodding a spiritual lack in his stepson. In buying the Dalai Lama's book, however, Ronnie has no idea that, as Harry tells Thelma in *Rest*, "I always kind of identified with him. He's about my age. I like to keep track of the guy. I have a gut feeling this'll be his year" (1236). From the time of his first flight south in *Run* when both he and the spiritual leader of Tibet are understood to be missing, Harry feels a kinship to this figure whose relationship to his divinity helps Rabbit in *Rest* understand the centrality of self to his own religious impulses: "the Dalai Lama," Rabbit decides there, "can no more resign godhead than Harry can resign selfhood" (1317). For readers unfamiliar with Rabbit's spiritual identifications, Updike explicates the connection by having Nelson immediately associate Ronnie's gift with the ex-Mt. Judge basketball teammate whom, although dead, Ronnie loathes: "Nelson is startled because, in unwrapping, the saintly Asian on the jacket at first peek suggests his late father, not so much physically as in the aura of sly assertiveness, a tentative tricky loveable something in the guarded smile" (330). Rabbit's "tricky loveable something" is constantly remembered in this novella, Updike's last visit to Diamond County, but the real purpose of this final return to Brewer is to dramatize two issues that *Rest* left gapingly unresolved: Nelson's relationship with the woman whom the dying Ruth Leonard, in the interim between *Rest* and "Remembered," revealed to be his half-sister, and his relationship with his father's memory. The resolutions of these relationships may, admittedly, somewhat too neatly fulfill the Dalai Lama's prophecy that "the very motion of our life is toward happiness"; the novella clearly seeks to confer Updike's benediction upon these characters who have played such an important role in his literary career and perhaps seeks, too, to leaven the bleak tetralogy close of *Rest*. Updike's benediction concludes on the same question with which *Redux* ends—"OK?"—except that in "Remembered" Updike seems to have attempted to elide the question mark.

Is family life sufficient compensation for the loss of belief in anything transcending the human? Janice thinks so: "Like Ronnie said," she thinks in "Rabbit Remembered," "we're alone. All we have is family, for what it's worth."[2] Nelson seems to think so. When his childhood friend Billy Fosnacht over lunch launches into a confession of his agonizing fears of death, Nelson responds, "It's a concept the mind isn't constructed to accept. So stop trying to force it to. Come on, eat. Enjoy. Have I told you, Billy, I've discovered I have a sister? No, I'm not kidding" (327). For the man who casually and consistently sacrifices his wife and children to his cocaine addiction in *Rest*, family has become in "Rabbit Remembered" the antidote to the dread of mortality. Harry's sister Mim, in whom many of Harry's anticommunal impulses live on, expresses surprise at the sudden commitment to the family Annabelle has inspired in Nelson: "You're quite a family man, Nelson, I don't know where you get it from. The Springer side, I guess. They were good Germans. The Angstroms never quite fit in"[3] (273).

Ben Turnbull's equivocal affirmation of family that provides the epigraph for this chapter delineates the reasons that family has become so important to Nelson, who "has not been raised to believe in anything above his father's head" (*Redux*, 548) and who was never afforded glimpses of the "transactions with the unseen world" that flickeringly illuminated Harry's existence. In "Remembered," Updike is dealing with characters who largely lack the spiritual dimension that animates and may even justify Rabbit Angstrom: the reduced and depleted world of "Remembered" recalls the Brewer reality that Updike invokes through Harry's eyes at the end of *Redux*:

> These mundane surfaces had given witness to his life; this cup had held his blood; here the universe had centered, each downtwirling maple seed of more account than galaxies. No more. Jackson Road seems an ordinary street anywhere. Millions of such American streets hold millions of lives, and let them sift through, and neither notice nor mourn, and fall into decay, and do not even mourn their own passing but instead grimace at the wrecking ball with the same gaunt facades that have outweathered all their winters. (590)

Streets sustaining lives drained of meaning, lives for which the best that can be said is that those living them are joylessly surviving—this is the diminished, deflated world of "Remembered," and the novella struggles to find in it the potential for a positive ending.

Janice's interior monologue exposes her flaccid agnosticism—she "has never not believed in a God of some sort but on the other hand never made a thing out of it like Mother or in his weird way Harry"

(210)—while Nelson's rehab-inspired view of things convinces him that "living to the next hit, the next scrounged blow-out, gives [addicts'] lives a point. Being clean exposes you to life's having no point" (266). Through Janice, Nelson, Pru, Annabelle, and Billy Fosnacht, Updike is trying hard to answer that question about the redemptiveness of family life in the affirmative,[4] but the narrative's warmth sometimes feels forced, and, despite the familial reunion and "movement toward happiness" on which the novella closes, it is difficult not to suspect that the uncompellingness of the novella's affirmation of family is as much a product of the withdrawal from the Rabbit saga of the only character who could imagine anything beyond the redeeming family as Updike's career-long ambivalence about the value of family. Significantly, many of the best moments in "Rabbit Remembered" seem not dramatizations of the virtues of family but products of the anarchic, antifamilial spirit of Harry Angstrom precipitated by his acts in the novels or living on in his son.

Before discussing how the survivors fare in post-Rabbit Brewer, I want briefly to address the challenge with which a Rabbit novella lacking Rabbit confronted Updike. Updike has argued that one of the strengths of the novel is that it allows the novelist "the potential of getting out of the hero's head and into someone else's," and he described *Run* as an "exercise in viewpoint" in which the perspectives of Ruth, Eccles, and Janice are presented in addition to the prevailing third-person limited perspective of Rabbit.[5] The novels subsequent to *Run* devote substantially less print to competing perspectives, and it seems fair to suggest that Updike had difficulty granting the other characters in the tetralogy the depth of insight and complexity of consciousness that is Harry's protracted four-novel-long religio/comedic meditation. The Rabbit novels are, of course, fully plotted works of fiction, but, as I've tried to show, what is most remarkable about them is less their continuing fable than their creation of thirty years of impressions, of one American's interior monologue and thoroughly subjective act of witness. Elizabeth Hardwick's description of what was a trilogy when she reviewed it effectively conveys this aspect of the novels: "Rabbit Angstrom is created out of recalcitrant materials, the high school basketball court and finally the Toyota dealership in Brewer. . . . But in Updike there are no staccato moments; it unwinds and unwinds, scene after scene, a long flow of attention and feeling."[6] Harry's "inner sense of himself," the narrator of *Rest* comments, "is of an innocuous passive spirit, a steady small voice, that doesn't want to do any harm, get trapped anywhere, or ever die" (1395); the voice of these novels dies with Harry, the withdrawal of the densely interrogatory textures of his witnessing leaving behind characters who have largely been the agents of architecture, plot. What remains, then, is not the mystery of whither goes humanity, but questions instead of what happens to Nelson and Janice and Annabelle. Of none of these characters could Updike have said what he did about Harry in 1990: that "Rabbit is good enough for me to like him. I've liked him for more than a thousand pages, and I like him because he's alive. When I put him on paper, he talks and walks, and acts like a character."[7] He acts like a character, I'd add, the "wandering thread of [whose] feelings leads" enough of somewhere to keep readers emotionally engaged for nearly fifteen hundred pages of prose, and whose tragically declining "transactions with the unseen world" (201) constitute the primary energy of that fascination.

Without Harry and his furtive sensations of the invisible and religious sense of Brewer as the magical site that spawned him, the Diamond County world Updike creates in "Remembered" seems diffuse and lacking in resonance: it becomes a familiar working-class American city populated by people who do some things and say many more but who would never understand the concept that Rabbit embodies of "salvation by sensibility." "Rabbit," Updike suggested in the *Rabbit Angstrom* introduction, "is like [Dostoevsky's] Underground Man, *incorrigible*; from first to last he bridles at good advice, taking direction only from his personal, also incorrigible God."[8] As protagonist of "Remembered," Nelson has only the anonymous "higher power" of twelve-step programs to place faith in, and if he isn't so secular as to constitute an exception to Updike's claim that, "My heroes, at least, are all struggling for some kind of inner certitude, illumination, or something,"[9] he isn't completely unlike Alma's son, Clark, in *Lilies*, who has for religious sensibility the fact that "he didn't know what to believe—he only knew he was going to die someday" (408). The characters in "Remembered," like Teddy in *Lilies*, invoke Updike's musing in his interview with T. M. McNally and Dean Stover shortly before he began writing *Rabbit at Rest*: "You wonder in a way, why write about people if they're just bundles of neurons and cartilage and going to live and die just like the other chickens in the yard?"[10] This novella, with its distinctly "feel-good" ending and prevailing will to closure, seeks to find something to affirm in the living on of the survivors of the Rabbit tetralogy, and that something seems initially to be what Rabbit initially ran from, what Nelson has also repeatedly fled, and what Updike's fiction has consistently depicted in the most ambivalent terms—family. If that dramatic trajectory in "Remembered" seems somewhat unpersuasive, it's because Nelson's more significant reconciliation with his father in the narrative takes the form of his embracing what for Harry had been a nearly sacred covenant—his commitment to the truth—and repudiating that element of his father's character that had marred Nelson's—and Annabelle's—life.

Arguably, the greatest challenge for Updike in writing this sequel—working with a protagonist he characterized as a "relatively humane but sort of sodden guy"[11]—was transforming Nelson into a compelling source of drama. At best, in *Run* and *Redux* he's a child victim of what Elizabeth Hartwick termed his parents' "domestic vagrancy": he is "the wounded, helpless, indignant witness" of Harry's and Janice's wanderings, as Updike described him.[12] The adult he has grown into in *Rich* and *Rest* has translated his victimization by his father—he never blames Janice for her *Redux* abandonment of him and his father for Charlie Stavros—into a justification for every failure he commits and personality flaw he possesses. (Accordingly, Janice is writing him a blank check for all future behavioral excesses in suggesting, after Pru and Harry have slept together in *Rest*, that Nelson can't be held responsible for any subsequent act he commits given this outrage his father has committed against him.) As I've suggested, Nelson in large part exacts from his father "the price Harry has to pay for being himself": he is a sort of son-as-superego who smashes up the cars Harry loves to sell at Springer Motors, unwittingly stymies Harry's bedding down with Cindy Murkett in the Caribbean by fleeing his pregnant wife in Brewer to run back to Kent State, and sucks the Toyota franchise up his nose through his cocaine addiction. When in *Rich* Melanie tells Nelson it's not his father's fault that Nelson is psychologically damaged, Nelson insists, "It *is*. . . . Everything's his fault . . . and he enjoys it, the way he looks at me sometimes you can tell that he's really eating it up, that I'm fucked up" (742). Nelson's complete unwillingness to take responsibility for the petulant complainer he evolves into—"it's not fair!" is his tetralogy-spanning mantra—renders him insufferable in *Rich*, and his becoming more "fucked up" on drugs in *Rest* augments his negative qualities, necessitating his rehabilitation at the end of that novel, followed by his potential redemption in "Remembered." Family is the star to which he somewhat equivocally hitches his wagon of self-redemption.

In a despondent moment in *Rest*, Harry briefly loses interest in the idea that he has fathered a daughter other than Becky, thinking of his *Rich* hope that Ruth spared his child "as an old story, as a song on the radio nobody's listening to" (1302). In the novel's final scene, however, he wants to tell Nelson, "*you have a sister*," but manages to convey only the word "sister," so that Nelson thinks his father is referring to Mim, who is en route to Brewer from Las Vegas. "If something does not soon happen to her," Harry thinks earlier of

Annabelle in *Rest*, "hers will become a silly empty face. Innocence will dull down into stupidity" (1313). It is Nelson's goal in "Remembered" to become the something that prevents Annabelle's from becoming that face, to make family redemptive for his half-sister by drawing her into his. That mission is complicated by his own reservations about family, his conviction that his father and Aunt Mim loved each other "with the heavy helplessness of blood, that casts us into a family as if into a doom" (272). By the time he has dedicated himself to his mission, however, family has acquired an even more negative aura in the novella.

The affirmation of family gets off to a bad start in "Remembered" when the first two words of the narrative identify the woman answering the doorbell at 89 Joseph Street as Janice Harrison. It is difficult to read Janice's widowhood-terminating marriage to Ronnie Harrison as confirmation of anything but Rabbit's oft-repeated unflattering characterization of her: she's dumb. Harry's consistently negative estimation of Ronnie is, of course, colored by their adolescent rivalry on the Mt. Judge high school basketball team, and by his inability to forgive Ronnie for having had Ruth sexually before Harry did; the fact that he's been cuckolding Ronnie with Thelma from the end of *Rich* to the end of Thelma's life adds an element of guilt, exacerbating the antipathy and contempt he feels for Ronnie. Consequently, Harry is anything but a neutral perceiver of Ronnie's character. Nonetheless, there seems clearly to be a judgment being passed on Janice's loyalty in "Remembered" for marrying the man Harry views as "just about his least favorite person in the world," the Brewerite who, all of Harry's life, has been "shadowing Harry with his ugly flesh, a reminder of everything sweaty and effortful in life Harry had hoped squeamishly to glide over and avoid" (1327). "Ronnie is always there," Harry thinks later in *Rest*, "like the smelly underside of his own body, like the Jockey underpants that get dirty every day" (1393). More significant than Harry's tendency to construe Ronnie as "body" to his "soul" is the fact that Harry's negative estimation of Ronnie is consistently validated by Ronnie's actions throughout "Remembered."

Despite referring to Annabelle as a "twat" and "con artist" who is the product of Harry's having "screwed this dead cow back in the dark ages," Ronnie agrees to Nelson's half-sister being invited to the Harrison family Thanksgiving. Provoked by alcohol and the familial tensions underlying this ill-advised Angstrom/Harrison reunion, Ronnie becomes increasingly irritable with Annabelle's defense of the Clinton administration during dinner, and peevishly confronts her as they're doing dishes. She asks him what her mother had been like when Ronnie knew her; he replies, "She'd fuck anybody." Then he wonders aloud, repeating it so Janice can hear, "I asked her how it felt being bastard kid of a whore and a bum." Recalling their discussion of Clinton's White House sexual indulgences, Ronnie adds for Janice's benefit, "I didn't ask her for a blow job, though" (300). Nelson responds to Ronnie's harassment of Annabelle by asking Janice the thoroughly reasonable question, "Why did you marry him? How could you do that to us?," but his suggestion that the marriage was a betrayal of Harry and Nelson points in the opposite direction of this scene's dramatic trajectory, which has its genesis in Ronnie's wife Thelma's funeral in *Rest*.

After the memorial service, Harry and Ronnie separate themselves from the mourners for a brief, acrimonious confrontation during which Ronnie accuses Harry of using Thelma without ever appreciating the love she gave him.[13] Harry's rejoinder to Ronnie's accusation comprises what seems to be his most gratuitously insensitive assertion in the tetralogy: "I *did* appreciate her. I did. She was a fantastic lay" (1394). Even granting Harry's inconstant commitment to telling the whole truth regardless of the cost, making such a comment to a widower mourning the death of his wife seems particularly inexcusable, a stunningly heedless act approaching Ronnie's treatment of Annabelle for cruelty. The fact that Harry's funeral outrage is left as an unresolved loose end in *Rest* is particularly surprising: although in the novel Ronnie and Harry subsequently play an amicable round of golf together, *Rest* ends with Harry never atoning for this offense, and underlying the "buried years of righteous resentment" Ronnie feels toward Harry that emerge during the awful holiday celebration in "Remembered" is, I'm suggesting, his memory of having been told at her funeral that Thelma "was a fantastic lay." Ronnie's Thanksgiving revenge is to turn Harry's characterization of Thelma against Annabelle's mother ("she'd fuck anybody"), adding, for good measure, that Annabelle "looks just like [Ruth], without the ginger in her hair, and cunt, my guess is" (301).

Updike doesn't usually allow his characters to nullify themselves this irretrievably in the reader's sympathies, and the incident reinforces Janice's deepening suspicions that "Ronnie married her just to score somehow on Harry" (217). But the ironies of Ronnie's bitter assault against Annabelle are multiple: by responding to "She was a fantastic lay" in this way, he has unwittingly brought Harry into the dismal Thanksgiving, and Nelson, as if inspired by his father's conjured presence, reacts by doing what Harry always does when things get claustrophobic. Earlier in the novella, Nelson recalled a conversation (from *Rich*) in which his father told him that he was being trapped into marriage by Pru's pregnancy just as Harry had been by Janice's, and that his son—whom he perceives as "too much me"—should do what Harry didn't do then: run (253).

Nelson doesn't run then, either, but Ronnie's onslaught, apparently provoked by his bitter recollections of Harry, convinces Nelson that he has no business living with his stepfather and mother, and thus the Angstrom heir walks out of Thanksgiving and Janice's familial home for good. Escaping the Springer homestead is exactly what Pru had always wanted Nelson to do before she and he separated, but Nelson "could never see the point with my mother sitting on all those rooms over in Mt. Judge. I didn't want to leave her alone. My mother" (250). Departing from 89 Joseph Street, consequently, not only transforms Nelson from the "agoraphobic mental cripple" (239) he has been perceiving himself as while living with Janice and Ronnie, but prepares the way for his reconciliation with Pru, who was so opposed to moving in with Janice that she, in *Rest*, engineers sleeping with Harry in order to render their inhabiting the same house again impossible. With a thoroughly inadvertent assist from Ronnie and the ghostly intercession of his father, Nelson is provoked into doing precisely what Harry does in the course of *Rich*: he liberates himself from his mother-in-law's house in order to move toward gaining a home of his own. When, a few days later, Janice apologizes for Ronnie's outburst, Nelson interrupts her: "No . . . it was clarifying. It showed me what a pipsqueak and leech I tend to be" (306). Even Ronnie Harrison's articulation of his ugly notion of truth is positive in this novella. Thus is the major dynamic of "Rabbit Remembered" established, one a little too explicitly probed by a pre-Thanksgiving dialogue between Nelson and Annabelle: Nelson explains that he wants to help her because, "Without your mother, you're stuck. You're not going anywhere. You're under a spell, and we've got to break it."

"Nelson," she replies, "are you sure it's my spell you're trying to break?" (283).

Nelson's "spell" is a condition of desolate stasis that many middle-aged white male protagonists of recent American literature and film experience: at age forty-four, he is separated from his wife, he lives with his mother and communicates with his children largely over the Internet; he has come to doubt the meaning and value of the therapeutic work he does, and he has begun to suspect that his unresolved relationship with his father is the cause for his state of psychic paralysis. He tells Ronnie as much after he's moved out of Janice's house: one of the reasons Nelson likes Ronnie is "that you and I are about the only people on earth my father still bugs. He bugs us because we wanted his good opinion and didn't get it. . . . He beat us out. You look at Annabelle and see living proof that he beat you out—you may have fucked Ruth but he knocked her up and he stares out of her face at you. Right?" (308). Figuring out how his father "beat him out" is part of Nelson's psychic burden in "Rabbit Remembered," the son needing to learn how to remember his father without being "bugged" by him.

Admittedly, dispelling Nelson's "spell" constitutes anything but a constant "motion toward happiness": dramatizing the process he must undergo in order to undo that spell involves the reanimation of numerous tensions generated in the Rabbit tetralogy. Following his father's death, Nelson attended and received a counselor's certificate from Hubert F. Johnson Community College[14] and has become a mental health counselor at Brewer's Fresh Start Adult Day Treatment Center. The client who troubles him most is Michael DiLorenzo, a schizophrenic who suffers "an illness that seems to be nothing other than himself, a rot of his most intimate ego, that voice within, where it was nestled supposedly safe in his skin" (228). His disease is egocentricity turned pathological, and the reader isn't surprised when Nelson compares his client to another, more psychologically sound, egotist: Michael, Nelson thinks, "peaked too early, like Dad in a way" (229). In his dreams, Nelson will conflate Michael and Harry into a father/child for whose condition he bears a terrible responsibility.

The therapeutic session Updike creates between Nelson and Michael, and then between Nelson and Michael's parents, is a vividly evoked case study in the potential lethalness of family: Michael's father insists that he never pressured his son to prepare himself to take over his dry cleaning business, but Michael's Christmas Eve suicide—he strangles himself with a plastic suit bag from his father's company—suggests the opposite. Before Michael's death, Nelson has a dream in which he pictures "a tall man practicing chip shots in the moonlight" in the small backyard behind 89 Joseph Street: "The man is bent over and intent, and a certain sorrow emanates from him in the grey-blue light." He undertakes his hitting with "patient concentration, as if on a task he has been assigned for eternity—the little studied half-swing, a slump-shouldered contemplation of the result, a disconsolate trundling another ball with the face of the club into position at the man's feet, and another studied swing" (275). Only on the phone with Annabelle does Nelson admit that this figure has his father's affect, his aura "toward the end. Before he ran south and died" (277). What makes the dream particularly disquieting for Nelson is that the Springer backyard is too small to hit golf balls in, and Harry never practiced his golf game: as Nelson explains to Annabelle, his father "just got up on the tee and expected to be terrific" (278).

As we've seen, Harry values golf primarily because he believes perfection is achievable on the golf course ("All you have to do is take a
simple, pure swing and puncture the picture in the middle with a ball
that shrinks in a second to the size of a needle-prick, a tiny tunnel into
the absolute," he thinks in *Rest*, tacitly recalling his "perfect shot" in
Run—"that would be *it*" [1100]). He doesn't believe that attaining
perfection demands practice, however, which he associates with rote
repetition. His perfect shot on the golf course with Eccles in *Run* is
precisely the opposite of what Nelson dreams: one simple swing, and
"That's it . . . that's *it*!"—the ball's flight visualizes Harry's belief and
confirms it, transforming Eccles's view of him in the process. Harry's
shot, in other words, proves the possibility of evolution, revelation,
change. The Sisyphean swings of Nelson's dreamed golfer suggests
the pointless repetitiveness of life that Harry complains of throughout *Rest* and from which he finally seeks escape on a basketball court,
but they also invoke the condition of many of Nelson's clients at
Fresh Start, Michael in particular. "Schizophrenics don't get wholly
better," Nelson dejectedly muses after the DiLorenzo interviews:
"They don't relate. They don't follow up. They don't hold it together" (239). Progress, change, growth are illusory for them: in telling Annabelle about his client's death, Nelson acknowledges that he
"thought [Michael] was getting better—more engaged and reporting
no auditory hallucinations. Shows how little I know" (334).

Nelson's golfer dream conflates two sources of anxiety: first, it expresses his guilt at ignoring his father's suicidal desolation in the last
weeks of Harry's life. (At the end of *Rest*, Pru alone calls Harry to
ask how he is passing all the solitary hours of his days of self-exile in
Florida—Nelson only calls seeking to persuade him to agree to Janice's plan of selling their Penn Park house. More significantly, Janice
initially buys the Florida condo in part to get Harry away from
Springer Motors so that Nelson can take over, and Nelson responds
to the arrangement by accusing Harry of doing nothing in Deleon
but playing golf; Nelson's dream frightens him because of its subcon-
scious acknowledgment that Nelson is responsible for the golfer's Sisyphean condition.) Second, the dream projects Nelson's sense of
failure arising from his incapacity to minister to his clients' illnesses;
in both sources of anxiety, unchangeability and its resultant despair
prevail. "The misery of the world," Nelson tells Annabelle at their
first lunch together, "That's what I kept thinking during my group
[therapy meeting] this morning—the pity of everything, all of us,
these confused souls trying so pathetically hard to break out of the
fog—to see through our compulsions, our needs as they chew us up.
I got panicky and let it get out of control," he tells Annabelle, "The

group ran me." (282). (Nelson, clearly, has grown sufficiently in Updike's estimation in "Remembered" that he has become an articulate critic of the helplessness of the merely human.)

When he learns of the suicide of the client he had attempted to rescue from the antisocial voices in his head, Nelson experiences the terrible guilt of a mother who has failed to save her child from death: "Nelson feels he is reaching down to bring something back, but his hands are soapy and he cannot bring it back, it sinks" (332). When he thinks of Michael again in a dark moment during the novella's valedictory drive around Brewer, Nelson has a thought that he doesn't know echoes his father's end of life conviction that *"There is no mercy"*: "Nelson tastes the dead iron at the core of even green planets. No fresh start, no mercy" (344). Nelson will never believe in any transcendent form of mercy, but he needs to experience a restoration of his faith in the new beginnings that the Fresh Start Adult Treatment Center promises its clients if he isn't to submit completely to despair, and it is his movement toward that restoration of belief in the efficacy of psychotherapy that the novel's ending delineates, one in which the ghostly golfer, in an alternate manifestation, plays a significant role.

Just as the group therapy sessions at Fresh Start seem to have reared out of Nelson's control, "it makes him weary just to think about his aging, uncontrollable family" (335). Consequently, through solving his familial dilemma, he resolves his professional conflict. Nelson has concluded from the Thanksgiving disaster that there was no point in his effort to include Janice and Ronnie in his relationship with Annabelle, because "my sister is something that concerns Dad and me, not you" (306). Annabelle is, Nelson tells Ronnie, "something my father left me to take care of, and I don't know how to do it" (308). His failed attempts to take care of her early in the novella partake of his own despair, since he wants "to give her her father, but when he holds out his hands, the dust pours through them, too fine and dead to hold. Time has turned the spectacular man to powder, in just ten years" (255). He discovers the way "to give her her father" during the drive that he, Pru, Billy Fosnacht, and Annabelle take through Brewer on New Year's Eve, 1999.

Nelson has brought the two couples together without a clear plan. Billy Fosnacht is an unhappy divorcee, the "gruesome friend" (as Skeeter characterized him) with whom Nelson was staying on the night that the Angstroms' Vista Crescent home burns in *Redux* and whose recent separation from his wife has left him preoccupied with thoughts of death. Annabelle has never married, for reasons that Nelson has intuited and that the scene dramatically bears out. Pru has brought Roy to visit his father for the New Year's holiday, but she also perceives Nelson differently since he has moved out of his mother's house, and thus agrees to this odd New Year's Eve double date. Continuing to worry that Annabelle "is too much for him to take on" (281) just as his father declines to see Annabelle's mother while he is in the hospital because "Maybe she'd be too much for me" (1315), Nelson engineers this New Year's Eve foursome, and when Annabelle tells him that she hopes he knows what he's doing in setting it up, he admits that he doesn't.

After the two couples watch *American Beauty*[15] at a discount movie house, Nelson gets disoriented coming out of the parking lot, and Pru offers directions, gratifying the desire he expresses earlier in the text: "he wants a woman to take over" (218). As they head into Brewer, he prods Annabelle to talk about Frank Byer, Ruth's husband, whom she thought to be her actual father for many years during her childhood. Having been set on course by Pru, "there is no stopping him, now that he and the Corolla are headed in the right direction." His impulsive sense that he is going in the right direction seems reinforced by his "persistent sensation that there is one more person in the car than the four of them"—an encouraging presence perhaps balancing out the sinisterly judgmental third person Janice feels in the apartment with her on the afternoon that Becky drowns and the one that Harry intuits in his Deleon condominium in his final days in *Rest*. Despite the discomfort he is clearly causing Annabelle, Nelson keeps pushing her toward the articulation of what she has never acknowledged to herself: that she hated Frank Byer, for molesting her, and that when he died, "I felt I'd killed him. Good for me!" Once she has disburdened herself of the sexual secret that has, in Nelson's view, impaired her relations with men, Billy comforts Annabelle's weeping while congratulating his friend's accomplishment: "Great going, Nelson. So that's psychotherapy."

"It helps to get things out in the open," Nelson responds (347).

Earlier in "Remembered," Nelson, regressing to his childhood's resentment tropisms, decides that "only for the powers that be does knowing things pay off. Only they can afford to know the truth" (264). Here, he proves that not only the "powers that be" can benefit from knowing what's true: he has given Annabelle her father by offering her Harry's capacity for truth-telling (the presence of that "fifth person in the car" in this moment is so strong that Nelson has "to strengthen his grip on the steering wheel" so as to maintain some control over the force inspiring his actions), and in so doing has redeemed, in his own eyes, the efficacy of his therapeutic practice with its dependency upon the patient excavation of truth. In order to effect this process, "[Nelson] needs to undress his sister in front of Billy"

(346), because only through figuratively revealing her true self to his inhibited friend will Billy be able to see through "[his] compulsions, [his] needs as they chew [him] up," and be able to make contact with this other solitary human being. Nelson has done what he needed to do for Annabelle, who tells him in the epilogue (wherein the "movement toward happiness" approaches a rampage) that she is seeing Billy seriously and they've talked of marriage; in the remainder of this scene, however, the "fifth person in the car"—whom Updike, with uncharacteristic candor, identified as Rabbit[16]—still has to help Nelson exorcise a ghost of his own.

As they enter downtown Brewer, the traffic lights blink off at Sixth and Weiser, the corner where Kroll's Department Store stood in Harry and Janice's childhoods. This piece of local geography has accrued great resonance in the Rabbit tetralogy: it's not only where Harry and Janice met, but its closing provoked Harry to think in *Rest* that, "If Kroll's could go, the courthouse could go, the banks could go. When the money stopped, they could close down God himself"[17] (715). In addition, in her last years, Ruth Leonard Byer works in an investment building across from the former Kroll's site, suggesting major sociocultural changes occurring in Brewer. Sixth and Weiser, then, is a site of epiphanies in the tetralogy, and is about to become one again. As if internalizing the history of changes, losses, and betrayals embedded here, Nelson feels a sudden surge of irrational anger at the nonfunctioning lights: "Decades of wrongs, hurts, unjust deaths press behind his eyes. He pushes down on the window locks. hooded kids with sparkle dust on their faces are crowding around the Corolla, and looking up the street toward Mt. Judge" (351). The "unjust deaths" Nelson typically thinks about are those of Becky and Jill, which he blames on Harry, but the context here suggests that it's his father's death that these "Hooded kids with sparkle dust on their faces" are evoking, since it was another black street kid—Tiger—who played Harry in his ultimately fatal basketball game. Nelson's characteristic response to being reminded of past slights and wrongs is to strike out at them, and by suddenly cutting him off, a Ford Exposition ("I hate SUVs. . . . ," Nelson thinks, "Pretentious gas-guzzlers, they think they own the road") offers itself as a target for his class-based resentments. Rather than creating an accident with the SUV and thereby reprising his late adolescent penchant for totaling automobiles ("I wish I'd smashed up all Dad's cars," he tells Melanie in *Rest*, "the whole fucking inventory" [741]), Nelson speeds through the intersection, calling on resourcefulness and driving skills to serve him rather than self-pitying anger. He shivers after getting through this intersection, feeling "as if a contentious spirit is leaving him."

Pru's response confirms Nelson's surprising triumph of coordination and driving skill: "Oh honey, that was great, the way you made that asshole chicken out. I think I wet my pants" (353). It's regrettable that Pru is reduced in this scene to a generic, pants-wetting rescued female, but the point is nonetheless clear: by refusing to play car crash revenge as he did in the Springer lot when his father repudiated Nelson's convertibles in *Rich*, Nelson has demonstrated a new sense of maturity, one that prompts Pru to offer to stay with him at his apartment that night—in honor, apparently, of his having proved that he's no longer "a pipsqueak." To make sense of this scene, it's necessary to recall Harry's response in *Rich* to Nelson's smashing of the convertibles he'd taken in trade in the lot: "He hasn't felt so close to breaking out of his rut since Nelson smashed those convertibles" (876). The "contentious spirit" that has left Nelson once the collision is averted is the impulsiveness of Harry Angstrom of which Nelson had been so aware earlier in the scene that he was obliged "to strengthen his grip on the steering wheel": Nelson has managed to break out of his rut—his "spell"—not by smashing cars, but by using coordination and fast reflexes to keep himself and his passengers safe. He has learned, in other words, to weigh, balance, and make choices among the complex inheritances bequeathed him by his father: he calls on Harry's devotion to truth-telling to dispel Annabelle's erotic stasis and to redeem her from her solitary life, but he rejects the lure of disaster so characteristic of Harry that he'd recognized in himself earlier ("He hungers for a hurricane, he realizes—for an upheaval tearing everything loose" [257]) as being a substantial source of the pains of his childhood, and of his half-sister's as well. At the stroke of midnight on January 1, 2000, Nelson has created for himself (with a little ghostly assistance) what Ronnie Harrison never does: a Rabbit Angstrom he can live with.

Epilogue:
The Closest Thing to
a Religious Experience

Clinging to a creed demolished everywhere you look, to a patriotism as obsolete as blood sacrifice, to a storybook small town that
never existed, least of all in the dingy thirties; . . . and now in this
present chapter of egocentric rambling slyly confessing to wanting, on the basis of a medieval or at best eighteenth century metaphysics, to preserve your miserable, spotty identity forever! What
about the big picture!!

           —from the original ending of *Self-Consciousness*

TERMINATING THIS STUDY OF A HIGHLY SELECTED PORTION OF JOHN
Updike's fiction with a discussion of "Rabbit Remembered" promises to ensure a predominantly upbeat closure. In the novella's epilogue, "And Beyond," Nelson has reunited with Pru (whose desire
to turn working for a living into a career seems to be moving toward
gratification) and his children, who clearly need a father at home, and
he has moved to Akron, Ohio, to live with them. Janice and Ronnie
have reached an age at which Florida will be easier on them than
Pennsylvania, and are soon to follow Nelson in departing Brewer, the
couple having decided to live in Janice's Deleon condominium. (Apparently, only readers of *Rest* would find Janice and Ronnie's inhabiting the place where Harry spends the final, agonizingly solitary days
of his life grotesque; sensitivity isn't among Janice's gifts, however,
and her marriage to Ronnie does little to alter the reader's perception
of her spiritual vapidity.[1]) The ride through Brewer that Nelson, Pru,
Annabelle, and Billy Fosnacht take on New Year's Eve 1999 is, for the
tetralogy's readers, a farewell tour of significant sites of Rabbitland,
the narrative ending on very much the same note that one of Updike's
best stories—"The Happiest I've Been"[2]—does: Nelson liberates
himself from the home that has simultaneously nurtured and stifled
him, but the fact that Annabelle and Billy Fosnacht seem bound
toward marriage will give him reason to return for visits.[3] The novel-

la's closing joke invokes Harry's—and Updike's—incessant ambivalence toward family. "If Billy and I get married," Annabelle asks Nelson on the phone, "will you give me away?' Says Nelson, "Gladly" (359). Nelson is glad to have a sister, and will as gladly give her away.

This predominantly glad closure is, of course, no more final or conclusive than are the endings of any of the Rabbit novels, or the resolutions of the chapters of *In the Beauty of the Lilies*, for that matter. Significantly, in fact, there are clear parallels between the narratives of the four Rabbit novels and the four chapters of *Lilies*, as if, in some sense, Updike were reprising the themes of the Rabbit saga in *Lilies*, rewriting the tetralogy and drawing some parallel conclusions.[4] At the end of *Run*, Rabbit's faith in "something that wants me to find it" has turned into a conviction that his hope that "somewhere there was something better for him than listening to babies cry and cheating people in used car lots" has killed his daughter; having been disappointed by the church window in which he futilely seeks the solace of light, and feeling that his inability to resolve the choices confronting him has nullified him—"in effect there was nobody there"—he looks up and "something in the block of brick three-stories" around him "makes him happy; the steps and windowsills seem to twitch and shift in the corner of his eyes, alive" (232). He pursues that vitality through attempting to flee, mindlessly and heedlessly, from his irreconcilable choices into its eternal present. At the end of the first chapter of *Lilies*, Clarence Wilmot is similarly seeking solace for lost faith in images of the ecstatic present—in his case, through those projected through kinetic images of life on movie screens. "Eyes had never before seen in this manner," *Lilies'* narrator explains: "impossibilities of connection and disjunction formed a magic, glittering sequence that left real time and its three dimensions behind" (106). Like Rabbit's realm of deliverance ("There is light, though, in the streetlights"), the movies are where Clarence seeks to flee from "his fall, his failure, his disgrace, his immediate responsibilities, his ultimate nullity" (108).

The Rabbit Angstrom who, after Becky's death in *Run*, "feels he will never resist anything again" (233), becomes the protagonist of *Redux*, a man so benumbed by his experiences in Eisenhower's America that he sleepwalks through the turbulent sixties, becoming a passive spectator of his existence as his wife deserts him for a lover and a girl for whom he has taken some measure of responsibility sinks into a fatal drug addiction. Like Teddy Wilmot's impassivity in *Lilies*, Harry's "frightened, hypnotized condition" in which "he can, do nothing, it seems, but ask questions" (349) is in large part provoked by the fact that he, again like Teddy, has "let all that"—Christianity—

"go." Both protagonists have retreated into a resentful withdrawal from God, a bruised spiritual sullenness: Harry blames God for refusing to pull the plug of the bathtub in which Becky drowned, Teddy blaming Him for the fact that "My poor Dad wanted to believe and needed to believe, and God just stayed silent" (201). Of both of them could be said what Teddy's wife says of her husband: he "just wants to get through this vale of tears . . . with minimal damage. It's as if he won't give God any satisfaction" (269). If either Teddy or Harry in *Redux* finds anything approaching redemption, the form it takes is that of domesticity. Visualizing Emily Sifford "at the end of a sudden straight road" of his life and determining to ask her to marry him is "the closest thing to a religious experience Teddy expected to have" (198), and the perfect beauty of the child their union produces further confirms the redemption that is their marriage. The narrator of *Redux* is more equivocal about the saving quality of the reunion of Janice and Rabbit, posing the rhetorical question—"OK?"—as they fall asleep together in the Safe Haven motel, far from the cultural dislocations of the sixties that both protagonist and author so clearly despise. All the vicissitudes of the Angstroms' marriage as they are depicted in *Rich* and *Rest* never completely contradict Harry's *Rest* judgment about their union: "What *was* there about Janice? It must be religious, their tie, it made so little other sense" (1235). In the last years of his life, Teddy offers a more prosaic but no less genuine affirmation of his domestic arrangements than Harry's: "Em and the postal department were mighty good to me" (419).

Because they share such a compelling sense of their protagonists' delight in negotiating the physical, material worlds around them, *Rabbit is Rich* and the Essie/Alma chapter of *Lilies* are probably the most palpably convergent of these Updike texts. Since their ego-driven relationship to the world is so positive, Harry of *Rich* and Essie/Alma share in common a thoroughgoing delight in being themselves. Essie's first significant feeling is an experience "of joy at being herself and not somebody else . . . She was so lucky to be herself and not them she sometimes felt dizzy with it; being who she was was like a steep shining cliff she stood on the edge of looking out over everything like a fair-haired girl in a story book she had about Scotland" (231). Updike occasionally imbues Rabbit with a similar sense of wonder at being himself—a mystical experience I've cited Updike marveling at in his own life through an insight he ascribes to Kierkegaard.[5] Because of the freedom to be unreflective that her physical beauty affords her ("The shell of illusion needed behind it only a certain poise, a stillness, for the audience to feel engaged," she believes, "It was better, in fact, not to reach out too boldly. . . . If God were too eager to please, who would worship Him?" [310]), Essie/Alma is more devoted in both moviemaking and life to skimming the surfaces than is Harry, whose interior monologue is ever registering and critiquing the world outside him and worrying it for hints of transcendence. Nonetheless, he thinks in *Rich* that "a water strider in a way is what the mind is like, those dimples at the end of their legs where they don't break the skin of the water quite" (830). As Updike constructs it, one of the mercies of middle age (and, consequently, of the mirroring narrative of *Rich*) consists in that Harry's sensibility is able to continue skimming the surface of the real in just this way throughout much of the novel, the protagonist at his most complacent moments feeling largely unimplicated in the natural processes that he witnesses.[6] Similarly, the movies Essie enjoys most are the ones in which women just skim along over everything, and the security and immunity that Harry acquires through buying a comfortable, insulating house of his own, she gains by making movies in which she feels "encased in a fine and flexible but impermeable armor; the bright island of make-believe . . . was a larger container, a well-lit spaceship, carrying her and the other actors into an immortal safety, beyond change and harm" (335). Essie "had known as a child she was the center of the universe and [in her early photographic sessions] the proof was accumulating, click by click" (280), and although the end of her narrative, like that of *Rich*, has begun to erode her certainty of that centrality (in *Lilies'* closing chapter, she tells a reporter that "the old Hollywood gave us a very artificially heightened sense of life and beauty, and it placed a terrible burden on everyone, actresses and audience alike" [46]), in the Essie/Alma chapter she remains a believer: "She, too, had her religion. She had trouble understanding how people could doubt God's existence: He was so clearly there, next to her, interwoven with her, a palpable pressure, as vital as the sensations in her skin, as dependable as her reflection in the mirror" (354). Although Harry is nothing like so confident of God's presence in his life, he nonetheless experiences moments of spiritual elation in *Rich*, which he characterizes in describing the gay minister contracted to marry Pru and Nelson: "nothing touches him; that's real religion" (803). "Essie/Alma" and *Rich* are clearly the sunniest portions of their larger narratives, deeply compelling depictions of human beings perceiving themselves in sync with the material world. If Rabbit is right in *Rich* when he thinks "there must be a good way to live" (745), these are the Updike narratives in which that way is most likely to emerge.

"Rabbit basks above that old remembered world, rich, at rest" (682) is Updike's summation of Harry's hard-won equanimity in

Rich, but his reintroduction of that sentence as an epigraph for *Rest* signals the darkening ethos of the latter novel, a mood paralleled by the grimness of the Clark/Esau/Slick chapter of *Lilies*. The son Alma produces is, by her own account, "a rather sullen, bland loser with little of the Wilmot sense of election or [his father's family's] continental flair" (360); in the final chapter of *Lilies*, Clark's deeply injured self-esteem leaves him vulnerable both to a crazed spiritual guru and a "sickness unto death" not unlike Rabbit's in *Rest*. The narrator of *Lilies* explains as Clark leads the Temple's women and children toward the deaths that Jesse has decreed as their fates, "There was nothing for him on the outside [of the Temple of True and Actual Faith] now, just hassle, and embarrassment for Mother. Whoremongers, sorcerers, the whole pack of supercilious shits" (486). Harry is no less demoralized by the venal materialism of humanity ("Rabbit realized the world was not solid and benign, it was a shabby set of temporary arrangements rigged up for the time being, all for the sake of money" [1469]), but he is more devastated by the diminution that he's experienced in his valuation of his interior life. His *Rich* view of his mind as "a water strider . . . those dimples at the end of their legs where they don't break the skin of the water quite" is transformed in *Rest* into pure anxiety: "Harry has trouble believing how his life is tied to all this mechanics [projected on a monitor during his angioplasty]—that the *me* that talks inside him all the time scuttles like a water-striding bug above this pond of body fluids and their slippery conduits. How could the flame of him ever have ignited out of such wet straw?" (1295). In *Rest*, Rabbit is repeatedly confronted with his own helpless involvement in the natural processes he viewed with such disinterested curiosity in *Rich*, and faced as well with the inescapable fate these godless mechanics of annihilation impose upon him. Without ever becoming fully conscious that he's seeking to flee the trap invoked in his insight that "it's hell, to be a creature. You are trapped in yourself, the genetic instructions, more strictly than in a cage" (1144), Harry provokes the fatal continuation of the basketball game with Tiger that tacitly dramatizes his concurrence with Dr. Morris's judgment that "sometimes it's time" (1513). Clark is displaying the same loyalty to self in his similarly self-destructive act of killing the "false prophet," rejecting as he does so the demeaning nickname—Slick—he has been given by Jesse and his lieutenants in derisive acknowledgment of his worldly mediational skills. "Slick, you fucker, I'll give you Slick," he yells as he shoots Jesse, thus ensuring that Jesse's armed lieutenants will "do him the favor" of murdering him in revenge. There is, as I've suggested, nothing "slick," in the meaning the novel's narrator ascribes to his action: "the living God had laid hold of him, the present-tense God beyond betting on" (486).

The Rabbit tetralogy ends with Harry assuring his son, "Well, Nelson, all I can tell you is it isn't so bad," (1516), and although the reader may puzzle over what the antecedent of "it" is in Harry's assertion, it seems clear that Harry's moment of "inspired certainty," analogous to Clark's moment of "hyperclarity" in the Lower Branch holocaust, takes place on the basketball court, and that God declines to be invited into his death even more markedly than, Updike argued, He does in *In the Beauty of the Lilies*. If *Rabbit at Rest* ends on a religious note, it is of the sort that Updike described in claiming that "although Harry is less specifically theological than [in] the last novel, in some way it's the most peaceful theologically because he's almost got beyond the vocabulary of theology and is acting out a religious event which is his own demise."[7] But then, neither of these narratives ends at these points, each of them having something approximating an epilogue.

The concluding scene of *Lilies*, as I've indicated, depicts Teddy watching news coverage of Clark's death on television, the scene emphasizing the point that, because of the reporters' ignorance of what happened at Lower Branch intersecting with Teddy's hearing difficulties and senility, this decent man with his diminished capacities is not clearly comprehending much of what he is perceiving or grasping its relevance to him. Before the final fiery confrontation with federal troops, Jesse complains that the tapes he's made and pamphlets of exegetical prophecy he has distributed in the thousands and the interviews he's sat for since the initial episode with Colorado police have done nothing to further his spiritual mission: "nothing, in any cosmic sense, had happened. The world remained insufficiently perturbed. It rolled on, untransformed" (472). Such, too, is the world's condition as it is dramatized in the closing scene in Teddy's living room: Teddy watches the news broadcast, oblivious of the potential sacramental meaning of Clark's sacrifice, in part because the NBC reporters don't see it, perceiving instead a generic narrative of heroism that Alma will be able to exploit to reanimate her dwindling screen career, and in part because "Teddy had no faith to offer; he had only the facts of daily existence. Weather, family news, local change" (412). The extermination of the self-proclaimed messiah ensures that his message of "faith as small as a mustard seed will see you through, but only faith" (473) will go unheard, and that the world will remain untransformed, numbly agnostic, routinely untranscendent, despite the occurrence of an event that at least one religious skeptic believed to have confirmed the existence of "the present-tense God beyond betting on." "Clark had done it to save them all" is Teddy's summation of the Temple of the True and Actual Faith's terminal day, emphasizing the children his grandson rescued; Updike's point, I think, is that the way that the Lower Branch confrontation plays itself out, a "false prophet" is eliminated, but no one is saved. In the absence of real consolation, we, like Teddy, fall back upon false solace: for him, the illusion that his wife rather than his cleaning woman sits at his side—for him and for us, the sour, fraudulent illusions incessantly projected by television.

Nelson is younger, sharper, and more resourceful than the declining Teddy, but I think Updike is making a similar point about the ordinary American by closing the Rabbit saga in "Rabbit Remembered" from Harry's son's perspective. As I've argued, the peripeteia in "Remembered" is thoroughly psychological and moral; the closest the novella comes to suggesting supernatural intercession may be the line, "Happiness for [Annabelle's deepening relationship with Billy Fosnacht] is already rising in him, like water trembling upward" (358), with its suggestions of a transformation into a positive key of the water in which Nelson's other sister, Becky, drowned. "Remembered" closes in affecting psychological epiphany and family reunion, but its therapeutic resolution also conjures up the question posed by Thomas Marshfield in *A Month of Sundays*: "Is this the end of therapy, a reshouldering of ambiguity, rote performance, daily grits, hollow vows, stale gratifications, receding illusions?" (213). In *Rich*, after all, Annabelle is the "destiny" Harry contrives for himself in an attempt to give his life the shape that God's withdrawal from it revoked; she's a "mysterious branch of his past which has flourished without him" (722), proof of possibility existing beyond his vision. In some sense, Nelson's absorption of Annabelle into his family as a way of reconciling himself with his father is, ironically, his therapist's way of demystifying her, metamorphosing her from "mysterious branch" of Harry's interior religious scenario to a half-sister for whom he feels sibling responsibility. Nelson's forging of a Harry Angstrom he can live with, in other words, resolves his psychic blockage while leaving achingly unresolved the validity of Harry's belief that his life has a shape transcending time's random successiveness and unaddressed his desire to experience a death he could live beyond. I want to close this study by reading the ending of *Lilies* and the close of Updike's last fictional visit to Diamond County as a conjoined testament to Updike's inability to resolve the basic conflict between Rabbit's—and Updike's own—realistic and religious impulses.

Clark's climactic act of heroism and untelevised religious epiphany in *Lilies* is Updike's means of dramatizing an idea that he has held, by his own account, since first reading Kierkegaard: the notion that genuine religious experience is incommunicable to others. "The relief of speech is that it translates me into the universal,"[8] Kierkegaard argues in *Fear and Trembling*, suggesting that the experience of belief moves the knight of faith out of the universal into human incommunicability. The tragic hero has support in the universal; the knight of faith has only himself alone, and this constitutes the dreadfulness of his situation. "Eagerly I took from Kierkegaard the idea that subjectivity too has its rightful claims, amid all the desolating objective evidence of our insignificance and futility and final nonexistence," Updike acknowledged in an essay on "A Book that Changed Me," anticipating Clarence's argument in *Lilies* that belief is a decision: "faith is not a deduction, but an act of will, a heroism. . . . After *Fear and Trembling*, I had a secret twist inside, a precarious tender core of cosmic defiance; for a time, I thought of all my fictions as illustrations of Kierkegaard."[9] Illustration number one, of course, is the kink in Rabbit's chest in *Run*, which he initially associates with his impulses toward freedom—his desire to "find an opening" in the field of personal diminishment and cloying domesticity he inhabits—and which he ultimately must destroy in himself because he perceives its having kept him away from home as having killed his daughter. The existence in himself of that "precarious tender core of cosmic defiance" is known only to Harry—to the other characters, his actions seem, as Eccles describes them, "monstrously selfish." The reader of the tetralogy, of course, also knows that Harry is animated by a subjectivity that seems—to Rabbit, at any rate—undeniably spiritual, and although the protagonist's faith dwindles over the course of the tetralogy, Harry retains much of his "twice-born" aura through the end of *Rest* because of his extreme sensitivity to manifestations of God's nonexistence. Kierkegaard's *Fear and Trembling* terminology seems, admittedly, ill-suited to Harry Angstrom, but the theologian's tragic hero/knight of faith distinction does help to account, I think, for the literary perseverance of Updike's protagonist: "Most men live in such a way under an ethical obligation that they can let sorrow be sufficient for the day, but they never reach this passionate concentration, this energetic consciousness. The universal may in a certain sense help the tragic hero to attain this, but the tragic hero is left all to himself. The hero does the deed and finds repose in the universal, the knight of faith is kept in constant tension" (89). Whether Rabbit possesses "this passionate concentration, this energetic consciousness" is probably open to debate; that his "furtive sensations of the invisible" keep him in a state of "constant tension" throughout the series seems fairly incontestable. Updike refuses to resolve that tension at the end of *Rest* for reasons Kierkegaard would applaud: there is no certainty, on this side of mortality, whether Harry is right in his despondent mood in *Redux* in thinking, "Rising, working, there is no reason any more, no reason for anything, no reason why not, nothing to breathe but a sour gas bottled in empty churches, nothing to rise by" (513)—whether his conclusion is justified in *Rest* that "*There is no mercy*" (1126).

As I've indicated, Nelson unknowingly echoes this latter phrase of Harry's in "Remembered," which, far from transforming him into a knight of faith, points up how difficult it is, in Updike's theological stance, to make conclusive claims about the spirituality of even the most superficially secular individuals. To put this another way, the external unrecognizability of the knight of faith problematizes all judgments about spiritual condition. "Whether the individual is in temptation (Anfechtung)," Kierkegaard insists, and Updike agrees, "or is a Knight of Faith only the individual can decide" (89)—and even the individual isn't so certain. Updike's Lutheranism, with its insistence upon the "otherness" and unreachability of God, intersects with his Kierkegaard-inculcated conviction that belief is seldom validated in any other than a highly subjective (and often ambiguous) spiritual sense—consider the experiences of spiritual solace Updike offers somewhat equivocally in "The Future of Faith"[10]—to produce a writer whose eschatological position is one of radical unknowability.[11] That unknowing, for Updike's reader—and, I'd speculate, for Updike as well—is often indistinguishable from not believing. In my reading of his oeuvre, the chronic unresponsiveness of God has cumulatively darkened Updike's vision in a way figured dramatically in Rabbit's parallel deepening doubts throughout *Rest*, a darkening reinforced by the loss of the "still center" of Updike's existence in Shillington occasioned by the orphanizing attendant upon his mother's death[12] and manifested in his work by his profoundly consolationless *The Afterlife* stories fictionalizing Linda Grace Hoyer Updike's demise. The significance of that place, and the meaning of its loss, is conveyed in Updike's poem, "Upon Becoming a Senior Citizen":

> I am your son; your mile grid of brick—
> the little terraces, the long back yards—
> contains my dream of order, here transposed
> to an eternal scale . . .
>
> A thumbnail held
> near enough to the eye blots out the sun;
> we hug those first years and their guardians
> so close to spite the years that took away
> the days of trolley cars, coal furnaces,
> leaf fires, knickers, and love from above.[13]

In "Why Rabbit Had to Go," Updike attributed the desolateness of
Rest to his mother's death's converging with the completion of the
first draft of the novel,[14] but a marked preoccupation with mortality
pervades as well *In the Beauty of the Lilies*—particularly in the off-
hand registering of major characters' deaths as afterthoughts to the
cataloguing of history's oblivious passage—and makes reading
through Ben Turnbull's unrelenting despair in *Toward the End of
Time* a thoroughly desolating experience. (The convergence of natural patterns and human meaning David Kern discovers in pigeons'
feathers is nowhere to be found in Ben Turnbull's perception of the
intricate beauty of pink laurels: "Amid such patterns infinitely multi-
plied, we make our aimless way; nature's graph paper, scored in
squares finer than a molecule's width, deserves tracing less coarse
than our erratic swoops of consciousness. All this superfine scaffolding, for what? The erection for a few shaky decades of a desperately
greedy ego that tramples through the microcosmic underbrush like a
blinded, lamenting giant" [189–90].) The fact that the two texts I'm
reading as Updike's major accomplishments in the novel close with
one protagonist deliberately inciting his own annihilation through an
act of sacrificial murder, while the other chooses the game that briefly
elevated his life as a vehicle for suicide, suggests the deep pessimism
of which the post-1989 Updike is capable, as does the poem ironically
titled "Song of Myself." Updike introduces into the poem the sentence fragment, "God, that dwindled residue," and then describes his
futile efforts to make prayer the entranceway to forgetful sleep:

> My mind mocks itself as I strive to pray,
> to squeeze from a dried-up creed
> enough anaesthetizing balm
> to enroll me among sleep's tranced citizenry
> who know no void nor common sense.

Against the power of these negations, however tentative or partial
they might be construed as being, what opposing affirmation can be
provided by a character who has "no faith to offer; he had only the
facts of daily existence. Weather, family news, local change" (412), or
by one whose creator describes him as "a relatively humane but sort
of sodden guy"?[15] The two letters Teddy writes to Clark while he's at
Lower Branch are full of "weather, family news, local change," which
actually comes as a welcome respite from Jesse's relentless "The-
ways-of-the-world-are-not-mine" biblical exegesis; more significantly, they also communicate the honesty and dignity of suffering
humanity, of a man mourning the loss of his wife and groping toward

faith through his memories of those in his family who, like her, believed. "I never minded other people believing," Teddy writes, "and
maybe being surrounded by two good believing women as I was freed
me up to coast along with the Lord's forbearance. Looking back I
wonder if Dad didn't believe more than he knew, and that's what
made him so serene at the end. I hope when my turn comes shortly I
make no more fuss than my old man" (417). Teddy's letters, like the
chapter Updike devotes to him, exemplify Updike's affirmation of the
ordinary, his literary endorsement of Howells's theory of the novel,
which held that its "method should be realism, which he once defined
as 'nothing more and nothing less than the truthful treatment of
material,' and its subject should be the common life of ordinary
Americans."[16] Teddy's commonplace witnessing of the world is valuable for Updike, I'm contending, for two contradictory reasons—one
eschatological/democratic, the other literary/spiritual/compensatory.
Because the mechanics of salvation, if they exist, are ultimately unknowable, Teddy's thoughtful agnosticism may render his soul as re-
deemable as that of a more conventional Christian. Kierkegaard's
theology and Updike's aesthetic alike egalitarianly assume that nothing is more unknowable from the outside than the state of soul of the
individual, except perhaps, the state of the soul known from the inside. "Simple human decency and self-respect" ought to do it" (490),
Teddy thinks at the end of *Lilies*, and, in Updike's eyes, maybe they
do. That such conventionality could testify to the condition of salvation is a paradox not unlike the one Updike expounded upon in his
own experience: "As a young person, I felt that thinking of myself
being suspended quite pointlessly in an immense void of indifferent
stars and mathematically operating atoms made it difficult to justify
action. To act because, if you don't, you'll get hungry—to act simply
because of a human reaction to stimuli—was not to act in a way that
gave shape to life. Justification was not there, and it was a problem for
me. I read the existentialists seeking a handle for something it had
been hard for me to grasp, and thinking about life in this way enabled
me to become involved in life as an average, enterprising, and organized person."[17] If existentialist texts can turn Updike into "an average, enterprising, and organized person," it seems equally possible
that conventionality can turn Teddy into a kind of saint.

The literary/spiritual/compensatory reason for Teddy's significance is that, in the absence of more elevated or ethereal subjects of
witness, Teddy is what we must understand. In his "Whitman's
Egotheism" essay, Updike quotes the good gray poet: "Whatever
may have been the case in years gone by, the true use for the imaginative faculty of modern times is to give ultimate vivification to facts, to

science, to common lives, endowing them with glows and glories and final illustriousness which belong to every real thing, and to real things only." Updike glosses Whitman's comment this way: "The mystery of Me proclaimed, what Emerson called the 'other Me'—the world itself—can be sung in its clean reality, and real things assigned the sacred status that in former times was granted to mysteries. If there is a distinctive 'American realism,' its metaphysics are Whitman's" (117). Teddy is worthy of literary scrutiny for the reasons that Howells offered for his use of ordinary materials: "I am not sorry for having wrought in common, crude material so much: that is the right American stuff. . . . I was always, as I still am, trying to fashion a piece of literature out of the life next at hand." Updike's appends to Howells's aesthetic credo what sounds to me a dourly secular gloss in concluding his "Howells as Anti-Novelist" essay: "It is hard to see more than eight decades later, what else is to be done."[18]

We have already seen much of the affirmation that Nelson's dramatic progress through "Rabbit Remembered" has to contribute to what I've characterized as the darkening landscape of Updike's fiction. For one thing, he manages, as A. O. Scott noticed, almost single-handedly to transform the tragedy of *Rest* into the comedy of "Remembered," the novella closing in a potential marriage.[19] That accomplishment, in keeping with a son who "has not been raised to believe in anything higher than his father's head" (325) and who has none of "this crazy dim faith" Harry had in himself from basketball or "being everybody's pet" (906) is thoroughly secular. Accordingly, the movements precipitated by Nelson in "Remembered" are all psychological, but nonetheless real: in *Rich*, Bessie Springer fires Charlie Stavros in order to make an opening for Nelson at Springer Motors, which suggests that Nelson has displaced Janice's lover. In *Rest*, Janice has Nelson displacing his father at the Toyota agency, thereby reiterating the Oedipal implications of Springer Motors' staffing practices. By walking out on Janice and her new husband, Nelson repudiates the idea that all of his power in the world derives from his mother's solicitude toward him.

In addition, Nelson's growth in maturity in other areas is not inconsiderable, much of it inculcating in him lessons Harry has had to learn. Among other revelations, he realizes that a father can be disappointed in his son and love him nonetheless, thus lessening his life-long, painful awareness that Harry held his nonathleticism and "little Springer hands" against him. "His son is a nerd," Nelson decides about Roy during a phone conversation with the boy, "a bore to his classmates and a nag to his teachers" (315). At the end of the call, Nelson tries to tell Roy he loves him, but his son has already hung up, the incident echoing Janice's comment to Ronnie and Nelson earlier in the novella, "Harry loved Nelson, it frustrated him that he could never express it properly" (222).

Of course, it is with Nelson's conflicted love for his father that "Rabbit Remembered" is primarily concerned, and one of his memories of Harry exemplifies that love while revealing the basic affirmative quality Updike ascribes to Nelson. "His father had been a rebel of a sort, and a daredevil," Nelson thinks, "but as he got older and tame he radiated happiness at just the simplest American things, driving along in an automobile, the radio giving off music, the heater giving off heat, delivering his son somewhere in this urban area that he knew block by block, intersection by intersection." (As we've already noticed, Nelson gets lost coming out of a Brewer Cineplex parking lot.) "At night, in the underlit ghostliness of the front seat, their two shadows were linked it seemed forever by blood. To Nelson as a child his own death seemed possible in so perilous a world but he didn't believe his father would ever die" (252).

Nelson's appreciation for his father's "happiness at just the simplest American things," and his own appreciation of thoroughly temporary pleasures, are the point here, and, since his father didn't live forever, Nelson's memory of these moments he shared with his father in the car is about as resonant as his affirmation gets.[20] Arguably, it is one of Updike's greatest strengths as a writer that he can evoke with equal power the human spiritual longing for what Wallace Stevens called "imperishable bliss" as well as the fervent embracing of a more earthbound and passing beauty, and despite his "soddenness," Nelson in "Remembered" exemplifies that aesthetic resignation. In one of his *Americana* poems, "A Rescue," Updike recalls feeling, in the poem's present, the satisfaction of having just written words that would "see print" and therefore maybe "last forever" through the eyes of those who read them. More satisfying still, however, was the ensuing act of rescuing a goldfinch from entrapment in a tool shed:

> Without much reflection, for once, I stepped
> to where its panicked heart
> was making commotion, the flared wings drumming,
> and with clumsy soft hands
> pinned it against a pane, held loosely cupped
> this agitated essence of the air,
> and through the open door released it,
> like a self-flung ball,
> to all that lovely perishing outdoors. (81)

"A Rescue" isn't "Sunday Morning," but the attempt to celebrate a reality that won't last over one that may is similar, as is the preference evoked in Updike's poem for natural beauty—"that lovely perishing outdoors"—over the memorial contrivances of the human mind. Nelson is no poet, but by embedding in him the memory of "his father and him in the front seat of the car, both of them having nothing to say but the silence comfortable, the shared forward motion satisfying" (251), Updike was granting him a secular sensibility that values what was because it recognizes that once it was "is." Nelson in "Remembered" embodies the truth that his cocaine addiction compelled his father to hear from Mr. Shimada as the Toyota representative withdraws the franchise from Springer Motors: "Things change is world's sad secret" (609).

Consequently, we leave the Rabbit saga as Nelson experiences the joy of a present moment ("Happiness for [Annabelle] is already rising in him, like water trembling upward") that is perhaps the only joy he is capable of knowing, but which is clearly genuine joy nonetheless. Nelson has come a long way from the petulant, "fucked-up" postadolescent who excoriates his father to Melanie in *Rich*, "He is bad, really bad. He doesn't know what's up, and he doesn't *care*, and he thinks he's so great. That's what gets me, his happiness. He is so fucking *happy!*" (741). In this, too, Nelson has become his father's son by the end of "Rabbit Remembered," for, as he tells Annabelle, quoting the Dalai Lama in their closing conversation, "The very motion of our life is toward happiness" (357). It is hard to see, more than a decade after Harry Angstrom's death, what else there is for Nelson to hope for.

Notes

PROLOGUE

Epigraph at the beginning of the chapter is from Updike, *"Franny and Zooey"* (review of *Franny and Zooey*, by J. D. Salinger), in *Assorted Prose* (New York: Alfred A. Knopf, 1965), 239.

1. Robert Frost, "The Constant Symbol," in *Robert Frost: Poetry and Prose*, ed. Edward Connery Lathem and Lawrance Thompson (New York: Holt, Rinehart, and Winston, 1972), 401.

2. Martin Amis's review of Updike's fourth collection of essays and criticism, *Odd Jobs*, points up the author-unto-himself aura that Updike's career emanates, one reproduced in his critics' general tendency to discuss his work in isolation from that of his contemporaries. Invoking the humanistic affirmativeness of *Odd Jobs'* reviews and essays, Amis suggested that "Updike sometimes seems a lonely and anachronistic figure in this age of irony and dread" (*The War Against Cliché* [New York: Vintage Books, 2002], 387).

3. Without denying the accuracy of the term, "Christian novelist," which is so often applied to him, Updike expresses his discomfort with the descriptor in "Remarks Upon Receiving the Campion Medal," in *John Updike and Religion: The Sense of the Sacred and the Motions of Grace*, ed. James Yerkes (Grand Rapids, Mich.: William B. Eerdmans, 1999), 3–6.

4. "Love as a Standoff" (review of *Victoria* by Knut Hamsun, trans. Oliver Stallybrass), in *Picked-Up Pieces* (New York: Alfred A. Knopf, 1975), 148.

5. A. O. Scott, "God Goes to the Movies" (review of *In the Beauty of the Lilies*), *Nation*, February 12, 1996, 26.

6. Birkerts included Updike in the "literary fathers" of contemporary American literature—Bellow, Roth, and Mailer—whose recent work, in its continued celebration of male narcissism, has been subject to the law of attrition. "The very thing that made these artists avatars of the self-seeking liberation of culture is now their unmaking," Birkerts argued. "Not because we, as a culture, have ceased to focus on ourselves, but because they, as writers, have fallen victim to the law of diminishing returns. The self, however grandiose, is finite; the wells do dry up." "Roth, Mailer, Bellow Running Out of Gas," *New York Observer*, October 13, 1997. David Foster Wallace's take-no-prisoners review of *Toward the End of Time* explains that "I think the reason so many of my generation dislike Mr. Updike and the other G[reat] M[ale] N[arcissists] has to do with these writers' radical self-absorption, and with their uncritical celebration of this self-absorption both in themselves and in their characters." "John Updike, Champion Literary Phallocrat, Drops One; Is This Finally the End for Magnificent Narcissists?" *New York Observer*, October 13, 1997.

7. Frank Gado, *First Person: Conversations on Writers and Writing* (Schenectady, N.Y.: Union College Press, 1973) 88.

8. Emerson, "The American Scholar," in *Oxford Writers: Ralph Waldo Emerson*, ed. Richard Poirier (New York: Oxford University Press, 1990), 52.

9. Updike revised Thelma's line in the *Rabbit Angstrom: A Tetralogy* (New York: Everyman Library, 1995) edition of *Rabbit at Rest* to "Harry, you're not actually God, it just feels that way to you" (1232). For note on Rabbit texts used in this study, see chapter 1, note 1.

10. "One Big Interview," in *Picked-Up Pieces*, 509.

11. "A Gift from the City," in *The Same Door* (New York: Alfred A. Knopf, 1968), 191.

12. "My Uncle's Death," in *Assorted Prose* (New York: Alfred A. Knopf, 1965), 203.

13. "Separating," in *Problems and Other Stories* (New York: Alfred A. Knopf, 1979), 117.

14. *Self-Consciousness: Memoirs* (New York: Alfred A. Knopf, 1989), 211.

15. *Memories of the Ford Administration* (New York: Alfred A. Knopf, 1992), 277.

16. "Special Message" to Purchasers of the Franklin Library Limited Edition of *Rabbit Redux*, reprinted in *Hugging the Shore: Essays and Criticism* (New York: Alfred A. Knopf, 1983), 859.

17. *John Updike in His Own Words*, videotape, IUP, 1996.

18. Marshall Boswell suggests that the Dalai Lama's appearances in the tetralogy consistently dramatize the link between Harry's perception of the sacredness of his past and egocentricity: since we all have what Updike calls a "subjective geography," "We are all, in a sense," Boswell concludes, "the Dalai Lama." *John Updike's Rabbit Tetralogy: Mastered Irony in Motion* (Columbia: University of Missouri Press, 2001), 44.

19. "Rabbit Remembered," in *Licks of Love: Short Stories and a Sequel* (New York: Alfred A. Knopf, 2000), 210.

20. "The Future of Faith: Confessions of a Churchgoer," *The New Yorker*, November 29, 1999, 85.

21. "Whitman's Egotheism," in *Hugging the Shore*, 110.

22. *John Updike in His Own Words.*

23. *Assorted Prose*, 289.

24. *The Comedy of Redemption: Christian Faith and Comic Vision in Four American Novelists* (Notre Dame: Notre Dame University Press, 1988), 182.

25. "One Big Interview," in *Picked-Up Pieces*, 504.

26. "The Dogwood Tree: A Boyhood," in *Assorted Prose*, 182.

27. Introduction to *The Poorhouse Fair* (New York: Alfred A. Knopf, 1977), xvii.

28. *Roger's Version* (New York: Alfred A. Knopf, 1986), 67.

29. "Melville's Withdrawal," in *Hugging the Shore*, 97–98.

30. George Hunt's *John Updike and the Three Secret Things: Sex, Religion, and Art*, John Neary's *Something and Nothingness: The Fiction of John Updike and John Fowles* (Carbondale: Southern Illinois University Press, 1992), and Marshall Boswell's *John Updike's Rabbit Tetralogy* all bring to their analyses of the Rabbit tetralogy the perspectives of Christian existentialism, and I am indebted to their insights into Updike's debt to Kierkegaard, Barth, and Tillich.

31. *Roger's Version*, 203.

32. Updike, "Why Rabbit Had to Go," *New York Times Book Review*, August 5, 1990, 24.

33. *In the Beauty of the Lilies* (New York: Alfred A. Knopf, 1996), 7.

34. "Hawthorne's Creed," in *Hugging the Shore*, 76.

35. "*Remembrance of Things Past* Remembered," in *Picked-Up Pieces*, 167.

36. "If the Salt Has Lost His Savor," an early version of "Pigeon Feathers" contained in Updike's papers at Harvard's Houghton Library (76M-76, 9), has David contest his mother's agnostic replies more explicitly: "'But why doesn't anybody know? Why won't anybody tell me? It's *important*, mother. Because if there's no immortality, there's no God'—to say 'God' to his mother was like swearing—'and if there's no God, there isn't anything'" (8).

37. *Toward the End of Time* (New York: Alfred A. Knopf, 1997), 25–26.

38. Frank Kermode's chronos/kairos distinction informs my thinking about both the changing cultural ethos of the Rabbit novels and the narratives' evolving shapes. "[C]*hronos* is 'passing time' or 'waiting time'—that which, according to Revelation, 'shall be no more'—and *kairos* is the season, a point in time filled with significance, charged with its meaning derived from its relation to the end." *The Sense of an Ending: Studies in the Theory of Fiction* (New York: Oxford University Press), 67.

39. "One of My Generation," in *Museums and Women* (New York: Alfred A. Knopf, 1972), 178.

40. "And I find I cannot imagine being a writer," Updike explained in an interview, "without wanting somehow to play, to make these patterns, to insert these secrets into my books and to spin out this music that has its formal side." "One Big Interview," in *Picked-Up Pieces*, 498.

41. Jeff Campbell, "Interview with John Updike," in *Conversations with John Updike*, ed. James Plath (Jackson: University Press of Mississippi, 1994), 92.

42. James Yerkes, ed., *John Updike and Religion: The Sense of the Sacred and the Motions of Grace* (Grand Rapids, Mich.: William B. Eerdmans, 1999), i. The passage derives from Updike's "Remarks on religion and contemporary American literature delivered at Indiana/Purdue University in Indianapolis, April, 1994," reprinted in *More Matter* (New York: Alfred A. Knopf, 1999), 850.

43. Introduction to *Soundings in Satanism*, ed. F. J. Sheed, in *Picked-Up Pieces*, 88.

44. "Bech Meets Me," in *Picked-Up Pieces*, 12.

45. David Malone's essay, "Updike 2020," provides a worthy admonition against excessively identifying Turnbull's positions with Updike's: "At one level . . . *Toward the End of Time* is a subtle criticism of Ben's solipsistic view of life, using both the negative example of his brutish callousness toward others' misfortune and an image pattern that suggests the effect that Ben's way of life has on people around him." *John Updike and Religion*, ed. James Yerkes, 91.

CHAPTER 1. THE TRUTH THAT SHALL MAKE YOU FREE

1. John Updike, *Rabbit, Run*, in *Rabbit Angstrom: A Tetralogy* (New York: Everyman Library), 201. A note on texts: the publication in 1995 of the Everyman Library *Rabbit Angstrom* with revisions, corrections, and a new introduction by Updike makes that edition of the Rabbit books the most authoritative, and the parenthetical page number following citations from the novels in the text refers to that cumulative text. To locate citations in the post-1995 Fawcett Ballantine trade paperbacks deriving from the Everyman Library edition plates, use the following formula:

Rabbit, Run	identical pagination
Rabbit Redux	subtract 267
Rabbit is Rich	subtract 623
Rabbit at Rest	subtract 1051

In those cases where there are significant disparities in wording of citations between the Everyman Library text and the first edition, I've indicated the revisions in endnotes.

2. Foreword, in *Hugging the Shore*, xviii.

3. A note on the protagonist's names: a not inconsiderable element in the rhetorical effectiveness of the Rabbit novels, is the fact that the protagonist has two names. Rabbit is his high school nickname, one which continues for him to be evocative of a time when he was rewarded for running; it's the name he associates with youthfulness, the purity of his impulses, fame, and self-esteem. Harry is his adult name, the one Eccles uses when he tells him "a terrible thing has happened to us," and as the tetralogy proceeds, other characters refer to him almost exclusively as Harry. A significant characteristic of Harry's, however, is that a substantial portion of his interior landscape remains "Rabbit," and although he can be as derisive toward his adolescent nickname as Ruth Leonard or ex-teammate Ronnie Harrison sometimes are, "Rabbit" is probably the name his eternally youthful soul—if he has one—answers to. In sum, there are few aspects of the conflicting impulses of Harold Angstrom's character that aren't contained within the binary opposition of his nicknames. Updike very skillfully varies the employment of these names in order to signal how Rabbit/Harry is perceiving himself in a given scene, the author simultaneously modulating the reader's distance from/closeness to him through this device.

4. There are passages in the tetralogy that reflect points of view other than Rabbit's—the perspectives of Ruth, Janice, Eccles, and Nelson are presented through interior monologue. The vast majority of the four novels' narrative is, however, dominated by Rabbit's subjective angle of vision, the highly elastic third-person limited narration Updike employs allowing him to shift fairly seamlessly from describing the protagonist's actions from an exterior point of view to unmediatedly registering Rabbit's impressions and perceptions. (George Searles effectively describes the prevailing narrative voice of the Rabbit novels in *The Fiction of Philip Roth and John Updike* [Carbondale: Southern Illinois University Press, 1985], 114.) "His day has been bothered by God" is not a third-person narrator's summation of Rabbit's day, in other words, but a third-person approximation of the character's thought and mood couched in language very close to Harry's own. In quoting from the *Rabbit Angstrom* texts I'll assume the reader's awareness of Updike's use of this perspective, which falls somewhere between first- and third-person narrative, and refrain from introducing every passage with "Through Updike's third-person limited narrative voice, Rabbit thinks . . . "

5. Rabbit's tropism toward unmitigated candor is mildly tempered in the Everyman edition of the novel, cited here, by his use of the hick term for prostitute, "hooer." In all earlier printings, Rabbit's question is markedly less facetious: "Were you really a whore?" (Alfred A. Knopf, 1970, 99).

6. George Caldwell, the protagonist of *The Centaur* (New York: Alfred A. Knopf, 1963), the novel initially conceived by Updike as representing a countertext juxtaposing Caldwell's selflessness against Rabbit's egocentricity, is similarly devoted to the pursuit of truth: strangers encountering his father, Peter Caldwell explains, find themselves "involved willy-nilly in a futile but urgent search for the truth" (83).

7. T. M. McNally and Dean Stover, "An Interview with John Updike," in *Conversations with John Updike*, ed. James Plath, 193.

8. Even Billy Fosnacht experiences a form of redemption in the tetralogy: in "Rabbit Remembered," Billy is not so "gruesome" as to prevent Nelson's half-sister, Annabelle Byer, from considering marrying him.

9. "The Man Within" (review of *Graham Greene: The Man Within*, by Michael Shelden), *The New Yorker*, June 26 and July 3, 1995, 184.

10. "Whitman's Egotheism," in *Hugging the Shore*, 117.

11. *In the Beauty of the Lilies* allows Updike to ascribe to messianic visionary Jesse Smith the argument that representation can be evil: "The color was overwhelmingly glorious," the Christian demagogue says of Hollywood movies, "and such a wealth of attention was paid to every detail that you thought you were looking upon reality itself. The devil's work is lovingly done—give Satan his due" (380.)

12. Jan Nunley, "Thoughts of Faith Infuse Updike's Novels," in *Conversations with John Updike*, 254.

13. "Howells as Anti-Novelist," in *Odd Jobs*, 171.

14. Norman Podhoretz, "A Dissent on Updike," in *Doings and Undoings: The Fifties and After in American Writing* (New York: Farrar, Straus, 1984), 257.

15. "Answer to 'Why Are We Here?,'" in *Odd Jobs*, 869.

16. "The Persistence of Evil," *The New Yorker*, July 22, 1996, 68.

17. "One Big Interview," 509.

18. "Midpoint," in *Midpoint and Other Poems* (New York: Alfred A. Knopf, 1969), 5.

19. "Answer," in *Odd Jobs*, 869.

20. As Updike eulogized his protagonist in an interview accompanying the publication of "Rabbit Remembered, "what was nice about [Harry] was that for all his limitations, he was interested—interested in passing phenomena and interested in the news and in changes of style, interested in the changes in the American costume, especially as it affected women." Charles McGrath, *New York Times Book Review*, November 19, 2000.

21. "Updike's American Comedies," in David Thorburn and Howard Eiland, eds., *John Updike: A Collection of Critical Essays* (Englewood Cliffs, N.J.: Prentice-Hall, 1979), 62.

22. The obvious dissimilarities between author and protagonist notwithstanding, Updike's tendency in interviews is to minimize rather than emphasize differences between himself and Rabbit. "Harry and I have a lot in common," he wrote in an introduction to the Easton Press edition of the Rabbit novels, "we grew up together, and are both white American males whose chief historical experiences have been the Depression, World War II, and the Cold War" (*More Matter*, 820). "Intellectually, I'm not essentially advanced over Harry Angstrom," he explained in "One Long Interview." "I went to Harvard, it's true, and wasn't much good at basketball; other than that, we're rather similar. I quite understand both his anger and passivity, and feeling of the whole Vietnam involvement as a puzzle, that something strange has gone wrong" (*Picked-Up Pieces*, 508). "Like Harry, I try to remain open," he subsequently suggested (509), and "Even the way Rabbit sits in front of his Linotype machine day after day [in *Redux*] reminded me of myself, the way I sit in front of the typewriter" (510).

23. Dr. Morris's thoroughly unwelcome advice to Harry at the end of *Rest* invokes the physical intruder that has encroached upon Harry's lifelong spiritual conversation with himself: "Get interested in something outside yourself, and your heart will stop talking to you" (1483).

24. "The Dogwood Tree: A Boyhood," in *Assorted Prose*, 185–86.

25. Rabbit's lamentation for lost youth seems to echo the epiphany of Dexter Green at the end of F. Scott Fitzgerald's "Winter Dreams": "'Long Ago,' [Green] said, 'there was something in me, but now that thing is gone, that thing is gone. I cannot cry, I cannot care. That thing will come back no more.'" *Babylon Revisited and Other Stories* (New York: Charles Scribner's Sons, 1960), 135.

26. Two essays on Updike's style from which I have benefited are John Flei-

schauer, "John Updike's Prose Style: Definition at the Periphery of Meaning," *Critique* 30 (Summer 1989): 277–89, and Philip Stevick, "The Full Range of Updike's Prose," in *New Essays on Rabbit, Run*, ed. Stanley Trachtenberg (Cambridge: Cambridge University Press, 1993), 31–52.

27. Elizabeth Tallent was, I think, among the earlier Updike critics to notice, in *Married Men and Magic Tricks: John Updike's Erotic Heroes* (Berkely, Calif.: Creative Arts Book Company, 1982), 79–80, that the novel's language becomes a net Rabbit feels himself trapped in in *Run*; I was introduced to the idea by James W. Hoffman's Contemporary American Literature class at the New School for Social Research in 1967.

28. Elizabeth Hardwick's review of *Rabbit is Rich* eloquently summed up this aspect of the then trilogy in asserting that, "These wonderful novels are acts of conservation, a gathering of plant specimens north of the Delaware River, a rare and lasting collection of the fertilities of Updike's genius." "Citizen Updike," in her *American Fictions* (New York: Modern Library, 1999), 251–64.

29. See Alice and Kenneth Hamilton, *The Elements of John Updike* (New York: Eerdmans, 1970); George W. Hunt, "Reality Imagination and Art: The Significance of Updike's 'Best Story,'" in William R. McNaughton, ed., *Critical Essays on John Updike* (Boston: G.K. Hall, 1982), 207–16; and James Plath, "Verbal Veneer: Updike's Middle Class Portraiture," in *Rabbit Tales*, ed. Lawrence R. Broer (Tuscaloosa: University of Alabama Press, 1998), 207–30. Edward Vargo," in "Making History in *Rabbit at Rest*" (in *Rabbit Tales*, 85) briefly draws parallels between Harry's perceptions and Updike's realism.

30. *"Remembrance of Things Past* Remembered," in *Picked-Up Pieces*, 163.

31. Sanford Pinsker argues for the significance of this anthropological function of the tetralogy in "Restlessness in the 1950s: What Made Rabbit Run," in *New Essays on Rabbit, Run*, 62.

32. "Religious Consolation," *The New Republic*, August 23, 1999, 43.

33. "Howells as Anti-Novelist," 177.

34. *Memories*, 360.

35. "How Does the Writer Imagine?" in *Odd Jobs*, 135.

36. Nunley, "Thoughts of Faith Infuse Updike's Novels," 254.

37. Updike was rich about a decade before Rabbit was: "Tonight I am a rich man," he declared in "Farewell to the Middle Class," published in Japan in 1969. The essay written for Suntory whiskey celebrates in something like the good spirits of *Rabbit is Rich* that the Updike family "is rich and everything goes." *Picked-Up Pieces*, 15.

38. *Assorted Prose*, 159.

39. Joyce Carol Oates, "So Young!" (review of *Rabbit at Rest*), *New York Times Book Review*, September 30, 1990, 1.

40. Updike, "Why Rabbit Had to Go," 24.

CHAPTER 2. WHERE ONLY A SCRIBBLE EXISTS

1. "The Original Ending of *Self-Consciousness*," in *Literary Outtakes*, ed. Larry Dark (New York: Fawcett Columbine, 1990), 328.

2. Henry Adams, *The Education of Henry Adams* (New York: Houghton Mifflin, 1946), 287, 289.

3. Adams, 500.

4. Updike summarizes that transition and its happy outcome in *Self-Consciousness*: "While I can now glimpse something a bit too trusting in the serene sense of

artistic well-being, of virtual invulnerability, that being published in *The New Yorker* gave me for over thirty years, the self who looked up to the empyrean of print from that dusty farm in Pennsylvania with its outhouse and coal-oil stove is not so remote from me that I can still think it anything less than wonderful to have become a writer" (222).

5. Nunley, "Thoughts of Faith Infuse Updike's Novels," 248. "You tend to get stuck on the books you read [past tense], and the books you were taught," he told Martha Davis Beck in 1996. "In a way, my aesthetic is a sort of midfifties modernism" ("An Interview with John Updike," *The Hungry Mind Review* [Spring 1996]: 22).

6. One of the numerous drafts of "Pigeon Feathers" in the Houghton Library's John Updike Collection memorializes Updike's brief intention to place the story in the present—1959—of the narrative's writing: he castigates himself for referring to war posters in David's room as revealing the inspiring experience's actual period. "Pigeon Feathers" (8), bMS Am 1793.1.

7. Updike fabricates a late middle-aged protagonist's visit to this lost paradise in "The Other Side of the Street" in *The Afterlife and Other Stories* (New York: Alfred A Knopf, 1994), 136–48.

8. "Remarks on the Occasion of E. B. White's Receiving the 1971 National Medal for Literature on December 2, 1971," in *Picked-Up Pieces*, 435.

9. Introduction to the Czech edition of *Of the Farm*, in *Picked-Up Pieces*, 83.

10. "The Sandstone Farmhouse," in *The Afterlife and Other Stories*, 129.

11. "The Brown Chest," in *The Afterlife and Other Stories*, 227

12. John Updike, "Pigeon Feathers," in *Pigeon Feathers and Other Stories* (New York: Alfred A. Knopf, 1962), 138.

13. The manuscript of "If the Salt Has Lost His Flavor," a very early draft of the story that became "Pigeon Feathers," omits the barn scene, terminating instead with David and his mother chiming in on a song David's grandfather is singing upstairs— "There is a happy land, far, far away, where saints in glory stand, bright, bright as day" (Houghton Library John Updike Collection, 76–76M, 9, 10). Of the autobiographical experience this scene memorializes, Updike has said, "This is the way it was, is. There has never been anything in my life quite as compressed, simultaneously as communicative to me of my own power and worth and of the irremediable grief in just living, in just going on" ("One Big Interview," 499). As "Pigeon Feathers" expanded, Updike cut the "happy land" song, using it in the resolution of another Olinger story, "Flight," in which Allen Dow recognizes through seeing the power that his mother's father has over her the tremendous power she has over him (*Pigeon Feathers*, 72–73) and which will henceforth figure substantially in his "just living, in just going on."

14. This scene enacts the fulfillment of a phobia Updike admits to having had as a child: "a morbid fear of spiders and insects—specifically, a fear that they would become very large, a frequent theme of the movies and adventure stories of my boyhood." *Self-Consciousness: Memoirs*, 50.

15. *The Comedy of Redemption*, 194–95. I cite Wood's chapter, "Updike as an Ironist of the Spiritual Life," repeatedly in *Rabbit (Un)Redeemed* because it seems to me to account better than do other Updike critical arguments for the remarkable absence of explicit references to scripture throughout Updike's fiction—and in Rabbit's head—for a self-professedly "Christian writer," and because Wood's description of Updike's ambivalence toward God seems to me thoroughly coherent and completely persuasive.

16. For an Updike story, "Pigeon Feathers" is unusually pervaded by elements of

the hero's adventure typology of Campbell's *The Hero with a Thousand Faces*. David is urged on to his adventure in the barn by his grandmother, initially "refusing the call" to confront and defeat his demons there. The barn in which his self-transformation begins is compared to a haunted forest, its doors-within-doors suggesting a mirroring of consciousness reinforcing the scene's repeated indications that in shooting the pigeons David is destroying an inadequate projection of himself.

17. That David's conception, articulated in the story's final sentence, contains an element of arrogance and even a modest attempt at divine extortion is suggested by its echoing of Eve in Milton's *Paradise Lost*: "Nor can I think that God, Creator-wise, / Though threatening, will in earnest so destroy / Us his prime creatures, dignified so high, / Set over all his Works, which in our Fall, / For us created, needs with us must fail / Dependent made; so God shall uncreate, / Be frustrate, do, undo, and labor lose, / Not well-conceiv'd of God, who though his Power / Creation could repeat, yet would be loath / Us to abolish, Lest the Adversary / Triumph and say; Fickle their state whom God / Most favors, who can please him long? Mee first / He ruined, now Mankind. Whom will he next? / Matter of scorn, not to be given the Foe" (book 9, 938–52). Merritt Y. Hughes, ed., *John Milton: Complete Poems and Major Prose* (Indianapolis: Odyssey Press, 1957), 400.

18. Nunley, 249.

19. Robert Detweiler was one of the early Updike critics to recognize "the possible irony in the whole performance" of David's embrace of the argument from design of God's existence. *John Updike* (Twayne Publishers, 1972), 63. Robert M. Luscher perpetuated this stance in suggesting that "David's affirmation of God's existence ... is more important as a strategy to cope with his fear of death rather than as a genuine religious commitment." *John Updike: A Study of the Short Fiction* (New York: Twayne Publishers, 1993), 32.

20. Updike's impolitic, unreconstructed and competitive side visible here emerges even in his highly civilized *New Yorker* reviews; consider this comment on Robert Frost: "In long retrospect, I think there was something salutary in seeing a revered man break loose from our consensual politics and raise the possibility that life, between great powers and old friends, is combat, and not clean combat at that. The pugnacious refusal not to let MacLeish's easy metaphor pass stemmed from the same independent, unaccountable, self-created, precariously maintained vigor ('There's a vigorous devil in me,' he once wrote Louis Untermeyer) that had lodged his best poems where they could not be got rid of" (review of Parini's *Robert Frost*, *The New Yorker*, March 15, 1999, 90–91).

21. Larry E. Taylor argued in *Pastoral and Anti-Pastoral Patterns in John Updike's Fiction* (Carbondale: Southern Illinois University Press, 1971) that David's mother is "associated with the archetypal pattern of the earth mother," while his father is "associated with mind and spirit." "These polarities that associate women with earth and matter and men with mind and spirit exist throughout Updike's fiction; marriage and sexual union are symbolic of 'the marriage of earth and heaven,' the reconciliation of warring pastoralism and anti-pastoralism" (56).

22. Considering one of his early paintings, Peter Caldwell comments, "Looking at this streak of black, I relived the very swipe of my palette knife, one second of my life which, in a remarkable way, had held firm. It was this firmness, I think, this potential fixing of a few passing seconds, that attracted me, at the age of five, to art. For it is at about that age, isn't it, that it sinks in upon us that things do, if not die, certainly change, wiggle, slide, retreat and shuffle out of all identity?" *The Centaur* (New York: Alfred A. Knopf, 1961), 62.

23. Introduction to *Self-Selected Stories of John Updike* (Tokyo: Shinchosha, 1996); reprinted in *More Matter*, 767–70.

24. Nunley, 253.

25. Updike, *Self-Consciousness*, 231.

26. Campbell, "Interview with John Updike," in *Conversations with John Updike*, 103.

27. *The Comedy of Redemption*, 197.

28. Adams, 455.

29. John Updike, "Packed Dirt, Churchgoing, A Dying Cat, A Traded Car," in *Pigeon Feathers and Other Stories*, 261. Compare Adams's invocation of the inconceivability of a God who torments human beings: "The idea that any personal deity could find pleasure or profit in torturing a poor woman, by accident, with a fiendish cruelty known to man only in perverted and insane temperaments, could not be held for a moment" (289).

30. That the David Kern stories are rooted in autobiography is no longer a controversial assertion; nonetheless, it seems surprising that, as late as *The New Yorker* proofs of "Packed Dirt" that Updike edited by hand so as to fictionalize it more significantly, the narrator's wife is named "Mary" (Updike's first wife's name), the hospital in England where she gives birth is "Oxford Hospital" (where Updike's first child was born), and the narrator's father refers to him as "Johnnie," which Updike replaces with "David." "Pigeon Feathers," bMS Am 1793.3, in Houghton Library Updike Collection, Harvard University.

31. John Updike, "The Heaven of an Old Home" (review of *Souvenirs and Prophecies: The Young Wallace Stevens*, by Holly Stevens), in *Hugging the Shore*, 610.

32. William H. Pritchard's inclination to perceive Updike primarily as "America's Man of Letters," I think, often prompts him to minimize the spiritual dynamisms of the author's work. Consequently, I would argue that Pritchard is insufficiently acknowledging the assertions of regret over lost spiritual certainties pervading the two fuguelike David Kern stories in his assertion that "the heart of these stories does not lie in the loss or recovery of faith, but rather in the familial and provincial affirmations enacted through conflict and tenuous resolution." *Updike: America's Man of Letters* (South Royalton, Vt.: Steelforth Press, 2000), 75.

33. "Solitaire," in *Museums and Women*, 78.

34. Henry Adams anticipated David Kern's and Alf Clayton's experiences of being undone by the pure excess of materials they seek to organize and systematize, the inundation eliciting from him one of those moments of postmodern self-reflection that make the *Education* seem as fully contemporary as an Updike novel: "Accidental education could go no further, for one's mind was already littered and stuffed beyond hope with the millions of chance images stored away in the memory. One might as well try to educate a gravel pit. The task was futile, which disturbed a student less than that, in pursuing it, he was becoming himself ridiculous" (353).

35. Campbell, "Interview with John Updike," 99.

36. "One Big Interview," in *Picked-Up Pieces*, 504.

37. "Novelist and Believer," in *Mystery and Manners* (New York: Farrar, Straus & Giroux, 1969), 168.

38. John Updike, "Leaves," in *The Music School* (New York: Alfred A. Knopf, 1966), 54.

Chapter 3. Upward Space

1. "Special Message" to Subscribers of the Franklin Library Edition of *Rabbit, Run*, in *Hugging the Shore*, 849–51.

2. *In the Beauty of the Lilies*, 18.

3. One of Updike's recent reintroductions of David Kern continues the Olinger-ite's convergence with Rabbit's progressively secular decline: in "Lunch Hour," collected in the 2000 collection, *Licks of Love*, Updike's formerly theologically inclined protagonist revisits Olinger and experiences nothing more spiritual than a desperate nostalgia for the girls he knew in high school, who are now as old as he is. In "The Walk with Elizanne" (*The New Yorker*, July 7, 2003, 66–71), Kern's memories of a high school crush take on a more eschatological cast. See note 5, below.

4. *John Updike in His Own Words*.

5. In his reluctance to picture an afterlife, Rabbit resembles his fabricator, who has seldom described the form that eternal life might take. One exception is Thomas Marshfield's explanation, in *A Month of Sundays* (New York: Alfred A. Knopf, 1975), of the "longing for immortality" as "a craving not for transformation into a life beyond imagining but for our *ordinary life*, the mundane life we so driftingly and numbly live to go on forever and forever. The only paradise we can imagine is this earth. The only life we desire is this one" (209). "The Walk with Elizanne," projects a similarly worldbound afterlife: "If Mamie was right and we live forever, David [Kern] thought, he could imagine no better way to spend eternity than taking that walk with Elizanne over and over, until what they said, whether they touched, whether or not he dared to hold her hand in his, and each hair of the fine black down on her forearms all came as clear as letters deep-cut in marble" (*The New Yorker*, July 7, 2003, 70–71). This is the "Blessed Man" idea rendered more eschatological still: the ideal is for human experience to turn into indelible words ("as clear as letters deep-cut in marble"), despite the fact that the event memorialized is basically trivial: David can't remember the woman who was the girl who inspired it when he's introduced to her at the Olinger High reunion, and he acknowledges toward the story's close that the walk with Elizanne he recalls so obsessively "was an adolescent flirtation that had come to nothing" (71).

6. Updike's "In Football Season" ends on a note similarly uniting youthful girl-hood, flowers, and spirituality: "Girls walk by me carrying their invisible bouquets from fields still steeped in grace, and I look up in the manner of one who follows with his eyes the passage of a hearse, and remembers what pierces him." *The Music School*, 8.

7. "Throughout *Rabbit Angstrom*," Marshall Boswell persuasively argues, "Updike employs water as the figurative element of death, an association made specific by baby Becky's drowning. By the same token, it is also a figure for the *nihil* from which creation emerges." *John Updike's Rabbit Tetralogy*, 63.

8. "Rabbit's failure to integrate his religious feeling," Stanley Trachtenberg summarized Edward P. Vargo's argument in *Rainstorms and Fire*, "with any paradigmatic myth or ritual act other than sports, sexuality, or running, or, briefly, in the rite of Christian burial prevents his meaningful or sustained communion with the unseen world." Introduction to *New Essays on Rabbit, Run*, 9.

9. "Intercession," in *The Same Door* (New York: Alfred A. Knopf), 206.

10. "Is There Life After Golf?" in *Picked-Up Pieces*, 98.

11. A frustrating round of golf in *Rest* provokes Harry to consider posing to his Jewish golfing partners an "unaskable question" he can't directly articulate: "how about death?" (1111). Later, at Club Nineteen, he thinks, but never says, *"Help me, guys. Tell me how you've gotten on top of sex and death so they don't bother you"* (1113).

12. Philip Stevick precisely defined the way in which the novel's present tense narration creates this aura of open-endedness: "Every thematic commentary on *Rabbit,*

Run remarks on the rootlessness and alienation that leave all the characters devoid of passion or resolve or even a stable sense of self. What such commentaries do not remark is that the style of the novel with its insistent present tense and its illusion of not having issued from a deliberate, recollecting mind, is an extraordinarily potent technique for dramatizing the terrible loneliness of these figures." Stevick, "The Full Range of Updike's Prose," *New Essays*, 48.

13. All editions before Everyman Library have "his grandfather's color stretched dense across the east." Perhaps Updike remembered that during Rabbit's drive south he associated the east with the urban congestion of Philadelphia, finally turning "instinctively right, north," as he heads back home (34).

14. "[W]hite and number one" is an addition Updike made in his Everyman Library revision (113), embellishing the scene's satire of Rabbit's narcissistic self-perception by adding racial identification as well as an allusion to the 1980s best-seller title, *Looking Out for Number One*, to Rabbit's vision of himself-as-ball. It is precisely this self-conception that comes to crisis in *Rabbit Redux*.

15. It's tempting to infer some convergence between the importance of Harry's grandfather remaining upstairs and Updike's profound recollection, cited in the previous chapter, of his own grandfather singing "There is a happy land far, far away" as the author and his mother listened from downstairs. "One Big Interview," 499.

16. Vargo, *Rainstorms and Fire* (Port Washington, N.Y.: Kennicat Press, 1973), 61.

17. *The Centaur*, 112.

18. "Rabbit's ecstatic 'That's *it*!' is simultaneously discovery and confirmation," Sanford Pinsker suggested, "a moment when confusion gives way to wordless certainty . . . this all-important *It* conflates God, the motions of grace, the pure camaraderie of sport, and, perhaps most important of all, the bracing possibility of a new, pristine chance at the next tee into a single image." "Restlessness in the 1950s," 71.

19. Sigmund Freud, *The Future of an Illusion*, trans. W. D. Robson-Scott (New York: Anchor Books, 1964), 25.

20. Ibid.

21. The name Tothero, which Hunt argues seems so perfectly to incorporate both child-hero and dead (German: tot)-hero (*John Updike and the Three Great Sacred Things: Sex, Religion, and Art* [Grand Rapids, Mich.: William B. Eerdmans, 1980] 41), appears to be a brilliant Updike fabrication, but "In the Cemetery High Above Shillington," a poem collected in *Americana and Other Poems* (New York: Alfred A. Knopf, 2001), 29, suggests that both this surname and Olinger (read o-linger) were not clever Updike creations but Shillington family names.

22. Harry seems to be inadvertently confirming Eccles's judgment when, in *Rest*, he marvels that he and Janice have stayed together through the years: "What was there about Janice? It must be religious, their tie, it made so little other sense" (1235).

23. In characterizing the Lutheran theology underlying Updike's fiction, Darrell Jodock implicitly explains Kruppenbach's refusal to engage in Eccles's peripatetic ritual of praise and blame: "the Lutheran tradition is not moralistic. That is, it does not think that right behavior determines a person's status or value before God, and it does not emphasize, formulate, or inculcate detailed moral guidelines." "What is Goodness?: The Influence of Updike's Lutheran Roots," in *John Updike and Religion*, ed. James Yerkes, 122.

24. No admirer of Eccles, George W. Hunt points out that the generic sermon the minister delivers on the Sunday when Rabbit attends his church dealing with "the forty days in the wilderness and Christ's conversation with the Devil" is so uninspiring that Rabbit hardly listens and the narrator blandly summarizes it. *John Updike and the Three Great Sacred Things*, 45.

25. In what may be a revisionist take on Rabbit's biography, *Rabbit is Rich* has Harry recalling attending Sunday school presided over by Kruppenbach (684). In giving Eccles his theological comeuppance, the Lutheran minister expresses no familiarity with Harry Angstrom or his family, though he hardly gives Eccles the opportunity to identify the family of his parish about whom Eccles has come to seek his counsel before ripping into his pastoral chastisement. George Hunt quoted Updike as saying that he perceived Kruppenbach "as the touchstone of the novel as I intended it. His life, including the motorcycles, is meant to be Barth in action" (*John Updike and the Three Great Sacred Things*, 43), but the Lutheran minister's withdrawal from the tetralogy save for Harry's brief recollection in *Rich* may provide substantiation for Ralph C. Wood's view that Kruppenbach is "Updike's comical impersonation of Karl Barth," the embodiment of a "transcendently alive but ethically irrelevant faith" no more efficacious for Harry than the "washed out and attenuated religion of Eccles" (*The Comedy of Redemption*, 215).

26. The Fawcett Crest paperback edition (New York, 1962), reinforcing Rabbit's intense involvement in the dictates of this ceremony, follows "[c]asting every care on thee" with "[h]e has done that; he feels full of strength" (244).

27. Until the publication of "Rabbit Remembered" in 2000, there seems no parallel justification for Harry's equally honest, equally callous assertion to Ronnie Harrison at his wife Thelma's funeral in *Rest*: "'Ronnie,' he whispers, 'I *did* appreciate her. I did. She was a fantastic lay'" (1394). It seems as much out of a desire to avenge himself on his dead rival that Harrison in "Remembered" has married and is thus "laying" Janice.

28. The first edition and 1970 revision use the more casual phrase, "the source of all things" (281), making this one of few revisions of the novel that gravitate away from Rabbit's diction for the purpose of clarifying an idea.

29. Eccles too will escape that cave, but he has to wait until Updike's Everyman Library revision of *Rabbit Redux* to do it. In the meeting between Rabbit and Eccles on a bus that Updike added to the *Rabbit Angstrom* edition (or, as Boswell suggests, deleted from the first edition of *Redux*?), the now ex-minister explains to Rabbit his certainty that "a very exciting thing is happening in Western consciousness." He is taking notes toward a book on the subject, asking Rabbit, "How does 'Out from Plato's Cave' strike you as a title?" (939). Boswell draws illuminating parallels between Updike's gay ministers, Eccles and Archie Campbell (*Rich*), in "The World and the Void: *Creatio ex Nihilo* and Homoeroticism in Updike's *Rabbit is Rich*," in *John Updike and Religion*, ed. James Yerkes, 168–70.

30. Donald J. Grenier described the climax of the burial scene this way: "Buoyed by a faith that Eccles does not have, forgiven by a God the mourners do not acknowledge, Rabbit feels unified with all the world as she leaps to heaven . . . He wants to forgive as he has been forgiven, to express his vision of the upward spaces, to begin again, but his unintentionally calloused remarks shock the mourners, who are unable to see the truth of his belief." *John Updike's Novels* (Athens: Ohio University Press, 1984), 60.

31. Marshall Boswell describes Harry's realization at the graveside in different, more Barthian terms: "Although Janice *was* in fact 'there,' her part in the death does not necessarily constitute her 'guilt.' Rather, she was merely one element in a string of physical events that God, in his Wholly Other indifference, let unwind." *John Updike's Rabbit Tetralogy*, 73.

32. *Self-Consciousness*, 98.

33. Nunley, "Thoughts of Faith Infuse John Updike's Novels," 253–54.

34. John Updike, "The Fork" (review of *The Final Years: Journals 1853–55 by Soren Kierkegaard*), in *Picked-Up Pieces*, 113.

35. *The Comedy of Redemption*, 195. Given Ralph C. Wood's perhaps unsurpassed exposition of the dark paradoxes permeating Updike's Christian beliefs, it surprises me to find him describing Rabbit's flight from the cemetery "as one of the most morally offensive scenes in our literature." Wood's reading of the then Rabbit trilogy (e.g., Rabbit slowly discovers that "grace does not abound amidst angelic flight from responsibility, but within the rich confines of temporal obligation" [217]) and his tendency to define the protagonist as a "sinner" seems to ascribe to the novels markedly more moralizing purposes than are evident in Wood's excellent explication of Updike's conflictual theology.

36. Updike, "The Fork," 121.

37. Soren Kierkegaard, *Fear and Trembling* and *The Sickness Unto Death*, trans. Walter Lowrie (Princeton: Princeton University Press, 1953), 72.

38. According to Ralph C. Wood, institutional American religion's failure to instill in Harry the capacity to "walk the straight line of a paradox" provides Updike with one of *Run*'s few unambiguous critiques: "The problem Updike poses for his characters is the same, he believes, that life thrusts upon every human being: how to walk this narrow divide [between finitude and infinity] without plunging into animal finitude or else orbiting into angelic infinity. The function of religion, in general, and the church in particular, is to teach us how to negotiate this hazardous path between opposites. That Angstrom is not thus instructed gives Updike the occasion for a stinging critique of contemporary American religion" (*The Comedy of Redemption*, 213).

39. Boswell interprets this dream as suggesting that "life . . . is an eclipsing of death—and vice versa. For every something, a nothing." "The World and the Void," 164.

40. "One Big Interview," 504.

41. For the majority of American literature's male protagonists, Mary Gordon has maintained, motion is what matters: "The image of the moving boy has been central in American writing. Motion is the boy's genius. He *must* be able to *move* freely. Quickly. The boy on his strong legs cuts through the world, through time, constricting space, the accidents of birth, class, limitation, law. He wriggles from under the crushing burden of fate. And fate's agent, the embodiment of unmoving weight, is female. She who does not move, who will not move, who cannot move. Who won't allow the boy to move." *Bad Boys and Dead Girls* (New York: Viking Press, 1991), 3–4.

42. John Updike, Introduction to *Rabbit Angstrom: Four Novels* (New York: Everyman's Library, 1995), xiv.

43. Jeff Campbell, "Interview with John Updike," 99.

44. "Whitman's Egotheism," in *Hugging the Shore*, 116.

CHAPTER 4. DESOLATE OPENNESS

1. *Rabbit, Run*'s title similarly evokes the narrator's sympathies: "the title is a piece of advice in the imperative mode," Updike has acknowledged, "though the man giving it was sitting at a desk in the upstairs room of a seventeenth-century house, overlooking a shady street corner in a small New England town." "Special Message" to Purchasers of the Franklin Library Limited Edition of *Rabbit, Run*," reprinted in *Hugging the Shore*, 849).

2. "The Harry Angstroms of this world—the men of *angst* who are really afraid," Kenneth and Alice Hamilton wrote in concluding their chapter on *Rabbit*,

Run, "are the ones who most need the light that proclaims on earth the light of heaven. When for them that light has gone out, there is no other way to take except 'the other way, down Summer Street to where the city ends,' and where the heart goes hollow." *The Elements of John Updike*, 155.

3. "Updike, Malamud, and the Fire Next Time," in *John Updike: A Collection of Critical Essays*, Thorburn and Eiland, eds., 44.

4. In "The Secret Integration," Thomas Pynchon evoked, through the perception of the preadolescents who constitute the story's collective protagonist, an analogous "desolate openness" embodied in a upscale suburban neighborhood of prefabricated houses: "[T]here was nothing about the little, low-rambling, more or less identical homes of Northumberland Estates to interest or haunt, no chance of loot that would be any more than the ordinary, waking-world kind the cops hauled you in for taking; no small immunities, no opportunities for hidden life or otherworldly presence: no trees, secret routes, shortcuts, culverts, thickets that could be made hollow in the middle—everything was out in the open, everything could be seen at a glance; and behind it, under it, around the corners of its houses and down the safe, gentle curves of its streets, you came back, you kept coming back, to nothing; nothing but the cheerless earth." *Slow Learner: Early Stories* (Boston: Little, Brown, 1984), 158.

5. Updike offered a similar apologia for his work's preoccupation with "shameful" things: "Down-dirty sex and the bloody mess of war and the desperate effort of faith all belonged to a dark necessary underside of reality that I felt should not be merely ignored, or risen above, or disdained. These shameful things were intrinsic to life, and though I myself was somewhat squeamish about sex and violence and religion, . . . they must be faced, it seemed to me, and even embraced" (*S-C*, 135).

6. Prescott argues that "In the end [Harry] can solve none of his problems and Updike must do all of it for him, ringing in death, fire and seduction to get Harry approximately back where he started." "Angstrom's Angst" (review of *Rabbit Redux*), *Newsweek*, November 15, 1971, 122D.

7. John Updike, "Special Message" to Purchasers of the Franklin Library Limited Edition of *Rabbit Redux*, reprinted in *Hugging the Shore*, 858.

8. The Vietnam War has proved an issue upon which nonveteran American writers have felt an extraordinarily protracted obligation to declare themselves, even long after its termination. In *A Prayer for Owen Meany* (New York: William Morrow, 1989), John Irving suddenly ascribes to his eleven-year-old title character a remarkable prescience about the war as it was being fought, the diminutive split-protagonist's liberal critique of American warmongering and military strategy (87–91) registering Irving's Vietnam stance at the cost of seriously compromising whatever credibility the predominantly symbolic Meany retained.

9. Perhaps one reason that Updike has been able convincingly to masquerade as a Jewish author in his Henry Bech stories is that he shares the notion of the absolute primacy of the self so central to many Jewish American writers. I discuss this much-remarked tendency of Jewish American literature in "The Bully Poetics of Stanley Elkin" chapter of *Reading Stanley Elkin* (Urbana-Champaign: University of Illinois Press, 1986), 1–20.

10. When *Redux* was published, Updike drew the parallel between Harry's occupation and his own in suggesting that "Like Harry, I'm hog fat, reactionary, passive. I'm a plugger. Even the way Rabbit sits in front of his Linotype machine day after day reminded me of myself, of the way I sit in front of the typewriter. . . ." (*Picked-Up Pieces*, 510).

11. Judie Newman's discussion of *Redux* in *John Updike* (New York: St. Martin's Press, 1988), 32–61, concentrates on the idea that Rabbit is "stranded in a typo-

graphic field" early in the novel. "Print still dominates Harry's perceptions," Newman argues, "and he remains trapped within the domination of the eye" (47) until his introduction to the countercultural, McLuhanite synthesis promulgated by Skeeter liberates him into the cultural ambiguities of the novel's close. Donald J. Greiner makes the useful point that many "of the columns [Harry] sets for the local newspaper are about Brewer's history, and thus he is always reminded how the traditional values of family and country are slipping away" (*John Updike's Novels*, 74).

12. Introduction to *Rabbit Angstrom: Four Novels*, xiv.

13. Harry's discomfort with technology in *Redux* becomes more personal and immediate in *Rest*, in which the "Godless technology" of angioplasty relegates him to national normalcy, revealing that he has, as Dr. Oman explains, ". . . a typical American heart, for his age and economic status et cetera" (1201).

14. "What did we expect [from *Ranger* photos]?" Updike asked rhetorically in a *New Yorker* "Talk of the Town" piece a month after the event: ". . . some message, some brief scrawl from God, a legible graffito on that blank and conspicuous surface." "We Looked Forward. . . ," *The New Yorker*, 40 (August 22, 1964), 23, reprinted in *Assorted Prose*, 74.

15. Janice's desertion of Rabbit mirrors precisely his *Rabbit, Run* desertion of her. He initially runs because she forgives his snappishness with her ("everything is forgiven, everything is the same" [15] he thinks before leaving); she leaves him because he fails to blame her for having an affair and refuses to prohibit her from seeing Charlie again.

16. Boswell offers a compelling argument for the presence in Updike's fiction of evil as Barth described it— "the reality behind God's back"—and summarizes the dark side of his faith in these terms: "Ever enthralled by paradox and tension-producing contradiction, Updike over the decades has fashioned himself into a Barthian believer with an existentialist's high regard for the void." "The World and the Void: *Creatio et Nihilo* and Homoeroticism in Updike's *Rabbit is Rich*," in *John Updike and Religion*, ed. James Yerkes, 165, 164.

17. Guy Davenport, *The New Republic*, December 31, 1971, 1473–74.

18. Brom Weber, *Saturday Review*, November 27, 1971, 54–55.

19. Updike signals the parallels between Rabbit's sexual adventuring in beginning relationships with Ruth and with Jill by having both characters respond to his question, "What do you do?" by saying "nothing," and by using the same language to describe the couples exiting the establishments where they've become acquainted: "With this Ruth he enters the street" (64); "With this Jill, then, Rabbit enters the street" (381).

20. Robert Alter, "Updike, Malamud, and the Fire This Time," in David Thorburn and Howard Eiland, eds., *John Updike: A Collection of Critical Essays*, 47.

21. Charles Thomas Samuels was one sympathetic reviewer of *Redux* puzzled by Rabbit's aphasic behavior in the novel—especially by his willingness to give Skeeter a home and his obliviousness to Skeeter's brutalizing of Jill through readdicting her to heroin. Samuels argues that the two explanations the novel offers—Harry tells Nelson that Jill will leave if he ejects Skeeter, and he is too paralyzed by despair and fear to intervene in the Jill/Skeeter relationship—don't really account for this nearly criminal level of passivity. "Updike on the Present," in *Critical Essays on John Updike*, 63–67.

22. "The tetralogy is about and not only in the last book," Updike has asserted, "a man's relationship with his coming death." Introduction to Easton Press uniform edition of the Rabbit Angstrom novels, in *More Matter*, 821.

23. Twenty-six years later, Updike could have been invoking Skeeter's ethic in

claiming that, "a cultural emphasis on individual freedom makes choosing evil a lively option" ("Persistence of Evil," *The New Yorker*, 22 July 1996, 65).

24. "One Big Interview," 510.

25. *Fighters and Lovers: Theme in the Novels of John Updike* (New York: New York University Press, 1973), 150. Markle's chapter on *Rabbit Redux* contains the most positive estimate of Skeeter in the Updike critical literature, her careful examination of the novel's language demonstrating persuasively how Skeeter (and blacks in the novel in general) are associated with vitality, whites with ghostliness and insubstantiality. "The two races," she contends, "are contrasted in terms similar to Eldridge Cleaver's 'primeval mitosis' theory: Whites have become all sterile, bodiless intellect (technology), and blacks are the physical—fertile, sexual" (157).

26. In an interview comment I cited earlier, Updike speculated that Skeeter's claims to godhead may have validity: "[I appeared surprised that among the critics] no one's given serious consideration to the idea that Skeeter, the angry black, might *be* Jesus. He *says* he is. I think probably he might be. And if that's so, people *ought* to be very nice to him" ("One Big Interview," in *Picked-Up Pieces*, 510). I assume Updike was suggesting that Skeeter is the sort of Christ figure that Flannery O'Connor introduces in "A Good Man is Hard to Find," a redeemer whose form of salvation is incommensurate with human moral comprehension. Beyond this understanding of Skeeter-as-Christ, I'm skeptical of Updike's comment because: 1) it renders Skeeter's treatment of Jill morally unintelligible; 2) Updike admits that he was himself "drug-dazed" from anesthesia for a broken leg when he made the assertion; and 3) the reporting of Skeeter's death in *Rabbit is Rich* communicates nothing of death and resurrection, and has absolutely no lasting effect on the single believer in Skeeter's divinity, Rabbit, who very seldom recalls his Black History mentor again in the tetralogy.

27. George W. Hunt attributed to Karl Barth's influence on Updike the fact his novels contain no truly "satanic" figures: "at best, 'Satan' can become, in Updike's phrase, 'a myth to teach us virtue.' . . . Instead [of such figures], we confront the more impersonal forces of Nothingness as they mingle with and obscure human creation." *John Updike and the Three Great Sacred Things*, 35.

28. In their final meeting, Skeeter insists to Harry that the drugs he gave Jill were "so cut [that] sugar water has more flash" (555). Nothing in the novel supports Skeeter's potentially exculpatory argument; the fact that he mistook the sound of the arsonists in the garage for Jill "coming to bug [him] to shoot her up again" (556) serves to confirm his complicity in her addiction.

29. "One Big Interview," in *Picked-Up Pieces*, 503.

30. In *Roger's Version*, Updike says no to another artificially induced form of religious belief: Dale Kohler's computer-generated "proofs" of God's existence.

31. Vargo, *Rainstorms and Fire: Ritual in the Novels of John Updike* (Port Washington, N.Y.: Kennicat Press, 1973), 173.

32. That Jill becomes Skeeter's primary victim is ironic, given that it was she who understood early on that "our egos make us deaf. Our egos make us blind. Whenever we think about ourselves, it's like putting a piece of dirt in our eye" (402).

33. Edward P. Vargo's compelling reading of the burning of the Angstrom house as a cleansing, redeeming immolation (*Rainstorms and Fire*, 167–70) seems to stumble on the fact that Rabbit, by his own account, remains "pretty screwed up" at the end of the novel.

34. "Special Message" to Purchasers of . . . *Rabbit Redux*, in *Hugging the Shore*, 858–59.

35. Mary Gordon, "Good Boys and Dead Girls"; Mary Allen, "John Updike's

Love of Dull Bovine Beauty," in Harold Bloom, ed., *Modern Critical Views: John Updike* (New York: Chelsea House Books, 1987), 93.

36. George Hunt, *John Updike and the Three Great Sacred Things*, 171.

37. Quoted in Jeff H. Campbell, "Middling, Hidden, Troubled America: John Updike's Rabbit Tetralogy," in Lawrence R. Broer, ed., *Rabbit Tales: Poetry and Politics in John Updike's Rabbit Novels*, 38.

38. Hunt, *John Updike and. . .*, 166. It seems pointed difference between *Redux* and *Rest* that in the earlier novel Mim arrives from California to mediate tensions and facilitate the restoration of order, whereas in the tetralogy's close she's still in flight when Harry's death renders her journey pointless.

39. Mim also engages in extended sociopolitical dialogues with Harry extending the novel's ideological emphases. The gist of her argument is that the American West has adapted to atheism more effectively than the East, Westerners becoming as hard and unsentimental as the cockroaches that have inhabited the desert for centuries. Updike may have some sympathy for her Didionesque perception of the Westernization of America, but it is not inconceivable that he loaded her down with so much loquaciousness in an attempt to divert the reader's attention from her thoroughly instrumental role in the novel.

40. Although it could be argued that Harry's moment of grief is insufficient response to Jill's death, one for which he bears some responsibility, it *is* nonetheless a response, and Mary Allen's failure to mention this scene in her critique of Harry's indifference to the girl's memory undermines the credibility of her argument in "John Updike's Love of Dull Bovine Beauty."

41. George W. Hunt offered a persuasive summary of the novel's moon landing architecture: "As the story opens, Rabbit is earthbound and unadventuresome; once Janice leaves, he ventures into the void; in the middle section, like the astronauts, part of him travels in orbit to the dark side of the moon (Skeeter), while another part begins a free fall, eventually stepping onto a new planet (Jill); the novel ends with his return to earth (Janice) and an ambiguous usage of the astronaut's confirmation (OK?)." *John Updike and. . .*, 175.

42. *The Comedy of Redemption*, 190.

43. "The Oven Bird," in *The Poetry of Robert Frost*, ed. Edward Connery Lathem (New York: Holt, Rinehart, Winston, 120.

Chapter 5. Domestic Peace

1. Harry's odd reference to "gas bottled in empty churches" represents his conflation of the "gentle tawny smell of sickness" that emanates from his mother's room with her anxiety about "a smell of gas escaping" in the house when he was a child. This mental image conjoining his mother, sickness, and domestic threat is introduced when Harry is riding a bus, prompting a prayer: "He bows his head and curtly prays, *Forgive me, forgive us, make it okay for her. Amen.* He only ever prays on buses. Now this bus has that smell" (*Redux*, 276).

2. Joseph Waldmeir's suggestive description of Mim—"deus ex machina from the dark side of the moon, sexual machine and uncompromising pragmatist from Las Vegas, the gambler's moon crater, epitome of artificiality and sterility"—accounts for her ability to arouse the silenced satirist in her brother. "*Rabbit Redux* Reduced," in Lawrence R. Broer, ed., *Rabbit Tales: Poetry and Politics in John Updike's Rabbit Novels*, 119–20. Waldmeir's characterization, I think, also points up a weakness in the novel: that Mim is so conscious of herself as embodying West Coast nihilism seems

to me indicative of the political overfreighting of *Redux*, as does the sociopolitical abstractness and sophistication of the conversations she and Harry engage in during her visit.

3. Paul Grey, "Perennial Promises Kept," *Time Magazine*, October 18, 1982, 74.

4. Stanley Elkin, *George Mills* (New York: E.P. Dutton, 1982), 297.

5. Michiko Kakutani, "Turning Sex and Guilt into an American Epic," *Saturday Review*, October 1981, 14.

6. *Something and Nothingness*, 77.

7. Thomas R. Edwards, "Updike's Rabbit Trilogy" (review of *Rabbit is Rich*), *The Atlantic*, October, 1981, 100.

8. Norman Mailer, "Some Children of the Goddess," in *Cannibals and Christians* (New York: Dial Press, 1966), 120.

9. Thomas Edwards was the first of Updike's critics to perceive these novels as having specific cultural foci: "If the first two Rabbit novels are religious and political respectively, *Rabbit is Rich* is clearly a story of the economic life." "Updike's Rabbit Trilogy," 100.

10. "Why Write?" in *Picked-Up Pieces*, 38.

11. T. M. McNally and Dean Stover, "An Interview with John Updike," in *Conversations with John Updike*, ed. James Plath, 203.

12. Updike; *Hugging the Shore*, 873. In a 1985 essay about her, Updike often praised his mother's ability to "name all the trees and flowers and birds in her woods," adding that "I wish I could, and, and try to learn the names from her now" ("Mother," in *Odd Jobs*, 69). It seems clear that he perceived her gift of matching vision and word as a link between himself and her as writers.

13. Mary O'Connell pushes this point further: "By emulating Horace [Smith] and assuming the role of a caretaker who cooperates with nature to create and sustain life, Rabbit is brought into a wholesome relation with the world. He begins to see nature as creative, death as part of the creative process, women as cooperative, and children (seeds) as like to be nurtured and surrendered." *Updike and the Patriarchal Dilemma*, 177.

14. Robert Frost, "The Constant Symbol," 401.

15. "How Does the Writer Imagine?," 135.

16. "Howells as Anti-Novelist," 189.

17. Updike, "The Heaven of an Old Home" (review of *Souvenirs and Prophecies: The Young Wallace Stevens*, by Holly Stevens), in *Hugging the Shore*, 610.

18. "Updike on Updike," *New York Times Book Review*, September 27, 1981, 35; *Hugging the Shore*, 871.

19. My generally sympathetic reading of Rabbit's character, one that seems to me compatible with Updike's prevailing attitude toward his protagonist, tends sometimes to minimize the character's negative qualities. It seems consistent with Rabbit's bourgeois insularity in the novel that he perceives the girl he doesn't yet know as Annabelle as a source of pleasure and meaning for his life, but never thinks about the life that his abandonment of Ruth imposed upon this daughter. In "Rabbit Remembered," Nelson displays far greater responsibility toward her than Harry ever does, and that fact generates whatever measure of happy ending the Rabbit saga can be said to have.

20. Kakutani, 14.

21. In explicating this pattern of the excitation of sexuality being replaced by the gratifications of wealth, Marshal Boswell borrows Tom Wolfe's term, "plutography," to suggest that Harry has moved from being provoked by pornography (pictures of prostitutes) to getting off on pictures of rich people. *John Updike's Rabbit Tetralogy*, 146.

22. Updike's own faith seems to be similarly uncentered on scripture. In the introduction, I quoted his comment invoking the deeper experience of religious wonder provoked by an acknowledgment of the magnitude of the universe as opposed to the mythos of Christ's sacrifice for humanity. The one biblical book Harry specifically refers to is "Ecclesiastes," which he characterizes as "the Lord's last word. There is no other word, not really." It is Babe's singing in Jimbo's Bar that has reminded him of the biblical text, however, and his description of her performance as "no woman's voice at all, and no man's, [but] is merely human, the words of Ecclesiastes" (373) secularizes the allusion. Updike's tendency to grant precedence to interior spiritual experience over the authority of scripture is a consistent element of his work, his characters (in the words of Stephen H. Webb) seeking God through "sinning boldly" and through "the paradoxes of faith" rather than in the revealed word of scripture. "Writing as a Reader of Karl Barth," in James Yerkes, ed., *John Updike and Religion*, 151.

23. A third novel, Updike predicted in 1971, "would have to be a different kind of book [from *Run* and *Redux]*—a short book, a pastoral book, an eclogue." "One Big Interview," in *Picked-Up Pieces*, 510.

24. Harry's perception of rain as validation of God's existence is an association that Updike clearly shares with him. "Rain is grace," Updike wrote in *Self-Consciousness*: "rain is the sky condescending to the earth; without rain, there would be no life" (41).

25. "One Big Interview," in *Picked-Up Pieces*, 504.

26. Whereas the *Babbitt* epigraph of *Rich* evokes the smug middle-class comfort of which Lewis's protagonist has become iconographic, the quotation from Stevens invokes the contrasting narrative of a bunny deluding itself that it has achieved safety from the peril of a cat. It seems clear that Updike is using the two epigraphs to suggest that Babbittlike Harry is so swaddled amid the comforts of middle-class American life that he risks self-inflation analogous to Stevens's rabbit's delusionary conclusion that "the little green cat is a bug in the grass." *The Collected Poems of Wallace Stevens* (New York: Alfred A. Knopf, 1978), 209.

27. Donald J. Greiner cites a *New York Times* article recording the fact that Nelson Angstrom's name was read in the graduation roll at Kent State at its 1982 commencement, but that no one appeared to accept the degree. *John Updike's Novels*, 99n10.

28. In one of the many father/son convergences in the novel, Nelson is here reacting against a mocking question that has plagued Harry's life as well. In *Run*, Ronnie Harrison asks it of him (157), and Janice poses the same question in *Redux* when Harry becomes skittish about the motel owner's perception of their renting the Safe Haven Motel room for the afternoon (612).

29. Quoted in Christopher Lasch, *The Culture of Narcissism* (New York: W.W. Norton, 1979), 211.

30. Harry's fondest sexual memory in *Run* is set in his father's car: "Mary Ann. Tired and stiff and lazily tough after a game he would find her hanging on the steps under the school motto and they would walk through the mulching wet leaves through white November fog to his father's new blue Plymouth and drive to get the heater warm and park. Her body a branched tree of warm nests yet always this touch of timidity. As if she wasn't sure, but he was much bigger, a winner. He came to her a winner, and that's the feeling he's missed since" (170). He feels like anything but a winner in *Rich* while driving his Corolla and contemplating his resentment at all the sex happening everywhere, which doesn't include him: "One world: everybody fucks everybody. When he thinks of all the fucking there's been in the world and the fucking there's going to be, and none of it for him, here he sits in this stuffy car dying, his heart just sinks" (936).

31. Updike's own resolution of this conflict between social conformity and asserting the self's aggressive impulses is, unsurprisingly, literary: "I'm willing to show good taste, if I can, in somebody else's living room, but our reading life is too short for a writer to be in any way polite. Since his words enter into the other's brain in silence and intimacy, he should be as honest and explicit as we are with ourselves" ("Interview with Helen Vendler," *New York Times Book Review*, April 10, 1977, reprinted in *Hugging the Shore*, 864).

32. In *Rest*, Harry attributes to his Jewish golf partners the same capacity to be spontaneous that Nelson in *Rich* resentfully ascribes to him, admiring "this ability that Jews seem to have, to sing and to dance, to give themselves to the moment" (1104).

33. The complete absence of dramatization of Nelson's departure and of his interior monologue as he flees Brewer reaffirms the point often made by bystanders of Rabbit's flights in *Run*: from the outside, the runner's flight looks like nothing but cowardice, immorality, and irresponsibility.

34. Pru's acquiescence to Nelson's explanation for abandoning her necessitates a certain suspension of credibility on the reader's part. When she arrives in Brewer, Pru expresses genuine dismay at Nelson's admission that he and Melanie have had an ongoing sexual relationship while Pru's friend was supposed to be helping Nelson deal with the fact of his soon becoming a father; it's difficult to believe that Pru's response to Nelson's having returned to Kent State (and thus Melanie) wouldn't include at least an expression of anxiety about their erotically reuniting.

35. The convergence of birth and Super Bowl was probably inspired by the fact that Updike's first grandchild was born on Super Bowl Sunday in 1981.

36. Judie Newman offers a careful explication of Harry's "growing awareness of the connection between money and anality" in *Rich* (*John Updike*, 73); Marshall Boswell (*John Updike's Rabbit Tetralogy*) expands upon her discussion of Janice as a "money slot" (145–46). Sally Robinson goes them both one better by suggesting that "the [Rabbit] novels' escalating interest in anal eroticism and homosexuality signals a perhaps unconscious desire on Updike's part to figure the disempowerment of white masculinity through a sexual metaphor. For it is the bodies of *men* which inflame Rabbit's interest throughout the series—from Skeeter's 'electric' body to the bodies of male porn stars Rabbit fantasizes about in *Rabbit at Rest.*" *Marked Men: White Masculinity in Crisis* (New York: Columbia University Press, 2000), 45.

37. Harry is thinking in *Rest* of these pictures of Webb and Cindy and his late middle-age dwindling sexual impulses when he contemplates how faded the world seems to him now: "And the lenses are always dusty and the things he looks at all look tired; he's seen them too many times before. A kind of drought has settled over the world, a bleaching such as overtakes old color prints, even the ones kept in a drawer" (*Rest*, 1099).

38. Updike made precisely the same point throughout *Couples* (New York: Alfred A. Knopf, 1968), particularly in the scene in which the couples move sleeping children from one room to another so that the adults can bed down with Tarbox neighbors to whom they're not married.

39. *Time Magazine* file, October 20, 1960. Used with permission of Time, Inc.

40. "As Good As It Gets," *John Updike and Religion*, ed. James Yerkes, 11.

41. "The World and the Void: *Creatio ex Nihilo* and Homoeroticism in *Rabbit is Rich*," in *John Updike and Religion*, ed. James Yerkes, 178–79.

CHAPTER 6. NOTHING IS SACRED

1. It seems significant that the reader's first image of Nelson Angstrom in the tetralogy depicts him sitting at Harry's accustomed place at the Angstroms' kitchen table, the son already having displaced his father in this Oedipal emblem.

2. As late as 1996, Updike could still wax lyrically about the spiritual uplift of basketball: "Getting off the ground, and that kind of lightness of basketball, and that kind of lightness when you play it. I never was very good, but the other day a basketball came into my hands, and like Proust's Madeleine, it brought back the whole sensation. I mean, the basketball itself is this tense orb that fits into your hands and wants to fly. It wants to go up and go into the hoop . . . It's all about height, isn't it?—if you can get higher than the other guy, then you're ahead. And so there's this whole antigravitational bliss of it, versus . . . our daily weight pulling us down." Martha Davis Beck, "An Interview with John Updike," *Hungry Mind Review* (Spring 1996): 17.

3. *John Updike's Rabbit Tetralogy: Mastered Irony in Motion*, 228.

4. Updike, "Why Rabbit Had to Go," *New York Times Book Review*, August 5, 1990, 24.

5. Ibid.

6. M. M. Bakhtin, *The Dialogic Imagination: Four Essays*, trans. Caryl Emerson and Michael Holquist (Austin: University of Texas Press, 1981), 216.

7. Campbell, "Interview with John Updike," 99.

8. James Kaplan, "Requiem for Rabbit," *Vanity Fair*, October 1990, 114.

9. Quoted in Dennis Farney, "Novelist Updike Sees Nation Frustrated by its Own Dreams," *Wall Street Journal*, September 16, 1992, A10.

10. Early in his career, Updike expressed doubts about the efficacy of writing about death: "Perhaps, indeed, Death (as opposed to dying, which is a species of living) is a better subject for meditation than for fiction, since it is, however conceived, unknowable, and emotional effects aimed from one conception of it can too easily, by a slight shift of philosophy, be evaded." "Snow from a Dead Sky," in *Assorted Prose*, 233.

11. Gail Caldwell, "Updike: Rabbit has His Final Say, But the Writer has More to Tell," *Boston Globe*, September 25, 1990, 66. Largely ignored by Updike's critics, Caldwell's very substantial interview/essay seems to me one of the most illuminating pieces published on him, primarily because her questions elicited such unusually candid and thoughtful responses from Updike.

12. Mary O'Connell argues persuasively that Harry's gluttony is reflective of his hatred of the body in favor of the spirit. *Updike and the Patriarchal Dilemma*, 211–12.

13. Beginning with the Memorial Day scene in *Run* in which Ruth swims in a public pool while Harry declines to enter the water because "cold is wet to him," Updike has characterized his protagonist as someone repulsed by watery depths and their inhabitants. While waiting in the hospital for Janice to give birth to Becky, he decides, "There is no God; Janice can die . . . he feels underwater, caught in chains of transparent slime, ghosts of the ejaculations he has spat into the mild bodies of women" (170). Elsewhere in *Rest* "underneath the sea [is] a murky cold world halfway to death. He really can't stand the thought of underwater, the things haunting it, eating each other, drilling through shells, sucking each other's stringing guts out" (1145). Only in *Rich* is he able to make peace between himself and water and disassociate the element from Godlessness, his ability to take a daily morning dip at Ma Springer's Poconos cabin partaking of "the love he feels for each phenomenon, and not for the first time in his life seeks to bring himself into harmony with the intertwining simplicities that uphold him, that were woven into him at birth" (745). In this antipathy for water, as in so many other psychological details of Rabbit's character, Updike embedded in him one of his own traits: a childhood dunking in a swimming pool had no lasting effects, "but the sensation lingered enough to make me dread water—its sting of chlorine, its indifferent coldness, its semi-opacity" (S-C, 88). This experience is fictionalized in "Trust Me" in *Trust Me and Other Stories* (New York: Alfred A. Knopf, 1987).

14. *Rest* explicates what *Rich* so effectively dramatizes in such compelling detail: that "What [Harry] enjoyed most, it turns out in retrospect, and he didn't know it at the time, was standing around in the showroom . . . waiting for a customer . . . shooting the bull with Charlie or whoever, earning his paycheck, filling his part in the big picture, doing his bit, getting a little recognition . . ." (1459–60). Wesley Kort ("Learning to Die: Work as Religious Discipline in Updike's Fiction," in *John Updike and Religion*, 190) finds the "big picture" defined in these terms secular and spiritually limited, but the *Rest* sentence seems to me effectively expressive of a level of male camaraderie untypical of the tetralogy and evocative of a deep affection for ordinary experience that occupies one pole of Updike's perception of existence.

15. Matthew Wilson, "The Rabbit Tetralogy: From Solitude to Society to Solitude Again," *Modern Fiction Studies* 37, 1 (Spring 1991): 23.

16. Updike, "The Man Within" (review of *Graham Greene: The Man Within*, by Michael Shelden), *The New Yorker*, June 26 and July 3, 1995, 184.

17. On the evidence of his twenty novels, first-person narration—rather than the third-person limited narration of the Rabbit novels—is Updike's perspective of choice. The voices of distinctly literary character/narrators such as Peter Caldwell in *The Centaur*, Joey in *Of the Farm*, Thomas Marshfield in *A Month of Sundays*, Roger Lambert of *Roger's Version*, Sarah Worth in *S*, and Ben Turnbull of *Toward the End of Time* might be said to combine to form a sort of ur-Updike narrative voice.

18. "Leaves," in *The Music School and Other Stories*, 53.

19. Updike discussed the influence of his mother's death on *Rest* in a "Special Message" for the Franklin Library's First Edition Society printing of *Rabbit at Rest*, reprinted in *Odd Jobs*, 869–72.

20. Updike, *The Coup* (New York: Alfred A. Knopf, 1978), v.

21. Updike, "Why Rabbit Had to Go," 24.

22. *The New Yorker*, June 16, 1997, 84. Reprinted in *Americana and Other Poems*, 37.

23. Mr. Shimada, the Toyota representative who pulls the plug on the Springer Motors franchise after Nelson's financial malfeasance has been revealed, is constantly metaphorized as a replacement for God in Harry's view, his negative critique of American "disciprine" making him a more judgmental deity than Harry's Deus absconditus usually seems.

24. In his extensive review of *Roger's Version* (1986), Frederick Crews argued that Updike seemed "less and less able to put together the God of mass liquidation and the Man of Sorrows; the redemptive end of the bargain evidently strikes him as a wild and ever more desperate uncertainty. The result," Crews concluded, "has been the growth of a belligerent, almost hysterical callousness" in Updike incarnated by *Roger's Version*. "Mr. Updike's Planet," *New York Review of Books*, December 4, 1986, 8.

25. *The Centaur*, 299.

26. Updike, "The Dogwood Tree: A Boyhood," in *Assorted Prose*, 182.

27. Updike, *Roger's Version*, 175.

28. In confirmation of the novel's faith/self duality, Updike revised "center of the universe" to "Harry, you're not actually God, it just feels that way to you" (1232) in the *Rabbit Angstrom* edition.

29. Harry has been interested in the Dalai Lama since his first trip south in *Run*, his fascination in *Rest* culminating in another articulation of the God/self dichotomy: "Do you still believe in God, if people keep telling you you *are* God?" (159).

30. Updike's *Rest* notes at Harvard's Houghton Library suggest that the first title he considered before arriving at *Rabbit at Rest* was "Rabbit Retired." MS stor 279 (1 of 4), John Updike Papers, Houghton Library, Harvard University, Cambridge.

31. Kyle A. Pasework argues that Updike intends for the reader to understand that Thelma, in not merely sexual terms, is a far more admirable Christian than Harry. "The Troubles with Harry: Freedom, America, and God in John Updike's Rabbit Novels," in *Religion and American Culture* 6,1 (Winter 1996): 1–33.

32. Harry's attempt to involve Mim in his sentimental recollection of his little sister's innocence in their last conversation is a failure: she not only can't remember the subsequent line of this song, but doesn't recall singing it. She has traveled too far from Mt. Judge/Brewer to be lured back from Las Vegas by her brother's desperate and needy nostalgia; it's appropriate, consequently, that she's still en route to Florida when Harry dies.

33. *Rabbit, Run* (New York: Alfred A. Knopf, 1960), 281.

34. "The Afterlife," in *The Afterlife and Other Stories*, 16.

35. "Poker Night," in *Trust Me and Other Stories*, 189.

36. "Special Message" for the Franklin Library's First Edition Society Printing of *Rabbit at Rest*," in *Odd Jobs*, 870.

37. Judie Newman argues persuasively that Pru intentionally seduces Harry for the express purpose of stymieing Janice's recently hatched plans to reunite the couples under the Springer roof. "*Rabbit at Rest*: The Return of the Work Ethic," in Lawrence Broer, ed., *Rabbit Tales* 201.

38. *The Poorhouse Fair* (New York: Alfred A. Knopf, 1977), 116.

39. Letter from Shillington resident and Updike high school classmate, Barry Nelson, October 19, 1997.

40. John Updike, *In His Own Words*.

41. James Baldwin anticipated Skeeter in making the argument that racism is a consequence of whites' inability to acknowledge the fact of their mortality. "Stranger in the Village," in *The Price of the Ticket: Collected Non-Fiction, 1948–85* (New York: St. Martin's/Marek, 1985), 88–89.

42. *The Music School and Other Stories*, 54

43. MS stor 279 (1 of 4), John Updike Papers, Houghton Library.

44. Introduction to the Easton Press's uniform edition of the four novels about Rabbit Angstrom, reprinted in *More Matter*, 821.

CHAPTER 7. ROOM FOR BELIEF

1. Kermode, *The Sense of an Ending*, 56.

2. The three boxes of *In the Beauty of the Lilies* materials Updike donated to the Houghton Library provide overwhelming evidence of the painstaking task of historical reconstruction involved in writing this "mountain of a book almost too steep for me" (letter to Carole Atkins Sherr). Among many other mail correspondences, Updike asked the Princeton Theological Seminary what time Clarence would have been likely to have been served dinner at Princeton at the turn of the century, compiled a library for Clarence's rectory study from a bibliography supplied by the Andover-Harvard Theological Library, received information about the process of Presbyterian demission from Westminster John Knox Press, learned from a number of New Jersey historians what Clarence would see from his train windows as he travels from Paterson to Jersey City in 1910 to begin the demission process, collected maps and descriptions of Philadelphia circa 1927 from which to construct Teddy's and Emily's honeymoon, contacted the postmaster general to ask how Teddy would have applied for his mail carrier's position, and so on.

3. "What You Deserve is What You Get" (review of *You Must Remember This* by Joyce Carol Oates), in *Odd Jobs*, 330.

4. Kermode, 48.

5. At the risk of foreshadowing my conclusion, I'll acknowledge that I cannot endorse the position of Charles Berryman, inspired in part by Gore Vidal's highly negative review of *Lilies*, that, "While it may not be fair to dismiss *In the Beauty of the Lilies* as a list 'of random objects,' the relentless piling up of details through four generations does tend to overwhelm the drama of religious decline." "Faith or Fiction: Updike and the American Renaissance," *John Updike and Religion*, 206. The "relentless piling up of details" of fictional historiography in *Lilies*, I'll argue, is at the very least Updike's attempt to compensate for the cultural attenuation of "the drama of religious decline."

6. Campbell, "Interview with John Updike," in *Conversations with John Updike*, 99.

7. "Special Message" for the Franklin Library's Signed First Edition Society Printing of *In the Beauty of the Lilies*, in *More Matter*, 831. Updike's most explicit description of God's being is conveyed in the phrase "a pocket in human nature that nothing else will fill." In *Roger's Version*, Roger Lambert imagines Dale Kohler's notion of faith: "Without it—faith, I mean, there's this big hole, and what's strange, the hole is a certain shape, that it just exactly fills. That He just exactly fills" (203). In *Lilies*, Essie Wilmot as a child thinks that "God was in the clouds and sent Jesus to earth to make Christmas and Easter, and His love pressed down from heaven and fit her whole body like bathwater in the tub" (233).

8. Updike had experienced some of the same difficulties turning James Buchanan's life into the play, *Buchanan Dying*, that Clayton has in making him the subject of a successful biographical study. *Memories of the Ford Administration* allowed Updike to translate his post–*Buchanan Dying* struggles with the refractory Buchanan biographical materials into a work of fiction. See "Special Message" for the Franklin Library Edition of *Memories of the Ford Administration*," in *More Matter*, 825–27.

9. A pop culture analogue of the sort of biographical narrative that Clayton condemns himself for producing are the "Biography" programs on cable station A&E. Seldom do these biographical sketches offer any thesis about their subject or attempt to connect one set of choices to other decisions s/he made. The message of this medium seems to be that the only understanding of human beings' lives available to us is through a linear delineation of what they did and what happened to them—there's no "why," but only a "*here* and a *there*."

10. "Why Write?" in *Picked-Up Pieces*, 35.

11. "The Original Ending of *Self-Consciousness*," in Larry Dark, ed., *Literary Outtakes*, 329. The problem with the "purely human," he suggests in *Self-Consciousness*, is "that when we try in good faith to believe in materialism, in the exclusive reality of the physical, we are asking our selves to step aside; we are disavowing the very realm where we exist and where things precious are kept—the realm of emotion and conscience, of memory and intention and sensation" (*S-C*, 250).

12. "The Man Within" (review of *The Man Within* by Michael Shelden), *The New Yorker*, June 26 and July 3, 1995, 187.

13. Updike, *In the Beauty of the Lilies* (New York: Alfred A. Knopf, 1996), 5. Further citations are to this edition and are given by page number in the text.

14. Updike's position on the existence of winners and losers might be gauged by the fact that in *Rest* he makes cocaine addict Nelson Angstrom a proponent of this Manichean ethic: when Janice explains to Nelson why he needs to enter a detoxification program, Nelson objects, "I'm a recreational user just like you're a social drinker. We need it. We losers need a lift" (1335).

15. Although not the dogmatic Calvinist that Orr is, Updike can occasionally take positions reminiscent of the laborer's condemnation of this world in favor of the next: "A certain pleasantly faded flower-child, hug-your-neighbor sweetness has replaced the sterner old dispensations," Updike wrote in "The Future of Faith." "[T]he social gospel of love, with its outreach to the losers of the world, including endangered species, has come inside" (85). Darrell Jodock examines the "sterner old disposition" of Updike's Lutheranism in "What is Goodness? The Influence of Updike's Lutheran Roots," in *John Updike and Religion*, 119–44.

16. *John Updike in His Own Words*.

17. Although Updike clearly has limited sympathy for Dreaver's theological stance, the point that he used Conner in *The Poorhouse Fair* to exemplify in his *Paris Review* interview with Charles Thomas Samuels seems to me largely uncontradicted by his subsequent work: "I'm not conscious of any piece of fiction of mine which has even the slightest taint of satirical intent. You can't be satirical at the expense of fictional characters, because they're your creatures. You must only love them, and I think that once I'd set Conner in motion I did to the best of my ability try to love him and let his mind and heart beat." "The Art of Fiction XLIII: John Updike," *Paris Review* 12 (Winter 1968): 108. Darryl Van Horne in *The Witches of Eastwick* may be the exception that proves the rule; see James Plath, "Giving the Devil His Due: Leeching and Edification of Spirit in *The Scarlet Letter* and *The Witches of Eastwick*," in *John Updike and Religion*, 220–22.

18. "The Future of Faith," 85.

19. Campbell, "Interview with John Updike," 94.

20. "The Pocket Nothing Else Will Fill: Updike's Domestic God," in *John Updike and Religion*, ed. James Yerkes, 59.

21. It seems significant that Rabbit too feels that existence has similarly been eviscerated by a worm: "The mechanically precise dark ghost of the catheter is the worm of death within him, Godless technology is fucking the pulsing wet tubes we inherited from the squid, the boneless sea-cunts" (1298).

22. *The Comedy of Redemption*, 190.

23. Updike's "Books Into Film" essay, inspired by the release of the film version of *The Witches of Eastwick*, similarly emphasizes the visual power and generic plotting of the medium to the exclusion of its art, approvingly citing Wolcott Gibbs's 1950s' characterization of film, which construes it as "an art form fundamentally based on the slow, relentless approach and final passionate collision of two enormous faces." "Books Into Film," in *Odd Jobs*, 38.

24. "The Future of Faith," 91.

25. Updike's identification with Clarence is clearly signaled through his burdening of the protagonist with a complex of speech-inhibitors derived from the writer's own physiology. Clarence's respiratory problem recalls Updike's asthma, and his speechlessness invokes the affliction that Updike recounts experiencing in the "Getting the Words Out" chapter of *Self-Consciousness*: "The paralysis of stuttering," he explains, "stems from the dead center of one's being, a deep doubt there." *Self-Consciousness*, 87.

26. Reaching upward to touch the ineffable is a recurrent expression of faith in Updike's fiction: in "Pigeon Feathers," David Kern lies in bed, reaching up in hopes of feeling Christ's touch on his fingertips, and Rabbit's onset of grief over Jill's death in *Redux* is precipitated by his dream of reaching up to touch "the ends of her hair where it must hang" above him, "only to wake to find his hands empty and Jill irretrievably gone" (597).

27. "Faith in Search of Understanding" (review of *Anselm: Fides Quaerens Intellectum*, by Karl Barth), *Assorted Prose*, 273–74.

28. James Wood, "John Updike's Complacent God," in *The Broken Estate: Essays on Literature and Belief* (New York: Random House, 1999), 196.

29. "How Does the Writer Imagine?" in *Odd Jobs*, 135.

30. Nunley, "Thoughts of Faith Infuse Updike's Novels," in *Conversations with John Updike*, 257.

31. After disclaiming the pulpit, Hartley Updike resorted to selling real estate, not encyclopedias, but the trajectory is similar: he had moved from invoking heaven to merchandizing the earth, and might thereby have inspired the profession his grandson assigned to the highly unspiritual Janice Angstrom as the appropriately materialistic occupation through which she supercedes her declining husband in *Rest*.

32. Teddy isn't the only Updike character who suffers paralyzing dread at the movies: "'No!,' Richard [Maple] said, suddenly terrified, as when sometimes in the movie theatre a vast pit of reality and eventual death opened underneath him, showing the flickering adventure on the screen to be a mere idle distraction from his life, a waste of minutes while his final minute was rapidly approaching" ("Grandparenting," in *The Afterlife*, 309). Fulham, the protagonist of "The Wallet," has a similar experience of withering terror in a movie theater in "The Wallet" (*Trust Me: Short Stories*, 224–25).

33. Updike wanted Emily, who is constantly associated with the greenhouse her parents own, to seem less a diminished thing than she perceives herself as being. In a highly uncharacteristic act of self-critique, "To Two of My Characters" (*Americana and Other Poems*, 44), Updike expresses doubt about having done both Emily ("a hothouse houri, dizzying") and Essie justice in *Lilies*. His meditation provoked by entering a real greenhouse, Updike acknowledged that "I wanted you to be beautiful, the both of you, / And here, among real flowers, fear I failed."

34. Essie's name change ironically telescopes the form her redemption of Clarence's disgrace takes. The surname that Hollywood moguls choose for Essie/Alma replaces the letter "I" in the word that describes Clarence's official withdrawal from his ministry—he was allowed to "demit" his office—with an "o," thus ensuring that her stage name memorialize not Clarence's fall but her popularity with her audience—her demotic appeal.

35. Dwight Garner, "'As Close as You Can Get to the Stars': The *Salon* Interview: John Updike," *Salon*, January 3, 2001.

36. "The Wallet," in *Trust Me*, 224.

37. The harrowing passivity of Clarence, Teddy, and Rabbit in *Redux* reflect the spiritual pessimism I earlier cited Ralph C. Wood as ascribing to Updike: "This celebrated incident [the church burning in *Couples*] points up the moral passivity of Updike's work: his reluctance to find fault and access blame, his conviction that our lives are shaped by forces too vast for mere mortals to master. There is a deep tragic pessimism pervading the entirety of his fiction. For Updike, as for few contemporary writers, there are problems that admit of no solution, that must be patiently endured, and that have their ultimate source as the primordial origin and end of life" (*The Comedy of Redemption*, 190).

38. Updike's afterword to *Lilies* cites three sources he consulted on the Waco incident, two of which characterize Koresh in terms not completely different from Updike's depiction of Jesse Smith. "David Koresh," the authors of *Madman in Waco* wrote, "personified the deepest, darkest, dreariest, and smuggest narcissism-induced stupidity." Brad Bailey and Bob Darden, *Madman in Waco: The Complete Story of the Davidian Cult, David Koresh and the Waco Massacre* (Waco, Tex.: WRS Publishing, 1993), 135. Updike's other source, *Inside the Cult*, was written by two disaffected former Branch Davidians, who acknowledge that "we had come to Mount

Carmel to expose [Koresh] as a cruel, maniacal, child-molesting, pistol-packing religious zealot who brainwashed his devotees into believing he was the Messiah, the reincarnation of Jesus Christ, and who would eventually lead them into an all-out war with the United States government and, finally, to their deaths." Marc Breault and Martin King, *Inside the Cult: A Member's Chilling, Exclusive Account of Madness and Depravity in David Koresh's Compound* (New York: Signet Books, 1993), 12.

39. Julian Barnes's highly positive review of *Lilies* emphasizes mediation over redemption in his reading of Clark's dying deed: "This may look like a redemptive act, but in fact it is just as movie-influenced as Clark's other deeds: he knows what to do less because of some moment of spiritual clarity than because the cliché of action movies insists that the compromised hero retain our sympathy by killing the bad guys and then dying himself." "Grand Illusion" (review of *In the Beauty of the Lilies*), *New York Times*, January 28, 1996.

40. In addition to the Branch Davidian works Updike cites, my primary source for information on Koresh and Waco is James D. Tabor and Eugene V. Gallagher, *Why Waco?: Cults and the Battle for Religious Freedom in America* (Berkeley: University of California Press, 1995).

41. The combination of television's distortedly fragmentary envisioning of the Long Branch culmination and Teddy's befuddled perception of the event make it difficult to agree with Donald Grenier's conclusion that "The religious aura that shapes [Updike's] canon, the acceptance of Karl Barth's rigorous theology, which insists that humanity must profess the first tenet of the Apostles' Creed, is more than the consistent asserting of personal faith; it is the unblinking commitment to a universal hope." "The World as Host: John Updike and the Cultural Affirmation of Faith," in *John Updike and Religion*, ed. James Yerkes, 262.

CHAPTER 8. A CONTENTIOUS SPIRIT

1. Campbell, "Interview with John Updike," in *Conversations with John Updike*, 34.

2. "Rabbit Remembered," in *Licks of Love: Stories and a Sequel* (New York: Alfred A. Knopf, 2000), 219.

3. Mim's comment invokes a significant theme in "Remembered"—Nelson's choosing between families. "It was drummed into him that he took after the Springers—little and dark-eyed, and something of a smooth operator like his grandfather, and he wonders now if he shouldn't let go of that. This sudden sister, this love child, is a chance to move closer to Dad, the Angstrom side within him" (319). His decision seems affirmed by Janice's thoughts about her Springer family in relation to the families of her two husbands: in her house, she is "surrounded by Koerner and Springer things: the Angstroms and Harrisons had contributed hardly a stick of furniture, they were nobodies in the county, they would leave nothing behind but their headstones" (304).

4. What I find little evidence of in Updike's novella is the convergence of familial and spiritual impulses he attributed to Andre Dubus's novella, *Voices from the Moon*, in which institutional religion continues to exert force. Updike argued that, "for Mr. Dubus, amid the self-seeking egos of secular America, the church still functions as a standard of measure, a repository of mysteries that can give scale and structure to our social lives. The family and those intimate connections that make families are felt by this author as sharing the importance of our souls, and our homely, awkward

movements of familial adjustment and forgiveness as being natural extensions of what
Pascal called 'the motions of Grace.'" "Ungreat Lives" (review of *Voices from the
Moon*, by Andre Dubus, and *Concrete*, by Thomas Bernhard), in *Odd Jobs*, 652).

5. Charlie Reilly, "A Conversation with John Updike," in *Conversations with
John Updike*, 133.

6. Elizabeth Hardwick, "Citizen Updike," in *American Fictions*, 263.

7. Melvyn Bragg, "Forty Years of Middle America with John Updike," in *Conversations with John Updike*, 221. Maybe the clearest evidence of Updike's sympathies in his doling out of perspectives is the fact that, although the points of view of
Nelson, Janice, Ruth, or Eccles inspire some sympathy in the reader for the characters, they seldom elicit laughter that isn't aimed at the character whose perspective
is being represented. Only Harry regularly wins the reader over through wit and
humor.

8. Introduction to *Rabbit Angstrom: Four Novels*, xxii.

9. Campbell, "Interview with John Updike," 95.

10. McNally and Stover, "An Interview with John Updike," in *Conversations with
John Updike*, 202.

11. Charles McGrath, "Going Home Again" (interview with John Updike), *New
York Times Book Review*, November 19, 2000, 3.

12. Introduction to *Rabbit Angstrom*, xvi.

13. Thelma's view of the relationship differs from Ronnie's: although she acknowledges loving more than she was loved by Harry, she locates in the affair the
explanation for God's imposition of lupus upon her. In his backwardly erotic way,
with Thelma, Rabbit continued to "give people faith."

14. The news article describing the burning of his Vista Crescent house that Harry
sets at Verity Press in *Redux* identifies Skeeter as Hubert Johnson, the convergence
of names seeming to suggest that Nelson continued to learn from Skeeter long after
the black man's death.

15. The relevance of *American Beauty*'s midlife crisis narrative to the Rabbit saga
is self-evident: as in *Redux*, the male protagonist, Lester Burnam, whom Pru describes as "a man who had never noticed . . . anything but his own selfish itches and
threatened ego" (343), is sexually attracted to a much younger woman. The two plots
diverge when Lester ceases sexual activity with the girl when she reveals that she is a
virgin, but Billy Fosnacht notices another potential parallel to *Redux*: "I was afraid
somebody's house was going to get burned down, either the hero's or the military
man's next to it" (344). Oddly, Billy doesn't recall the night the Angstrom house
burns—perhaps because as Nelson and Harry leave the Fosnacht apartment, Billy
accuses his mother of being a "whore" for sleeping with Nelson's father. A. O.
Scott's review of *Licks of Love* argues that *American Beauty* "tries to turn Updike's
realism into Gothic, and to impose a ready-made tragic vision on a story that turns
out to have been a comedy all along." "Still Wild About Harry," *New York Times*,
November 19, 2000.

16. "I tried to imagine Harry not just as an absence but also as some kind of
ghostly presence, nudging these two children toward reunion and happiness."
Charles McGrath, "Going Home Again".

17. The remarkable significance attributed to the closing of Kroll's in *Rest* is, I
think, difficult to account for without introducing as context the closing of Reading,
Pennsylvania's Pomeroy's, a department store in which Updike's mother (like the
mother in "A Sandstone Farmhouse") worked for three years during his early childhood. See "Mother," in *Odd Jobs*, 68. The department store is crucial to Rabbit for
its Christmas display, because he feels that it was as if "God himself put them there

to light up this darkest time of the year" (1469). "My own deepest sense of self has to do with Shillington," Updike wrote in *Self-Consciousness*, "and (at a certain slant) the scent or breath of Christmas" (220).

EPILOGUE

In the epigraph from this deleted ending of *Self-Consciousness*, Updike has "Oppositional Other" mock many of the values he has affirmed throughout his memoirs. Larry Dark, ed., *Literary Outtakes*, 328–29.

1. Few of Updike's interview comments have ever surprised me as much as his comment to Charles McGrath, "I love Janice—she's a survivor, it turns out," because Updike's unsympathetic depiction of Janice seems to me one of the constants of the Rabbit saga. As I read it, the tetralogy implicitly endorses Harry's feeling from *Redux* forward that he continues to mourn Becky in a way that Janice seems not to ("Women and nature forget," he decides [298]), and, as I've suggested previously, her effort to move herself and Harry back into the Springer homestead in *Rest* closely resembles Linda Grace Hoyer Updike's traumatic relocation of her husband and son from Shillington to her childhood home. In addition, Janice's guilty admission after Harry's first heart attack that "being a widow won't be so bad," and her feeble prayer following Harry's massive myocardial infarction—*"Dear God, dear God, . . . do what you think best"* (1514)—make the reader think Harry is right not to take her very seriously. Mary O'Connell's point that Janice undergoes a moment of compelling grief when she arrives at the Florida hospital is persuasive (*Patriarchal Dilemma*, 223), but then in "Remembered" she has married Ronnie Harrison and become a social snob as well, describing Ruth as "this dead slut [who] forced this girl on us" (260) and condescending to both of her husbands' families: "the Angstroms and Harrisons had contributed hardly a stick of furniture [to the Springer family house], they were nobodies in the county, they would leave nothing behind but their headstones" (304).

2. *The Same Door: Short Stories*, 220–42.

3. In testament to the fact that this is also Updike's farewell tour of Brewer/Reading, he added a new sentence to the "About the Author" blurb of *Licks of Love*, which "Remembered" closes. The blurb, which had remained largely unchanged in his books for a decade, ends with "He lives in Massachusetts."

4. Julian Barnes's review of *Lilies* anticipates my comparison between the four Rabbit novels and four chapters of *Lilies* in describing *Lilies* as "a compressed tetralogy." "Grand Illusion," 2.

5. "The mystery that more puzzled me as a child was the incarnation of my ego—that omnivorous and somehow pre-existent I—in a speck so specifically situated amid the billions of history. Why was I I? The arbitrariness of it astounded me; in comparison, nothing was too marvelous." *Assorted Prose*, 182. The negative pole of this mystery is contemplated by George Caldwell in *The Centaur*: "how could his father's seed, exploding into an infinitude of possibilities, have been funneled into this, this paralyzed patch of alien land, these few cryptic faces, those certain walls of [his high school class-] Room 204?" (298).

6. "The inner curve" of the Rabbit trilogy, Margaret Morganroth Gullette argued in *Safe at Last in the Middle Years* (Berkeley: University of California Press, 1988), consists in Updike's "deconstructing . . . the confused animosities of adolescence and early manhood, and replacing the decline narrative they produced with belated, at first tentative, and then more assured progress narratives" (83).

7. *John Updike in His Own Words*.

8. *Fear and Trembling*, 122.

9. "A Book that Changed Me," in *Odd Jobs*, 844.

10. See, for instance, the two potential divine intercessions he cites in his "The Future of Faith" essay: during an attack of terror while visiting a New England women's college, Updike found a self-help book that eased his anxiety and allowed him to sleep; in Florence, shortly before writing "The Future of Faith," another spiritual crisis was allayed by a rainstorm: "The rain was furious. I was not alone. God was at work—at ease, even . . . I lay down beside [my wife] and fell asleep amid the comforting, busy, self-careless drumming. All this felt like a transaction, a rescue" (91). As I've indicated, rain for Rabbit is "the last proof left to him that God exists" (*Rich*, 733).

11. To cite Ralph C. Wood one final time, "Updike is haunted, in fact, by God's withdrawal from history. Ours is an age of anxiety not only because a certain spiritual vacancy has invaded and hollowed out our lives. It is not God's death, Updike argues, but his absence that creates such inward emptiness. With Matthew Arnold and a great cloud of Christian witnesses, Updike agrees that we live in the twilight of Christendom. We dwell at the ebbing edge of a once brimming sea of faith. The cosmos no longer resounds with the supernal music of the spheres; it echoes instead with the 'melancholy, long, withdrawing roar' of Dover Beach. . . . That this enormous something called the cosmos should have come from nothing is, for Updike, unthinkable. Yet he cannot discern God unambiguously anywhere in the world; on the contrary, he is haunted by God's deep duality. At times God appears to be a cretinous Mangler who causes much of the world's pain. Yet he is also the gracious creator who has so generously endowed his creation that it sings of his goodness rather than his malevolence" (*Comedy*, 192–93).

12. Updike describes his mother's death as making him an orphan in a footnote to *Self-Consciousness* which, for reasons unexplained, does not appear in the memoir. See "Footnotes to *Self-Consciousness*," in *Odd Jobs*, 869.

13. *Americana and Other Poems*, 34, 37.

14. "Why Rabbit Had to Go," 1.

15. McGrath, "Going Home Again."

16. "Howells as Anti-Novelist," 169.

17. Gado, *First Person*, 89.

18. "Howells as Anti-Novelist," 189.

19. A. O. Scott, "Still Wild About Harry."

20. Joyce Carol Oates eloquently summarized Updike's affirmation of quotidian life at the end of "Updike's American Comedies": "The charge that Updike is too fascinated with the near infinitesimal at the cost of having failed to create massive, angry works of art that more accurately record a violent time is unfair, because it is far more difficult to do what Updike does. Like Chiron/Caldwell, he accepts the comic ironies and inadequacies of ordinary life" (*Modern Critical Views: John Updike*, ed. Harold Bloom, 68).

Works Cited

Adams, Henry. *The Education of Henry Adams*. New York: Houghton Mifflin, 1946.

Allen, Mary. "John Updike's Love of Dull Bovine Beauty." In *Modern Critical Views: John Updike*, ed. Harold Bloom, 69–96. New York: Chelsea House Books, 1987.

Alter, Robert. "Updike, Malamud, and the Fire Next Time." In *John Updike: A Collection of Critical Essays*, ed. David Thorburn and Howard Eiland, 39–50.

Amis, Martin. Review of *Odd Jobs: Essays and Criticism*, by John Updike. In *The War Against Cliché*, 384–88. New York: Vintage Books, 2002.

Bailey, Brad, and Bob Darden. *Madman in Waco: The Complete Story of the Davidian Cult, David Koresh and the Waco Massacre*. Waco, Tex.: WRS Publishing, 1993.

Bailey, Peter J. *Reading Stanley Elkin*. Urbana-Champaign: University of Illinois Press, 1986.

Bakhtin, M. M. *The Dialogic Imagination: Four Essays*, trans. Caryl Emerson and Michael Holquist. Austin: University of Texas Press, 1981.

Baldwin, James. "Stranger in the Village." In *The Price of the Ticket: Collected Non-Fiction, 1948–85, 79–90*. New York: St. Martin's/Marek, 1985.

Barnes, Julian. "Grand Illusion." Review of *In the Beauty of the Lilies*, by John Updike. *New York Times*, January 28, 1996.

Beck, Martha Davis. "An Interview with John Updike." *Hungry Mind Review* (Spring 1996): 16–17, 22, 58–59.

Berryman, Charles. "Faith or Fiction: Updike and the American Renaissance." *John Updike and Religion*, 195–207.

———. "Updike Redux: A Series Retrospective." In *Rabbit Tales: Poetry and Politics in John Updike's Rabbit Novels*, ed. Lawrence R. Broer, 17–33.

Birkerts, Sven. Review of *Rabbit at Rest* by John Updike. In *American Energies: Essays on Fiction*, 251–54. New York: William Morrow, 1992.

———. "Roth, Mailer, Bellow Running Out of Gas." *New York Observer*, October 13, 1997.

Bloom, Harold, ed. *Modern Critical Views: John Updike*. New York: Chelsea House Books, 1987.

Boswell, Marshall. *John Updike's Rabbit Tetralogy: Mastered Irony in Motion*. Columbia: University of Missouri Press, 2001.

———. "The World and the Void: *Creatio ex Nihilo* and Homoeroticism in *Rabbit is Rich*." In *John Updike and Religion: The Sense of the Sacred and the Motions of Grace*, ed. James Yerkes, 162–79.

Bragg, Melvyn. "Forty Years of Middle America with John Updike" (1990). In *Conversations with John Updike*, ed. James Plath, 221–28.

Breault, Marc, and Martin King. *Inside the Cult: A Member's Chilling, Exclusive Ac-*

count of Madness and Depravity in David Koresh's Compound. New York: Signet Books, 1993.

Broer, Lawrence R., ed. *Rabbit Tales: Poetry and Politics in John Updike's Rabbit Novels.* Tuscaloosa: University of Alabama Press, 1998.

Buck, Paula R. "The Mother Load: A Look at Rabbit's Oedipus Complex." In *Rabbit Tales: Poetry and Politics in John Updike's Rabbit Novels,* ed. Lawrence R. Broer, 150–69.

Caldwell, Gail. "Updike: Rabbit has His Final Say, But the Writer has More to Tell." *Boston Globe,* September 25, 1990, 61, 66.

Campbell, Jeff. "Interview with John Updike" (1976). In *Conversations with John Updike,* ed. James Plath, 84–104.

———. "Middling, Hidden, Troubled America: John Updike's Tetralogy." In *Rabbit Tales: Poetry and Politics in John Updike's Rabbit Novels,* ed. Lawrence R. Broer, 34–49.

Campbell, Joseph. *The Hero with a Thousand Faces.* Princeton: Princeton University Press, 1949.

Crews, Frederick. "Mr. Updike's Planet." Review of *Roger's Version. New York Review of Books,* December 4, 1986, 4–14. Reprinted in *The Critics Bear It Away: American Fiction and The Academy,* 168–86. New York: Random House, 1992.

Davenport, Guy. Review of *Rabbit Redux. The New Republic,* December 31, 1971, 1473–74.

Detweiler, Robert. *John Updike.* New York: Twayne Publishers, 1972.

Diamond, George. "Chaos and Society: Religion and Social Order in Updike's *Memories of the Ford Administration.*" In *John Updike and Religion: The Sense of the Sacred and the Motions of Grace,* ed. James Yerkes, 243–56.

Edwards, Thomas R. "Updike's Rabbit Trilogy." Review of *Rabbit is Rich. The Atlantic,* October, 1981, 100.

Elkin, Stanley. *George Mills.* New York: E.P. Dutton, 1982.

Ellison, Ralph. *Invisible Man.* New York: Random House, 1952.

Emerson, Ralph Waldo. "The American Scholar." In *The Oxford Writers: Ralph Waldo Emerson,* ed. Richard Poirier, 39–52. New York: Oxford University Press, 1990.

Farney, Dennis. "Novelist Updike Sees Nation Frustrated by its Own Dreams" (interview with John Updike). *Wall Street Journal,* September 16, 1992, A10.

Fitzgerald, F. Scott. "Winter Dreams." In *Babylon Revisited and Other Stories,* 114–35. New York: Charles Scribner's Sons, 1960.

Fleischauer, Charles. "John Updike's Prose Style: Definition at the Periphery of Meaning." *Critique* 30 (Summer 1989): 277–89.

Freud, Sigmund. *The Future of an Illusion.* Translated W. D. Robson-Scott. New York: Anchor Books, 1964.

Frost, Robert. "The Constant Symbol." In *Robert Frost: Poetry and Prose,* ed. Edward Connery Lathem and Lawrance Thompson, 400–405. New York: Holt, Rinehart, Winston, 1972.

———. "The Oven Bird." In *The Poetry of Robert Frost,* ed. Edward Connery Lathem, 120. New York: Holt, Rinehart, Winston.

Gado, Frank. *First Person: Conversations on Writers and Writing.* Schenectady, N.Y.: Union College Press, 1973.

Garner, Dwight. "'As Close as You Can Get to the Stars': The *Salon* Interview: John Updike." *Salon*, January 3, 2001, 1–4.

Gordon, Mary. "Good Boys and Dead Girls." In *Good Boys and Dead Girls*, 17–22. New York: Viking Press, 1991.

Greiner, Donald J. *John Updike's Novels.* Athens: University of Ohio Press, 1984.

———. "The World as Host: John Updike and the Cultural Affirmation of Faith." In *John Updike and Religion: The Sense of the Sacred and the Motions of Grace*, ed. James Yerkes, 262.

Grey, Paul. "Perennial Promises Kept," *Time Magazine*, October 18, 1982, 72–81.

Gullett, Margaret Morganroth. *Safe at Last in the Middle Years.* Berkeley: University of California Press, 1988.

Hamilton, Alice, and Kenneth Hamilton. *The Elements of John Updike.* Grand Rapids, Mich.: Eerdmans, 1970.

Hughes, Merritt Y., ed. *John Milton: Complete Poems and Major Prose.* Indianapolis: Odyssey Press, 1957.

Hunt, George W., SJ. *John Updike and the Three Great Sacred Things: Sex, Religion, and Art.* Grand Rapids, Mich.: Eerdmans, 1980.

———. "Reality Imagination and Art: The Significance of Updike's 'Best Story.'" In *Critical Essays on John Updike*, ed. William R. McNaughton, 207–16.

Irving, John. *A Prayer for Owen Meany.* New York: William Morrow, 1989.

Jodock, Darrell. "What is Goodness? The Influence of Updike's Lutheran Roots:" In *John Updike and Religion: The Sense of the Sacred and the Motions of Grace*, ed. James Yerkes, 119–44.

Kakutani, Michiko. "Turning Sex and Guilt into an American Epic." Review of *Rabbit is Rich. Saturday Review*, October 1981, 14.

Kaplan, James. "Requiem for Rabbit." Review of *Rabbit At Rest. Vanity Fair*, October 1990, 114.

Kermode, Frank. *The Sense of an Ending: Studies in the Theory of Fiction.* New York: Oxford University Press, 1967.

Kierkegaard, Søren. *Fear and Trembling* and *The Sickness Unto Death.* Translated Walter Lowrie. Princeton: Princeton University Press, 1953.

Kort, Wesley. "Learning to Die: Work as Religious Discipline in Updike's Fiction." In *John Updike and Religion: The Sense of the Sacred and the Motions of Grace*, ed. James Yerkes, 180–94.

Lasch, Christopher. *The Culture of Narcissism.* New York: W. W. Norton, 1979.

Lassiter, Victor K. "*Rabbit is Rich* as a Naturalistic Novel." *American Literature* 61, 3 (October 1989): 429–45.

Luscher, Robert M. *John Updike: A Study of the Short Fiction.* New York: Twayne Publishers, 1993.

Mailer, Norman. "Some Children of the Goddess." In *Cannibals and Christians*, 104–30. New York: Dial Press, 1966.

Markle, Joyce B. *Fighters and Lovers: Theme in the Novels of John Updike.* New York: New York University Press, 1973.

McGrath, Charles. "Going Home Again." *New York Times Book Review*, November 19, 2000, 3–4.

McNally, T. M., and Dean Stover. "An Interview with John Updike" (1987). In *Conversations with John Updike*, ed. James Plath, 192–206.

McNaughton, William R., ed. *Critical Essays on John Updike*. Boston: G. K. Hall, 1982.

Mendes, Sam, dir. *American Beauty*. Dreamworks Pictures, 1999. DVD, Dreamworks Home Entertainment, 2000.

Newman, Judie. *John Updike*. New York: St. Martin's Press, 1988.

———. "*Rabbit at Rest*: The Return of the Work Ethic." In *Rabbit Tales: Poetry and Politics in John Updike's Rabbit Novels*, ed. Lawrence R. Broer, 189–206.

Nunley, Jan, "Thoughts of Faith Infuse Updike's Novels" (1993). In *Conversations with John Updike*, ed. James Plath, 248–59.

Oates, Joyce Carol. "So Young!" Review of *Rabbit at Rest*. *New York Times Book Review*, September 30, 1990, 1, 43. Reprinted as "John Updike's Rabbit" in *Where I've Been, and Where I'm Going: Essays, Reviews and Prose*, 161–65. New York: Plume Books, 1999.

———. "Updike's American Comedies." In *John Updike: A Collection of Critical Essays*, ed. David Thorburn and Howard Eiland, 53–68. Englewood Cliffs, N.J.: Prentice-Hall, 1979.

O'Connell, Mary. *Updike and the Patriarchal Dilemma*. Carbondale: Southern Illinois University Press, 1996.

O'Connor, Flannery. "Novelist and Believer." In *Mystery and Manners*. New York: Farrar, Straus & Giroux, 1969.

Olster, Stacey. "Rabbit Rerun: Updike's Replay of Popular Culture in *Rabbit at Rest*." *Modern Fiction Studies* 37, 1 (Spring 1991): 45–61.

Pasewark, Kyle A. "The Troubles with Harry: Freedom, America, and God in John Updike's Rabbit Novels." *Religion and American Culture* 6,1 (Winter 1996): 1–33.

———. "An Umbrella Blowing Inside Out: Paradoxical Theology and American Culture in the Novels of John Updike." In *John Updike and Religion: The Sense of the Sacred and the Motions of Grace*, ed. James Yerkes, 101–18. Grand Rapids, Mich.: Eerdmans, 1999.

Pinsker, Sanford. "Restlessness in the 1950s: What Made *Rabbit, Run*?" In *New Essays on Rabbit, Run*, ed. Stanley Trachtenberg, 53–76. Cambridge: Cambridge University Press, 1993.

Plath, James, ed. *Conversations with John Updike*. Jackson: University of Mississippi Press, 1994.

———. "Verbal Veneer: Updike's Middle Class Portraiture." In *Rabbit Tales: Poetry and Politics in John Updike's Rabbit Novels*, ed. Lawrence R. Broer, 207–30.

Podhoretz, Norman. "A Dissent on Updike." In *Doings and Undoings: The Fifties and After in American Writing*, 254–58. New York: Farrar, Straus & Giroux, 1984.

Prescott, Peter. "Angstrom's Angst." Review of *Rabbit Redux*. *Newsweek*, November 15, 1971, 122D.

Pritchard, William H. *Updike: America's Man of Letters*. South Royalton, Vt.: Steerforth Press, 2000.

Ra'ad, Basem. "Updike's New Version of Myth in America." *Modern Fiction Studies* 37, 1 (Spring 1991): 25–34.

Raban, Jonathan. "Rabbit's Last Run." Review of *Rabbit at Rest*. *Washington Post Book World*, September 30, 1990, 1, 15.

Reilly, Charlie. "A Conversation with John Updike" (1978). In *Conversations with John Updike*, ed. James Plath, 124–50.

Ristoff, Dilvo I. "Appropriating the Scene: The World of *Rabbit at Rest*." In *Rabbit Tales: Poetry and Politics in John Updike's Rabbit Novels*, ed. Lawrence R. Broer, 50–69.

Robinson, Sally. *Marked Men: White Masculinity in Crisis.* New York: Columbia University Press, 2000.

Samuels, Charles Thomas. "The Art of Fiction XLIII: John Updike." *Paris Review* 12 (Winter 1968): 85–117.

———. "Updike on the Present." Review of *Rabbit Redux.* In *Critical Essays on John Updike*, ed. William R. McNaughton, 63–67.

Schiff, James A. *John Updike Revisited.* New York: Twayne Publishers, 1998.

———. "The Pocket Nothing Else Will Fill: Updike's Domestic God." In *John Updike and Religion: The Sense of the Sacred and the Motions of Grace*, ed. James Yerkes. Grand Rapids, Mich.: Eerdmans, 1999.

Scott, A. O. "God Goes to the Movies." Review of *In the Beauty of the Lilies. The Nation*, February 12, 1996, 25–28.

———. "Still Wild About Harry." Review of *Licks of Love. New York Times*, November 19, 2000, 1–3.

Searles, George. *The Fiction of Philip Roth and John Updike.* Carbondale: Southern Illinois University Press, 1985.

Stevens, Wallace. "The Rabbit as King of the Ghosts." In *The Collected Poems of Wallace Stevens*, 209. New York: Alfred A. Knopf, 1978.

Tabor, James D., and Eugene V. Gallagher. *Why Waco?: Cults and the Battle for Religious Freedom in America.* Berkeley: University of California Press, 1995.

Tanner, Tony. "A Compromised Environment." In *City of Words*, 273–94. New York: Harper and Row, 1973. Reprinted in *Modern Critical Views: John Updike*, ed. Harold Bloom, 37–56.

Taylor, Larry E. *Pastoral and Anti-Pastoral Patterns in John Updike's Fiction.* Carbondale: Southern Illinois University Press, 1971.

Thorburn, David, and Howard Eiland, eds. *John Updike: A Collection of Critical Essays.* Englewood Cliffs, N.J.: Prentice Hall, 1979.

Time Magazine Stringer File: John Updike Interview. October 20, 1960.

Trachtenberg, Stanley. Introduction in *New Essays on Rabbit, Run*, ed. Stanley Trachtenberg, 1–29. New York: Cambridge UP, 1993.

Updike, John. "The Afterlife." In *The Afterlife and Other Stories*, 3–19.

———. *The Afterlife and Other Stories.* New York: Alfred A. Knopf, 1994.

———. Afterword in *In the Beauty of the Lilies*, 493.

———. *Americana and Other Poems.* New York: Alfred A. Knopf, 2001.

———. "Answer to 'Why Are We Here?'" In *Odd Jobs*, 869.

———. *Assorted Prose.* New York: Alfred A. Knopf, 1965.

———. "Bech Meets Me." In *Picked-Up Pieces*, 10–13.

———. "The Blessed Man of Boston, My Grandmother's Thimble, and Fanning Island." In *Pigeon Feathers and Other Stories*, 227–45.

———. "Books Into Film." In *Odd Jobs*, 36–39.

———. "A Book that Changed Me." In *Odd Jobs*, 844.

———. "The Brown Chest." In *The Afterlife and Other Stories*, 225–33.

———. *The Centaur.* New York: Alfred A. Knopf, 1961.

———. *The Coup.* New York: Alfred A. Knopf, 1978.

———. "The Dogwood Tree: A Boyhood." In *Assorted Prose*, 151–87.

———. "Emersonianism." In *Odd Jobs*, 148–68.

———. "Faith in Search of Understanding." Review of *Anselm: Fides Quaerens Intellectum*, by Karl Barth. In *Assorted Prose*, 273–81.

———. "Farewell to the Middle Class." In *Picked-Up Pieces*, 15.

———. "Footnotes to *Self-Consciousness.*" In *Odd Jobs*, 865–69.

———. Foreword in *Hugging the Shore*, xv–xx.

———. "The Fork." Review of *The Last Years: Journals, 1853–55*, by Søren Kierkegaard. In *Picked-Up Pieces*, 107–22.

———. "*Franny and Zooey.*" Review of *Franny and Zooey*, by J. D. Salinger. In *Assorted Prose*, 234–39.

———. "The Future of Faith: Confessions of a Churchgoer." *The New Yorker*, November 29, 1999, 84–91.

———. "A Gift from the City." In *The Same Door: Short Stories*, 163–93.

———. "Grandparenting." In *The Afterlife and Other Stories*, 298–316.

———. "Hawthorne's Creed." In *Hugging the Shore*, 73–79.

———. "The Heaven of an Old Home." Review of *Souvenirs and Prophecies: The Young Wallace Stevens*, by Holly Stevens. In *Hugging the Shore*, 603–16.

———. "How Does the Writer Imagine?" In *Odd Jobs*, 122–37.

———. "Howells as Anti-Novelist." In *Odd Jobs*, 168–89.

———. *Hugging the Shore: Essays and Criticism.* New York: Alfred A. Knopf, 1983.

———. "If the Salt Has Lost His Savor." An early draft of "Pigeon Feathers." John Updike Papers, Houghton Library, Harvard University (76M–76, 9).

———. "Intercession." In *The Same Door*, 193–209.

———. "In Football Season." In *The Music School*, 3–8.

———. *In the Beauty of the Lilies.* New York: Alfred A. Knopf, 1996.

———. "In the Cemetery High Above Shillington." In *Americana and Other Poems*, 29.

———. Introduction to the Czech edition of *Of the Farm*. In *Picked-Up Pieces*, 82–83.

———. Introduction to the Easton Press edition (1993) of the Rabbit novels. In *More Matter*, 816–21.

———. Introduction in the 1977 edition of *The Poorhouse Fair*, xvii–xix.

———. Introduction in *Rabbit Angstrom: Four Novels*, ix–xxiv.

———. Introduction in *Soundings in Satanism*, ed. F. J. Sheed, 87–91. In *Picked-Up Pieces*.

———. "Is There Life After Golf?" In *Picked-Up Pieces*, 98–106.

———. *John Updike: Early Stories.* New York: Alfred A. Knopf, 2003.

———. *John Updike in His Own Words.* Videotape. Pittsburgh: IUP, 1996.

———. "Leaves." In *The Music School and Other Stories*, 52–56.

———. *Licks of Love: Short Stories and a Sequel.* New York: Alfred A. Knopf, 2000.

———. "Love as a Standoff." Review of *Victoria*, by Knut Hamsun, trans. Oliver Stallybrass. In *Picked-Up Pieces*, 148–53.

———. "Lunch Hour." In *Licks of Love and Other Stories*, 16–27.

———. "The Man Within." Review of *Graham Greene: The Man Within*, by Michael Shelden. *The New Yorker*, June 26 and July 3, 1995, 182–89.

———. "Melville's Withdrawal." In *Hugging the Shore*, 80–105.

———. *Memories of the Ford Administration*. New York: Alfred A. Knopf, 1992.

———. "Midpoint." In *Midpoint and Other Poems*, 3–44.

———. *Midpoint and Other Poems*. New York: Alfred A. Knopf, 1969.

———. *A Month of Sundays*. New York: Alfred A. Knopf, 1975.

———. "More Love in the Western World." In *Assorted Prose*, 283–99.

———. *More Matter*. New York: Alfred A. Knopf, 1999.

———. "Mother." In *Odd Jobs*, 67–69.

———. *Museums and Women and Other Stories*. New York: Alfred A. Knopf, 1972.

———. *The Music School*. New York: Alfred A. Knopf, 1966.

———. "My Father, on the Verge of Disgrace." In *Licks of Love*, 44–60.

———. "My Uncle's Death." In *Assorted Prose*, 200–209.

———. *Odd Jobs: Essays and Criticism*. New York: Alfred A. Knopf, 1991.

———. *Of the Farm*. New York: Alfred A. Knopf, 1965.

———. "On Becoming a Senior Citizen." *The New Yorker*, June 16, 1997, 84. Reprinted in *Americana and Other Poems*, 37.

———. "One Big Interview." In *Picked-Up Pieces*, 491–519.

———. "One of My Generation." *Museums and Women*, 175–81.

———. "The Original Ending of *Self-Consciousness*." In *Literary Outtakes*, ed. Larry Dark, 328–29. New York: Fawcett Columbine, 1990.

———. "Packed Dirt, Churchgoing, A Dying Cat, A Traded Car." In *Pigeon Feathers and Other Stories*, 246–79.

———. "The Persistence of Evil." *The New Yorker*, July 22, 1996, 62–65.

———. *Picked-Up Pieces*. New York: Alfred A. Knopf, 1975.

———. "Pigeon Feathers." In *Pigeon Feathers and Other Stories*, 116–50.

———. *Pigeon Feathers and Other Stories*. New York: Alfred A. Knopf, 1962.

———. "Pigeon Feathers." John Updike Papers, Houghton Library, Harvard University, bMS Am 1793.3.

———. "Poet on the Fault Line." Review of *Robert Frost*, by Jay Parini. *The New Yorker*, March 15, 1999, 84–91.

———. "Poker Night." In *Trust Me: Short Stories*, 182–89.

———. *The Poorhouse Fair: With an Introduction by the Author*. New York: Alfred A. Knopf, 1977.

———. *Problems and Other Stories*. New York: Alfred A. Knopf, 1979.

———. *Rabbit Angstrom: A TETRALOGY*. New York: Everyman Library, 1995.

———. *Rabbit at Rest*. New York: Alfred A. Knopf, 1990.

———. *Rabbit at Rest* manuscript #2. John Updike Papers, Houghton Library, Harvard University, MS stor 279 (1 of 4).

———. *Rabbit Redux*. New York: Alfred A. Knopf, 1971.

———. "Rabbit Remembered." In *Licks of Love: Short Stories and a Sequel*, 177–359.

———. *Rabbit is Rich*. New York: Alfred A. Knopf, 1981.

————. *Rabbit, Run.* New York: Alfred A. Knopf, 1960.

————. *Rabbit, Run.* New York: Fawcett Crest, 1962.

————. *Rabbit, Run.* Alfred A. Knopf, revised edition, 1970.

————. "Religious Consolation." *The New Republic,* August 23, 1999, 43.

————. "Remarks on the Occasion of E. B. White's Receiving the 1971 National Medal for Literature on December 2, 1971." In *Picked-Up Pieces,* 434–37.

————. "Remarks on Religion and Contemporary American Literature Delivered at Indiana/Purdue University in Indianapolis, April, 1994." In *John Updike and Religion: The Sense of the Sacred and the Motions of Grace,* ed. James Yerkes, n.p. Reprinted in *More Matter,* 850.

————. "Remarks Upon Receiving the Campion Medal." In *John Updike and Religion: The Sense of the Sacred and the Motions of Grace,* ed. James Yerkes, 3–6.

————. "Remembrance of Things Past Remembered." In *Picked-Up Pieces,* 162–68.

————. *Roger's Version.* New York: Alfred A. Knopf, 1986.

————. *The Same Door: Short Stories.* New York: Alfred A. Knopf, 1968.

————. "The Sandstone Farmhouse." In *The Afterlife and Other Stories,* 103–35.

————. *Self-Consciousness: Memoirs.* New York: Alfred A. Knopf, 1989.

————. "Separating." In *Problems and Other Stories,* 116–31.

————. "Snow from a Dead Sky." In *Assorted Prose,* 233.

————. "Solitaire." In *Museums and Women,* 78–84.

————. "Special Message" for the Franklin Library's First Edition Society Printing of *Rabbit at Rest.*" Franklin Center, Pa.: Franklin Library, 1990, n.p. Reprinted in *Odd Jobs,* 869–72.

————. "Special Message" for the Franklin Library's Signed First Edition Society Printing of *In the Beauty of the Lilies.*" Franklin Center, Pa.: Franklin Library, 1996, n.p. Reprinted in *More Matter,* 831–33.

————. "Special Message" for the Franklin Library Signed First Edition Society Printing of *Memories of the Ford Administration.*" Franklin Center, Pa.: Franklin Library, 1992, n.p. Reprinted in *More Matter,* 825–27.

————. "Special Message" to Purchasers of the Franklin Library Limited Edition of *Rabbit Redux.* Franklin Center, Pa.: Franklin Library, 1981, n.p. Reprinted in *Hugging the Shore,* 858–59.

————. A "Special Message" to Subscribers of the Franklin Library Edition of *Rabbit, Run.* Franklin Center, Pa.: Franklin Library, 1977, n.p. Reprinted in *Hugging the Shore,* 849–51.

————. "To Two of My Characters." In *Americana and Other Poems,* 44.

————. *Toward the End of Time.* New York: Alfred A. Knopf, 1997.

————. *Trust Me: Short Stories.* New York: Alfred A. Knopf, 1987.

————. "Ungreat Lives." Review of *Voices from the Moon* by Andre Dubus and *Concrete,* by Thomas Bernhard. In *Odd Jobs,* 649–56.

————. "Updike on Updike." *New York Times Book Review,* September 27, 1981, 35. Reprinted in *Hugging the Shore,* 871.

————. "The Walk with Elizanne." *The New Yorker,* July 7, 2003, 67–71.

————. "The Wallet." In *Trust Me: Short Stories,* 222–37.

————. "We Looked Forward . . ." *The New Yorker,* August 22, 1964, 23. Reprinted in *Assorted Prose,* 74.

———. "What You Deserve is What You Get." Review of *You Must Remember This*, by Joyce Carol Oates. *Odd Jobs*, 329–35.

———. "Whitman's Egotheism." In *Hugging the Shore*, 106–17.

———. "Why Rabbit Had to Go." *New York Times Book Review*, August 5, 1990, 1, 24–25.

———. "Why Write?" In *Picked-Up Pieces*, 35.

Vargo, Edward. "Cornchips, Catheters, Toyotas: Making History in *Rabbit at Rest*." In *Rabbit Tales: Poetry and Politics in John Updike's Rabbit Novels*, ed. Lawrence R. Broer, 70–88.

———. *Rainstorms and Fire: Ritual in the Novels of John Updike*. Port Washington, N.Y.: Kennicat Press, 1973.

Vendler, Helen. "Interview with John Updike." *New York Times Book Review*, April 10, 1977, 3, 28. Reprinted in *Hugging the Shore*, 862–65.

Waldmeir, Joseph. "*Rabbit Redux* Reduced." In *Rabbit Tales: Poetry and Politics in John Updike's Rabbit Novels*, ed. Lawrence R. Broer, 111–28.

Wallace, David Foster. "John Updike, Champion Literary Phallocrat, Drops One; Is This Finally the End for Magnificent Narcissists?" *New York Observer*, October 13, 1997, 1–4.

Webb, Stephen H. "Writing as a Reader of Karl Barth: What Kind of Religious Writer is John Updike Not?" In *John Updike and Religion: The Sense of the Sacred and the Motions of Grace*, ed. James Yerkes, 145–61.

Weber, Brom. Review of *Rabbit Redux*. *Saturday Review*, November 27, 1971, 54–55.

Wills, Garry. "Long Distance Runner." Review of *Rabbit at Rest*. *New York Review of Books*, October 25, 1990, 11–14.

Wilson, Matthew. "The Rabbit Tetralogy: From Solitude to Society to Solitude Again." *Modern Fiction Studies* 37, 1 (Spring 1991): 5–24.

Wood, James. "John Updike's Complacent God." In *The Broken Estate: Essays on Literature and Belief*, 196. New York: Random House, 1999.

Wood, Ralph C. *The Comedy of Redemption: Christian Faith and Comic Vision in Four American Novelists*. Notre Dame: University of Notre Dame Press, 1988.

Yerkes, James. "As Good as it Gets: The Religious Consciousness in John Updike's Literary Vision." In *John Updike and Religion: The Sense of the Sacred and the Motions of Grace*, ed. James Yerkes, 9–30. Grand Rapids, Mich.: Eerdmans, 1999.

———, ed. *John Updike and Religion: The Sense of the Sacred and the Motions of Grace*. Grand Rapids, Mich.: Eerdmans, 1999.

Index

Page numbers in **boldface** refer to major discussions of the entry

289